Bankruptcy for Paralegals

Janette J. Anderson, J.D., Esq.
Attorney at Law

PRENTICE HALL PARALEGAL SERIES

Prentice Hall
Upper Saddle River, New Jersey 07458

Library of Congress Cataloging-in-Publication Data

Anderson, Janette J.
    Bankruptcy for paralegals / Janette J. Anderson.
      p.   cm.
    Includes index.
    ISBN 0-13-360058-0
    1. Bankruptcy—United States. 2. Legal assistants—United States—
Handbooks, manuals, etc. I. Title.
KF1524.3.A53 1996
346.73'078—dc20
[347.30678]   96-22733
                                           CIP

Acquisitions Editor: Elizabeth Sugg
Director of Production and Manufacturing: Bruce Johnson
Managing Editor: Mary Carnis
Editorial/Production Supervision and
   Interior Design: Inkwell Publishing Services
Cover Director: Jayne Conte
Manufacturing Buyer: Edward O'Dougherty

© 1997 by Prentice-Hall, Inc.
A Division of Simon & Schuster
Upper Saddle River, New Jersey 07458

Printed in the United States of America

10 9 8 7 6 5 4 3 2 1

ISBN 0-13-360058-0

Prentice-Hall International (UK) Limited, *London*
Prentice-Hall of Australia Pty. Limited, *Sydney*
Prentice-Hall Canada Inc., *Toronto*
Prentice-Hall Hispanoamericana, S.A., *Mexico*
Prentice-Hall of India Private Limited, *New Delhi*
Prentice-Hall of Japan, Inc., *Tokyo*
Prentice-Hall of Southeast Asia Pte. Ltd., *Singapore*
Editora Prentice-Hall do Brasil, Ltda., *Rio de Janeiro*

Contents

Preface   *vii*

1
Introduction   *1*

General Introduction   *1*
Policy of Bankruptcy Law   *2*
Structure of Bankruptcy Law   *4*
Bankruptcy Code   *4*

History of Bankruptcy Law   *7*
Appendix A: The Bankruptcy Reform Act of
    1994   *13*

2
Infrastructure of a Bankruptcy Case   *21*

Parties   *21*
The Bankruptcy Court System   *24*
Stare Decisis or Precedent of Bankruptcy Case
    Law   *26*
The Bankruptcy Code   *27*

The Bankruptcy Estate   *29*
Exemptions   *35*
Abandonment   *37*
Chronological Events in Bankruptcy Proceedings
    in Chapter 7 and Chapter 13 Cases   *40*

3
Varieties of Bankruptcy Chapters   44

Introduction   44
Description of the Chapters   45

Eligibility Requirements of Each Chapter   49
Comparison of Bankruptcy Chapters   60

4
Initial Documentation   67

Introduction   67
Petition   69
Schedule A (Real Property)   73
Schedule B (Personal Property)   73
Schedule C (Property Claimed as Exempt)   80
Schedule D (Creditors Holding Secured Claims)   80
Schedule E (Creditors Holding Unsecured Priority
    Claims)   83
Schedule F (Creditors Holding Unsecured
    Nonpriority Claims)   85
Schedule G (Executory Contracts and Unexpired
    Leases)   85

Schedule H (Codebtors)   85
Schedule I (Current Income)   85
Schedule J (Current Expenditures)   92
Summary of Schedules   94
Chapter 7 Individual Debtor's Statement of
    Intention   94
Statement of Financial Affairs   94
Disclosure of Compensation of Attorney for
    Debtor   110
Notice of Available Chapters   111
Master Mailing List   111
Bankruptcy Doc Prep Operations   115

5
Automatic Stay   118

Definition   119
Policy   120
Specific Enumerated Actions Prohibited by
    Stay   123
Duration   125
Statutory Exclusions from the Automatic Stay   125

Stay Relief   137
Stay Relief Burden of Proof   145
Hearing on Stay Relief Motions   145
Expedited Stay Relief   146
Codebtor Stay   146
Violations of the Automatic Stay   148

6
Discharge   154

Introduction   154
Denial of Discharge   155
Nondischargeability of Certain Obligations   156
Plaintiffs in Nondischargeability Actions   170

Sanctions Available to Debtor   173
Applicability of Section 523 to Chapters 7, 11, and
    13   173
Effect of Discharge   173

7
Dismissal/Conversion   178

Introduction   178
Administrative Dismissal   179
Dismissal Due to Lack of Eligibility   184
Creditor Requested Dismissal   186

Substantial Abuse Filing   190
Voluntary Dismissal   192
Effect of Dismissal   194
Conversion   195

8
Voidable Transfers *199*

Introduction *199*
Duties of Legal Assistants in Voidance Actions *200*
Preferences *201*
Fraudulent Conveyances *218*
Postpetition Transfers *229*

Collection of Voidable Transfers *231*
Authority to Bring Voidable Transfer Actions *231*
Statutes of Limitations on Voidable Transfer
Actions *233*

9
Creditor Status, Priority, and Distribution Rights *241*

Introduction *241*
Secured Creditors *242*
Priority Creditors *244*
Unsecured Creditors *247*
Punitive-Type Debts *248*
Postpetition Interest *248*

Surplus to Debtor *249*
Superpriority Creditors *249*
Super Superpriority Creditors *250*
Filing Proofs of Claim *250*
Allowance of Claim *251*

10
Chapter 7 Practice *256*

Introduction *256*
Debtor's Role *257*
Debtor's Rights *260*
Trustee *273*

Creditors *277*
General Timeline for Chapter 7 *278*

11
Chapter 13 Practice *283*

Introduction *283*
Parties: Roles, Duties, and Rights *284*
Confirmation Process *293*
Formulation of a Plan *312*

Modification of Chapter 13 Plans *314*
Revocation of Confirmation *314*
Chapter 13 Discharge *315*

12
Chapter 11 Practice *320*

Introduction *320*
Parties: Duties and Rights *321*
The Confirmation Process *332*
Chapter 11 Plan and Confirmation *335*
Appendix A: U.S. Trustee's Office
Requirements *341*

Appendix B: Sample Employment
Application *367*
Appendix C: U.S. Trustee's Office Employment
Guidelines *380*

13
Bankruptcy Procedure and Discovery   *403*

Introduction   *403*   Discovery in Bankruptcy   *415*
Bankruptcy Procedure   *404*

Glossary   *419*

Index   *429*

Preface

Bankruptcy for Paralegals is an introductory bankruptcy manual for legal assistants. The scope of the book ranges from detailed procedural aspects of common bankruptcy litigation practice to the policy and history behind bankruptcy law. Moreover, *Bankruptcy for Paralegals* provides practical insight into the differences of each chapter of the Bankruptcy code, the impact of the substantive rights and duties of parties within each chapter, along with appropriate procedures and deadlines to protect such rights. It also contains an analysis of basic litigation issues such as stay relief, avoidance actions, dismissal, nondischargeability, and confirmation matters.

ACKNOWLEDGMENTS

Many experts contributed their advice to the accuracy of this work. In particular, we would like to thank Myra Harris, American Institute; Robert Loomi, Spokane Community College; Anne Kastle, Edmonds Community College; Lorraine Crozier and Daird Hubbard, Keis College; and George Schrader, Auburn University at Montgomery.

Special acknowledgment is given to The Law Offices of Jeffrey S. Shinbrot, of Beverly Hills, California, not only for allowing me the great amount of time necessary to put together these materials but for supporting and assisting me in their production. The attorneys and paraprofessionals of The Law Offices of Jeffrey S. Shinbrot deserve special recognition here due to their continuing remarkable commitment to all practicing legal assistants by supporting and helping me in this undertaking.

Additionally, special recognition is given to Robert Mothershead, PC, Attorneys at Law, of Phoenix, Arizona and all the staff paraprofessionals there for their extraordinary efforts in making contributions to this work.

Finally, a heartfelt personal acknowledgment is indispensable for Emily Joy and Patricia Joy for their support and encouragement in the preparation of this work.

1 *Introduction*

GENERAL INTRODUCTION

Throughout the history of civilization individuals and businesses have faced financial straits. Unemployment, illness, fire, flood, mismanagement and inability to compete due to advancing technology all may trigger a person's inability to pay bills. The person who owes the debt is called a *debtor*. The person to whom the debt is owed is called a *creditor. Bankruptcy* is the legal system developed to resolve the effects of financial crises.[1] *Bankruptcy law* in the United States attempts to strike a balance between the rights of debtors and the rights of creditors with built-in safeguards and protections for each.

The filing of a bankruptcy petition suspends the normal operation of rights and obligations between the debtor and creditors. The essence of bankruptcy law is to rearrange the rights and liabilities between debtors and creditors. Collections, lawsuits, foreclosures, repossessions, seizures and levies are all brought to a halt. Liens become subject to avoidance as do certain preferential payments made in favor of certain creditors above other creditors. Fraudulent transfers and obligations are also subject to avoidance.

The Bankruptcy Court is an arena for virtually every type of law including those which typically come to mind such as taxes, Uniform Commercial Code (UCC) security interest laws, real estate deeds of trust or mortgage laws, as well as general civil litigation for breaches of contract.

1

However, the Bankruptcy Court is also called upon frequently to resolve legal issues in areas not commonly thought of as being adjudicated in Bankruptcy Court such as inheritance law,[2] securities law,[3] environmental law,[4] domestic relations law,[5] criminal law,[6] pension law,[7] trust law,[8] fraud,[9] and entertainment law.[10]

In essence, bankruptcy operates as a collective execution for all creditors on all the assets of the debtor. This execution takes place whether the assets are actually in the possession of the debtor or a third party. The principal function of bankruptcy is to implement in a single proceeding, the entitlement of all the creditors.

The collective nature of bankruptcy replaces each individual creditor's collection remedies. This prevents the individual creditors' race to the courthouse steps in an attempt to collect from the debtor before all the rest of the creditors. Bankruptcy, through its collective execution, ensures that all creditors of equal rank will be treated equally.

Moreover, such collective execution in one forum, namely the Bankruptcy Court, reduces costs associated with each creditor racing to the courthouse to grab a judgment and execute against the debtor's property. In this way creditors are benefited by the administrative efficiencies of this collective proceeding. Finally, the collective nature of the bankruptcy proceeding is more likely to increase the aggregate pool of assets available to creditors by prohibiting a disadvantaged piecemeal liquidation of the debtor's assets.

POLICY OF BANKRUPTCY LAW

There are four basic goals in bankruptcy law. The first is to convert property of the debtor into cash and distribute it among creditors equally. The second is to give the debtor a fresh start. The third is to provide an economical administrative forum for bankruptcy. The final goal is to continue the law-based orderliness of the open credit economy in the event of a debtor's inability or unwillingness to pay his or her debts.

The first goal is often expressed as making the equitable distribution of the debtor's assets among his or her creditors. In other words, creditors of equal status must be treated equally and equitably. While equality of distribution among all creditors is a central policy of the Bankruptcy Code, exceptions are made by granting priority status to certain claims and subordinating others. For example, priority is given to such claims as prepetition wages and benefits of a debtor's employees, "layaway" deposits of a debtor's customers, overdue alimony or child support, and taxes.[11] Under the central policy of equal distribution, creditors of equal priority (or rank) receive a pro rata share of the debtor's property. However, when there is not enough to go around, the bankruptcy judge apportions assets among creditors within the same priority.[12]

The next goal in bankruptcy is to relieve the honest debtor from the weight of oppressive indebtedness and permit the debtor to start afresh, freed from the obligations and responsibilities arising from a poor business decision, illness, or unemployment. Bankruptcy provides to the honest but unfortunate debtor, who surrenders for distribution the property owned at the time of bankruptcy, a new opportunity in life and a clear field for future effort unhampered by the pressure and discouragement of preexisting debt.[13]

This "fresh start" is implemented by allowing the individual debtor to keep certain property as exempt and by providing a discharge that releases the individual debtor from liability on prepetition debts and claims. Exemptions are intended to allow a debtor to keep certain property needed for a fresh start to make sure the debtor will not be left destitute and therefore a public charge (i.e., on welfare). Note that there is no constitutional right to a discharge.[14] In fact, only an individual (i.e., not a corporation, partnership, etc.) is granted a discharge in a liquidation Chapter 7 case.[15]

The third goal in bankruptcy is to provide a forum for the collective execution and processing of the debtor's assets. This reduces the administrative expenses in liquidation and distribution of the debtor's property, as well as providing a quick way to achieve such liquidation and distribution. This goal is fulfilled through lessened costs and more uniform results made possible by current bankruptcy law.

The final goal in bankruptcy is to provide substantive laws regarding treatment of creditors and their claims and liens in bankruptcy. These bankruptcy laws indirectly impact credit terms and practices by lenders through their anticipation and/or preparation in the event a borrower ultimately files bankruptcy. One of the basic philosophies of bankruptcy is the protection of private credit to promote commerce. In essence, the stability of how creditors are treated in the event of bankruptcy impacts the lending standards and risk factors associated with open credit.

For example, commonly high interest rates are provided on unsecured loans (such as credit cards) but lower interest rates are available to secured loans (such as vehicle loans). The disparity in interest reflects the creditors' risk in the event of bankruptcy. Essentially, unsecured loans are the last in the distribution of assets (if any remain). Secured loans, on the other hand, are first to receive either the amount of their lien or the return of the collateral. Accordingly, the stability of the treatment of creditors through bankruptcy promotes commerce by allowing open credit based upon the particular risk factors as articulated through the Bankruptcy Code.

STRUCTURE OF BANKRUPTCY LAW

The Congressional power to enact bankruptcy legislation comes from the Bankruptcy Clause in the Constitution. The United States Constitution, Article I, Section 8, Clause 4 provides that Congress shall have the power to establish uniform laws on the subject of bankruptcies throughout the United States. The uniformity required under the Bankruptcy Clause is geographical, not personal. In other words, such clause does not forbid Congress to distinguish among classes of debtors, although it does prohibit Congress from enacting bankruptcy laws that specifically apply to the affairs of only one named debtor.

Additionally, the uniformity requirement does not prohibit Congress from recognizing that state laws do not treat commercial transactions in a uniform manner. In fact bankruptcy laws recognize the laws of the state in certain situations. For example, whether a debtor has rights to certain property depends upon state law. Even if such recognition leads to different results in different states, the uniformity requirement in the Bankruptcy Clause does not require the elimination of any differences among the states. For example, Congress can give effect to the allowances of exemptions prescribed by state law without violating the Bankruptcy Clause's uniformity requirement (i.e., the homestead exemption allowed to a debtor in California may be different in amount than the homestead exemption allowed to a debtor in Texas or Florida).

BANKRUPTCY CODE

The Bankruptcy Code is codified as Title 11 of the United States Code. The Bankruptcy Code is divided into eight chapters: 1, 3, 5, 7, 9, 11, 12, and 13. Citation to the Bankruptcy Code should be in Arabic numbers (not by Roman numerals, which were used under the prior Bankruptcy Act). For example, the operative statute for distribution to creditors is 11 U.S.C. Section 726. Section 726 is within Chapter 7 of Title 11. Another example includes definitions contained in 11 U.S.C. Section 101. Section 101 is within Chapter 1 of Title 11.

All bankruptcy cases are commenced under one of the operative chapters of the Code. That is, Chapter 7 (liquidation), Chapter 9 (municipal reorganization), Chapter 11 (business reorganization), Chapter 12 (family farmer reorganization), or Chapter 13 (wage-earner reorganization). The other chapters in the Code, Chapter 1 (general provisions), Chapter 3 (case administration), and Chapter 5 (creditors, debtors, and the estate), contain provisions that generally apply to cases under Chapter 7, 11, 12 or 13. However, the provisions within each operative chapter (i.e., Chapters 7, 9, 11, 12, and 13) apply only to cases under that chapter.

Title 28 of the United States Code is also known as the Judicial Code. Title 28 also contains a number of provisions relating to bankruptcy, including:

- Bankruptcy judges in regular active service constituting a unit of the District Court to be known as Bankruptcy Court.
- The District Courts' referring of cases and proceedings to the bankruptcy judges.
- The retirement or removal of bankruptcy judges.
- The recall to service of retired bankruptcy judges.
- The prohibition against nepotism for employees of the Bankruptcy Court and the judges.
- The authority of the U.S. Attorney General to investigate acts of the trustees in bankruptcy cases, the United States trustee system.
- The appropriateness of trustees of a bankruptcy case to sue or be sued.
- Abstention of cases, appropriateness of venue, jury trials, removal of claims to the bankruptcy court, bankruptcy fees, the power of the Supreme Court to promulgate Bankruptcy Rules, etc.

Title 18 of the United States Code contains provisions regarding bankruptcy crimes. Title 18 of the United States Code is under "Crimes and Criminal Procedure." Section 152 of Title 18 is the heart of the bankruptcy crimes statutes. It attempts to cover all the possible methods by which a debtor or any other person may attempt to defeat the Bankruptcy Code through an effort to keep assets from being equitably distributed among creditors.[16]

Basically 18 U.S.C. Section 152 criminalizes the following offenses:

1. *Concealment offenses,* such as concealment of property during a bankruptcy proceeding, or knowing or fraudulent transfer or concealment of property in contemplation of bankruptcy, concealment destruction or falsification of documents relating to the property or financial affairs of the debtor, knowingly withholding any reported information from the court or the trustee, fraudulently receiving property belonging to the bankruptcy estate and thereby aiding and abetting its concealment.

2. *False oaths* in relation to an actual bankruptcy case, including oral statements or testimony in a court proceeding, written information and statements made in bankruptcy under the penalty of perjury, false entries in documents regarding the debtor's property or financial affairs.

3. *Offenses by creditors,* including filing a false proof of claim, giving or receiving money or property for acting or agreeing not to act with respect

to a bankruptcy case—i.e., bribery and extortion, side-bar-type agreements between a creditor and a debtor relating to the concealment, secretion or removal of property implicate a creditor in criminal activity.

Additionally, 18 U.S.C. Section 153 criminalizes fraud and embezzlement by trustees or officers of the court. Further, 18 U.S.C. Section 154 attempts to insure the objectivity of trustees and other court officers by providing for fines and removal from office for unlawfully benefiting from their position. Finally, 18 U.S.C. Section 155 makes it a crime for any party, including attorneys, to fraudulently enter into a fee agreement for services rendered with respect to the bankruptcy case, if the fee is to be paid from property of the estate (i.e., fee splitting).

Bankruptcy Rules

As noted, Title 28 grants the Supreme Court of the United States the authority to prescribe rules for the practice and procedure in cases under the Bankruptcy Code. Note that such rules cannot abridge, enlarge, or modify any substantive rights. Accordingly, the Federal Rules of Bankruptcy Procedure (F.R.Bankr.P.) apply to all bankruptcy proceedings (i.e., cases and matters to be resolved in bankruptcy).

Bankruptcy proceedings can take place in the administrative case (via motion and response), which are merely handled within the original case number of the particular bankruptcy case; take the form of a contested matter (also via motion and response), which are given a separate contested matter letter (i.e., Contested Matter A or Contested Matter B); or, in more complex matters, take the form of an Adversary proceeding (i.e., Adv. No. 96-123). Whether a matter must be delineated a Contested Matter or an Adversary is prescribed in the F.R.Bankr.P. 7001 or 9014.

Local Rules

Each District Court, by action of a majority of the judges therein, may make and amend rules governing practice and procedure in all cases and proceedings within the District Court's bankruptcy jurisdiction that are not inconsistent with the F.R.Bankr.P. Additionally, the District Court may further authorize the bankruptcy judges within such district to make additional bankruptcy rules. Therefore, legal assistants will need to be familiar with the District Court local rules as well as with the Bankruptcy Court local rules within their district.

For example, Arizona District Court local rules prescribe that all discovery disputes require personal consultation between the litigants' attorneys. An affidavit of such personal consultation must be included in any motion to resolve such dispute before the court will entertain such motion. Accordingly, any discovery dispute in bankruptcy court must comply with the local District Rules and attach an affidavit of counsels' personal consultation efforts.

Here is an additional example of the local rules for a Bankruptcy Court. In the Bankruptcy Court for the Central District of California, a local bankruptcy rule prescribes the order in which a debtor's initial documentation (statements and schedules) must be submitted to the clerk's office.

Official Forms

Together with the Bankruptcy Rules, the Official Bankruptcy Forms govern procedure in cases under the Bankruptcy Code. Local court rules may not prohibit or limit the use of the Official Forms. The Official Forms prescribed by the Judicial Conference are to be observed and used with such alterations as may be appropriate (such as combining forms or rearranging their contents to permit more economical use of such forms).

The use of the Official Forms is subject to a "rule of substantial compliance." In other words, a document for which an Official Form is prescribed generally will meet the standard of substantial compliance if the document contains the complete substance of (i.e., all the information required by) the Official Form. Homemade versions of the Official Forms, which attempt to minimize the number of pages, condense the words, and eliminate detailed instructions, may also:

- Omit the debtors' declarations under the penalty of perjury.
- Reduce type size.
- Have been unsatisfactorily completed. (For example, suppose the preparer has drawn arrows and circled pertinent information in black marker, used black marker to delete portions of the printed parts of the forms, marked other parts of the form with "whiteout" to delete either printed or typed material, and completed parts of the form by hand rather than typing them.)

This fails to comply with F.R.Bankr.P. 1002(a), 1007(b), 1008, and 9009 and may not be used by the debtors for petitions, schedules, and statements.

HISTORY OF BANKRUPTCY LAW

It is important for a legal assistant to understand the antiquity of the origins of bankruptcy law in order to comprehend its direction from the early goals of punishment of debtor to the more current policy of giving a debtor affirmative relief. Also, a general knowledge of the important historical revisions of American bankruptcy law ensures that a legal assistant will understand any analysis of the former Bankruptcy Act within current case law that applies (or contrasts) former U.S. bankruptcy laws.

Finally, details of the more current amendments along with the appropriate amendment dates are important to ensure the soundness of a legal assistant's research. Knowledge of such amendments will cue the savvy legal assistant to research whether particular case law has been overruled by statutory amendments to the Bankruptcy Code. In other words, the legal assistant will be prepared to ascertain whether such case law is a proposition of law long rooted in bankruptcy history or merely an old case that has been since overruled by statute and no longer applies. Accordingly, it is a vital research tool to know when recent amendments to the Bankruptcy Code occurred (in relation to the date of the case law located) so that the legal assistant can check to make sure the relevant statute is the same now as when the bankruptcy case was published.

The term "bankruptcy" is commonly believed to come from the Latin term *banca rotta,* or "broken bench" from medieval days when a sign of a merchant's insolvency was his broken stand in the marketplace. However, as with many other American laws, U.S. bankruptcy law's history is rooted in English Law. English remedies for bankruptcy between the 13th and 16th centuries were akin to punishment for a crime. Accordingly, the practice of debt slavery was widespread. Also, imprisonment was a common response to the failure to pay debts.

In fact, the laws of this early time and the harsh attitudes prevalent in England toward insolvency is shown in the following English Court's statement upon imprisoning an insolvent person:

> [N]either the plaintiff at whose suit he is arrested, nor the sheriff who took him in is bound to find him meat, drink, or clothes; but he must live on his own, or on the charity of others; and if no man will relieve him, let him die in the name of God ...[17]

In other words, insolvent persons were put into debtors' prisons and left to die if their family did not bring them food and clothing. In fact this harsh treatment of debtors is also demonstrated by the law of the English Parliament, which ordered that any debtor who could not demonstrate that his bankruptcy was due to misfortune would suffer pillory and the loss of an ear.[18]

During this time creditors were allowed access to a debtor's property and to any rents thereon. However, protected from creditor's seizure were actions against certain property of the debtor (namely oxen and beasts of plough). Albeit limited, from these beginnings sprang the initial thrust of a creditor's remedy against *property* of the debtor and not the debtor himself, as well as limited protection of the debtor's property through what are currently known as "exemptions." Accordingly, the development of bankruptcy law was clearly away from a creditor-based, punitive model of debt proceedings to one that is primarily an affirmative debtor's remedy. Granted this development was neither direct nor rapid, it nonetheless progressed in this direction.

In the United States the subject of bankruptcy was considered at the Federal Convention of 1787 where an Article was enacted allowing the Legislative Department (i.e., Congress) the power to establish uniform laws on the subject of bankruptcies. The founding fathers adopted this clause with practically no debate since the power of establishing uniform laws of federal bankruptcy was seen as intimately connected with the regulation of commerce. This would prevent fraud where the parties or their property were in, or could be removed into, different states.[19]

The first legislation regarding bankruptcy was the Bankruptcy Act of 1800 and was enacted in the wake of the financial panics of the 1790s and the imprisonment of many debtors, including prominent persons. While the 1800 Act was available to be triggered only by creditors and only traders, merchants, and brokers were eligible debtors, certain exemptions from liquidation were afforded debtors as to particular items (i.e., clothing, furnishings, etc.). However, a debtor was released from prison under the 1800 Act only if his debts were discharged.

After the 1800 Act was repealed in 1803, no bankruptcy legislation existed for 35 years. The states were left to deal with their residents' financial distress. During this time an increased tendency emerged that focused on bankruptcy as a debtor's remedy culminating in the potential for a discharge from existing debts. Thereafter, the Bankruptcy Act of 1867, the first comprehensive statute dealing with bankruptcy, was enacted and provided for debtor-initiated proceedings. The Act of 1867 was repealed after about a decade due largely to the abuses associated with the administration of the cases.

Next, the Bankruptcy Act of 1898 (the immediate forerunner of the Code) was enacted and allowed a debtor's discharge without creditors' consent in liquidation cases. Likewise, the course of bankruptcy law away from punitive measures and toward remedial measures for a debtor was acknowledged in the Act of 1898. The purposes of the 1898 Act were to give the debtor the most liberal remedies in voluntary proceedings and in every possible way protect those who are honest from unjust prosecution and at all times from persecution. Additionally, the Act was meant to protect the rights of creditors, giving them ample protection, but leaving no cruel weapon in their hands. Lastly, the Act was enacted since a law was necessary that would be inexpensive and simple in its operation.[20]

For over 70 years the Bankruptcy Act of 1898 was the only bankruptcy law. In essence, it was a statute conceived in the horse and buggy era that was still performing in the jet age of high technology. The Act was becoming counterproductive as the world changed, including the growth of consumer credit, the development of modern concepts of commercial financing, and the construction and expansion of new and different systems of payment. These changes in credit methods severely cramped the application of the Bankruptcy Act of 1898.

The Bankruptcy Reform Act of 1978 (the Bankruptcy Code) was the immediate successor to the Bankruptcy Act of 1898. The Bankruptcy Code is, basically, the same as we now know it except for later amendments. The first amendments were in 1982 (technical errors corrected as well as clarifying and substantive changes with respect to securities and commodities) and the Bankruptcy Amendments and Federal Judgeship Act of 1984 (BAFJA).

The BAFJA was implemented in response to a U.S. Supreme Court decision that was devastating in its breadth, *Northern Pipeline Construction Co. v. Marathon Pipe Line Co.*, 458 U.S. 50 (1982). In essence, the Supreme Court ruled that the Reform Act of 1978 was unconstitutional and that bankruptcy judges did not have the authority to hear and determine bankruptcy cases as was granted in the 1978 Reform Act.[21] Accordingly, BAFJA was enacted, placing the exclusive jurisdiction of bankruptcy cases within the District Court power with the bankruptcy court being a "unit" of the District Court. BAFJA also differentiated between "core" and "noncore" matters and the bankruptcy court's power to hear and adjudicate such matters.

Thereafter, the Bankruptcy Code was amended in 1986. This legislation was a combination of statutes to implement the U.S. Trustee system, to authorize additional bankruptcy judgeships, and to enact Chapter 12 (family farmer reorganization.) Further amendments were made in 1988 that included certain retiree benefits protection in bankruptcy, added restitution as a nondischargeable claim, and amended certain provisions of Chapter 9 (municipal reorganization). The 1990 Amendments were technical amendments, which affected complex lending and financing agreements regarding commodities or foreign transactions (such as swap agreements, forward contracts, margin payments, settlement payments, and repurchase agreements). Additionally, the 1990 Amendments excepted the automatic stay for licensing bodies for educational debtors, made certain student loans nondischargeable, added DUI injuries as nondischargeable, and made restitution in Chapter 13 nondischargeable.

On October 22, 1994 Congress enacted the Bankruptcy Reform Act of 1994 (referred to as the "1994 Amendments"). (See Appendix A to this chapter.) The 1994 Amendments brought sweeping change to much of the Code. The 1994 Amendments apply prospectively. In other words, the 1994 Amendments are applicable to all cases filed after October 22, 1994.

CONCLUSION

Bankruptcy law in the United States is contained in distinct federal statutes (i.e., Title 11) and has unique bankruptcy courts. Bankruptcy has evolved from the idea of punishing a debtor to granting relief to a debtor. However, both the policy of bankruptcy as well as the bankruptcy statutes protect creditors' rights as well. Since it is a relatively new law and is constantly being amended, bankruptcy law is always evolving. This evolution, in addition to other areas of law being adjudicated within the bankruptcy forum, makes bankruptcy practice very interesting and challenging.

REVIEW QUESTIONS

1. What are the four policy goals underlying bankruptcy law?
2. Who enacts bankruptcy law and where do they obtain their power to enact such laws?
3. Where is the bankruptcy law located?
4. Who makes bankruptcy rules which govern procedure? What about local rules?
5. What is the most recent amendment to the Bankruptcy Code? When was the effective date for such amendment?

ENDNOTES

[1] Creditor and debtor rights outside the bankruptcy arena are governed by state law. Such non-bankruptcy rights and remedies are beyond the scope of this text.

[2] Property received through inheritance within 180 days of the petition date is considered estate property.

[3] Chapter 11 reorganization plans are permitted to swap debt for equity (i.e., stock) without registering such stock with the Securities and Exchange Commission.

[4] Toxic waste site property is often a clash in whether a property may be abandoned from the estate.

[5] Alimony, child support, and property settlement agreements arise in nondischargeability actions and may be treated as priority claims in distribution rights; community property may be sold or community assets used for distribution.

[6] Restitution fines issues are often resolved in dischargeability actions.

[7] Employee pension claims are given priority. Further, Federal ERISA statutes exclude such plans as estate property.

[8] Spendthrift trusts are excluded from property of the estate.

[9] Claims based upon debtor's fraud are nondischargeable. Fraudulent conveyances are voidable. Debtor's fraud in bankruptcy renders him ineligible for discharge.

[10]Note: Kim Bassinger's bankruptcy filing brought about by an alleged breach of her entertainment contract to perform in a movie.

[11]11 U.S.C. Section 507.

[12]*In re American Reserve Corp.*, 840 F.2d 487 (7th Cir. 1988).

[13]*Local Loan Co. v. Hung*, 292 U.S. 234 (1934).

[14]*U.S. v. Kras*, 409 U.S. 434 (1973).

[15]But corporations and other business entities may be granted a discharge under a reorganization Chapter 11 case. This fulfills an underlying policy of bankruptcy law of preservation of jobs of a debtor business by virtue of the business's rehabilitation.

[16]*U.S. v. Goodstein*, 883 F.2d 1362 (7th Cir. Ill. 1989), cert. denied 494 U.S. 1007 (1990).

[17]*Namby v. Scott*, 86 Eng. Rep. 781, 786 (Exch., 1659).

[18]21 Jac.I.C. 19 (1623).

[19]Madison, The Federalist No. 42.

[20]H.R. Rep. 65 (to accompany S. 1035), 55th Cong., 2nd Sess. (incorporation H.R. Rep. 1228 [to accompany H.R. 8110], 54th Cong., 1st Sess.), pp. 29-30.

[21]Bankruptcy judges are not Article III judges, i.e., not appointed for life and their salaries subject to reduction by Congress.

A The Bankruptcy Reform Act of 1994

On October 22, 1994 Congress enacted the Bankruptcy Reform Act of 1994 (hereinafter "1994 Amendments"). The 1994 Amendments brought sweeping change to much of the Code. The 1994 Amendments apply prospectively. In other words, the 1994 Amendments are applicable to all cases filed after October 22, 1994.

The details of these current amendments, along with the appropriate amendment dates and applicability of the 1994 Amendments, are important to ensure the soundness of a legal assistant's research. Knowledge of the 1994 Amendments will alert the savvy legal assistant to research whether particular case law (even as recent as 1993 or early 1994 cases) has been overruled by the 1994 statutory amendments to the Bankruptcy Code.

In this way the legal assistant will be prepared to ascertain whether case law is a "proposition of law long rooted in bankruptcy history" or merely an old inapplicable case that has been overruled by statutory amendments to the Code. Accordingly, it is a vital research tool to know the date and applicability of the 1994 Amendments to the Bankruptcy Code in relation to the date of the case law located so that measures can be taken to ensure the particular statute is identical to when such a case was determined.

The more significant modifications brought about by the 1994 Amendments follow.

TITLE I—IMPROVED BANKRUPTCY ADMINISTRATION

101. Expedited hearing on automatic stay. The final stay lift hearing "concludes" within 30 days of the preliminary stay lift hearing. Note: Prior law merely required the final hearing be "commenced" within 30 days of preliminary hearing. Also, preliminary hearings must occur within 30 days of motion. The policy of this amendment is to ensure speedy conclusions of stay lift hearings and therefore save time and money. [11 U.S.C. Section 362(e).]

102. Expedited filing of plans under Chapter 11. Any extensions or reductions in a debtor-in-possession's 120-day exclusive period within which to file a plan is appealable as of right. [11 U.S.C. Section 1121, 28 U.S.C. Section 158(a).]

103. Expedited procedure for reaffirmation of debts. No hearing is required when the debtor is adequately represented by counsel. Further, additional language must be included in any reaffirmation agreement. Namely, that such reaffirmation agreement is not required under law, and under the attorney's affidavit that debtor has been advised of the ramifications of the reaffirmation agreement and any subsequent default. [11 U.S.C. Section 524(c).]

104. Powers of bankruptcy courts. Bankruptcy Courts are given power to hold status conferences [11 U.S.C. Section 105]; appeals are permitted if a party is denied its motion for abstention [28 U.S.C. Section 1334(c)(2)]; and procedures for setting up a Bankruptcy Appellate Panel (BAP) and the authority of such BAP to hear appeals in each Circuit are provided [28 U.S.C. Section 158(b).]

105. Participation by Bankruptcy Administrator at meetings of creditors and equity security holders. In states where there is no U.S. Trustee, then the Bankruptcy Administrator has the same powers as the U.S. Trustee to preside at the 341 First Creditors' Meeting. [28 U.S.C. Section 581.]

106. Definitions re: eligibility to serve on Chapter 11 committees. This section clarifies that pension benefit guarantors are eligible to serve on Chapter 11 Official Committees. [11 U.S.C. Section 1102.]

107. Increased incentive compensation for trustees. This section increases the amount the court may approve in compensation to Chapter 7 trustees to 25% of the first $5,000 in disbursements to creditors, 10% of additional amounts up to $50,000, 5% of additional amounts up to $1,000,000, and 3% of any amounts in excess of $1 million.[1]

---

[1]Prior compensation for Chapter 7 trustees was 15% of first $1,000 disbursed, 6% of next $2,000 disbursed and 3% of any additional funds disbursed.

108. *Dollar adjustments.*   This section makes the following upward dollar adjustments: increases the debt limits to be eligible for Chapter 13 to $250,000 unsecured debt and $750,000 secured debt[2] [11 U.S.C. Section 109(e)]; increases the aggregate amount of debt owed to creditors from a minimum in involuntary cases to $10,000[3] [11 U.S.C. Section 303(b)]; increases amounts allowed to certain priority creditors, employee pension, wages, lay-away priority [11 U.S.C. Section 507]; increases virtually all exemption amounts [11 U.S.C. Section 522(d)]; and provides for automatic increases in these dollar amounts at three-year intervals (due to inflation) [11 U.S.C. Section 104].

109. *Premerger notification.*   This section extends the antitrust review period for submissions to the Department of Justice and Federal Trade Commission in regard to mergers or acquisitions.[4] [11 U.S.C. Section 363(b)(2).]

110. *Allowance of creditor committee expenses.*   This section permits members of official committees court-approved reimbursement of actual and necessary out-of-pocket expenses (such as travel and lodging). [11 U.S.C. Section 503(b).]

111. *Bankruptcy court injunctions.*   This section provides a procedure (a trust) for handling future personal injury or wrongful death claims associated with mass tort injuries regarding asbestos. [See *Johns-Manville Corp*, 843 F.2d 636 (2nd Cir. 1988); 11 U.S.C. Section 524(g).]

112. *Authority of a bankruptcy court to conduct jury trials in civil proceedings.* The bankruptcy court can hold such jury trials if specifically designated by the district court and also only with the consent of the parties. [28 U.S.C. Section 157(c).]

113. *Sovereign immunity.*   This section waives a government's sovereign immunity in certain specified categories allowing recovery of money, declaratory judgments, and injunctive relief against such government entity. [11 U.S.C. Section 106(c).]

114. *Service of process on insured deposit institutions.*   Allows such service to be effective upon certified mail in a contested or adversary proceeding. (Previously service was achieved by first class mail.) [F.R.Bankr.P. 7004.]

---

[2]From $100,000 unsecured and $350,000 secured.

[3]From $5,000.

[4]See generally Section 7A of the Clayton Act [15 U.S.C. Section 18(a)], which requires parties to a merger or acquisition to notify the Department of Justice and the Federal Trade Commission and wait a specified period of time before completing the transaction, to allow for review of its competitive implications.

115. *Meetings of creditors and equity security holders.*   This section requires the Chapter 7 trustee to orally examine the debtor regarding certain informational questions. [11 U.S.C. Section 341.]

116. *Tax assessment.*   This section provides a new exception to the automatic stay for audits, demand for tax returns, assessment of uncontested tax liability, as well as making certain tax assessments and demand for payment of such assessments. [11 U.S.C. Section 362(b)(9).]

117. *Additional trustee compensation.*   This section provides that the Chapter 7 trustee will receive an extra $15 in addition to the $45 already provided.

TITLE II—COMMERCIAL BANKRUPTCY ISSUES

201. *Aircraft equipment and vessels, rolling stock equipment.*   This section protects all lease financing agreements and all debt financing agreements. In essence, this section deletes the requirement of the creditor being a purchase money lender on such equipment. [11 U.S.C. Sections 1110, 1168.]

202. *Limitation on liability of noninsider transferee for avoided transfer.*   This section basically overrules the *DePrizio* line of cases[5] (see Chapter 8, "Avoidable Transfers," for discussion). [11 U.S.C. Section 547.]

203. *Perfection of purchase money security interest.*   Grants a purchase money lender a 20-day period to perfect (prior law was 10 days). [11 U.S.C. Section 547(c)(3).]

204. *Continued perfection.*   Certain actions by creditors under the Uniform Commercial Code are permitted to maintain the secured position of the creditor and do not violate the automatic stay. [11 U.S.C. Section 362 and 546.]

205. *Impact of lease rejection on leases.*   This section enables lessees to retain their rights under a leasehold (such as amount and timing of payment; right to use, possess, sublet, or assign). [11 U.S.C. Section 365.]

206. *Contents of plan.*   This section prohibits the modification of the rights of a secured creditor who is solely secured by a debtor's principal residence in Chapter 11 cases. [11 U.S.C. Section 1123(b).]

207. *Priority for sales representatives.*   Sales representatives are entitled to the same priority status as employees. [11 U.S.C. Section 507(a)(3).]

---

[5]*In re V.N. DePrizio Construction Co.*, 847 F.2d 1186 (7th Cir. 1989); *In re C & L Cartage Co.*, 899 F.2d 1490 (6th Cir. 1990); and *In re Robinson Brothers Drilling*, 892 F.2d 850 (10th Cir. 1989).

208. *Production payments.* Estate property excludes production payments (oil or gas produces) sold by a debtor prepetition. [11 U.S.C. Sections 101 and 541.]

209. *Sellers rights to reclaim goods.* This section gives trade creditors ten extra days postpetition to use reclamation rights. [11 U.S.C. Section 546(c)(1).]

210. *Investment of funds of the estate.* The court can approve certain investments of estate money. [11 U.S.C. Section 345(b).]

211. *Selection of private trustees in Chapter 11 cases.* Creditors in Chapter 11 cases can elect their own Chapter 11 trustee. [11 U.S.C. Section 1104.]

212. *Rights of general partnership trustee against general partners.* The trustee has a claim against general partners for partnership deficiency to the extent the partner is personally liable under state law. [11 U.S.C. Section 723(a).]

213. *Impairment of claims and interests.* Cash payments to creditors as of the effective date no longer leave a class unimpaired unless they are paid interest as well. [11 U.S.C. Section 1124.] This section also disallows proofs of claim that are not timely filed. [11 U.S.C. Section 502.]

214. *Protection of security interest in postpetition rents.* Cash collateral perfection as well as certain hotel rents that constitute cash collateral are articulated in this section. [11 U.S.C. Section 552.]

215. *Netting of swap agreements.* This section includes spot foreign exchange agreements within the definition of "swap agreements." [11 U.S.C. Section 101(55).]

216. *Limitation of avoiding powers.* This section clarifies the statute of limitations of a trustee's avoiding powers. [11 U.S.C. Section 546(a)(1).]

217. *Small business.* This section defines "small business" (debtor with debts less than $2 million and not in the real estate business). Such small business debtors are allowed to preclude the appointment of creditors committees, have a 100-day exclusivity period to file a plan, and may hold a combination disclosure statement approval/plan confirmation hearing. [11 U.S.C. Section 101(51C), 1102(a), 1121(e), 1125.]

218. *Single-asset real estate.* Defines "single-asset real estate" (real estate generates substantially all of debtor's income; debts amount to less than $4 million). The automatic stay relief provides an additional section for creditors for single-asset real estate (if no plan filed within 90 days or debtor has not commenced monthly payments). [11 U.S.C. Sections 101(51B), 362(d)(3).]

219. *Leases of personal property.* Sixty days postpetition a debtor must perform all obligations under certain leases. [11 U.S.C. Section 365(b)(1).]

220. *Exemptions for small business investment companies.* Small business investment companies, as licensed by the Small Business Administration, are ineligible to file for bankruptcy. [11 U.S.C. Section 109(h).]

221. *Payment of taxes with borrowed funds.* Makes such loans nondischargeable. [11 U.S.C. Section 523(a)(14).]

222. *Return of goods.* Allows debtors to return unsold goods in order to offset debts. [11 U.S.C. Section 546.]

223. *Proceeds of money order agreements.* Excludes from estate property the proceeds from money orders sold within 14 days of the petition. [11 U.S.C. Section 541(b)(1).]

224. *Trustee's duties; professional fees.* Requires the U.S. Trustee to invoke procedural guidelines regarding professional fees in bankruptcy. [28 U.S.C. Section 586(a)(3)(A).]

225. *Notices to creditors.* All notices to creditors must set forth the debtor's name, address, and tax identification number.

TITLE III—CONSUMER BANKRUPTCY ISSUES

301. *Period for curing default on principal residence.* Safeguards Chapter 13 debtors' rights to cure default in their home mortgage at least through completion of foreclosure sale under state law. [11 U.S.C. Section 1322(b)(3) and (5).]

302. *Nondischargeability of fine under Chapter 13.* Adds criminal fines as nondischargeable in Chapter 13. [11 U.S.C. Section 1328(a)(3).]

303. *Impairment of exemptions.* Provides a simple arithmetic test to determine if a lien impairs an exemption regarding the debtor's right to avoid such lien. [11 U.S.C. Section 522(f).]

304. *Protection of child support and alimony.* Automatic stay does not apply to the establishment of paternity or support, or to modification of support actions. [11 U.S.C. Section 362(b)(2).] Priority status is afforded to past support obligations. [11 U.S.C. Section 507(a)(7).] Debtors cannot avoid judicial liens securing alimony or support. [11 U.S.C. Section 522(f)(1).] Certain property settlement obligations in a divorce are nondischargeable. [11 U.S.C. Section 523(a)(15).] Bona fide support payments are not subject to avoidance. [11 U.S.C. Section 547(c)(7).]

305. *Interest on interest.*   No interest is required on mortgage arrears cured through a plan. Overrules *Rake v. Wade*, 113 S.Ct. 2187 (1993). [11 U.S.C. Section 506(b).]

306. *Exceptions to discharge.*   Presumption of fraud increases amount of money as well as prepetition reach-back period. [11 U.S.C. Section 523(a)(2)(C).]

307. *Payments under Chapter 13.*   Trustee should commence making payments as soon as possible after confirmation of Chapter 13 plan. [11 U.S.C. Section 1326(a)(2).]

308. *Bankruptcy petition preparers.*   Creates standards and penalties for bankruptcy petition preparers (i.e., "doc prep"). In essence, doc preps must provide their personal identification on the bankruptcy filing and must give a copy of the documents to the debtor. Further, if doc preps engage in fraud, incompetence, or a deceptive act, the debtor is allowed actual damages, statutory damages of $2,000 or twice the amount paid to the preparer plus attorney's fees and costs. The doc prep person is also subject to injunctions to prevent further work in the bankruptcy preparation business. [11 U.S.C. Section 110.]

309. *Fairness to condominium and cooperative owners.*   Certain homeowners association dues are nondischargeable. [11 U.S.C. Section 523(a)(16).]

310. *Nonavoidability of a security interest on tools and implements of trade, animals, and crops.*   Limits certain debtors' lien avoidance regarding exempt property (tools of trade) over $5,000. [11 U.S.C. Section 522(f).]

311. *Conversion of case under Chapter 13.*   In conversion from Chapter 13 to Chapter 7, the property acquired after the Chapter 13 petition but prior to the Chapter 7 conversion is remitted to the debtor.

312. *Bankruptcy fraud.*   Increases penalties to fines of no more than $5,000 or imprisonment of not more than 5 years, or both. [18 U.S.C. Section 152.]

313. *Protection against discriminatory treatment of applications for student loans.* Ensures that applicants for student loans are not denied benefits due to prior bankruptcy filings. [11 U.S.C. Section 525(c)(1).]

TITLE IV—GOVERNMENTAL BANKRUPTCY ISSUES

401. *Exception from automatic stay for postpetition property taxes.*   Excepts from the stay the creation or perfection of ad valorem property taxes. [11 U.S.C. Section 362(b)(18).]

402. *Municipal bankruptcy.*   Clarifies eligibility for municipal bankruptcy filing. [11 U.S.C. Section 901.]

Severability; Effective Date; Application

The effective date of the 1994 Amendments is the enactment date, October 22, 1994. The 1994 Amendments apply prospectively (i.e., to all cases filed after October 22, 1994).

2 *Infrastructure of a Bankruptcy Case*

It is your first day on the job at a downtown bankruptcy firm. You get a telephone call from a man who says he is the trustee *in a case where your firm represents the* debtor. *The trustee says creditors have communicated to him that* bankruptcy estate *assets are missing. The Trustee wants to know if the debtor has claimed an* exemption *on this property. If not, the trustee is going to report it to the* Bankruptcy Court.

Who are the players in bankruptcy? How do they interact? Is there a special court for bankruptcy? Bankruptcy seems to have a language all its own. What do some of these bankruptcy terms mean?

PARTIES

Many parties are involved in each bankruptcy case. Each of these parties, or participants, plays an independent and important function, depending on the boundaries the Code places on their roles. However, all of these parties at some point in the case must interact with one another in order to achieve their specific objectives. Accordingly, a bankruptcy paralegal must be familiar with the nature of all these participants and their roles in a bankruptcy case.

A *debtor* is in every case. A debtor is the person or entity that files bankruptcy.[1] A debtor may be an individual, a husband and wife, a corporation, a partnership, a nonprofit corporation, a railroad, or even a municipality.[2] Debtors generally owe money to others and seek relief from such obligations through protection under the Code. However, despite the common misconception, it is not a requirement that debtors be insolvent.

In fact, debtors often file bankruptcy in order to reorganize their debts. This allows debtors to pay their obligations in a practical manner that meets their budget or means. Under the Code, reorganization cases also often allow debtors to relieve themselves of burdensome obligations, such as unprofitable leases or unfavorable mortgage terms.

Creditors also exist in every bankruptcy. Creditors are owed money or other obligations from the debtor. Each creditor holds a *claim*, or right to payment or an equitable remedy.

Creditors who hold claims against the debtor may be unsecured creditors, secured creditors, or priority creditors. *Unsecured creditors* are those who hold a claim against the debtor that is not secured by collateral, such as credit card debts. *Secured creditors* are those who hold a claim against the debtor that is secured by a lien upon the property of the estate, such as a car loan or a mortgage. *Priority creditors* are unsecured creditors who hold claims against the debtor that are given preference in any repayment distribution. Some claims Congress has afforded statutory priority include back alimony or support, taxes, wages to employees, etc.[3]

From a practical standpoint, it is best to include all potential "claimants" as creditors at the outset and alert the supervising attorney to the circumstances of a questionable creditor in a case.

The *trustee* is the official representative of the estate. The trustee exercises his or her statutory powers principally for the benefit of the unsecured creditors. A trustee in such capacity can sue or be sued and holds numerous administrative powers and specified duties. All Chapter 7 cases require a trustee to be chosen from a panel of private trustees maintained by the U.S. Trustee's Office to serve in a particular region. Immediately upon filing a petition, the U.S. Trustee appoints a trustee to serve as an interim trustee until the 341 First Creditor's Meeting. At the 341 Meeting the interim trustee becomes the permanent trustee unless another person is elected.

The duties of a trustee in Chapter 7 are to locate and take possession of all estate property. Thereafter, the trustee converts such property into cash. After the property has been liquidated into cash, the trustee makes distributions to the claimants in the order of priority. Finally, a Chapter 7 trustee has a duty to expeditiously close the estate.

In Chapter 11, a trustee (who replaces the debtor-in-possession) is authorized to operate the debtor's business. The Chapter 11 trustee also must investigate and file a report on the debtor's conduct, financial condition, and business operations. The Chapter 11 trustee also reports on the advisability of continuing the business of the Chapter 11. The Chapter 11 trustee may also file a plan of reorganization.

Note: Trustees are always appointed in liquidation cases (Chapter 7) and consumer reorganization cases (Chapter 13). However, trustees are seldom appointed in commercial reorganization cases (Chapter 11). Instead, the debtor assumes the role of a trustee as *debtor-in-possession*.

In Chapter 13 cases, the U.S. Trustee usually appoints a standing trustee. The Chapter 13 trustee must advise at the confirmation hearing regarding the proposed plan, furnish nonlegal advice to the debtor, and make sure that the debtor begins and maintains monthly plan payments. *Confirmation* is when the Court formally approves a plan that outlines the means and manner of repayment to creditors. Additionally, the Chapter 13 trustee makes distributions of payments to the creditors once the plan has been confirmed. The Chapter 13 trustee also investigates and makes an official report regarding the debtor's conduct, financial condition, business operations, and the advisability of continuation of the business.

An *examiner* investigates certain charges of fraud, dishonesty, incompetence, or mismanagement of the past or present management of a Chapter 11 debtor. An examiner is appointed only when a trustee has not been appointed in a Chapter 11 case. A debtor-in-possession retains its property and continues to operate its business even if an examiner is appointed. The examiner also advises as to the continuation of the Chapter 11 debtor's business.

The *United States Trustee* assumes many of the administrative responsibilities of a bankruptcy. This includes appointment and supervision of bankruptcy trustees, appointment of official committees, etc. The U.S. Trustee is appointed by the Attorney General for a term of five years.

The *creditors' committee* in a Chapter 11 reorganization case is a committee of unsecured creditors appointed by the U.S. Trustee's Office. This official committee usually consists of those willing persons holding the seven largest unsecured claims against the debtor. A creditors' committee assists in consulting with the debtor-in-possession or with a trustee and also participates in the formulation of an acceptable plan of reorganization. Note: In very large Chapter 7 liquidation cases, the unsecured creditors will elect a creditors' committee that consists of between 3 and 11 unsecured creditors to consult with the trustee about the administration of the estate.

Equity security holders are the holders of shares in a debtor corporation or partnership interests in a debtor partnership. Such equity security holders may also form an official committee similar to that of the unsecured creditors' committee.

Professional persons are those persons hired by the trustee, debtor-in-possession, or official committee (unsecured creditors' committee, equity security holders' committee). Such professionals may include the debtor's attorney, trustee's attorney, official committee's attorneys, accountants, auctioneers, property managers, etc. All professionals employed by the estate in the bankruptcy must have their employment authorized by the Bankruptcy Court by application. Additionally, all compensation to such professionals must be authorized by the Bankruptcy Court. Note: The compensation of such professionals is through estate property as an administrative expense.[4]

THE BANKRUPTCY COURT SYSTEM

District Courts have original and exclusive subject matter jurisdiction over all Bankruptcy Code cases.[5] District Courts also have original, but not exclusive, subject matter jurisdiction over civil proceedings arising under the Code (core matters) or those arising in, or related to, the Code (noncore matters).[6]

Notwithstanding the District Court's original jurisdiction, the District Court is allowed to make wholesale blanket references of both core[7] and noncore[8] matters to the Bankruptcy Court.[9] This is done as a matter of course in all districts throughout the United States.

The Bankruptcy Court is a "unit" of the District Court.[10] The District Court may provide that all cases and/or proceedings shall be referred to the Bankruptcy Court.[11] Bankruptcy Courts may hear and enter final orders in all core matters and may hear all noncore matters referred to them by the District Courts.[12] However, the Bankruptcy Court may not enter final orders in noncore matters unless all parties consent.[13] Without consent, the Bankruptcy Court submits proposed findings of fact and conclusions of law to the District Court. The District Court may then review such findings and conclusions de novo upon a timely request of any party.[14]

Accordingly, the jurisdiction of the Bankruptcy Court is derived entirely from the jurisdiction of the District Court. The District Court (and therefore, consequentially, the Bankruptcy Court) has exclusive jurisdiction over all property, wherever located, of the debtor as of the commencement of such case, as well as over property of the estate.[15]

Since the District Court has original jurisdiction over all bankruptcy cases, it retains the power to withdraw, in whole or in part, any core or noncore matter referred to the bankruptcy court, either sua sponte or upon motion of any party for "good cause."[16] A mandatory withdrawal of the reference (to bring the matter before the district court) applies in proceedings involving questions of federal and bankruptcy law and in personal injury tort and wrongful death claims.

Motions to withdraw the reference are to be filed with the Bankruptcy Clerk's office even though the District Court shall hear and adjudicate such motion.[17]

Bankruptcy Judges

Bankruptcy judges are appointed to 14-year terms by the Court of Appeals [28 U.S.C. Section 152(a)] (as opposed to life appointments of District Court judges).

Appeals from the Bankruptcy Court

Four avenues exist for appealing a judgment or order of the Bankruptcy Court. First, a party may always move the Bankruptcy Court who rendered such judgment or order to reconsider under F.R.Bankr.P. 9024.[18] Otherwise, a Bankruptcy Court order or judgment may be appealed to either a Bankruptcy Appellate Panel (BAP) or to the District Court.

A BAP is a tribunal composed of three bankruptcy judges from the districts within the circuit. The BAP is empowered to act as an intermediary appellate court between the Bankruptcy Court and the Circuit Court. The BAP has appellate jurisdiction over all final judgments, orders, and decrees of bankruptcy courts, as well as discretionary jurisdiction over all interlocutory[19] judgments, orders, and decrees of Bankruptcy Courts.[20]

All parties to the appeal must consent to review by the BAP. If a party does not wish an appeal to proceed to the BAP, an objection to the referral of the appeal must be filed. If such objection is filed, the appeal to the BAP is referred back to the District Court.

Additionally, the first and primary appellate review for judgments and orders (absent consent to the BAP) is the District Court. The District Court has appellate jurisdiction over all final judgments, orders, and decrees of Bankruptcy Courts, as well as discretionary appellate jurisdiction over all interlocutory judgments, orders, and decrees.[21] An appeal to the district court may be brought only in the judicial district in which the bankruptcy court is located. For example, an appeal from the Bankruptcy Court sitting in the Central District of California goes to the District Court in the Central District of California and cannot be appealed to the District Court in Arizona, Oregon, or even the Northern District of California.

A final judgment, order, or decree of a BAP or District Court may be appealed to the Circuit Court of Appeals.[22] For example, any appeal from a judgment of any District Court in California is appealed to the 9th Circuit Court of Appeals, any from a District Court in Georgia is to the 11th Circuit Court of Appeals, etc. Finally, all appeals from decisions of any Circuit Court of appeals are to the U.S. Supreme Court.[23]

STARE DECISIS OR PRECEDENT OF BANKRUPTCY CASE LAW

The Bankruptcy Code is a relatively new law compared with many other areas of law. Consequently, bankruptcy law is continuously evolving. Moreover, the Bankruptcy Code is amended frequently; for example, note the Bankruptcy Reform Act of 1994. Consequently, many cases regarding bankruptcy issues are published constantly to interpret new amendments or to interpret long-standing Code sections based on new factual twists. A majority of these cases are from the Bankruptcy Court that is the trial level court. Other published cases are from appeals from the Bankruptcy Court and are therefore from either the District Court or a Bankruptcy Appellate Panel. Still further on the appeal chain are the bankruptcy cases from the Circuit Courts. Finally, the Supreme Court of the United States regularly hears and publishes cases on bankruptcy matters, most often when the circuits are split on particular issues.

Accordingly, it is important for a legal assistant to realize which of these myriad of cases is controlling when researching a particular issue. Controlling cases are *stare decisis* or precedent for cases that follow in that jurisdiction. *Stare decisis*, or *precedent*, is the principle of law holding that, when a court has determined a legal issue (such as interpretation of a statute), it will adhere to that principal and apply it to all future cases where the facts are substantially the same, regardless of whether the parties and property are the same. *Stare decisis* or precedent serves to bind the same court or other courts of lower rank in subsequent cases when the very point is again in controversy.

All rulings of the Supreme Court of the United States bind all Bankruptcy Courts throughout the nation. However, always ensure that any Supreme Court bankruptcy cases have not been specifically overruled by Amendments to the Bankruptcy Code. For example, the recent Supreme Court case of *Rake v. Wade*, 113 S.Ct. 2187 (1993) resolved an issue (Chapter 13 "cure" not allowed interest) where several Circuit Courts had come to differing results. However, the 1994 Amendments enacted 11 U.S.C. Section 1322(e) in its entirety to specifically overrule *Rake v. Wade*.

Directly under the Supreme Court are the Circuit Court cases. All Circuit Court cases bind all District Court decisions, BAP decisions, and trial-level Bankruptcy Court decisions *within that circuit*. All courts outside the circuit are not bound by such decision; however, it may be persuasive. For example, the 9th Circuit publishes a decision regarding mortgage foreclosures and whether they may be avoided as fraudulent conveyances. All district courts within the 9th Circuit, such as Northern District of California, District of Washington, District of Arizona, Southern District of California, the 9th Circuit BAP, and District Courts in Oregon are *bound* by the 9th Circuit's decision regarding this issue. Further, all Bankruptcy Courts (trial-level courts) within every state of that circuit are also bound by the Circuit Court's decision. However, the 6th Circuit is not bound by any 9th Circuit decision, nor are any District Courts outside the 9th Circuit. Further, no trial-level Bankruptcy Courts outside the 9th Circuit are bound by this decision. At best, the decision may serve as persuasive, should no controlling precedent exist in that particular Circuit.

Under the Circuit Courts are the District Courts. All decisions by the District Court serve as precedent for all the Bankruptcy Courts within that district. Note: District Court cases do not serve as precedent upon one another. For example, the Northern District of California publishes a case regarding the appropriate sanctions for "bankruptcy mills." All Bankruptcy Courts within the Northern District of California are bound by this decision. However, the District Court in the Southern District of California or the Central District of California is not bound by such a decision (although it holds strong persuasive weight). Needless to say, no District Court in New York is bound by the Northern District of California's case, let alone any Bankruptcy Court in New York.

Finally, Bankruptcy Courts publish a substantial number of cases as well. Often the Bankruptcy Court, as a trial court, hears and determines many unique as well as many common issues that arise time and again. Also, it is not unusual for parties not to appeal certain decisions of the Bankruptcy Court due to the time and expense of such appeal in relation to the benefit should they prevail on appeal. Accordingly, the Bankruptcy Court has a unique, up-close view of many bankruptcy issues. Moreover, unlike the Supreme Court, the Circuit Courts, or the District Courts, the Bankruptcy Court only hears and determines bankruptcy matters and is therefore very well versed with even the most esoteric bankruptcy issues.

However, Bankruptcy Court cases (the trial court level) hold no precedent for any other court. Bankruptcy Court cases often are persuasive, especially when the Bankruptcy Court is in the same district or even circuit. Note, even bankruptcy cases outside the district may prove sufficiently persuasive if they are well reasoned and there is no existing precedent.

THE BANKRUPTCY CODE

The Bankruptcy Code is Title 11 of the United States Code. Title 11 is divided into eight chapters. Chapters 1, 3, and 5 are called the *omnibus* administrative chapters, which are generally applicable to all cases. Chapters 7, 9, 11, 12, and 13 are the chapters under which particular relief is sought (i.e., issues specific to cases filed as Chapter 7 will be found within Title 11, Chapter 7 of the

Code.) Note that most of the chapters are odd numbers. Congress specifically designed the Bankruptcy Code this way to allow substantial amendments through even-numbered chapters. For example, Chapter 12 was added in its entirety in 1986 as an experimental chapter available only to family farmers. Congress recognized that most family farmers were ineligible for Chapter 13 and Chapter 11 was too complicated, time-consuming, expensive and unworkable for family farmers.

Chapter 1—Definitions (11 U.S.C. Sections 101-109)

Section 101 provides definitions of all words and phrases used throughout Title 11. Section 102(1) defines the term "after notice and a hearing." Section 103 defines which of the provisions of Chapter 1, 3, and 5 apply in cases filed in Chapters 7, 9, 11, 12, and 13. Section 105(5) is the provision that allows the bankruptcy court to use general equity powers. Section 109 defines who is eligible to be a debtor under cases filed in Chapters 7, 9, 11, 12, and 13.

Chapter 3—Case Administration (11 U.S.C. Sections 301-366)

Chapter 3 contains the automatic stay provisions. Additionally, Chapter 3 deals with how a case is commenced, and outlines the officers in bankruptcy and how they are compensated. Chapter 3 also deals with some basic administrative matters in cases. Additionally, Chapter 3 includes provisions regarding the use, sale, or lease of estate property, and the executory contract provisions of the Code.

Chapter 5—Creditors, the Debtor, and the Estate (11 U.S.C. Sections 501-599)

Chapter 5 includes how a creditor gets its claim before the estate and how that claim is handled. Chapter 5 also deals with the debtor's duties and benefits, including the right to and effect of the discharge. Finally, Chapter 5 defines the "estate" and contains the trustee's avoiding powers.

Chapter 7—Liquidation (11 U.S.C. Sections 701-766)

This is the first affirmative relief chapter of the Code. Chapter 7 is liquidation or "straight bankruptcy" with no reorganization aspects. Chapter 7 deals with the appointment of a trustee and his or her duties. Chapter 7 instructs how the estate is collected, liquidated, and distributed. Finally, this chapter contains provisions regarding stockbroker liquidation and commodity broker liquidations.

Chapter 9—Municipality Reorganizations (11 U.S.C. Sections 901-946)

Chapter 9 deals with general administration matters of municipal reorganizations as well as the filing, confirmation, and effect of the Chapter 9 plan.

Chapter 11—Reorganization (11 U.S.C. Sections 1101-1174)

Chapter 11 is business or commercial reorganization where the debtor proposes the method and means to repay creditors through a plan. Chapter 11 includes the various parties in interest found in a Chapter 11 case and their roles. Chapter 11 also deals with plan formulation, confirmation, and postconfirmation matters.[24]

Chapter 12—Family Farmer Reorganizations (11 U.S.C. Sections 1201-1231)

Chapter 12 is available exclusively to "family farmers" as defined under the Code. This chapter is designed to give family farmers a fighting chance to reorganize their debts and keep their land. Chapter 12 was enacted as an experimental chapter in 1986 and included a sunset clause of seven years. In other words, Chapter 12 would be repealed in 1993 if Congress did not act further. However, in 1993 Congress extended the Sunset Provision to October 1, 1998. Chapter 12 includes provisions of the various parties in a Chapter 12 case such as the codebtor and trustee as well as their roles. Chapter 12 also specifies a farmer's plan formulation, confirmation, and postconfirmation matters.

Chapter 13—Individual Debt Adjustment (11 U.S.C. Sections 1301-1330)

Chapter 13 is known as wage earner reorganization. It is designed to allow individuals with regular income to reorganize by consolidating their debts and making one payment to the trustee. Chapter 13 is not available to business entities such as corporations or partnerships. Chapter 13 includes administrative matters and the role of the Chapter 13 trustee. This chapter also includes provisions regarding the formulation and confirmation of a wage earner's plan as well as postconfirmation matters.

THE BANKRUPTCY ESTATE

11 U.S.C. Section 541 describes the property that becomes "estate property" as well as the time within which to calculate whether property is estate property. The commencement of a case (i.e., the filing of a bankruptcy petition) cre-

ates an estate. Therefore, at the point in time that a bankruptcy is filed, the property of the estate is determined and the rights of third parties are fixed. Imagine a snapshot being taken at the precise moment a debtor files a bankruptcy. All property the debtor owns at that moment becomes estate property.

In general, estate property includes both tangible and intangible property, property recovered by the trustee, and property in the hands of a third party. Intangible property is something that cannot be touched, such as accounts receivable. The bankruptcy estate also encompasses possible lawsuits held by the debtor. Estate property further includes community property of the debtor and the debtor's nonfiling spouse. Estate property also includes certain property acquired within six months of the petition through inheritance, in a property settlement with the debtor's spouse, or as a beneficiary of a life insurance policy.

The estate property is comprised of six categories delineated in 11 U.S.C. Section 541(a) regardless of where the property is located or who holds the property. Therefore, the location of the property or whoever has possession of the property is immaterial. For example, property seized by the IRS before the petition is filed remains the property of the estate which the IRS may have to return. [*U.S. v. Whiting Pools, Inc.*, 462 U.S. 198 (1983).]

The categories of property included as estate property are:

1. *All legal or equitable interests of the debtor in property as of the commencement of the case.* This section includes every conceivable interest of the debtor in property, including all forms whether tangible or intangible, personal or real, causes of action, leasehold interests, or possessory interests. For example, a debtor's accounts receivable are property of the estate.[25] A debtor's contingent interest in earnest money deposited in escrow is estate property.[26]

However, even if the property is included in the estate, it does not change the nature of the property. Accordingly, if the debtor has a limited interest in the property, such interest remains limited as estate property. In short, the debtor's rights are not expanded beyond what existed at the commencement of the case. For example, if certain property of the debtor was subject to a constructive trust, then the estate takes such property subject to the restrictions of the constructive trust.[27]

This limitation is especially important in the area of prebankruptcy transfers, such as a foreclosure. If the foreclosure is completed prior to bankruptcy it would leave the debtor, and thus the estate, with no rights in the property. See *In re Kleitz*, 6 B.R. 214 (Bankr. Nev. 1989) (where sale was completed 30 minutes before the bankruptcy was filed, such property is not estate property). However, if the debtor has a right to redeem the property under state law, then such redemption rights would pass through to the estate.

Additionally, even if property is subject to exemption (11 U.S.C. Section 522, discussed below) by the debtor, such property becomes property of the estate. Merely listing the property as exempt does not exclude the property from the estate. However, thereafter such property is excluded from the estate once the exemption is approved by the court.[28]

Also, any interest that the debtor has under state law in any property held in a tenancy by the entirety, tenancy in common, or joint tenancy becomes property of the estate.[29] State law determines the nature and extent of the debtor's interests in these tenancies. Once state law has fixed the character of an interest in property, federal bankruptcy law mandates such interest be included as estate property.

Further, leases, contracts, or options for the sale of land also become property of the estate. For example, a debtor's unexpired lease for commercial property, or license to operate a hospital,[30] or contracts to perform maintenance services,[31] are property included in the bankruptcy estate.

Whatever interest the debtor has in personal property also becomes property of the estate. Even when property is repossessed, the debtor retains an interest until a sale occurs. Therefore, even if a car is repossessed before bankruptcy is filed, a debtor has both legal title to the car and equitable rights to cure the default and redeem the vehicle. Accordingly, the repossessed car is property of the estate regardless of who has physical custody.[32]

Additionally, when the debtor merely holds property as a bailee and title remains in the bailor, the estate acquires only such rights as held by the debtor (namely, physical possession). Therefore, the estate holds the property only as a bailee and the bailor can recover the property or its proceeds from the estate.

Also, any cause of action (i.e., a potential lawsuit) belonging to the debtor at the time of the bankruptcy filing is property of the estate. If the trustee does not reject the cause of action, he or she stands in the shoes of the debtor. Accordingly, personal injury actions,[33] actions against the government, contract actions,[34] actions for injuries to property of the debtor, and the rights of a debtor corporation to bring suit against its stockholders, members, directors, or officers all become property of the estate.

Property held by the debtor as a trustee for another is included in the estate but only to the extent of the debtor's interest. However, property held in trust for the debtor is included in the estate (except where the restrictions of 11 U.S.C. Section 541(c)(2) apply, discussed below).

2. *All interests of the debtor and the debtor's nonfiling spouse in community property as of the petition date, provided that such property is either under the sole, equal, or joint management and control of the debtor, or the property may be liable for* *a claim against the debtor.* A bankruptcy petition by one spouse passes all community property into the estate. Accordingly, all of a debtor's separate and community property is property of the estate, even though the debtor's spouse is not a debtor.[35] Therefore, a spouse filing in one of the eight community property states[36] cannot protect community property from becoming property of the estate. For example, even though only one spouse files bankruptcy, the real estate held by both the debtor and spouse as community property becomes property of the estate (provided such property is subject to the joint control of debtor).[37]

3. *Any interest in property that the trustee recovers as a voidable transaction.* This includes property that the trustee successfully recovers in a voidance action.[38]

4. *Any interest in property ordered transferred to the estate through a successful voidance action.* This includes property where the trustee is successful in a voidable transfer action and the Bankruptcy Court orders the property to be turned over to the estate.

5. *Certain "after acquired property."* If acquired within six months of the petition date, any interest acquired (a) by bequest, devise, or inheritance, (b) as a result of a property settlement agreement with the debtor's spouse or divorce decree, or (c) as a beneficiary of a life insurance policy or of a death benefit plan.

To further this, F.R.Bankr.P. 1007(h) requires the debtor to file a supplemental schedule showing any interests acquired after the date the petition was filed. Accordingly, any property acquired by the debtor up to 180 days after the petition through bequest, devise, or inheritance under a will,[39] through property settlement in a divorce decree, or by receiving benefits of a life insurance policy become estate property and must be reported.

6. *Proceeds, product, offspring, rents, or other profits from property of the estate (except postpetition earnings of an individual debtor).* For example, if an unencumbered apartment building is estate property, then all postpetition rents paid from the tenants would be estate property as well.

The estate generally includes the right to payment earned before bankruptcy, even if actual payment occurs later. This includes such things as commissions[40] or termination pay.[41] However, wages earned postpetition are not part of the debtor's Chapter 7 estate.[42] Note: Postpetition earnings in Chapter 13 and Chapter 12 cases are property of the estate.[43]

Despite the broad scope of estate property, property specifically excluded from becoming property of the estate is statutorily articulated in 11 U.S.C. Section 541(b). Such excluded property, that is not considered property of the estate, includes the following:

1. Any power that the debtor may exercise solely for the benefit of an entity other than the debtor. Property the debtor holds in trust for another, for example, is therefore not property of the bankruptcy estate.[44]

2. Any interest of the debtor in a nonresidential real property lease that has terminated by its own conditions prior to the filing of the petition. Therefore, a nonresidential lease (commercial property) that has expired by virtue of its own terms prepetition is not estate property.

3. Any license or accreditation or ability to participate in financial aid programs of a debtor that is an educational institution. This section eliminates the assertion by a debtor-school that it has a property interest in its accreditation status, state licensure, or the right to participate in financial aid programs for its students.

4. Any interest of the debtor pursuant to a farmout agreement in liquidate or gaseous hydrocarbons (excluding the consideration given the debtor for such a farmout agreement). A *farmout agreement* is a written agreement by which the owner of a right to produce liquid or gaseous hydrocarbons on property has agreed to transfer and assign all of that party's right to another entity in order for that entity to produce liquid or gaseous hydrocarbons. This paragraph excludes from estate property any interest that a debtor could recover in real property through a farmout agreement. In essence, this section prevents a debtor from undoing the agreement and reclaiming the property interest previously transferred in the farmout agreement.

5. Any interest in cash arising from the sale of the debtor of a money order (that is made within 14 days before the petition and that prohibits the debtor to commingle funds of such proceeds with property of the debtor). This section excludes from the bankruptcy estate proceeds from money orders sold within 14 days of the bankruptcy petition pursuant to an agreement prohibiting the commingling of such sale proceeds with property of the debtor. To benefit from this section, the money order issuer must have acted, prior to the petition, to require compliance with the commingling prohibition.[45]

Property becomes property of the estate regardless of any provisions in an agreement or transfer instrument that would apply outside the bankruptcy arena that (1) restricts or conditions a transfer of the debtor's interest in such property, or (2) is conditioned upon the debtor's insolvency, the debtor's filing bankruptcy, or the appointment of a trustee in bankruptcy that allows a termination of the debtor's interest in the property.

This provision strikes down limitations that restrict or condition transfer of the debtor's interest. Therefore provisions that restrict transfer of the debtor's assets into the estate are void. Accordingly, nonbankruptcy contractual provisions are unenforceable when they prevent a debtor's property interest from becoming part of the bankruptcy estate.[46]

Also, limitations that are conditioned on the insolvency or financial condition of the debtor or on the appointment of a custodian of the debtor's property are also void. Therefore, clauses limiting, modifying, or terminating a debtor's interest in property upon the filing of a bankruptcy petition are invalid.[47] Such clauses are commonly referred to as *ipso facto clauses* and are of no effect.

For example, disability benefits become property of the estate, despite restrictions on transfer.[48] Also, state liquor laws prohibiting the transfer of a liquor license cannot keep the license from becoming property of the estate.[49]

A major exclusion from estate property is as follows: The debtor is a beneficiary of a trust and the trust does not allow the debtor to transfer this beneficial interest to anyone. This prohibition against any transfer is called a restriction on the transfer. While most restrictions on the transfer of the debtor's interest in property are invalid, restrictions on the transfer of a debtor's beneficial interest *in a trust* are preserved. However, the restrictions must be enforceable under applicable nonbankruptcy laws. In essence, this protects spendthrift trusts from becoming estate property. However, such spendthrift trusts must be impenetrable under state law spendthrift trust statutes. Also, the Supreme Court announced that ERISA-qualified plans (retirement accounts) are excluded from the estate. The debtor's beneficial interest in these retirement accounts is restricted by applicable nonbankruptcy law, namely the federal provisions under ERISA.

Finally, property in which the debtor holds only legal title also becomes property of the estate, but only to the extent of the debtor's legal title to such property. This section was enacted to preserve the status of bona fide secondary mortgage market transactions. Therefore, mortgages or interests in them that are sold in the secondary market should not be included in the debtor's estate.[50] The purpose of this section is twofold: (1) to insure that secondary mortgage market sales, as they are currently structured, are not subject to challenge by the trustees in bankruptcy and (2) to insure that the purchasers will be able to obtain what they have purchased from the debtor without the trustees attacking the transactions as a loan from the purchaser to the seller.

EXEMPTIONS

Exempt property is protected from the reach of creditors. Exemptions are provided by every state and by federal bankruptcy law in order to protect debtors and their families from destitution. Exemptions (along with discharge) are the principal means by which bankruptcy's "fresh start" is achieved.

Debtors in bankruptcy must claim their exemptions in order to enjoy them; thereafter exempt property revests in (or goes back to) the debtor and is no longer property of the estate. Note: Any objection to a debtor's claimed exemptions must occur within 30 days of the conclusion of the 341 First Creditors' Meeting. [F.R.Bankr.P. 4003(b).] If no objection is timely made, the property claimed as exempt is automatically exempt under 11 U.S.C. Section 522(l). [*Taylor v. Freeland & Kronz*, 112 S.Ct. 1644 (1992).] However, only individual debtors are allowed to exempt property from the bankruptcy estate. In short, no corporation, partnership, business association, etc. is allowed any exemptions whatsoever.

Exemptions can be claimed in any bankruptcy chapter that an individual can file (i.e., Chapters 7, 11, 12, or 13). In most Chapter 7 cases, the exempt property will be the only property that the debtors can keep. All other property (estate property) is liquidated and the proceeds are distributed to creditors.

Under 11 U.S.C. Section 522(b), debtors may claim from the federal exemption list unless applicable state law specifically does not so authorize. This is the "opt-out" provision that allows states to restrict bankruptcy debtors only to exemptions available under state (nonbankruptcy) law.[51]

If a state has not "opted out," then the debtor may claim from the federal list of exemptions found in 11 U.S.C. Section 522(d). However, a debtor must claim either the state exemptions or the federal exemptions within 11 U.S.C. Section 522(d). Mixing and matching federal and state exemptions is not permissible.[52]

Additionally, each joint debtor (i.e., each spouse) can assert an exemption against the same item of property. This effectively doubles the exemptible amount in that item.[53] However, joint debtors must both claim under either the state exemptions or the federal exemptions. For example, a husband cannot choose state exemptions in a joint case where the wife chooses federal exemptions.

The list of federal exemptions available under 11 U.S.C. Section 522(d) is as follows:[54]

1. The debtor's interest in real estate or personal property that the debtor uses as a residence in the value of $15,000.

2. The debtor's interest not to exceed $2,500 in value in one motor vehicle.

3. The debtor's interest not to exceed $400 in any particular item or $8,000 in aggregate value, in household furnishings, household goods, wearing apparel, appliances, books, animals, crops, or musical instruments, that are held primarily for the personal, family, or household use of the debtor or a dependent of the debtor.

4. The debtor's aggregate interest, not to exceed $1,000 in value, in jewelry held for personal, family, or household use.

5. The debtor's aggregate interest in any property not to exceed in value $800 plus up to $7,500 of any unused amount of the exemption provided under paragraph 1 (homestead).

6. The debtor's aggregate interest, not to exceed $1,500 in value, in any tools of trade.

7. Any unmatured life insurance contract owned by the debtor, other than a credit life insurance contract.

8. The debtor's aggregate interest, not to exceed in value $8,000 in any unmatured life insurance contract under which the insured is the debtor.

9. Professionally prescribed health aids for the debtor or dependent.

10. The debtor's right to receive:

    a. A social security benefit, unemployment compensation, or a local public assistance benefit.

    b. A veterans' benefit.

    c. A disability, illness, or unemployment benefit.

    d. Alimony, support, or separate maintenance, to the extent reasonably necessary for the support of the debtor and any dependents.

    e. A payment under a stock bonus, pension, profit sharing, annuity, or similar plan or contract on account of illness, disability, death, age, or length of service, to the extent reasonably necessary for the support of the debtor and any dependent (with exceptions).

11. The debtor's right to receive, or property that is traceable to:

    a. An award under a crime victim's reparation law.

    b. A payment on account of wrongful death to the extent reasonably necessary for the support of the debtor and dependents.

    c. The payment under a life insurance contract to the extent reasonably necessary for the support of the debtor and dependents.

d. A payment not to exceed $15,000 on account of personal bodily injury (excluding pain and suffering or compensation for actual pecuniary loss) of the debtor.

e. A payment in compensation of loss of future earnings to the extent reasonably necessary for the support of the debtor and dependents.

ABANDONMENT

Abandonment under 11 U.S.C. Section 554 removes property from the bankruptcy estate and returns the property to the debtor as though no bankruptcy had occurred. There are two justifications for abandonment before a case is closed: (1) The property is of inconsequential value to the estate, or (2) the property is burdensome to the estate.

For example, assume an individual debtor filed Chapter 7 (liquidation) and had an apartment complex valued at $500,000. The apartment complex would become property of the estate upon the filing of the petition. However, also assume a mortgage existed on the apartment complex in the amount of $500,000. In this situation, the apartment complex is of inconsequential value to the estate since the trustee cannot liquidate (sell) the property, pay off the mortgage, pay off the sales costs, and have any remaining funds to distribute. In fact, the apartment complex may even be burdensome since certain property taxes or property management fees may be accruing. Therefore, the trustee may determine to abandon the property from the estate. Once abandoned, the property revests (goes back to) the debtor.

Also, a debtor may file a motion to compel the trustee to abandon property. Using our preceding example, the property is worth $500,000 and the underlying mortgage is $464,000. Assume the costs for a trustee to sell the property would be about $36,000 (i.e., realtor's commissions, closing costs, etc.). Again, the property is of inconsequential value *to the estate*. The property may be abandoned and revested in the debtor. In this case, the debtor will be able to keep the $36,000 worth of equity in the property, notwithstanding that no exemption may exist for such equity.

Also, secured creditors often request that property be abandoned from the estate. Once the property is abandoned, it becomes property of the debtor. However, the duration of the automatic stay on a *debtor's* property is not as long as the automatic stay on *estate* property. The automatic stay continues on estate property until such property is no longer property of the estate. The automatic stay continues on debtor's property only until the debtor gets a discharge, the case is closed, or the case is dismissed. In essence, if the property is abandoned to the debtor and the debtor gets a discharge relatively shortly thereafter, the automatic stay is no longer in effect against the property and the secured creditor can foreclose.

Further, upon the closing of a case, property that has been scheduled by the debtor but not administered is deemed abandoned.[55] Note: Unscheduled concealed assets are not abandoned upon closing because they were never "administered."

The ability of trustees to abandon property is limited where violations of environmental laws may exist on the property.[56] For example, a court may not authorize abandonment of a hazardous waste site without imposing conditions that will adequately protect the public's health and safety.

Midlantic Nat'l Bank v. N.J. Dept. of Environmental Protection
474 U.S. 494 (1986)

Powell, J. [Quanta Resources Corp. (Quanta)] processed waste oil at facilities located in New York and New Jersey. The New Jersey Department of Environmental Protection (NJDEP) discovered that Quanta had violated a provision of the operating permit for the New Jersey facility by accepting oil contaminated with a toxic carcinogen. During negotiations with NJDEP for the cleanup of the New Jersey site, Quanta filed a petition for reorganization under Chapter 11 of the Bankruptcy Code, and after NJDEP had issued an order requiring cleanup, Quanta converted the action to a liquidation proceeding under Chapter 7. An investigation of the New York facility then revealed that Quanta also accepted similarly contaminated oil at that site. The trustee notified the creditors and the Bankruptcy Court that he intended to abandon the property under §544(a) of the Bankruptcy Code, which authorized a trustee to "abandon any property of the estate that is burdensome to the estate or that is of inconsequential value to the estate." The City and State of New York objected, contended that abandonment would threaten the public's health and safety, and would violate state and federal environmental law. The Bankruptcy Court approved the abandonment, and, after the District Court affirmed, an appeal was taken to the Court of Appeals for the Third Circuit. Meanwhile, the Bankruptcy Court also approved the trustee's proposed abandonment of the New Jersey facility over NJDEP's objection, and NJDEP took a direct appeal to the Court of appeals.]

* * *

[W]hen Congress enacted §544, there were well-recognized restrictions on a trustee's abandonment power. In codifying the judicially developed rule of abandonment, Congress also presumably included the established corollary that a trustee could not exercise his abandonment power in violation of certain state and federal laws. The normal rule of statutory construction is that if Congress intends for legislation to change the interpretation of a judicially created concept, it makes that intent specific. * * * The Court has followed this rule with particular care in construing the scope of bankruptcy codifications. If Congress wishes to grant the trustee an extraordinary exemption from nonbankruptcy law, "the intention would be clearly expressed, not left to be collected or inferred from disputable considerations of convenience in administering the estate of the bankrupt." * * *

Neither the Court nor Congress has granted a trustee in bankruptcy powers that would lend support to a right to abandon property in contravention of state or local laws designed to protect public health or safety. As we held last Term when the State of Ohio sought compensation for cleaning the toxic waste site of a bankruptcy corporation:

> Finally, we do not question that anyone in possession of the site—whether it is [the debtor] or another in the event the receivership is liquidated and the trustee abandons the property or a vendee from the receiver *or the bankruptcy trustee*—must comply with the environmental laws of the State of Ohio. Plainly, that person or firm may not maintain a nuisance, pollute the waters of the State, or refuse to remove the source of such conditions." *Ohio v. Kovacs,* 469 U.S. 274 (1985) (emphasis added).

Congress has repeatedly expressed its legislative determination that the trustee is not to have carte blanche to ignore nonbankruptcy law. Where the Bankruptcy Code has conferred special powers upon the trustee and where there was no common-law limitation on that power, Congress has expressly provided that the efforts of the trustee to marshal and distribute the assets of the estate must yield to governmental interests in public health and safety. *Infra,* at 760-761. One cannot assume that Congress, having placed these limitations upon other aspects of trustees' operations, intended to discard a well-established judicial restriction on the abandonment power. * * *

Thus, where a governmental unit is suing a debtor to prevent or stop a violation of fraud, *environmental protection,* consumer protection, *safety, or similar police or regulatory laws,* or attempting to fix damages for violation of such a law, the action or proceeding is not stayed under the automatic stay. H.R.Rep. No. 95-595 (emphasis added); S.Rep. No. 95-898 (emphasis added); U.S. Code Cong. & Admin. News 1978, pp. 5838, 6299. * * *

In light of the Bankruptcy trustee's restricted pre-1978 abandonment power and the limited scope of the other Bankruptcy Code provisions, we conclude that Congress did not intend for §544(a) to pre-empt all state and local laws. The Bankruptcy Court does not have the power to authorize an abandonment without formulating conditions that will adequately protect the public's health and safety. Accordingly, without reaching the question whether certain state laws imposing conditions on abandonment may be so onerous as to interfere with the bankruptcy adjudication itself, we hold that a trustee may not abandon property in contravention of a state statute or regulation that is reasonably designed to protect the public health or safety from identified hazards. Accordingly, we affirm the judgments of the Court of Appeals for the Third Circuit.

Under Section 554, specific property of the estate may be abandoned in three ways. First the trustee or debtor-in-possession may state its intention to abandon and give parties in interest an opportunity for hearing. Next, a motion by a party in interest can seek an order compelling the trustee to abandon. Finally, the failure of the trustee to administer the property as scheduled by the debtor before the case is closed will result in automatic abandonment.

F.R.Bankr.P. 6007 specifies two different procedures for requesting abandonment, depending upon which party initiated the abandonment request. The notice procedure found in 11 U.S.C. Section 554(a) and Rule 6007(a) applies only to the trustee or debtor-in-possession (DIP). Under this section the trustee (or DIP) may abandon the property once notice to all parties has been provided without a hearing if there are no objections. Otherwise, all other parties in interest must file a motion to require the abandonment of the property under Rule 6007(b). This motion commences a contested matter under Rule 9014. A hearing is set in due course, and notice of such motion and hearing is provided to all creditors. Objections to such abandonment are due within 15 days of such notice.

CHRONOLOGICAL EVENTS IN BANKRUPTCY PROCEEDINGS IN CHAPTER 7 AND CHAPTER 13 CASES

1. *The petition date* triggers the automatic stay and changes ownership of all debtor's property to that of estate property. It is also the reach-back period starting date for prepetition preferences or fraudulent conveyances.[57].

2. *Appointment of trustee/interim trustee.*

3. *Remainder of statements and schedules* are due (F.R.Bankr.P. 1007) 15 days after petition as well as the Chapter 13 plan if it is not already on file.

4. The *341 First Creditors' Meeting* is usually within six weeks of the petition. Attendance of debtor is required.

5. *Objections to exemptions* are due within 30 days after the *conclusion*[58] of the First Creditors' Meeting (or the filing of any amendment to the list of exemptions). [F.R.Bankr.P. 4003(b).]

6. The *Chapter 7 deadline for complaints* to determine the dischargeability of any specific debt under 11 U.S.C. Section 523(c) or complaints objecting to the debtor's entire discharge under 11 U.S.C. Section 727(a) is 60 days from the *first date*[59] set for the 341 First Creditors' Meeting. [F.R.Bankr.P. 4004(a), 4007(c).] For Chapter 13 cases, discharge complaints are due as the Court shall fix (Court must give 30 days' notice of date fixed). [F.R.Bankr.P. 4007(d).]

7. Creditors file *proofs of claim*. Under F.R.Bankr.P. 3003(c) the deadline is 90 days after the *first date*[60] set for the 341 First Creditor's meeting.

8. In a Chapter 13 case, a hearing is conducted to confirm the plan.

9. The *discharge order* is entered.

10. *Closure of case.*

CONCLUSION

The bankruptcy process involves a special type of federal court which hears exclusively bankruptcy cases and is called the Bankruptcy Court. Also, bankruptcy law is federal law and included in Title 11 of the United States Code. The titles and roles of parties in each bankruptcy case are identical, namely the debtor, creditors, or trustee. The filing of a bankruptcy petition transforms most of a debtor's property to that of estate property. Property of the estate can be removed from the bankruptcy by a debtor claiming it as exempt or through abandonment.

REVIEW QUESTIONS

1. What is a debtor?

2. What is a creditor?

3. What is a trustee and what are the duties of a trustee in each chapter?

4. What is an unsecured creditors committee and what are its duties?

5. What is property of the estate? What is excluded from property of the estate?

6. What is an exemption? Has your state "opted out" of the federal exemptions? If so, where are your state exemption laws found? Give an example of an exemption allowed in your state.

7. What is abandonment? What are the two criteria for abandonment?

ENDNOTES

[1]Note: Debtors may also have bankruptcy filed against them in involuntary cases.

[2]See Chapter 3 of this text for eligibility requirements for each bankruptcy chapter.

[3]See Chapter 9 of this text, "Creditor Status, Priority, and Distribution Rights" for further detailed analysis of creditor status.

[4]See Chapter 12, "Chapter 11 Practice," for more detailed discussion of employment applications, fee applications, etc.

[5]28 U.S.C. Section 1334(a).

[6]28 U.S.C. Section 1334(b).

[7]*Core proceedings* include matters concerning the administration of the estate, proceedings affecting liquidation of assets and the adjustment of the debtor-creditor relationship; counterclaims against persons filing claims against the estate; turnover orders; orders to obtain credit; orders determining preferences and fraudulent conveyances; proceedings concerning the automatic stay; discharge and dischargeability actions; actions regarding the validity, priority, and extent of liens; confirmation of plans; orders approving the use, lease or sale of property, and the allowance/disallowance of claims (excluding personal injury or wrongful death tort claims). [28 U.S.C. Section 157(d)(2).]

[8]All proceedings that are not core are "noncore." A *noncore proceeding* is a civil proceeding that, in the absence of a petition in bankruptcy, could have been brought in a district court or a state court. *In re Colorado Energy Supply, Inc.,* 728 F.2d 1283 (10th Cir. 1984).]

[9]28 U.S.C. Section 157(a).

[10]28 U.S.C. Section 151.

[11]28 U.S.C. Section 157(a).

[12]28 U.S.C. Sections 157(b)(1), (c)(1).

[13]28 U.S.C. Section 157(c)(2).

[14]28 U.S.C. Section 157(c)(1).

[15]28 U.S.C. Section 1334(d).

[16]28 U.S.C. Section 157(d).

[17]F.R.Bankr.P. 5011.

[18]A notice of appeal to a higher court deprives the bankruptcy court of jurisdiction to entertain a motion for reconsideration.

[19]*Interlocutory orders* merely decide one aspect of the case without disposing of the case in its entirety on the merits. An example of an interlocutory order is an order granting stay relief in a bankruptcy case.

[20]28 U.S.C. Section 158(b).

[21]28 U.S.C. Section 158(a).

[22]28 U.S.C. Section 158(d).

[23]28 U.S.C. Sections 1254, 1252, 1651, Supreme Court Rule 19(1)(b).

[24]Chapter 11 also outlines provisions unique to railroad reorganizations.

[25]*In re Crysen/Montenay Energy Co.,* 902 F.2d 1098 (2nd Cir. 1990).

[26]*In re Turner*, 29 B.R. 628 (Bankr. D. Me. 1983).

[27]*In re Flight Transp. Corp. Secur. Litigation*, 730 F.2d 1128 (8th Cir. 1984).

[28]*In re Sherk*, 918 F.2d 1170 (5th Cir. 1990).

[29]An interest in property held by the debtor as a co-owner is subject to sale if the requirements of Section 363(h) are met.

[30]*In re Saugus General Hospital, Inc.*, 4 B.C.D. 1160 (Bankr. Mass. 1978).

[31]*In re Da-Sota Elevator Co.*, 939 F.2d 654 (8th Cir. 1991).

[32]*In re Willis*, 34 B.R. 451 (Bankr. M.D. N.C. 1983).

[33]*In re Cottrell*, 876 F.2d 540 (6th Cir. 1989).

[34]*Lambert v. Fuller Co.*, 122 B.R. 243 (E.D. Pa. 1990).

[35]*In re Merlino*, 62 B.R. 836 (Bankr. W.D. Wash. 1986).

[36]Arizona, California, Idaho, Louisiana, Nevada, New Mexico, Texas and Washington.

[37]*In re Ward*, 74 B.R. 465 (Dist. N.J. 1987) aff'd 837 F.2d 124 (3rd Cir. 1988).

[38]See Chapter 8, "Voidable Transfers," for detailed discussion of such voidance actions.

[39]*In re Chenoweth*, 143 B.R. 527 (S.D. Ill. 1992) aff'd 3 F.2d 111 (7th Cir. 1993).

[40]*In re Scanlon*, 10 B.R. 245 (Bankr. S.D. Cal. 1981).

[41]*In re Marshburn*, 5 B.R. 711 (Bankr. Colo. 1980).

[42]*In re Hellums*, 772 F.2d 379 (7th Cir. 1985).

[43]Sections 1306 and 1207.

[44]*In re R & T Roofing Structures & Commercial Framing, Inc.*, 887 F.2d 981 (9th Cir. 1989).

[45]H.R. Rep. 103-834, 103rd Cong., 2nd Sess. 32 (Oct. 4, 1994); 140 Cong. Rec. H10769 (Oct. 4, 1994).

[46]*In re Draughon Training Inst.*, 119 B.R. 921 (Bankr. W.D. La. 1990).

[47]*In re Railroad Reorganization Estate*, 133 B.R. 578 (Bankr. D. Del. 1991).

[48]*In re Howell*, 4 B.R. 102 (Bankr. M.D. Tenn. 1980).

[49]*In re Matto's, Inc.*, 9 B.R. 89 (Bankr. E.D. Mich. 1981).

[50]Often the seller of the mortgage retains the original mortgage notes and related documents and the purchaser records the purchase under state recording statutes. The retention of the mortgage documents by the seller and the decision by the purchaser not to record do not impair the character of secondary mortgage market transactions.

[51]Most states have "opted out" of the federal bankruptcy exemptions.

[52]*In re Bradley*, 960 F.2d 502 (5th Cir. 1992) cert. denied, 113 S.Ct. 1412 (1993).

[53]*John T. Mather Memorial Hospital, Inc. v. Pearl*, 723 F.2d 193 (2nd Cir. 1983).

[54]Substantial increases in the exempt amounts were added through the 1994 Amendments as listed.

[55]11 U.S.C. Section 544(c)

[56]*Midlantic Nat. Bank v. New Jersey Dept. of Environmental Protection*, 474 U.S. 494 (1986).

[57]See Chapter 8, "Voidable Transfers."

[58]Often the 341 First Creditors' Meetings are continued. However, the 30-day deadline runs from the *conclusion* or the last of such continued 341 Meetings.

[59]Often the 341 First Creditors' Meetings are continued. However, the 60-day deadline runs from the *first* date set for such meeting.

[60]Note, often the 341 First Creditors' Meetings are continued. However, the 90-day deadline runs from the *first* date set for such meeting.

3

Varieties of Bankruptcy Chapters

You spent all yesterday afternoon with a client who is going to file bankruptcy. As a paralegal you went over every detail of the client's financial problems, each creditor, the client's monthly living expenses and income, and why the client needs to file bankruptcy. Now, the supervising attorney ask you whether the client can file Chapter 13 or if Chapter 11 is necessary. Also, the attorney asks you if Chapter 7 might be best for the client.

What are the differences between these types of bankruptcy cases? What are the results if the client filed one type of case instead of another? What does it take for a client to be able to file one type of bankruptcy case as opposed to another?

INTRODUCTION

Three basic types of bankruptcies are typically found in each district: Chapter 7 (liquidation cases), Chapter 13 (wage earner reorganization), and Chapter 11 (commercial reorganization). Additionally, in some jurisdictions such as the Midwest, Chapter 12 (family farmer) cases are often filed. Finally, Chapter 9 cases (municipality reorganization), such as a city or a county, are quite rare throughout the United States.

Following are descriptions of the chapters, a comparison of the basic chapters as well as a detailed analysis of the eligibility requirements for each chapter.[1] This shall provide a broad overview of the general scheme and purposes of the different bankruptcy chapters. Armed with this basic general information, the legal assistant may proceed to further detailed analysis of the practice necessary for each of the separate bankruptcy chapters contained later in this text in Chapter 10 ("Chapter 7 Practice"), Chapter 11 ("Chapter 13 Practice"), and Chapter 12 ("Chapter 11 Practice").

DESCRIPTION OF THE CHAPTERS

There are basic similarities among all the bankruptcy chapters. For example, the parties are the same regardless of the chapter chosen, including the debtor, creditors, and someone acting as a trustee. Further, the debtor is always required to file the initial documentation and attend the 341 First Creditors' Meeting. However, the fundamental difference between the chapters is whether the goal is to liquidate or reorganize. Liquidation is simply collecting all the available assets, selling them, and distributing the proceeds to creditors. Reorganization is formulating a method to repay creditors, usually over time. If reorganization is the aim, then the Bankruptcy Code provides a selection of reorganization chapters that a debtor may file. Each of the reorganization chapters furnishes the debtor with a different means to reorganize.

Chapter 7

Chapter 7 is the liquidating bankruptcy and is also known as "straight bankruptcy." In Chapter 7, individual debtors relieve themselves of all unsecured debt in order that they may have a "fresh start." In Chapter 7 a trustee is appointed to investigate, collect, sell, and distribute all estate assets.

However, in individual Chapter 7 cases, the debtor is allowed to retain exempt property.[2] Exempt property (to the extent such property does not exceed the specified exemption amount) is not collected or sold by the trustee. *Exempt property* is that which a debtor may claim under federal law or that is provided under state law if the state has "opted out" of the federal exemption scheme. Exemptions generally allow individual debtors to retain equity in (up to the specified amount) their home, car, tools of trade, health aids, alimony/support payments, certain types of insurance payments, etc. Note that only individuals are entitled to claim exemptions. Corporations, partnerships, business associations, etc. are not entitled to claim exemptions.

Once the Chapter 7 trustee has collected and sold all nonexempt assets of the estate, a distribution is made to creditors. A creditor's status determines the hierarchy of the payment distribution. For example, a secured creditor shall receive payment before an unsecured creditor. Likewise, a priority creditor such as a tax authority shall receive payment before the unsecured creditors.[3] Note: Unsecured creditors are the last to be paid. In most Chapter 7 cases not enough funds exist to make any payment whatsoever to unsecured creditors.

Once a Chapter 7 case is filed, the individual debtor receives a "discharge" of all but a few specific unsecured debts. Chapter 6 of this text contains a detailed analysis of "nondischargeable" obligations under 11 U.S.C. Section 523. This discharge permanently enjoins (or stops) any further collection attempts on amounts debtor owed. Once a debt is discharged, a creditor cannot bring a state court lawsuit, cannot contact the debtor via correspondence or telephone, and cannot attach liens on the debtor's property or garnish the debtor's wages. Note: Discharge is not available for debtors who display misconduct in attempting to defraud their creditors or conceal assets from the Court.[4]

However, a discharge in Chapter 7 is available only to individuals. The discharge provisions of 11 U.S.C. Section 727(a)(1) require that a debtor be an individual before the court may grant a discharge. Accordingly, Chapter 7 corporate debtors, partnership debtors, and the like are not entitled to discharge.

When the trustee finishes liquidating the estate by selling and distributing all nonexempt assets, the trustee files a final report. This report contains information such as the assets recovered, the amount received by the trustee in liquidation of those assets, and the amount of distribution to creditors. After the final report is filed and distributions are made, the court closes the case.

Chapter 9

Under 11 U.S.C. Section 109(c) only a municipality or other political subdivision that is unable to pay its debts as they mature and that is not prohibited by state law from proceeding under Chapter 9 is permitted to be a Chapter 9 debtor. The municipality must generally be authorized to file a Chapter 9 petition by its state legislature or a state governmental officer.

Chapter 9 is an extremely rare form of relief. The most prominent recent example of a Chapter 9 bankruptcy is Orange County, California. However, other examples include cities (City of South Tucson, Arizona[5] and Wapanucka, Oklahoma), irrigation districts, school districts, etc. Chapter 9 cases entail the filing of a plan of reorganization by a municipality. However, due to its rarity and complexity, Chapter 9 bankruptcy shall not be dealt with in this text.

Chapter 11

Chapter 11 cases are known as "business reorganizations" or "commercial reorganizations." However, an individual may also file for relief under Chapter 11. Chapter 11 cases are commonly the most complex and involved of the bankruptcy chapters. Imagine a Chapter 11 for an individual with multiple commercial buildings. While all general Chapter 11 requirements are still necessary from such an individual, the undeniable complexity of such individual's Chapter 11 will never reach the magnitude found within a large commercial Chapter 11 such as *In re Landmark Hotel & Casino, Inc.* (where debtor operated a large hotel and casino) or within publicly traded Chapter 11 cases such as *America West Airlines, Inc.* (where debtor operated an airline company) or *In re Revco Drug Stores, Inc.* (where debtor operated a nationwide chain of drugstores).

In Chapter 11, the debtor commonly remains in control of the business as well as the debtor's assets and is known as the debtor-in-possession. As debtor-in-possession, the debtor has all the fiduciary duties of a trustee in Chapter 7 cases. This means that the debtor-in-possession acts in the place of the trustee to represent the interests of all the creditors of the estate.

In addition to the regular statements and schedules to be filed with the Court, a Chapter 11 debtor-in-possession is required to provide a myriad of detailed information to the U.S. Trustee's Office and start paying U.S. Trustee's quarterly fees. Additionally, all professionals hired by the Chapter 11 estate (including the bankruptcy attorney, accountants, property managers, etc.) must apply and become authorized to act on behalf of the estate. Additionally, creditors' committees may be formed (and possibly equity holders' committees) to oversee the administration of the case.

Thereafter, issues of cash collateral and stay relief are usually initiated shortly after a case is filed. Further, short deadlines are imposed upon the debtor-in-possession within which to assume or reject commercial real estate leases (within shopping centers).

Additionally, the Chapter 11 debtor is given an exclusive period within which to propose a plan of reorganization. A Chapter 11 plan of reorganization is a document which outlines the manner and means in which creditors will be repaid. This plan must be accompanied by a disclosure statement. A disclosure statement describes in great detail the proposed plan, history of the debtor, details regarding the debtor's business operation, and illustrates how the plan would be beneficial to creditors. These documents may consists of hundreds of pages of text along with numerous exhibits. If the debtor-in-possession's exclusivity period lapses, then any party in interest may file a plan, including creditors and creditors' committees.

Once a plan is filed and the disclosure statement is approved by the court, the creditors may vote on the plan. The plan proponent (one who submits the plan) is required to send the plan and disclosure statement to all creditors along with a ballot by which the creditor accepts or rejects such plan. Should the plan be accepted by the creditors (or a sufficient number of the creditors), the plan is thereafter confirmed.

Needless to say, often Chapter 11 cases take substantial time and effort just to get to the confirmation stage. Equally apparent, Chapter 11 cases, due to the complexity and involvement of the parties, is very costly to the Chapter 11 estate in administrative expenses alone (i.e., debtor's attorney's fees, accountant's fees, creditors committee's attorney's fees, U.S. Trustee's quarterly fees, auctioneer's, realtors, and expert witnesses such as appraisers fees, etc.). Accordingly, individuals with relatively low debts often file for the less expensive and more expeditious Chapter 13 as opposed to Chapter 11.

Chapter 12

Chapter 12 is designed to meet the specific needs of family farmers and to give them a fighting chance to reorganize their debts and keep their land.[6] Chapter 12 is modeled primarily after Chapter 13, but some of the provisions are also from Chapter 11 and still others are unique. Most family farmers have too much debt to be eligible for Chapter 13. Further, Chapter 11 administrative requirements along with Chapter 11 treatment of undersecured debt (more liens on the property than the property is worth) often make Chapter 11 unfeasible for family farmers.

The most important feature of Chapter 12 is the ability to write down secured debt to the value of the property and then repay the secured debt over an extended period of time. Chapter 12 is a voluntary chapter and only the debtor may file a plan. The Chapter 12 plan must be filed within 90 days of the petition. Further, a confirmation hearing on such plan must be concluded 45 days after the plan is filed.

Like Chapter 13, under Chapter 12 a trustee is appointed to supervise and disburse payments to creditors. Otherwise, the debtor remains in possession of its assets and controls sales of estate assets. Such sales of farm equipment or farmland may be made even if the sales would not qualify under other chapters of the Code. Chapter 12 plan payments also last between three and five years to unsecured creditors, after which debtors receive their discharge. Finally, Chapter 12 debtors have their own unique eligibility requirements which are discussed in detail below.

Chapter 13

Chapter 13 is a "wage earner" reorganization case. Chapter 13 is intended to be an uncomplicated system for individuals to repay their debts under the Bankruptcy Code supervision and protection. Only individuals (or husbands and wives) who are wage earners may file Chapter 13. No corporations, partnerships, business associations, etc. may file Chapter 13. Wage earners may be traditional wage earners, business owners (sole proprietors), farmers, service persons, professionals, retirees, welfare or disability recipients, or other individuals as long as they receive regular income.

Chapter 13 debtors file plans that do not, necessarily, pay 100% in full to all creditors. A wage earner's excess income (that extra income after paying for monthly living expenses, such as food, insurance, utilities, etc.) is used to fund the plan. Additionally, Chapter 13 plan repayment schedules are three years at a minimum and can last no longer than five years.

Most Chapter 13 plans provide for the "cure" of one or more secured liens. To "cure" is to bring current prepetition defaults on secured claims such as late house payments or tardy car payments. Creditors are not allowed to vote either in favor or against a Chapter 13 debtor's proposed plan. Once the final payment has been made, the Chapter 13 debtor receives a "discharge." Accordingly, the discharge in Chapter 13 cases is delayed at least three years and may not take place until some five years beyond the filing of the initial petition.

Finally, to qualify for Chapter 13, a debtor must not exceed certain debt limits, which are articulated below.

ELIGIBILITY REQUIREMENTS OF EACH CHAPTER

Chapter 7

Chapter 7 relief is available to almost all types of debtors. Under 11 U.S.C. Section 109(b) eligibility requirements, a "person" may be a Chapter 7 debtor. "Person" includes individuals as well as businesses, such as corporations, partnerships, sole proprietorships, etc. However, governmental units, railroads, domestic insurance companies, banks, savings and loans associations, and credit unions may not liquidate under Chapter 7.[7] Also, a husband and wife may file a "joint" petition where together their case is treated as one case. However, there is no Bankruptcy Code authority for any other entities to jointly file for relief (such as a corporation and its president filing jointly or two general partners filing a joint individual petition).[8]

Additionally, the definition of "person" eligible for Chapter 7 relief does not include a probate estate.[9] However, a person declared incompetent (through conservatorship or guardianship state court proceedings) may qualify as a debtor as long as a guardian or next friend acts for the incompetent to file the bankruptcy and is able to perform the debtor's duties.[10] The rationale for allowing incompetents to be debtors is the consideration of equal protection and due process, which require the protection of the bankruptcy laws be equally available to such persons.[11]

Chapter 11

As in Chapter 7, Chapter 11 relief is available to all types of debtors, including individuals, corporations, partnerships, sole proprietorships, etc. However, unlike Chapter 7, Chapter 11 is statutorily not available to stockbrokers or commodity brokers. Also unlike Chapter 7, railroads are permitted to file for relief under Chapter 11.

Even unincorporated, not-for-profit associations, such as religious associations, fall within the definition that outlines eligibility for Chapter 11 relief. Accordingly, a church may file Chapter 11. [See *The Miracle Church of God in Christ*, 119 B.R. 308 (Bankr. M.D. Fla. 1990).]

However, trusts may file Chapter 11 only if they are "business trusts." Bankruptcy relief under Chapter 11 is available for all trusts created for the purpose of transacting business, whose beneficiaries make monetary contributions to the enterprise (i.e., a business trust).[12] In essence, a business trust eligible for Chapter 11 must be established for the purpose of conducting business and not merely to preserve the trust res for beneficiaries.[13]

Criteria for disqualification under Chapter 11 due to lack of being a business trust are:

1. The trust has never engaged in business.
2. The res of the trust (such as a residence) is incapable of being operated as a business.
3. No active bank accounts exist, or lines of credit or books and records; no employees, business address, or separate creditors exist.
4. The trust is a mere estate planning device.
5. The trust is in fact some type of family arrangement.[14]

Chapter 13

The eligibility requirements for Chapter 13 are that the debtor must be:

1. Only an individual,
2. with regular income,
3. who owes as of the petition date noncontingent, liquidated debts,
4. in an amount less than $250,000 unsecured and $750,000 secured.[15]

Note: Stockbrokers and commodity brokers are excluded from eligibility under Chapter 13.

The "individual" requirement of Chapter 13 precludes partnerships and corporations from eligibility. Even if a corporation is owned by only one shareholder, it is still ineligible for Chapter 13.[16] Further, probate estates are also excluded from Chapter 13.[17] However, a person declared mentally incompetent may qualify for Chapter 13.[18]

Additionally, the term "individual" under Chapter 13 includes an individual and the individual's spouse who may file a joint petition and pay one filing fee.[19] Both spouses are eligible to file a joint petition under Chapter 13 even if one spouse is unemployed.[20] However, once a debtor files separately (without the spouse), the petition cannot later be amended to include the spouse as a copetitioner. In joint cases of spouses, both spouses' assets, incomes, and liabilities are combined to determine eligibility.

The "regular income" requirement is defined as an individual whose income is sufficiently stable and regular to enable the individual to make payments under a Chapter 13 plan.[21] Therefore, the debtor's income must exceed living expenses.[22] This extra income is called *disposable income.*

The *regular income* requirement may include debtors on welfare,[23] disability benefits,[24] and social security, fixed pension or incomes of those who live on investment incomes. Self-employed persons may also have regular income sufficient to qualify for Chapter 13, such as salespersons or attorneys in private practice. Further, unemployment compensation may qualify as regular income,[25] as may regular child support payments.[26] Additionally, farmers may have regular income for Chapter 13 eligibility purposes.

The debts limits of Chapter 13 are qualified to include only "noncontingent and liquidated" debts. The Code specifically excludes "disputed" debts, those that a debtor contests as not being owed or has other counterclaims, setoffs, affirmative defenses, or mitigating circumstances.[27] Therefore, disputed debts are included within the amount of debt for eligibility purposes.

Debts are generally "contingent" if the debtor's legal duty to pay (his or her liability) does not come into existence until triggered by the occurrence of a future event that was reasonably within the presumed contemplation of the parties at the time the original relationship between the parties was created.[28] For example, recent cases recognize that tort claims are noncontingent debts and therefore counted in the debt limits for Chapter 13.[29] The rationale is that, even if such tort claims have not been reduced to judgment, the conduct that gave rise to the tort claim has occurred and liability is not dependent on any future event.[30] Accordingly, tort claims are counted in the debt limit calculation of Chapter 13 eligibility.

Even if a state court judgment has been entered but appealed by the debtor with the appeal still pending, the claim is noncontingent.[31] The liability has already attached and the claim is not contingent on the occurrence of any future event. Since the liability has attached, the debt is noncontingent, even if later the debtor may win the appeal.

Most contract claims against the debtor will be noncontingent. This is so even if the debtor may dispute liability or assert counterclaims. The debtor's liability arises when the parties enter into the contract and no further act is necessary to trigger liability. Therefore, contract claims are included in the debts for eligibility purposes.

However, a majority of cases find that a Chapter 13 debtor's guarantee of a debt is contingent since the debtor's liability will not occur until certain other conditions occur.[32] In other words, the guarantor has no liability unless and until the principal defaults. Accordingly, obligations that may arise due to a debtor's guarantee are generally not counted in the debt limitations of Chapter 13.

Also, for "noncontingent" purposes regarding partnership debts, inclusion of a partnership's potential obligations on an individual debtor depends on state law. When a partner is principally liable on a partnership debt under state law (such as Ohio, Texas, or South Dakota), all partnership debt is included as noncontingent. However, where a partner is liable only after creditors satisfy their claims from partnership assets under state law (such as Montana), the partnership debt is contingent and therefore excluded.

Next, the debt limits of Chapter 13 require the debts included be "liquidated." Whether a debt is liquidated turns on whether it is subject to ready determination and precision in computation of the amount due. Ready determination depends on the distinction between whether a simple hearing to determine the amount of debt will be sufficient or if an extensive and contested evidentiary hearing is necessary (where substantial evidence is required to establish the amount of liability).[33]

Where a debtor has admitted liability for a specific amount, the debt is liquidated and included in the eligibility calculation.[34] If the amount of the claim cannot be calculated, the debt is "unliquidated" and excluded from the debt limits. For example, damages that cannot be ascertained with precision are unliquidated.

Once "noncontingent and liquidated" issues are resolved, to determine eligibility for Chapter 13 the unsecured debts must not exceed $250,000 and the secured debts must not exceed $750,000. However, the timing and procedure for evaluation of debts become crucial.

As a general rule, the amount of the debt is determined as of the petition date.[35] Some courts determine eligibility by accepting the characterization (noncontingent and liquidated) and amount of the debt as set forth in the debtor's schedules as long as those schedules have been filed in good faith.[36] Other courts allow more extensive litigation of the amount and characterization of debt even if the schedules are prepared in good faith to determine if a Chapter 13 debtor is eligible.[37] Finally, other courts fully litigate all issues concerning claims allowance which may affect the amount or characterization of a debt.[38]

In Re Loya
123 B.R. 338 (9th Cir.BAP 1991)

Ollason, J. * * * Debtor was a professional tax preparer who occasionally advised his clients regarding tax shelters. In 1983 and 1984 he suggested to 86 of his clients that they invest in a certain aggressive tax shelter. That shelter ultimately failed both as an investment and as a tax shelter. All of the investors knew of the failure of the investment by late 1985.

In 1989, debtor filed a Chapter 13 petition listing the 86 investors as disputed claimants. He valued most of their claims at zero. Most of the claimants had not filed suit or otherwise pursued their claims. One claimant had a judgment for $18,814 against debtor arising from the failed tax shelter and two others had lawsuits pending.

Ten of the 86 investors filed proofs of claim alleging losses from the tax shelter scheme. Debtor object to all of them, principally alleging that they were barred by the statute of limitations. * * *

11 U.S.C. §109(e) forbids Chapter 13 relief if the debtor has greater than $100,000 [pre-1994 Amendments] in noncontingent, liquidated unsecured debts. A debt is noncontingent if all events giving rise to liability occurred prior to the filing of the bankruptcy petition. As explained in *In re Fostvedt*, 823 F.2d 305, 306 (9th Cir. 1987), "the rule is clear that a contingent debt is 'one which the debtor will be called upon to pay only upon the occurrence or happening of an extrinsic event which will trigger the liability of the debtor to the alleged creditor.'" The fact that most of the claims here have not be reduced to judgment does not render them contingent. * * * A tort claim ordinarily is not contingent as to liability; the events that give rise to the tort claim usually have occurred and the liability is not dependent on some future event that may never happen. It is im-

material that the tort claim is not adjudicated or liquidated, or that the claim is disputed, or indeed that it has any of the many other characteristics of claims under the Code.

Because the advice that gave rise to these claims has already been given and acted upon, these claims are noncontingent.

The question now turns to the issue of liquidation. * * * "[C]ontract debts (even though disputed) are considered liquidated and tort claims are not." That statement is generally correct but must be taken in its proper context. * * * The concept of liquidation has been variously expressed. The common thread ... has been ready determination and precision in computation of the amount due ... Some cases have stated the test as to whether the amount due is capable of ascertainment by reference to an agreement or by simple computation.

Therefore, whether a debt is liquidated or not for purposes of 11 U.S.C. §109(e) does not depend strictly on whether the claim sounds in tort or in contract, but whether it is capable of ready computation. For the same reason, whether a debt is liquidated does not depend on whether it is disputed. Thus a disputed debt which is capable of ready determination is liquidated. * * * The definition of "ready determination" turns on the distinction between a simple hearing to determine the amount of a certain debt, and an extensive and contested evidentiary hearing in which substantial evidence may be necessary to establish the amounts or liability.

It is not entirely clear where the line must be drawn between a simple hearing and a complex one, but this case does not require that we do so. From the record now before us, it appears that many of the claimants will readily admit that their claims have been barred by the statute of limitations. Accordingly it appears that only the briefest of hearings will be needed. Since the investors' claims are capable of ready determination and computation, they are liquidated for purposes of 11 U.S.C. §109(e).

Since the amount of the liquidated debt owed to many of the tax shelter claimants may be zero, the debtor may have less than $100,000 in unsecured, noncontingent, liquidated debts. It appears that the bankruptcy court misapplied the law in concluding that the full amount of these disputed claims must be included as the liquidated debt for the purposes of section 109(e). For that reason we remand for a redetermination of eligibility consistent with this decision.

Another wrinkle in the debt limits of Chapter 13 is whether certain claims are secured or unsecured. In Chapter 13 certain secured debts are allowed to be "stripped down" under 11 U.S.C. Section 506(a). In other words, if the property upon which the lien is based is worth less than the amount of the lien, the lien is reduced to the value of the property. The lien amount is therefore treated as the secured debt. The remainder of the lien (i.e., the undersecured portion) is thereafter treated as an unsecured debt.

Courts have reached different results as to whether the secured claims should be split by the strip-down provisions of 11 U.S.C. Section 506(a) in order to determine if the debtor is eligible. Some courts leave the determination of the extent of the secured claim for a later stage in the Chapter 13 proceedings and therefore consider the whole claim as secured.[39] However, a majority of the courts apply strip-down at the eligibility stage and therefore split the claim into secured and unsecured claims at the threshold of each Chapter 13.[40]

The impact of splitting the claim may benefit the debtor for eligibility purposes. For example, presume a debtor owes $800,000 as a secured claim on a commercial building that is worth $700,000. Through strip-down the secured amount of the claim would become $700,000 and the extra $100,000 will be treated as unsecured. This would allow the debtor to be eligible within the $750,000 secured claim maximum.

However, the impact of splitting claims may also preclude the debtor from eligibility under Chapter 13. Presume the debtor had $200,000 unsecured debt. Additionally, the debtor owed $500,000 as a secured claim on a commercial building that was worth only $400,000. The effect of strip-down would increase the amount of unsecured debt by $100,000. Therefore, the unsecured debt would total $300,000 and disqualify the debtor under Chapter 13. This is regardless of the fact that the original secured amount before strip-down ($500,000) was well within the $750,000 secured debt limits.

Chapter 12

Only a family farmer with regular annual income may be a debtor under Chapter 12.[41] "Regular income" means a family farmer whose annual income is sufficiently stable and regular to enable the farmer to make payments under a Chapter 12 plan. *Family farmer* may be an individual, or an individual and spouse, engaged in a farming operation. Further, the individual and spouse must have debts[42] below $1,500,000. Additionally, 80% of the debts (excluding the debts for the farmer's residence) must arise out of "farming operations" owned or operated by the individual. Also, more than 50% of the individual's gross income for the year before the bankruptcy must be derived from farming operations. [43] Even though most Chapter 12 debtors will have had losses in their farming operation the year before bankruptcy, the 50% income test deals with *gross* income.

The vast amount of contention relating to Chapter 12 eligibility is whether a debtor was engaged in farming and whether income is farm income (i.e., the "farming operation" test). Under the Code, *farming operation* includes farming, tillage of the soil, dairy farming, ranching, production or raising of crops, poultry, or livestock, and production of poultry or livestock products in an unmanufactured state.[44]

For example, a landlord's proceeds from farmland rentals may or may not constitute income from a "farming operation."[45] Sale of farm machinery is included as farm income.[46] Sale of farmland is not included as farm income.[47] Income from trucking cattle is farm income.[48] Crop dusting is not a farming operation.[49] Saw mill operations are farming operations.[50] Harvesting citrus crops for others is not a farming operation.[51] Horse breeding and training are not farming operations.[52] Timber harvest is a farming operation.[53] Chicken manure operation was not farm income.[54] A puppy farm is a farming operation.[55] A contract to share milk proceeds is farm income.[56] The training and horse riding aspects of a horse ranch are not farm income.[57]

Additionally, corporations and partnerships may also qualify as "family farmers" who are eligible for Chapter 12. Permitting corporations and partnerships to be Chapter 12 debtors is a departure from the usual Chapter 13 requirement that the debtor be only an individual. However, such business entities must meet the following six-part test:

1. Fifty percent of the outstanding stock or equity must be held by one family, or by one family and the relatives of the members of such family.

2. The family or relatives of the family must conduct the farming operation.

3. More than 80% of the value of the entity's assets must be related to the farming operation.

4. The entity's aggregate debts must not exceed $1,500,000.

5. Not less than 80% of the entity's aggregate debts as of the petition must arise from the farming operation (excluding the debt on the dwelling owned by the entity, but used as a residence by a shareholder or partner).[58]

6. If the entity is a corporation, any issued stock must not be publicly traded.

In Re Cloverleaf Farmer's Co-Op.
114 B.R. 1010 (Bankr.D.S.D. 1990)

Ecker, J. * * * Cloverleaf consists of seven families, a Hutterite colony of seventy-six individuals, living under a co-operative organization formally incorporated June 14, 1977. Cloverleaf's principal officers include: Vice President Herman J. Wipf, Secretary/Treasurer Don J. Hofer, Director Henry Wipf, and Director Phillip Tschetter. Cloverleaf's fourteen equity owners, all of which own a 7.14 percent interest, include Don Hofer, Herb

Wipf, John Wipf, Paul Tschetter, Johnny Wipf, Jr., Val Tschetter, Walter Wipf, Phillip Tschetter, Henry Wipf, Josh Hofer, Jake Hofer, Mike Hofer, Johnny Hofer, and Jimmy Wipf. Don Hofer's family tree, depicted in Appendix A, notes Don's family relationship to some stockholders.

Cloverleaf maintains about 1,350 tillable acres. Donald Hofer credibly testified the co-operative actively farms the land. Its members exclusively farmed until the past two difficult years forced some of Cloverleaf's members to work off the farm. Farmed crops include corn, barley, wheat, and beans. Farming equipment is borrowed from a third party because Valley National Bank, in 1989, foreclosed on a delinquent loan, thereby taking collateralized farming equipment and livestock.

* * * The SBA recorded a second mortgage it took on the realty in the county where the property is located when it loaned about $155,100 to Cloverleaf during 1981 and 1982. * * *

ISSUES

I. Who is included in the family of a Section 101(17) "family farmer" when Section 101(39) defines a relative to include all those related by affinity or consanguinity within the third degree as determined by the common law. * * *

Congress enacted Chapter 12 to protect the family farmer entity in which a family is engaged in farming operations while some family members may own the farm but have substantial nonfarm income to sustain themselves. A bankrupt must meet numerous tests to qualify as a Chapter 12 debtor. * * *

Subsection (B) [of §101(17)] sets the needs for a corporation or partnership to qualify for Chapter 12. The pertinent Subsection (B) requirement demands one family and the relatives of the members of such family own more than fifty percent of the farming corporation. A court may not strain Bankruptcy Code definitions in order to grant statutory family farmer status to entities not squarely fitting Bankruptcy Code requirements. * * *

The word, "co-operative" is not expressly listed as an entity type permitted to file Chapter 12. A co-operative is defined as a corporation or association organized to render economic services without gain to itself or its members who own and control it. (citations omitted). A co-operative, in South Dakota, is organized like and subject to rules governing a corporation. (citations omitted). Because a co-operative is a corporate body and a corporation may qualify as a family farmer, Cloverleaf achieves the Bankruptcy Code's qualification of a corporation as a family farmer provided other prerequisites are met. The SBA's sole allegation that Cloverleaf fails to qualify as a family farmer is that Cloverleaf's majority ownership is not held by a single family and the relatives of such family as required by Section 101(17)(B).

The majority of stock ownership of a "family farmer" corporation (co-operative) must be held by a family and the relatives and members of such family, not to any other entity. (citations omitted). Congress requires majority ownership in a farming corporation be owned by one family and its relatives because Congress' intent is to protect the small family farm in Chapter 12. (citations omitted).

The key to family membership is that a "relative" means individual related by affinity or consanguinity within the third degree as determined by the common law, or individual in a step or adoptive relationship within such third degree. 11 U.S.C. §101(39). The definitions terms are not further defined in the Bankruptcy Code. * * *

"Consanguinity" means * * * the connection or relation of persons descended from the same stock or common ancestor. * * * Consanguinity is synonymous with "kindred," whereas "affinity" is the connection between married persons and the kindred of the other. * * *

Consanguinity "degrees" measure the relationship between a person and his relatives. * * * Each generation is called a degree * * *.

Cloverleaf's members all live on the farm and, except for the last two years, only farmed. Chapter 12 was intended to rehabilitate dedicated family farmers such as this debtor. * * *

Applying the single count common law measure of consanguinity starts with Don Hofer's generation, as it appears to be the youngest generation of stockholders. Ascending three degrees leads to Don's great-grandfather, Joseph Wipf. Anyone sharing Joseph Wipf as a common ancestor is within the third level of consanguinity as determined by the common law. Any spouse of such family member also falls within the definition of family member since affinity counts as a relative under Section 101(39). The nine individuals within the third level of affinity or consanguinity, as determined by the common law, are Jake Hofer, Josh Hofer, Johnny Wipf, Jr., Donald Hofer, Walter Wipf, Johnny Hofer, John Wipf, Herb Wipf, and Henry Wipf. These shareholders constitute 9/14's or sixty-four percent of the equity ownership. Cloverleaf meets the statutory requirements of a "family farmer" since the Don Hofer family owns greater than half of the co-operative's equity.

Order denying motion to dismiss voluntary Chapter 12 bankruptcy petition.

Note: The 50% gross income test is not applicable for corporations and partnerships under Chapter 12. Further, the $1,500,000 limit is applicable only to aggregate debts of the entity. Therefore, the owners of the Chapter 12 business entity may have individual debts in excess of that amount.

Joseph Wipf

Jacob Wipf

Samuel Hofer — Margaret Wipf

John Wipf*

Herb Wipf*   Henry Wipf*

John Hofer

Joshua Hofer

Jake Hofer*   Mike Hofer   Josh Hofer*   Johnny Wipf, Jr.*—Elizabeth Hofer   Donald Hofer*   Dorothy Hofer—Walter Wipf*   Johnny Hofer*

KEY NUMBER SYSTEM

*Indicates shareholder status in Cloverleaf Farmer's Co-operative.

COMPARISON OF BANKRUPTCY CHAPTERS

The differences between the most common chapters of bankruptcy (Chapter 7, Chapter 13, and Chapter 11) hinge on three components: (1) the effect of each chapter, (2) the eligibility of the debtor to file under each chapter, and (3) the costs and time involved with each chapter. The following is a comparison of each chapter's critical components.

The "effect," or goal, of each chapter is ultimately "how much obligation may a debtor discharge." In Chapter 7, *individuals* are entitled to discharge all unsecured debts, provided such debts are not excluded from dischargeability under 11 U.S.C. Section 523. Every provision of 11 U.S.C. Section 523 is applicable to Chapter 7 debtors to eliminate certain debts from discharge. Chapter 7 does not discharge a debtor from secured debts. Generally, liens survive on a debtor's property regardless of a Chapter 7 discharge. For example, a house mortgage or car loan or tax lien will not be discharged and remain in place even after a discharge. However, corporations, partnerships and other entities are not entitled to a discharge in Chapter 7 whatsoever.

Chapter 13 also allows debtors to discharge all unsecured debts (which have not otherwise been paid through the plan). However, the Chapter 13 discharge is greater than a discharge in Chapter 7. Only certain portions of the nondischargeable sections within 11 U.S.C. Section 523 are applicable to Chapter 13 cases. The Chapter 13 discharge under 11 U.S.C. Section 1328(a) is often called a *super discharge.*

For example, only spouse/child support, student loans, drunk driving and criminal restitution claims remain nondischargeable. Therefore, other claims that would otherwise be nondischargeable in Chapter 7 under 11 U.S.C. Section 523 are discharged in Chapter 13. These claims include fraud, fiduciary embezzlement, willful and malicious injuries, government fines, property settlement claims in divorce, homeowners' association dues, etc.

A Chapter 13 also allows debtors to keep nonexempt assets which would be surrendered in a Chapter 7. For example, a Chapter 13 debtor would be able to keep a speedboat as long as the unsecured creditors were paid through the plan as much as the speedboat could be sold for.

Also, Chapter 13 allows a debtor to "strip down" certain secured debts. This means the debtor need only pay the value of the property and not the entire secured claim. For example, suppose a debtor bought a sports car and still owed the financing company $10,000 on the car. However, the car is now only worth $5,000. Chapter 13 allows the debtor to pay only $5,000 to the financing company and the rest of the amount is discharged.

Additionally, often the primary goal of a debtor in Chapter 13 is to "cure" a delinquent secured loan. The cure provisions of Chapter 13 allow the debtor to make up back payments to secured creditors over time through a plan. These cure payments are in addition to the regular monthly payments to the secured creditor. This allows Chapter 13 debtors to keep property such as their home or automobile which would otherwise be subject to foreclosure or repossession.

Chapter 11 discharge for individuals parallels the discharge of Chapter 7. In essence, all nondischargeability provisions of 11 U.S.C. Section 523 apply to individual Chapter 11 debtors. However, Chapter 11 allows corporations and other business entities to obtain a discharge through the Chapter 11 plan if the debtor remains in business after bankruptcy.

Chapter 11 also allows debtors to strip down certain secured loans as discussed above. Further, Chapter 11 also includes the "cure" provisions afforded in Chapter 13 which allow a debtor to make up back payments. However, Chapter 11 permits a debtor greater flexibility to restructure payments to creditors than Chapter 13. For example, a Chapter 11 debtor may propose to strip down a mortgage to the value of the property and repay this amount over a period of ten years.

The "eligibility" of each of the chapters is also a critical difference among the chapters. A detailed discussion of the eligibility requirements of each chapter was discussed above. Generally, business entities file Chapter 11 in order to receive a discharge. Individuals file Chapter 11 if the debt limit of Chapter 13 is exceeded.

Finally, the last component of the differences between the various chapters consists of the costs and efforts of the debtor in pursuing each chapter (i.e., time involved, attorney's fees, etc.). Chapter 7 cases are the swiftest and easiest to administer and are therefore the least expensive for a debtor to pursue. A Chapter 7 debtor need only file the initial documentation, cooperate with the trustee, and appear at the 341 First Creditors Meeting and discharge hearing. Note that many jurisdictions have eliminated the requirement for a debtor to appear at a discharge hearing. The discharge is granted to an individual Chapter 7 debtor within a few months of the petition date. At this point, the debtor has emerged from bankruptcy, is allowed to keep all exempt property, and is freed from all prepetition unsecured debts.

However, Chapter 13 cases are more complex than Chapter 7. Chapter 13 requires a formulation of a plan to repay creditors. The Chapter 13 plan requires the debtor to remain in bankruptcy and make monthly payments for three to five years before a discharge is granted. A Chapter 13 is usually much more expensive than Chapter 7 since the bankruptcy attorney must formulate a plan and attend confirmation hearings. Accordingly, to file a Chapter 13 case is usually more costly and requires more stamina than Chapter 7.

Chapter 11 is an involved, complicated, lengthy process that requires an extensive amount of time and costs for a Chapter 11 debtor. Initially, the Chapter 11 debtor is required to file more extensive documentation regarding assets in addition to the statements and schedules. Throughout the Chapter 11 the debtor is required to file monthly financial statements and pay quarterly fees to the U.S. Trustee's Office. The Chapter 11 debtor actively participates in the formulation of the plan and is often required to attend hearings on litigated matters such as cash collateral and stay relief. Meanwhile, the Chapter 11 debtor is expected to pay all professionals. This may include appraisers, expert witnesses, accountants, official creditors' committee's attorneys and the debtor's bankruptcy attorney. These expenses can be quite burdensome. For example, some law firms will not agree to represent a Chapter 11 debtor unless a large retainer is provided before the bankruptcy is filed, such as $50,000. Accordingly, a cost-benefit analysis should be used in conjunction with the effect of each chapter as well as the eligibility requirements in choosing which chapter is most beneficial for a potential debtor.

Dewsnup v. Timm
502 U.S. 410 (1992)

Blackmun, J. * * * On June 1, 1978, respondents loaned $119,000 to petitioner Aletha Dewsnup and her husband, T. LaMar Dewsnup, since deceased. The loan was accompanied by a Deed of Trust granting a lien on two parcels of Utah farmland owned by the Dewsnups.

Petitioner defaulted the following year. Under the terms of the Deed of Trust, respondents at that point could have proceeded against the real property collateral by accelerating the maturity of the loan, issuing a notice of default, and selling the land at a public foreclosure sale to satisfy the debt. (citations omitted)

Respondents did issue a notice of default in 1981. Before the foreclosure sale took place, however, petitioner sough reorganization under Chapter 11 of the Bankruptcy Code, 11 U.S.C. §1101 *et seq.* That bankruptcy petition was dismissed, as was a subsequent Chapter 11 petition. In June 1984, petitioners filed a petition seeking liquidation under Chapter 7 of the Code, 11 U.S.C. §701 *et seq.* Because of the pendency of these bankruptcy proceedings, respondents were not able to proceed to the foreclosure sale. See 11 U.S.C. §362.

In 1987, petitioner filed the present adversary proceeding in the Bankruptcy Court for the District of Utah seeking, pursuant to §506, to "avoid" a portion of respondents' lien. Petitioner represented that the debt of approximately $120,000 then owed to respondents exceeded the fair market value of the land and that, therefore, the Bankruptcy Court should reduce the lien to that value. According to petitioner, this was compelled by the interrelationship of the security-reducing provision of §506(a) and the lien-voiding provision of §506(d). Under §506(a) ("An allowed claim of a creditor secured by a lien on property in which the estate has an interest ... is a secured claim to the extent of the value of such creditor's interest in the estate's interest in such property"), respondents would have an "allowed secured claim" only to the extent of the judicially determined value of their collateral. And under §506(d) ("To the extent that a lien secures a claim against the debtor that is not an allowed secured claim, such lien is void"), the court would be required to void the lien as to the remaining portion of the respondents' claim, because the remaining portion was not an "allowed secured claim" within the meaning of §506(a).

The Bankruptcy Court refused to grant this relief. * * * Petitioner-debtor takes the position that §506(a) and §506(d) are complementary and to be read together. Because, under §506(a), a claim is secured only to the extent of the judicially determined value of the real property on which the lien is fixed, a debtor can void a lien on the property pursuant to §506(d) to the extent the claim is no longer secured and thus is not "an allowed secured claim." In other words, §506(a) bifurcates classes of claims allowed under §502 into secured claims and unsecured claims; any portion of an allowed claim deemed to be unsecured under §5406(a) is not an "allowed secured claim" within the lien-voiding scope of §506(d).

* * * §506 of the Bankruptcy Code and its relationship to other provisions of that Code do embrace some ambiguities. * * * Therefore, we hold that §506(d) does not allow petitioner to "strip down" respondents' lien, because respondents' claim is secured by a lien and has been fully allowed pursuant to §502. Were we writing on a clean slate, we might be inclined to agree with petitioner that the words "allowed secured claim" must take the same meaning in §506(d) as in §506(a). But given the ambiguity in the text, we are not convinced that Congress intended to depart from the pre-Code rule that liens pass through bankruptcy unaffected.

* * * Apart from the reorganization proceedings, see 11 U.S.C. §§616(1) and (10) (1976 ed.), no provision of the pre-Code statute permitted involuntary reduction of the amount of a creditor's lien for any other reason other than payment on the debt. Our cases reveal the Court's concern about this. * * *

Congress must have enacted the Code with a full understanding of this practice. See H.R. Rep. No. 95-595, p 357 (1977), U.S.Code Cong. & Admin. news 1978, pp. 5787, 6313 ("Subsection (d) permits liens to pass through the bankruptcy case unaffected").

When Congress amends the bankruptcy laws, it does not write on a clean slate. (citations omitted) Furthermore, this Court has been reluctant to accept arguments that would interpret the Code, however vague the particular language under consideration might be to effect a major change in pre-Code practice that is not the subject of at least some discussion in the legislative history.

* * * But, given the ambiguity here, to attribute to Congress the intention to grant a debtor the broad new remedy against allowed claims to the extent that they become "unsecured" for purposes of §506(a) without the new remedy's being mentioned somewhere in the Code itself or in the annals of Congress is not plausible, in our view, and is contrary to basic bankruptcy principles.

The judgment of the Court of Appeals is affirmed.

CONCLUSION

Essentially, bankruptcy allows a debtor to either liquidate or reorganize. The various chapters a debtor may choose to file bankruptcy under permit either liquidation or reorganization. The reorganization chapters each contain different requirements for repayment and distinct provisions which may allow a debtor flexibility. Also, each chapter has its own eligibility requirements in order to be a debtor. Finally, the costs and effort required by the debtor vary significantly among the available chapters under the Bankruptcy Code.

REVIEW QUESTIONS

1. What chapter is the liquidation bankruptcy case?
2. What chapters are the reorganization bankruptcy cases?
3. What are the eligibility requirements for Chapter 13?
4. What does Chapter 13 permit which is not allowed in Chapter 7?
5. Which chapter requires the most expense and effort on the debtor's part?
6. Which chapter is the swiftest and easiest for a debtor?
7. What are the differences between Chapter 13 and Chapter 11?
8. Why would an individual file a Chapter 11 instead of a Chapter 13?
9. Why would a business entity file a Chapter 11 instead of a Chapter 7?

ENDNOTES

[1]The eligibility requirements for Chapter 9 cases are omitted due to the rarity of cases.

[2]See 11 U.S.C. Section 522.

[3]See Chapter 9, "Creditor Status, Priority, and Distribution Rights," for a detailed analysis of creditor priority.

[4]See Chapter 6 of this text for a detailed analysis of denial of discharge under 11 U.S.C. Section 727.

[5]*In re City of South Tucson*, Case No. 83-00866 (Ariz. 1984).

[6]H.R. Rep. No. 958, 99th Cong., 2d Sess. 48 (1986).

[7]Banking institutions and insurance companies are excluded from liquidation under bankruptcy laws because other bodies provide for alternative liquidation under various regulatory laws.

[8]*In re Morris Plan Co.*, 62 B.R. 348 (Bankr. N.D. Iowa 1986).

[9]*In re Walters*, 113 B.R. 602 (Bankr. D. S.D. 1990).

[10]See *In re Jones*, 97 B.R. 901 (Bankr. S.D. Ohio 1989); *In re Zawisza*, 73 B.R. 929 (Bankr. E.D. Pa. 1987).

[11]*Id.*

[12]*In re Medallion Realty Trust*, 103 B.R. 8 (Bankr. D. Mass. 1989).

[13]*In re Metro Palms I Trust*, 153 B.R. 922 (Bankr. M.D. Fla. 1993).

[14]*In re Ophir Trust*, 112 B.R. 956 (Bankr. E.D. Wis. 1990); *In re Jay M. Weisman Irrevocable Children's Trust of 1981*, 62 B.R. 286 (Bankr. M.D. Fla. 1986).

[15]Increased by the 1994 Amendments from $100,000 unsecured and $350,000 secured.

[16]*In re La Cache Land Co.*, 54 B.R. 629 (E.D. La. 1985).

[17]*In re Jarrett*, 19 B.R. 413 (Bankr. M.D. N.C. 1982).

[18]*In re Zawisza*, 73 B.R. 929 (Bankr. E.D. Pa. 1987).

[19]28 U.S.C. Section 1930(a)(1).

[20]*In re McLeroy*, 106 B.R. 147 (Bankr. W.D. Tenn. 1989).

[21]11 U.S.C. Section 101(30).

[22]*In re Anderson*, 21 B.R. 443 (Bankr. N.D. Ga. 1981).

[23]*In re Iacovoni*, 2 B.R. 256 (Bankr. D. Utah 1980).

[24]*In re Howell*, 4 B.R. 102 (Bankr. M.D. Tenn. 1980).

[25]*In re McMonagle*, 30 B.R. 899 (Bankr.D. S.D. 1983); contra *In re Donohue*, 81 B.R. 714 (Bankr. S.D. Fla. 1987).

[26]*In re Taylor*, 15 B.R. 596 (Bankr. D. Arizona 1981).

[27]*In re Burgat*, 68 B.R. 408 (Bankr. D. Colo. 1986).

[28]*In re All Media Properties, Inc.*, 5 B.R. 126 (Bankr. S.D. Tex. 1980), aff'd 676 F.2d 193 (5th Cir. 1981).

[29]*In re Loya*, 123 B.R. 338 (Bankr. 9th Cir. BAP 1991).

[30]*In re McGovern*, 122 B.R. 712 (Bankr. N.D. Ind. 1989).

[31]*In re King*, 126 B.R 777 (N.D. Ill. 1991).

[32]*In re Fischel*, 103 B.R. 44 (Bankr. N.D. N.Y. 1989)

[33]*In re Wenberg*, 94 B.R. 631 (9th Cir. BAP 1988) aff'd 902 F.2d 769 (9th Cir. 1990).

[34]*In re Furey*, 31 B.R. 495 (Bankr. E.D. Pa. 1983).

[35]See *In re Lamar*, 111 B.R. 327 (Dist. Nev. 1990); *In re Cole*, 3 B.R. 346 (Bankr. S.D. W.Va. 1980).

[36]See *In re Pearson*, 773 F.2d 751 (6th Cir. 1985); *In re Robertson*, 84 B.R. 109 (Bankr. S.D. Ohio 1988); *In re Jerome*, 112 B.R. 563 (Bankr. S.D. N.Y. 1990); *In re Young*, 91 B.R. 730 (E.D. La. 1988).

[37]See *In re Koehler*, 62 B.R. 70 (Bankr. D. Neb. 1986); *In re Perry* 56 B.R. 663 (Bankr. M.D. Ga. 1986).

[38]*In re McGovern*, 122 B.R. 712 (Bankr. N.D. Ind. 1989); *In re Lucoski*, 126 B.R. 332 (S.D. Ind. 1991).

[39]*In re Pearson*, 773 F.2d 751 (6th Cir. 1985).

[40]See *In re Balbus*, 933 F.2d 246 (4th Cir. 1991); *In re Miller*, 907 F.2d 80 (8th Cir. 1990); *In re Day*, 747 F.2d 405 (7th Cir. 1984).

[41]11 U.S.C. Section 109(f).

[42]Noncontingent, liquidated.

[43]*In re Roberts,* 78 B.R. 536 (Bankr. C.D. Ill. 1987).

[44]11 U.S.C. Section 10 (21).

[45]See *In re Tim Wargo & Sons, Inc.,* 869 F.2d 1128 (8th Cir. 1989) (farmland rentals not farm income); contra *In re Vernon,* 101 B.R. 87 (Bankr. E.D. Mo. 1989) (rent is farm income).

[46]*In re Burke,* 81 B.R. 971 (Bankr. S.D. Iowa 1987).

[47]*In re Sohrakoff,* 85 B.R. 848 (Bankr. E.D. Cal. 1988); *In re Van Fossan,* 82 B.R. 77 (Bankr. W.D. Ark. 1987).

[48]*In re Guinnane,* 73 B.R. 129 (Bankr. D. Mont. 1987).

[49]*In re Van Air Flying Service, Inc.,* 146 B.R. 816 (Bankr. E.D. Ark. 1992).

[50]*In re Miller,* 122 B.R. 360 (Bankr. N.D. Iowa 1990).

[51]*In re Blackwelder Harvesting Co.,* 106 B.R. 301 (Bankr. M.D. Fla. 1989).

[52]*In re Cluck,* 101 B.R. 691 (Bankr. E.D. Okla. 1989).

[53]*In re Sugar Pine Ranch,* 100 B.R. 28 (Bankr. D. Or. 1989).

[54]*Federal Bank v. McNeal,* 77 B.R. 315 (S.D. Ga. 1987) aff'd 848 F.2d 170 (11th Cir. 1988).

[55]*In re Maike,* 77 B.R. 832 (Bankr. D. Kan. 1987).

[56]*In re Welch,* 74 B.R. 401 (Bankr. S.D. Ohio 1987).

[57]*In re McKillips,* 72 B.R. 565 (Bankr. N.D. Ill. 1987).

[58]Noncontingent, liquidated.

4 *Initial Documentation*

First thing in the morning your supervising attorney brings you an apple box full of a client's old bills, loan documents, deeds of trust, lease agreements, and other important papers. The client is coming in at noon to sign off on an emergency bankruptcy filing to stop a foreclosure. You are assigned to prepare the emergency paperwork this morning. Also, you are to prepare the remaining initial documents to be filed later this week. If any information is missing, you are supposed to let the client know today so he can gather it for you.

What types of documents does it take to start a bankruptcy? What information do you need? What is an emergency filing? What do the documents look like? What are they called? Is it important that they be accurate?

INTRODUCTION

The start of every bankruptcy case requires certain documents to be filed with the Court. These documents include comprehensive information about the debtor's assets and obligations as well as specific information regarding the debtor's financial affairs. As a paralegal, the most important and frequent tasks you will be required to perform are compiling and drafting the initial documents on behalf of debtors or examining and analyzing these documents if representing creditors or trustees. Accordingly, the paralegal must ensure the accuracy and completeness in the preparation or the analysis of these important documents.

Since the information contained in the initial documentation is specific to each debtor, a comprehensive questionnaire is the most efficient manner to obtain information. Some law firms allow the debtors to fill these questionnaires out themselves, while other law firms require the paralegal to assist the debtors. Note: Since most questionnaires must be extensive to acquire the necessary information, most debtors require the help of the paralegal in understanding the questions or the information required even if debtors are to complete the questionnaires themselves.

Practice hint: While a variety of questionnaires exist, some are more difficult than others for debtors to complete due to the phrasing of questions or format, etc. Therefore, it may save you considerable time if you were to compile an understandable and easy-to-use questionnaire.

Once the information is obtained, the paralegal must draft the initial documents. These documents include:

> The petition.
>
> Schedule A (real property).
>
> Scheduled B (personal property).
>
> Scheduled C (exempt property)
>
> Schedule D (secured claims)
>
> Schedule E (priority claims).
>
> Schedule F (unsecured claims).
>
> Schedule G (executory contracts).
>
> Schedule H (codebtors).
>
> Schedule I (statement of income).
>
> Schedule J (statement of expenses).
>
> Summary of schedules.
>
> §521 statement of intent.
>
> Statement of financial affairs.
>
> Rule 2016(b) statement of attorney compensation.
>
> Notice of available chapters.
>
> The master mailing list.

Often bankruptcy cases are filed in an emergency situation. For example, a debtor may seek to file bankruptcy mere hours or minutes before a scheduled Trustee's Sale of real property in order to avoid losing the property. Under such circumstances, it is virtually impossible to prepare and file all the initial documentation. However, the Bankruptcy Court may allow a case to be initially filed with only a certain few of these documents, such as the petition and master mailing list, and allow the remaining documents to be filed within the next few days. This is called an emergency filing. As a paralegal, you should check the local rules of the Bankruptcy Court in which you will be practicing to determine if an emergency filing is allowed and, if so, which documents are required in an emergency situation.

The initial documents may be manually typed on a typewriter onto forms. However, a variety of computer programs are also available to readily generate the initial documentation in the form required. Bear in mind that the information entered into the computer must still be accurate in order to ensure complete and accurate statements and schedules. Remember, the debtor will be signing these documents and declaring under the penalty of federal perjury that the documents are correct. The ramifications of inaccurate statements and schedules filed with the Bankruptcy Court cannot be overemphasized. Incorrect statements and schedules could lead to dismissal based upon bad faith, could prevent a debtor's discharge under 11 U.S.C. Section 727, or could even subject a debtor to criminal penalties under 18 U.S.C. Section 152 of fines of $500,000 and imprisonment of 5 years or both.

Despite whether the forms are generated manually or by a computer program, the ultimate documents generated are essentially identical in format.

PETITION

The petition starts off the case. A sample of the form for the initial documentation is included in Figure 4-1. Remarkably, the petition includes the following crucial information within only about two pages. The petition contains basic information about the debtor, including debtor's name, address, social security number or tax identification number, and nature of debtor's business, if any. The petition also states the approximate number of creditors, the extent of assets and liabilities, states the number of employees, and whether any funds might be available for distribution to creditors.

All related bankruptcy cases are also listed. These may include a partnership bankruptcy when an individual partner is filing or a corporate bankruptcy when a subsidiary is filing and vice-versa. Additionally, all bankruptcies filed by the debtor within the last six years are listed.

The petition also contains certain jurisdictional information, including the district within which the case is filed (i.e., Northern District of California; Dis-

```
———— United States Bankruptcy Court ———— VOLUNTARY PETITION ————
      DISTRICT OF ARIZONA
```

IN RE _____	NAME OF JOINT DEBTOR _____
JOHN DOE CORPORATION _____	N/A
ALL OTHER NAMES _____	ALL OTHER NAMES _____
	N/A
None	
SOC. SEC./TAX I.D. No. _____	SOC. SEC./TAX I.D. NO. _____
None_____	N/A
STREET ADDRESS OF DEBTOR _____	STREES ADDRESS OF JOINT DEBTOR ___
	N/A

```
LOCATION OF PRINCIPAL ASSETS OF BUSINESS DEBTOR   ———————————
  N/A
VENUE   _____
```

Debtor has been domiciled or has had a residence, principal place of business, or principal assets in this District for 180 days immediately preceding the date of this petition or for a longer part of such 180 days than in any other District.

```
——————————————————— INFORMATION REGARDING DEBTOR ———————————
```

TYPE: Corporation: NOT Publicly held	CHAPTER OF BANKRUPTCY CODE
NATURE: Business	UNDER WHICH THE PETITION
A. TYPE OF BUSINESS	IS FILED: 11
Commodity Broker	FILING FEE
	Attached
B. BRIEFLY DESCRIBE NATURE OF BUSINESS	

STATISTICAL/ADMINISTRATIVE INFORMATION —— ATTORNEY NAME(S)/ADDRESS——
Debtor estimates that, after any exempt property excluded and administrative expenses paid, NO funds will be available for distribution to unsecured creditors.

bar #

```
                        __(aard
               range    code)
  NO. OF CREDITORS 1-15      (1)
 ASSETS (thousands) Under 50 (1)
LIABIL. (thousands) Under 50 (1)
    NO OF EMPLOYEES 0        (1)
EQUITY SEC. HOLDERS 0        (1)
```

———————————————————————————————— THIS SPACE FOR COURT USE ONLY

FIGURE 4-1a. Petition (page 1).

Name of Debtor: Case No.:
JOHN DOE CORPORATION

Debtor intends to file a plan within the time allowed by statute, rule, or order of the court.

———————— PRIOR BANKRUPTCY CASE FILED WITHIN LAST 6 YEARS ————————
Location Where Filed _____ Case Number ____ Date Filed ____
No Prior Bankruptcies

——PENDING BANKRUPTCY CASE FILED BY ANY SPOUSE, PARTNER, OR AFFILIATE——
Name of Debtor _____ Case Number ____ Date Filed ____
No Pending Bankruptcies

Relationship ————————District ————————Judge ————————

——————————————— REQUEST FOR RELIEF ———————————————
Debtor requests relief in accordance with the chapter of title 11 United States Code specified in this petition.
———————————————————SIGNATURES ———————————————

Attorney signature   Date
——————————— CORPORATE OR PARTNERSHIP DEBTOR ———————————
I declare under penalty of perjury that the information provided in this petition is true and correct, and that the filing of this petition on behalf of the debtor has been authorized.

                                      Date

——————————————— EXHIBIT A ———————————————
|X| Exhibit A is attached and made a part of this petition.
_____ INDIVIDUAL CHAPTER 7 DEBTOR WITH PRIMARILY CONSUMER DEBTS ____
I am aware that I may proceed under Chapter 7, 11, 12, or 13 of title 11, U.S. C., understand the relief available under such chapter, and choose to proceed under chapter 7 of such title. If I am represented by an attorney, Exhibit B has been completed.

Signature of Debtor   Signature of Joint Debtor

Date: _____

——————————————— EXHIBIT B ———————————————
I, the attorney for the debtor(s) named in the foregoing petition, declare that I have informed the debtor(s) that the debtor(s) may proceed under chapter 7, 11, 12, or 13 of title 11 United States Code, and have explained the relief available under such chapter.

Signature of Attorney   Date

FIGURE 4-1b. Petition (page 2).

Attorney for the Petitioner

UNITED STATES BANKRUPTCY COURT FOR THE
DISTRICT OF ARIZONA

In re   Case No.:
JOHN DOE CORPORATION
Debtor   Exhibit A

                                         Chapter 11

1. Debtor's employer identification number is:

2. If any of debtor's securities are registered under section 12 of
   the Securities and Exchange Act of 1934, the SEC file number is:

3. The following financial data is the latest available information
   and refers to debtor's condition on:

   a. Total assets: 0.00
   b. Total liabilities: 0.00

		Amount	Approximate no. of holders
Fixed, liquidated secured debt:		0.00	1
Contingent secured debt:		0.00	0
Disputed secured claims:		0.00	0
Unliquidated secured debt:		0.00	0
Fixed, liquidated unsecured debt:		0.00	0
Contingent unsecured debt:		0.00	0
Disputed unsecured claims:		0.00	0
Unliquidated unsecured debt:		0.00	0

   No. of shares of preferred stock:
   No. of shares of common stock:

   Comments, if any:
   None

4. Brief description of debtor's business:
   None

5. List the name of any person who directly or indirectly owns,
   controls, or holds with power to vote, 20% or more of the voting
   securities of debtor:
   None

6. List the names of all corporations, 20% or more of the outstanding
   voting securities of which are directly or indirectly owned,
   controlled, or held, with power to vote, by debtor:
   None

Figure 4-1c. Petition (page 3).

trict of Maryland, Rockville Division, etc.) and the appropriateness of the venue of such district (i.e., the debtor has lived or had a principal place of business in that district for 180 days). The petition also states the chapter of the Bankruptcy Code under which the debtor is seeking relief.

The next set of documents includes all the assets of the debtor. These assets include real and personal property, tangible and intangible property, and assets wherein the debtor wholly or partially holds an ownership interest. Assets should be listed even if the value is dubious or if the property is to be declared exempt or is excluded from the estate.

SCHEDULE A (REAL PROPERTY)

Real property may be both commercial or residential property. Also, certain unique types of real property may be included on Schedule A, such as time share interests. See Figure 4-2. Schedule A requires the description and location of the property, such as the address and/or legal description. The nature of debtor's interest in the property, such as co-owner, joint tenant, or 100% interest is also included. The current market value of the property is also listed regardless of any underlying lienholders or the amounts of the liens. Thereafter, the amounts of any secured claims upon the property (i.e., liens) are also specified. Also, whether the property is in the debtor's possession or in the possession of some third party, such as a receiver, is included.

SCHEDULE B (PERSONAL PROPERTY)

All personal property of the debtor of whatever kind is listed within Schedule B. See Figure 4-3. Additionally, the description of the specific property must be indicated. Finally, the current market value of the debtor's interest in the property must be stated (without deducting any secured claim or any amount claimed as exempt). Current market value is the amount the debtor could possibly sell the property for. The specific types of property that are separately enumerated in Schedule B are as follows:

1. *Cash on hand.* All cash carried upon the debtor's person or which may be found in the debtor's home or otherwise is to be listed here.

2. *Checking, savings, or other financial accounts, certificates of deposit, or shares in banks, savings and loan, thrift, building and loan and homestead associations, or credit unions, brokerage houses, or cooperatives.* Basically, this requests information regarding all checking and savings accounts of

In re JOHN DOE CORPORATION
        Debtor

Case No. (if known)

SCHEDULE A - REAL PROPERTY

Description and location of property	Current market value of debtor interest in the property without deducting any secured claim or exemption
Nature of Debtor interest in property	Amount of secured claim

None

Total: 0.00

FIGURE 4-2. Schedule A.

In re   JOHN DOE CORPORATION
       Debtor   Case No. (if known)

SCHEDULE B - PERSONAL PROPERTY

Type of property _____ Description and location of property	Current market value of debtor interest in property without deducting any secured claim

1. Cash on hand.
   None
2. Checking, savings, or other financial accounts, certificates of deposit, or shares in banks, savings and loan, thrift, building and loan, and homestead associations, or credit unions, brokerage houses, or cooperatives.
   None
3. Security deposits with public utilities, telephone companies, landlords, and others.
   None
4. Household goods and furnishings, including audio, video, and computer equipment.
   None
5. Books, pictures, and other art objects, antiques, stamp, coin, record, tape, compact disc, and other collections or collectibles.
   None
6. Wearing apparel.
   None
7. Furs and jewelry.
   None
8. Firearms and sports, photographic, and other hobby equipment.
   None
9. Interests in insurance policies.
   None
10. Annuities.
    None
11. Interests in IRA, ERISA, Keogh, or other pension or profit sharing plans.
    None
12. Stock and interests in incorporated and unincorporated businesses.
    None
13. Interests in partnerships or joint ventures.
    None
14. Government and corporate bonds and other negotiable and non-negotiable instruments.
    None
15. Accounts receivable.
    None

FIGURE 4-3a. Schedule B (page 1).

16. Alimony, maintenance, support, and property settlements to which the debtor is or may be entitled.
    None
17. Other liquidated debts owing debtor including tax refunds.
    None
18. Equitable or future interests, life estates, and rights or powers exercisable for the benefit of the debtor other than those listed in Schedule of Real Property.
    None
19. Contingent and noncontingent interests in estate of a decedent, death benefit plan, life insurance policy, or trust.
    None
20. Other contingent and unliquidated claims of every nature, including tax refunds, counterclaims of the debtor, and rights to setoff claims.
    None
21. Patents, copyrights, and other intellectual property.
    None
22. Licenses, franchises, and other general intangibles.
    None
23. Automobiles, trucks, trailers, and other vehicles or accessories.
    None
24. Boats, motors, and accessories.
    None
25. Aircraft and accessories.
    None
26. Office equipment, furnishings, and supplies.
    None
27. Machinery, fixtures, equipment, and supplies used in business.
    None
28. Inventory.
    None
29. Animals.
    None
30. Crops - growing or harvested.
    None
31. Farming equipment and implements.
    None
32. Farm supplies, chemicals, and feed.
    None
33. Other personal property of any kind not already listed.
    None

                                    Total: 0.00

FIGURE 4-3b. Schedule B (page 2).

the debtor. Such information should include the name and address of the banking institution as well as the account number of the checking or savings account. This category also pertains to accounts within brokerage houses (such as investment accounts).

3. *Security deposits with public utilities, telephone companies, landlords, and others.* This requests information regarding any lease deposits the debtor may have, all telephone and/or long distance company, electricity, or gas deposits. The name and address of the entity holding the deposit, any account number, and the amount of the deposit should be included.

4. *Household goods and furnishings, including audio, video, and computer equipment.* Basically, all items of furniture in the debtor's house must be included here. Some law firms simply choose to state "bedroom furniture" while others choose to itemize all pieces of furniture (i.e., king-size bed, nightstand, dresser, etc.). Additionally, all audio equipment (stereos, walkmans), video equipment (VCR, video camera), and computer equipment (IBM computer) should be articulated. Again, the value of these household goods should be included.

5. *Books, pictures, and other art objects, antiques, stamp, coin, record, tape, compact disc, and other collections or collectibles.* Here, all libraries, pieces of art, antiques, and collections of virtually every type are listed along with their values.

6. *Wearing apparel.* Basically, this entails only "men's clothing" or "women's clothing" for most cases. However, a commercial resales debtor of clothing may have an extensive detailed list. Additionally, some commercial debtors may also have work uniforms to list in this category.

7. *Furs and jewelry.* Mink stoles, wedding rings, watches, costume jewelry, etc. should be listed here.

8. *Firearms and sports, photographic, and other hobby equipment.* Guns, mountain bikes, cameras, surf boards, trampolines, etc. should be placed in this category.

9. *Interests in insurance policies.* Name the insurance company of each policy, and itemize the surrender or refund value of each. Whole life insurance policies, term life insurance policies, etc. should be placed herein with the current surrender value for each policy, if any. Also, the address of the insurance company and account number should be included.

10. *Annuities.* Itemize and name each issuer. All annuities from retirement or in settlement of past lawsuits should be itemized. Additional information including the name and address of the annuity issuer and the account number should also be included.

11. *Interests in IRA, ERISA, Keogh, or other pension or profit sharing plans.* All retirement devices, along with the names and addresses of the institutions holding the plans and account numbers, should be listed here.

12. *Itemized stock and interests in incorporated and unincorporated businesses.* The debtor's shares in corporations, public or private, as well as interests in business associations should be articulated in this category.

13. *Itemized interests in partnerships or joint ventures.* The debtor's share of any general partnership, limited partnership, or one-time joint venture, along with the percentages of such holdings should be included here.

14. *Government and corporate bonds and other negotiable and non-negotiable instruments.* Government savings bonds, publicly or privately issued bonds in corporations, promissory notes, etc. should be categorized here.

15. *Accounts receivable.* All funds owed to debtor, along with the entity who owes such money, as well as the address and account number, should be included in this section.

16. *Alimony, maintenance, support, and property settlements to which the debtor is or may be entitled.* Give particulars. All payments owed as of the petition date resulting from a domestic relation case, including spousal support, child support, or other property settlement should be provided here. Additionally, the domestic relation state court case number should be included.

17. *Other liquidated debts owing to the debtor, including tax refunds.* Give particulars. Federal and/or state tax refunds that are due, along with the period of time that such refunds result from, as well as other liquidated debts, are to be included here.

18. *Equitable or future interests, life estate and rights or powers exercisable for the benefit of the debtor other than those listed in the Schedule of Real Property.* All remainder interests in property or other such future interests that are not included in Schedule A should be articulated here.

19. *Contingent and noncontingent interests in estate of a decedent, death benefit plan, life insurance policy, or trust.* All benefits flowing from inheritances, interests within a buy-sell corporate stock agreement, beneficial interests in life insurance policies, and/or beneficial interests in any type of trust should be itemized in this category.

20. *Other contingent and unliquidated claims of every nature, including tax refunds, counterclaims of the debtor, and rights to setoff claims.* Give the estimated value of each. This category includes all potential lawsuits where the debtor may hold some type of monetary claim, whether such claim has yet been liquidated. This would include claims of per-

sonal injury, even if such claim had not yet been initiated, litigated, or reduced to judgment.

21. *Patents, copyrights, and other intellectual property.* Give particulars. All rights of the debtor through licenses or actual holdings of copyrights or patents as well as other intellectual property (such as computer programs created by debtor) should be itemized here, along with patent and/or copyright numbers, if any.

22. *Licenses, franchises, and other general intangibles.* Give particulars. Should the debtor hold an interest under a franchise agreement (i.e., to run a McDonalds'), a license, etc., it should be listed here.

23. *Automobiles, trucks, trailers, and other vehicles and accessories.* All cars, trucks (commercial and otherwise), motorcycles, mopeds, along with accessories (camper shells, etc.) should be indicated here.

24. *Boats, motors, and accessories.* Include sailboats, speedboats, fishing boats, kayaks, and all parts thereto.

25. *Aircraft and accessories.* Include all airplanes, hang gliders, etc.

26. *Office equipment, furnishings, and supplies.* All desks, adding machines, fax machines, typewriters, file cabinets, and office supplies should be included in this section.

27. *Machinery, fixtures, equipment, and supplies used in business.* Movable equipment as well as permanent fixtures that the debtor has installed in the course of business should be included in this category.

28. *Inventory.* All items that the debtor has on hand to sell should be specifically listed, along with wholesale and potential retail prices.

29. *Animals.* Usually the individual debtor need not list a family pet. However, should the debtor be a farmer or owner of such animals as pedigree dogs or Arabian horses, those animals, along with their values, should be included.

30. *Crops—growing or harvested.* Give particulars. For farmers the specifics of the crops already harvested and those yet to be yielded should be articulated here.

31. *Farming equipment and implements.* Again for farmers, the identity of the specific farming equipment should be listed.

32. *Farm supplies, chemicals, and feed.* Again, for farmers, all seeds, fertilizer, etc. should be categorized here.

33. *Itemized other personal property of any kind not already listed.* This is the "catch-all" section of the personal property list. Should an item not be included in another specific section, it should be listed here.

SCHEDULE C (PROPERTY CLAIMED AS EXEMPT)

The next schedule is a list of all the debtor's claimed exemptions. See Figure 4-4. The exempt property is described along with the property's full value. Then the specific exemption law providing for the exemption is stated (i.e., for a homestead, either 11 U.S.C. Section 522(d)(1) or A.R.S. Section 1101 under Arizona law). Also, the value of the claimed exemption is stated.

Either exemptions are claimed under federal law [11 U.S.C. Section 522(d)], or a state may have "opted out" of the federal exemption scheme. If the state has opted out, then state exemption laws are the only available exemptions (i.e., a debtor cannot pick and choose or mix and match federal and state exemptions). Legal assistants should ascertain if the state where they are practicing uses federal or state exemptions and thereafter become exceptionally familiar with the nature and amounts provided for each exempt property.

Additionally, the trustee and/or party in interest has only a very limited time to object to a debtor's claimed exemption. F.R.Bankr.P. 4003 provides that all objections to claimed exemptions are barred after 30 days past the conclusion of the 341 meeting (or past any amendments by the debtor to the list of claimed exemptions). [See *Taylor v. Freeland,* 112 S.Ct. 1644 (1992).] This bar is complete, even though there may not be any good faith basis within which to claim such exemption.[1]

Schedules C through G list the debtor's liabilities. These schedules list the creditors of the estate divided into certain categories or "classes." Such classes include secured creditors, priority creditors, and unsecured creditors.[2]

SCHEDULE D (CREDITORS HOLDING SECURED CLAIMS)

All creditors holding claims secured by property of the debtor as of the petition date must be listed. See Figure 4-5. Such secured interests may include mortgages, judgment liens, garnishments, statutory liens (such as a tax lien), deeds of trust, UCC-1 security interest, etc. Initially, the creditor's name, address, and account number should be included. Additionally, the nature of the lien (i.e., first deed of trust, judgment lien, etc.) as well as a description of the underlying collateral should be specified. Also, the market value of the property is included (not subtracting any lien amounts). The amount of the secured creditor's claim is stated. Further, the unsecured portion of the creditor's claim is listed, if any. (Note: The unsecured portion is that which is "stripped down" under 11 U.S.C. Section 506.) Claims are also identified as contingent, unliquidated, or disputed. Finally, if any other entity holds the property jointly with the debtor, such co-ownership is identified.

In re   JOHN DOE CORPORATION
        Debtor   Case No. (if known)

               SCHEDULE C - PROPERTY CLAIMED AS EXEMPT

Debtor elects the exemptions to which debtor is entitled under:

| Description of property | Current market value of property |
| Specify exemption law and value claimed exempt | without deducting exemption |

None

Figure 4-4. Schedule C.

In re JOHN DOE CORPORATION
       Debtor   Case No. (if known)

              SCHEDULE D - CREDITORS HOLDING SECURED CLAIMS

Creditor's name and complete mailing address including zip code	Amount of claim without deducting value of collateral
Date claim was incurred, nature of lien, and description and market value of property subject to the lien	Unsecured portion, if any

Account no.:   Claim amount:
<< Incomplete >   Unsecured: unknown

Date incurred:
Nature of lien:
Claim is: Fixed and liquidated.
Collateral description: :<< Incomplete >
Collateral market value:
Lien seniority: 0
Total collateral value: 0.00

                                    Subtotal this page: 0.00
                                               Total: 0.00

FIGURE 4-5. Schedule D.

SCHEDULE E (CREDITORS HOLDING UNSECURED PRIORITY CLAIMS)

All claims entitled to priority are listed within Schedule E according to type of priority. See Figure 4-6. The name, address, and account number, if any, are included. The date the claim was incurred and consideration for the claim is articulated. The total amount of the claim is stated as well as the amount that is entitled to priority. Such priority claims are also identified as contingent, unliquidated, or disputed. A listing of the categories of priority claims is as follows:

1. *Extensions of credit in an involuntary case.* These are claims arising in the ordinary course of debtor's business or financial affairs after the commencement of the case but before the earlier of the appointment of a trustee or the order for relief under 11 U.S.C. Section 507(a)(2).

2. *Wages, salaries, and commissions.* Wages, salaries, and commissions, including vacation, severance, and sick leave pay owed to employees, and certain sales commissions earned, up to a maximum of $4,000[3] per employee, earned within 90 days immediately preceding the filing of the original petition, or the cessation of business, whichever occurred first, to the extent provided in 11 U.S.C. Section 507(a)(3).

3. *Contributions to employee benefit plans.* Money owed to employee benefit plans for services rendered within 180 days immediate preceding the filing of the original petition, or the cessation of business, whichever occurred first, to the extent provided in 11 U.S.C. Section 507(a)(4).

4. *Certain farmers and fishermen.* Claims of certain farmers and fishermen, up to a maximum of $4,000[4] per farmer or fisherman, against the debtor, as provided in 11 U.S.C. Section 507(a)(5).

5. *Deposits by individuals.* Claims of individuals up to a maximum of $1,800[5] for deposits for the purchase, lease, or rental of property or services for personal, family, or household use, that were not delivered or provided pursuant to 11 U.S.C. Section 507(a)(6).

6. *Claims for spousal support/child support.*[6]Alimony and child support as long as such liability is actually in the nature of support and is not assigned to another entity according to 11 U.S.C. Section 507(a)(7).

7. *Taxes and certain other debts owed to governmental units.* Taxes, customs duties, and penalties owing to federal, state, and local governmental units as provided in 11 U.S.C. Section 507(a)(8).

8. *Commitment to federal depository institutions' regulatory agency.* Claims based on a commitment to an authority to maintain the capital of an insured depository institution as set forth in Section 507(a)(9).

In re JOHN DOE CORPORATION
       Debtor   Case No. (if known)

       SCHEDULE E - CREDITORS HOLDING UNSECURED PRIORITY CLAIMS

|X| Debtor has no creditors holding unsecured priority claims.

TYPES OF PRIORITY CLAIMS:

| | Wages, Salaries, and Commissions

     Wages, salaries, and commissions, including vacation, severance,
     and sick leave pay owing to employees, up to a maximum of $4000
     per employee, earned within 90 days immediately preceding the
     filing of the original petition, or the cessation of business,
     whichever occurred first, to the extent provided in 11 U.S.C.
     sec. 507(a)(3).

| | Contributions to Employee Benefit Plans

     Money owed to employee benefit plans for services rendered
     within 180 days immediately preceding the filing of the original
     petition, or the cessation of business, whichever occurred first
     to the extent provided in 11 U.S.C. sec. 507(a)(4).

| | Certain Farmers or Fishermen

     Claims of certain farmers or fishermen, up to a maximum of $4000
     per farmer or fisherman, against the debtor, as provided in 11
     U.S.C. sec. 507(a)(5).

| | Deposits by Individuals

     Claims of individuals up to a maximum of $1800 for deposits for
     the purchase, lease, or rental of property or services for
     personal, family, or household use, that were not delivered or
     provided. 11 U.S.C. sec. 507(a)(6).

| | Taxes and Certain Other Debts Owed to Governmental Units

     Taxes, customs duties, and penalties owing to federal, state,
     and local governmental units as set forth in 11 U.S.C. sec.
     507(a)(8).

| | Commitments to Maintain Capital of Insured Depository Institution

     Claims based on commitments to the FDIC, RTC, Director of the
     Office of Thrift Supervision, Controller of the Currency, or
     Board of Governors of the Federal Reserve System, or their
     predecessors or successors, to maintain the capital of an
     insured depository institution. 11 U.S.C. sec. 507(a)(9).

Figure 4-6. Schedule E.

SCHEDULE F (CREDITORS HOLDING UNSECURED NONPRIORITY CLAIMS)

All creditors holding unsecured claims without priority are listed within Schedule F. See Figure 4-7. The name, mailing address, and account number are included. Additionally, the date the claim was incurred and the consideration for such claim is included (i.e., credit card, personal loan, etc.). All claims subject to setoff are indicated. Claims are also identified as contingent, unliquidated, or disputed. Finally, the amount of the claim is stated.

SCHEDULE G (EXECUTORY CONTRACTS AND UNEXPIRED LEASES)

All executory contracts, those contracts upon which some performance remains to be done, and unexpired leases (such as a car lease or commercial property lease) are described. See Figure 4-8. The name and mailing address of the other party to the lease or contract are indicated. Also, a description of the contract or lease and nature of the debtor's interest in the property are included. Schedule G requires that all nonresidential real property leases be specifically identified. Finally, if any government contracts are involved, the contract number is to be included.

SCHEDULE H (CODEBTORS)

The names and addresses of all codebtors are included in Schedule H if the codebtors are not spouses in a jointly filed case. See Figure 4-9. Codebtors are persons or entities who are liable on any debts previously listed in the schedules. This includes all guarantors and cosigners. Additionally, the name and address of the creditor to whom the codebtor is also liable are listed.

SCHEDULE I (CURRENT INCOME)

Schedule I (current income) along with Schedule J (current expenditures) provides the debtor's monthly budget. See Figure 4-10. Initially in Schedule I, the debtor's marital status and names, ages, and relationships of all dependents are identified. Next, the debtor's occupation, the name and address of the debtor's employer, and the length of the employment are listed. Next, the debtor's gross monthly average income (via wages, salary, and/or commis-

In re JOHN DOE CORPORATION
      Debtor

Case No. (if known)

SCHEDULE F - CREDITORS HOLDING UNSECURED NONPRIORITY CLAIMS

Creditor's name and complete mailing address including zip code Date claim was incurred and consideration for claim. If claim is subject to setoff, so state.	Amount of claim

None

Subtotal this page:	0.00
Total:	0.00

FIGURE 4-7. Schedule F.

86

In re   JOHN DOE CORPORATION
        Debtor   Case No. (if known)

         SCHEDULE G - EXECUTORY CONTRACTS AND UNEXPIRED LEASES

Name and mailing address, including zip code, of other parties to lease or contract.	Description of contract or lease and nature of debtor interest. State whether lease is for non-residential real property. State contract number of any governmental contract.

None

Figure 4-8. Schedule G.

In re   JOHN DOE CORPORATION
        Debtor   Case No. (if known)

SCHEDULE H - CODEBTORS

Name and address of codebtor	Name and address of creditor

None

FIGURE 4-9. Schedule H.

In re _____ ,   Case No. _____

               Debtor   (If known)

SCHEDULE I – CURRENT INCOME OF INDIVIDUAL DEBTOR(S)

The column labeled "Spouse" must be completed in all cases filed by joint debtors and by a married debtor in a chapter 12 or 13 case whether or not a joint petition is filed, unless the spouses are separated and a joint petition is not filed.

Debtor's Marital Status:	DEPENDENTS OF DEBTOR AND SPOUSE		
Married	NAMES _____	AGE	RELATIONSHIP
			Wife
		6	Daughter

EMPLOYMENT:	DEBTOR	SPOUSE
Occupation	Machine Operator	Clerk
Name of Employer		.
How long employed	10 Years	3 Years
Address of Employer	California	, California

Income: (Estimate of average monthly income)	DEBTOR	SPOUSE
Current monthly gross wages, salary, and commissions (pro rate if not paid monthly)	$ 2,236.00	$ 1,000.00
Estimated monthly overtime	$ 0.00	$ 0.00
SUBTOTAL	$ 2,236.00	$ 1,000.00
LESS PAYROLL DEDUCTIONS		
a. Payroll taxes and social security	$ 496.00	$ 270.00
b. Insurance	$ 0.00	$ 0.00
c. Union dues	$ 0.00	$ 0.00
d. Other (Specify None None)	$ 0.00	$ 0.00
SUBTOTAL OF PAYROLL DEDUCTIONS	$ 496.00	$ 270.00
TOTAL NET MONTHLY TAKE HOME PAY	$ 1,740.00	$ 730.00
Regular income from operation of business or profession or farm (attach detailed statement)	$ 0.00	$ 0.00
Income from real property	$ 0.00	$ 0.00
Interest and dividends	$ 0.00	$ 0.00
Alimony, maintenance or support payments payable to the debtor for the debtor's use or that of dependents listed above.	$ 0.00	$ 0.00
Social security or other government assistance (Specify) None None	$ 0.00	$ 0.00
Pension or retirement income	$ 0.00	$ 0.00
Other monthly income None None	$ 0.00	$ 0.00
(Specify) None None	$ 0.00	$ 0.00
None None	$ 0.00	$ 0.00
TOTAL MONTHLY INCOME	$ 1,740.00	$ 730.00

TOTAL COMBINED MONTHLY INCOME $ 2,470.00   (Report also on Summary of Schedules)

Describe any increase or decrease of more than 10% in any of the above categories anticipated to occur within the year following the filing of this document:

FIGURE 4-10a. Schedules I and J (page 1).

In re _____,   Case No. _____
                Debtor   (If known)

SCHEDULE I – CURRENT INCOME OF INDIVIDUAL DEBTOR(S)
(Continuation Sheet)

DEPENDENTS OF DEBTOR – (Cont.)		
NAMES	AGE	RELATIONSHIP
	10	Daughter

Describe any increase or decrease of more than 10% in any of the above categories anticipated to occur within the year following the filing of this document (Cont.):

DEBTOR

SPOUSE

FIGURE 4-10b. Schedules I and J (page 2).

In re _____ , Case No. _____
　　　　　　　　　　Debtor　　　　　　　　　　　　　　　　　　　　(If known)

SCHEDULE J – CURRENT EXPENDITURES OF INDIVIDUAL DEBTORS

　　　Complete this schedule by estimating the average monthly expenses of the debtor and the debtor's family. Pro rate any payments made bi-weekly, quarterly, semi-annually, or annually to show monthly rate.

☐ Check this box if a joint petition is filed and debtor's spouse maintains a separate household. Complete a separate schedule of expenditures labeled "Spouse."

Rent or home mortgage payment (include lot rented for mobile home)	$	1,250.00
Are real estate taxes included? Yes __✔__ No _____		
Is property insurance included? Yes __✔__ No _____		
Utilities Electricity and heating fuel	$	50.00
Water and sewer	$	60.00
Telephone	$	80.00
Other None	$	0.00
Home Maintenance (Repairs and upkeep)	$	40.00
Food	$	400.00
Clothing	$	40.00
Laundry and dry cleaning	$	50.00
Medical and dental expenses	$	20.00
Transportation (not including car payments)	$	140.00
Recreation, clubs and entertainment, newspapers, magazines, etc.	$	50.00
Charitable contributions	$	0.00
Insurance (not deducted from wages or included in home mortgage payments)		
Homeowner's or renter's	$	0.00
Life	$	0.00
Health	$	0.00
Auto	$	0.00
Other None	$	0.00
Taxes (not deducted from wages or included in home mortgage payments)		
(Specify) None	$	0.00
Installment payments (In chapter 12 and 13 cases, do not list payments to be included in the plan)		
Auto	$	357.72
Other None	$	0.00
Other None	$	0.00
Alimony, maintenance and support paid to others	$	0.00
Payments for support of additional dependents not living at your home	$	0.00
Regular expenses from operation of business, profession, or farm (attached detailed statement)	$	0.00
Other None	$	0.00
TOTAL MONTHLY EXPENSES (Report also on Summary of Schedules)	$	2,537.72

(FOR CHAPTER 12 AND 13 DEBTORS ONLY)
Provide the information requested below, including whether plan payments are to be made bi-weekly, monthly, annually, or at some other regular interval.

A. Total projected monthly income	$	_____
B. Total projected monthly expenses	$	_____
C. Excess income (A minus B)	$	_____
D. Total amount to be paid into plan each _____	$	_____
(interval)		

FIGURE 4-10c. Schedules I and J (page 3).

sions), as well as any estimated overtime income, is stated. From this gross amount, payroll deductions (such as payroll taxes and social security, insurance, union dues, etc.) are itemized. Then the total "net" monthly take-home pay is stated.

Additional income is also itemized. Such income may be from the operation of a business, profession, or farm. Income from real property is also included as additional income as well as income from interest and dividends. Alimony and child support are also listed as additional income. All government assistance (such as social security income) is listed within the additional income category. Finally, pension or retirement income is listed as additional income.

Thereafter, the debtor's total monthly income is calculated (and listed) by adding the net monthly income and the additional monthly income. If two individual spouses are filing a joint petition, the combined monthly total income (income of both debtors) is calculated and listed. Finally, any anticipated increase or decrease of more than 10% in the debtor's income is stated.

SCHEDULE J (CURRENT EXPENDITURES)

The average monthly living expenses of the debtor and the debtor's family are estimated and listed in Schedule J. The itemized expenses are categorized as follows:

Rent or home mortgage payments (including lot rental for a mobile home), including real property taxes and property insurance.

Utilities (including electricity, heating fuel, water and sewer, telephone, and homeowners' association dues).

Home maintenance (repairs and upkeep).

Food.

Clothing.

Laundry and dry cleaning.

Medical and dental expenses.

Transportation (not including car payments, but such items as bus fare, gasoline, subway, etc.).

Recreation, clubs and entertainment, newspaper, magazines, etc.

Charitable contributions (church tithing, etc.).

Insurance (not otherwise deducted from wages or included in the home mortgage payments), including homeowner's or renter's insurance, life insurance, health insurance, and auto insurance.

Taxes (not deducted from wages or included in the home mortgage payments).

Installment payments (other than payments to be included in a Chapter 12 or 13 plan), including car payments, boat payments, etc.

Alimony, maintenance, and support paid to others.

Payments for support of additional dependents not living at your home (for example, extra payments to help a retired mother or a child in college).

Regular expenses from the operation of a business, profession, or farm (it is necessary to attach a detailed statement of such expenses).

The debtor's total monthly expenses are added together and the total listed. In Chapters 13 and 12, the total amount of projected monthly income and expenses is also stated along with the excess income (monthly income greater than monthly expenses). Also for Chapters 13 and 12, the total amount to be paid monthly into a plan is stated.

Note: For a business debtor, such as a corporate Chapter 11 debtor, the expenses would not be "living expenses" but rather business operating expenses. An example of most of the major categories of such expenses is as follows:

Rent/mortgage payment

Repair/upkeep

Electricity and heating fuel

Water and sewer

Telephone

Garbage

Security

Other Utilities

Insurance

Taxes

Installment payments on equipment

Rent/lease payments

Maintenance of equipment

Advertising

Bank service charges

Interest

Depreciation

> Office expenses
> Dues and publications
> Laundry or cleaning
> Supplies and materials
> Freight
> Travel and entertainment
> Wages and salaries
> Commissions
> Employee benefit programs
> Pension/profit sharing plans
> Production costs

SUMMARY OF SCHEDULES

This schedule merely reiterates the total amounts of assets of the debtor (divided into real and personal property), as well as the total amount of the obligations of the debtor (divided into secured claims, priority claims, and unsecured claims). Additionally, the total monthly income and expenses (from the budget) are stated. See Figure 4-11.

CHAPTER 7 INDIVIDUAL DEBTOR'S STATEMENT OF INTENTION

In this section the debtor states his or her intention with respect to secured debts that are consumer debts. See Figure 4-12. Such intention is either to surrender the underlying property or to retain the underlying property through redemption or reaffirmation. Additionally, the debtor states whether the secured creditor's lien will be sought by the debtor to be avoided under 11 U.S.C. Section 522(f).[7]

STATEMENT OF FINANCIAL AFFAIRS

A detailed listing of the debtor's past financial history is included in the Statement of Financial Affairs, which must be filed by every debtor, regardless of the chapter filed. See Figure 4-13. Following is a listing of the specific questions on the statement of financial affairs, the meaning of such questions if not apparent, and the relevancy of each question to the trustee and/or creditors of the estate:

UNITED STATES BANKRUPTCY COURT FOR THE
DISTRICT OF ARIZONA

In re JOHN DOE CORPORATION
       Debtor   Case No. (if known)

_____ SUMMARY OF SCHEDULES _____

Schedule name	No. Sheets	Assets	Liabilities	Other
X (mark if attached)				
____ A - Real Property	1	0.00	_____	
____ B - Personal Property	2	0.00	_____	
____ C - Property Claimed as Exempt	1	_____		
____ D - Creditors Holding Secured Claims	1	_____	0.00	_____
____ E - Creditors Holding Unsecured Priority Claims	1	_____	0.00	_____
____ F - Creditors Holding Unsecured Nonpriority Claims	1	_____	0.00	_____
____ G - Executory Contracts and Unexpired Leases	1	_____		
____ H - Codebtors	1	_____		
____ Current Income of Corporate Debtor	N/A	_____		0.00
____ Current Expenditures of Corporate Debtor	2	_____		0.00

Summary Sheet	1	*************************************		
Total No. Sheets	12	*************************************		
Total Assets ->		0.00	********************	
Total Liabilities ->			0.00	*******
Total No. of Creditors ->			1	*******

FIGURE 4-11. Summary of Schedules.

United States Bankruptcy Court

<u>Central</u> **District of** <u>California</u>

In re _____   Case No. _____

          Debtor

                                            Chapter   <u>Seven</u>

CHAPTER 7 INDIVIDUAL DEBTOR'S STATEMENT OF INTENTION

1. I, the debtor, have filed a schedule of assets and liabilities which includes consumer debts secured by property of the estate.

2. My intention with respect to the property of the estate which secures those consumer debts is as follows:

     a.   *Property to Be Surrendered.*

Description of Property	Creditor's Name
1. _____	_____
2. _____	_____
3. _____	_____

     b.   *Property to Be Retained. [Check applicable statement of debtor's intention concerning reaffirmation, redemption, or lien avoidance.]*

	Description of property	Creditor's name	Debt will be reaffirmed pursuant to § 524(c)	Property is claimed as exempt and will be redeemed pursuant to § 722	Lien will be avoided pursuant to § 522(f) and property will be claimed as exempt
1.	Purchase money lien on 1995 Toyota Camry	Bank of America	✔		
2.	3rd deed of trust on		✔		·
3.	First deed of trust on		✔		
4.	4th deed of trust on		✔		
5.	2nd deed of trust on		✔		

3. I understand that § 521(2)(B) of the Bankruptcy Code requires that I perform the above stated intention within 45 days of the filing of this statement with the court, or within such additional time as the court, for cause, within such 45-day period fixes.

Date: _____   _____

                                        Signature of Debtor

Date: _____   _____

                                        Signature of Joint Debtor

FIGURE 4-12. Debtor's Statement of Intention.

UNITED STATES BANKRUPTCY COURT FOR THE
DISTRICT OF ARIZONA

In re   JOHN DOE CORPORATION
        Debtor
                                            Case No. (if known)

STATEMENT OF FINANCIAL AFFAIRS

---

1. Income from employment or operation of business.

NONE
|X| State the gross amount of income the debtor has received from
       employment, trade, or profession, or from operation of debtor's
       business form the beginning of this calendar year to the date
       this case was commenced. State also the gross amounts received
       during the two years immediately preceding this calendar year.

---

2. Income other than from employment or operation of business.

NONE
|X| State the amount of income received by the debtor other than
       from employment, trade, profession, or operation of the
       debtor's business during the two years immediately preceding
       the commencement of this case.

---

3. Payments to creditors.

NONE
|X| a. List all payments on loans, installment purchases of goods or
       services, and other debts, aggregating more than $600 to any
       creditor, made within 90 days immediately preceding the
       commencement of this case.

NONE
|X| b. List all payments made within one year immediately preceding
       the commencement of this case to or for the benefit of
       creditors who are or were insiders.

---

4. Suits and administrative proceedings, executions,
garnishments, and attachments.

NONE
|X| a. List all suits and administrative proceedings to which the
       debtor is or was a party within one year immediately preceding
       the filing of this bankruptcy case.

NONE   b. Describe all property that has been attached, garnished or

FIGURE 4-13a. Statement of Financial Affairs (page 1).

|X| seized under any legal or equitable process within one year immediately preceding the commencement of this case.

---

5. Repossessions, foreclosures, and returns.

NONE
|X| List all property that has been repossessed by a creditor, sold at a foreclosure sale, transferred through a deed in lieu of foreclosure or returned to the seller, within one year immediately preceding the commencement of this case.

---

6. Assignments and receiverships.

NONE
|X| a. Describe any assignment of property for the benefit of creditors made within 120 days immediately preceding the commencement of this case.

NONE
|X| b. List all property which has been in the hands of a custodian, receiver or court-appointed official within one year immediately preceding the commencement of this case.

---

7. Gifts.

NONE
|X| List all gifts or charitable contributions made within one year immediately preceding the commencement of this case except ordinary and usual gifts to family members aggregating less than $200 in value per individual family member and charitable contributions aggregating less than $100 per recipient.

---

8. Losses.

NONE
|X| List all losses from fire, theft, other casualty or gambling within one year immediately preceding the commencement of this case or since the commencement of this case.

---

9. Payments related to debt counseling or bankruptcy.

NONE
|X| List all payments made or property transferred by or on behalf of the debtor to any persons, including attorneys, for consultation concerning debt consolidation, relief under the bankruptcy law or preparation of a petition in bankruptcy within one year immediately preceding the commencement of this case.

FIGURE 4-13b. Statement of Financial Affairs (page 2).

In re JOHN DOE CORPORATION
       Debtor   Case No. (if known)

       Filing fee: 150.00
_____

       10. Other transfers.

NONE   List all other property, other than property transferred in the
|X| ordinary course of the business or financial affairs of the
       debtor, transferred either absolutely or as security within one
       year immediately preceding the commencement of this case.
_____

       11. Closed financial accounts.

NONE   List all financial accounts and instruments held in the name of
|X| the debtor or for the benefit of the debtor which were closed,
       sold, or otherwise transferred within one year immediately
       preceding the commencement of this case.
_____

       12. Safe deposit boxes.

NONE   List each safe deposit box or other box or depository in which
|X| the debtor has or had securities, cash, or other valuables
       within one year immediately preceding the commencement of this
       case.
_____

       13. Setoffs.

NONE   List all setoffs made by any creditor, including a bank, against
|X| a debt or deposit of the debtor within 90 days preceding the
       commencement of this case.
_____

       14. Property held for another person.

NONE   List all property owned by another person that the debtor holds
|X| or controls.
_____

       15. Prior address of debtor.

NONE   If the debtor has moved within the two years immediately
|X| preceding the commencement of this case, list all premises
       which the debtor occupied during that period and vacated prior
       to the commencement of this case.
_____

FIGURE 4-13c. Statement of Financial Affairs (page 3).

In re JOHN DOE CORPORATION
        Debtor   Case No. (if known)

16. Nature, location, and name of business.

NONE a. For individuals, list the names and addresses of all
|X| businesses in which the debtor was an officer, director,
      partner, or managing executive of a corporation, partnership,
      sole proprietorship, or was a self-employed professional within
      the two years immediately preceding the commencement of this
      case, or in which the debtor owned 5 percent or more of the
      voting or equity securities within the two years immediately
      preceding the commencement of this case.

NONE b. If the debtor is a partnership, list the names and addresses
|X| of all businesses in which the debtor was a partner or owned 5
      percent or more of the voting securities, within the two years
      immediately preceding the commencement of this case.

NONE c. If the debtor is a corporation, list the names and addresses
|X| of all businesses in which the debtor was a partner or owned 5
      percent or more of the voting securities, within the two years
      immediately preceding the commencement of this case.

17. Books, records, and financial statements.

NONE a. List all bookkeepers and accountants who within the six years
|X| immediately preceding the filing of this bankruptcy case kept
      or supervised the keeping of books of account and records of
      the debtor.

NONE b. List all firms or individuals who within the two years
|X| immediately preceding the filing of this bankruptcy case have
      audited the books of account and records, or prepared a
      financial statement of the debtor.

NONE c. List all firms or individuals who at the time of the
|X| commencement of this case were in possession of the books of
      account and records of the debtor.

NONE d. List all financial institutions, creditors, and other parties
|X| including mercantile and trade agencies, to whom a financial
      statement was issued within the two years immediately preceding
      the commencement of this case by the debtor.

FIGURE 4-13d. Statement of Financial Affairs (page 4).

In re   JOHN DOE CORPORATION
        Debtor   Case No. (if known)

18. Inventories.

NONE   a. List the dates of the last two inventories taken of your
|X| property, the name of the person who supervised the taking of
        each inventory, and the dollar amount and basis of each
        inventory.

NONE   b. List the name and address of the person having possession of
|X| the records of each of the two inventories reported in a.,
        above.

---

19. Current Partners, Officers, Directors, and Shareholders.

NONE   a. If the debtor is a partnership, list the nature and
|X| percentage of partnership interest of each member of the
        partnership.

NONE   b. If the debtor is a corporation, list all officers and
|X| directors of the corporation, and each stockholder who directly
        or indirectly owns, controls, or holds 5 percent or more of
        the voting securities of the corporation.

---

20. Former partners, officers, directors, and shareholders.

NONE   a. If the debtor is a partnership, list each member who
|X| withdrew from the partnership within one year immediately
        preceding the commencement of this case.

NONE   b. If the debtor is a corporation, list all officers or
|X| directors whose relationship with the corporation terminated
        within one year immediately preceding the commencement of this
        case.

---

21. Withdrawals from a partnership or distributions by a
    corporation.

NONE   If the debtor is a partnership or corporation, list all
|X| withdrawals or distributions credited or given to an insider,
        including compensation in any form, bonuses, loans, stock
        redemptions, options exercised and any other prerequisite
        during one year immediately preceding the commencement of this
        case.

FIGURE 4-13e. Statement of Financial Affairs (page 5).

In re JOHN DOE CORPORATION
       Debtor   Case No. (if known)

(The penalty for making a false statement or concealing property is
a fine of up to $500,000 or imprisonment for up to 5 years or both.
18 U.S.C. secs. 152 and 3571.)

DECLARATION

I, _____,
for JOHN DOE CORPORATION named as the debtor in this case, declare
under penalty of perjury that I have read the foregoing Statement of
Financial Affairs, consisting of 6 sheets (including this
declaration), and that it is true and correct to the best of my
information and belief.

Signature: _____ Date: _____

FIGURE 4-13f. Statement of Financial Affairs (page 6).

1. *Income from employment or operation of business.* State the gross amount of income the debtor has received from employment, trade, or profession, or from operation of the debtor's business from the beginning of this calendar year to the date this case was commenced. State also the gross amounts received during the two years immediately preceding this calendar year. If a joint petition is filed, state the income for each spouse separately.

> In essence, the debtor's annual income and source of such income for the prior three years is included in this section.

> Creditors find this information useful to determine if a nondischargeability action based upon fraud (11 U.S.C. Section 523(a)(2) may be feasible. Chapter 13 and Chapter 12 trustees find this information valuable in determining whether a debtor's proposed plan payments are feasible based upon the past earning history of debtor.

2. *Income other than from employment or operation of a business.* State the amount of income received by the debtor other than from employment, trade, profession, or operation of the debtor's business during the two years immediately preceding the commencement of this case. Give particulars.

> Income such as social security benefits, alimony/child support, disability, retirement, etc. should be included in this question.

> Again, creditors find this information useful to determine if a nondischargeability action based upon fraud (11 U.S.C. Section 523(a)(2) may be feasible. Chapter 13 and Chapter 12 trustees use this to determine whether a debtor's proposed plan payments are feasible based upon the past earning history of debtor.

3. *Payments to creditors:*

a. List all payments on loans, installment purchases of goods or services, and other debts, aggregating more than $600 to any creditor, made within 90 days immediately preceding the commencement of this case.

> Any unusual payments made outside the ordinary course of the debtor's customary business affairs to any creditor should be listed here as well as amounts paid to any one creditor over $600.

> > The trustee shall use this information to determine if a voidable preference has been made that favors the creditor over all other creditors of the same priority.[8]

b. List all payments made within one year immediately preceding the commencement of this case to or for the benefit of creditors who are or were insiders.

All payments of any type made to a person who is an insider (i.e., relative, partner, officer, director, etc.) and made within one year prepetition should be listed in this section.

The trustee shall use this information to determine if a voidable fraudulent conveyance or preference has been made to the detriment of creditors of the estate.[9]

4. *Suits, executions, garnishments and attachments:*

a. List all suits to which the debtor is or was a party within one year immediately preceding the filing of this bankruptcy case.

This question inquires whether the debtor has been a defendant or plaintiff in a lawsuit and, if so, requires recording the outcome of the lawsuit.

The trustee shall use this information to determine if a voidable fraudulent conveyance or preference has been made to the detriment of creditors of the estate.[10]

b. Describe all property that has been attached, garnished, or seized under any legal or equitable process within one year immediately preceding the commencement of this case.

If debtor's property has been taken through legal process (such as an IRS seizure, a wage garnishment, or a sheriff's levy), such property and details should be itemized here.

Again, the trustee shall use this information to determine if a voidable fraudulent conveyance or preference has been made to the detriment of creditors of the estate.[11]

5. *Repossessions, foreclosures, and returns.* List all property that has been repossessed by a creditor, sold at a foreclosure sale, transferred through a deed in lieu of foreclosure or returned to the seller, within one year immediately preceding the commencement of this case.

Information as stated should be listed.

Again, the trustee shall use this information to determine if a voidable fraudulent conveyance or preference has been made to the detriment of creditors of the estate.[12]

6. *Assignments and receiverships:*

a. Describe any assignment of property for the benefit of creditors made within 120 days immediately preceding the commencement of this case.

All assignments (voluntary or involuntary) and any appointments of a receiver should be noted here.

Again, the trustee shall use this information to determine if a voidable fraudulent conveyance or preference has been made to the detriment of creditors of the estate.[13]

b. List all property that has been in the hands of a custodian, receiver, or court-appointed official within one year immediately preceding the commencement of this case.

All state court receivers appointed upon the debtor's property should be listed, along with the identity and address of such receiver, information regarding the state court proceedings, date of the state court receivership order, and description and value of the property.

Again, the trustee shall use this information to determine if a voidable fraudulent conveyance or preference has been made to the detriment of creditors of the estate.[14]

7. *Gifts.* List all gifts or charitable contributions made within one year immediately preceding the commencement of this case except ordinary and usual gifts to family members aggregating less than $200 in value per individual family member and charitable contributions aggregating less than $100 per recipient.

Extraordinary gifts, including gifts to charities (such as church tithing), should be specified, including the name and address of the person/organization, relationship to the debtor, date of gift, and description and value of the gift.

Again, the trustee shall use this information to determine if a voidable fraudulent conveyance, preference or a postpetition transfer has been made to the detriment of creditors of the estate.[15]

8. *Losses.* List all losses from fire, theft, other casualty, or gambling within one year immediately preceding the commencement of this case or since the commencement of this case.

As stated, all losses from these events should be listed, along with the description and value of the property, the description of the circumstances, whether the loss was covered at all by insurance, and the date of the loss.

The trustee and/or creditors will find this information useful to determine if certain assets have disappeared (concealment of assets by the debtor).

9. *Payment related to debt counseling or bankruptcy.* List all payments made or property transferred by or on behalf of the debtor to any persons, including attorneys, for consultation concerning debt consolidation, relief under the bankruptcy law, or preparation of a petition in bankruptcy within one year immediately preceding the commencement of this case.

> List all payments made to anyone regarding preparation for bankruptcy. The information should include the name and address of the person paid, the date of payment, and the amount of funds/property paid or transferred.

Under the 1994 Amendments, specific criteria are enumerated for document preparation services regarding bankruptcy. The penalty for violation of such criteria involves monetary sanctions. The trustee will find such information useful in pursuit of "doc prep" agencies who do not follow the specific guidelines.

10. *Other transfers.* List all property, other than property transferred in the ordinary course of the business or financial affairs of the debtor, transferred either absolutely or as security within one year immediately preceding the commencement of this case.

> This is a "catch-all" question for all transfers not previously listed, including the debtor's providing of a lien or security interest.

Again, the trustee shall use this information to determine if a voidable fraudulent conveyance or preference has been made to the detriment of creditors of the estate.[16]

11. *Closed financial accounts.* List all financial accounts and instruments held in the name of the debtor or for the benefit of the debtor that were closed, sold, or otherwise transferred within one year immediately preceding the commencement of this case. Include checking, savings, or other financial accounts, certificates of deposit, or other instruments, as well as shares and share accounts held in banks, credit unions, pension funds, cooperatives, associations, brokerage houses and other financial institutions.

> As stated, all closed financial accounts should be listed, including the name and address of the institution (bank), type and number of account, amount of final balance, and date of closure of such account.

Again, the trustee shall use this information to determine if a voidable fraudulent conveyance or preference has been made to the detriment of creditors of the estate.[17] Additionally, the trustee and/or creditors will find this information useful to determine if estate assets have been concealed.

12. *Safe deposit boxes.* List each safe deposit or other box or depository in which the debtor has or had securities, cash, or other valuables within one year immediately preceding the commencement of this case.

As stated, list all safe deposit boxes, with the name of the depository and address, description of contents, date of transfers/surrender, and names of all with access to the box.

The trustee and/or creditors will find this information useful in investigating possible assets of the estate and/or concealment of such assets.

13. *Setoffs.* List all setoffs made by any creditor, including a bank, against a debtor or deposit of the debtor within 90 days preceding the commencement of this case.

If a bank uses funds from one account to pay amounts owed on an entirely different account (i.e., funds from the checking account to pay overdue installment on car loan), such setoff should be listed here. The name and address of the creditor, date of setoff and amount of setoff should be included.

This information is useful to determine if fraudulent conveyances, preferences, or improper statutory setoffs have occurred.[18]

14. *Property held for another person.* List all property that is owned by another person but that the debtor holds or controls.

As stated, all property held by debtors that is not their own should be listed, along with the name and address of the owner, description and value of the property, and its location.

The trustee, in the investigation for estate assets, must be alerted if the debtor is merely holding property that belongs to another. Such property is not estate property and cannot be liquidated by the trustee.

15. *Prior address of debtor.* If the debtor has moved within the two years immediately preceding the commencement of the case, list all premises that the debtor occupied during that period and vacated prior to the commencement of this case.

As stated, list all addresses of the debtor for two years.

The trustee and/or creditors shall use this information to determine if venue is proper in the jurisdiction in which the case is filed.

Questions 16–21 are to be completed by debtors that are corporations or partnerships and by any individual debtor who is or was (within two years before filing bankruptcy) any of the following: an officer, director, managing executive, or owner of more than 5% of the voting securities (stock) of a corporation; a partner, other than a limited partner, a sole proprietor, or otherwise self-employed.

16. *Nature, location, and name of business:*

a. If the debtor is an individual, list the names and addresses of all businesses in which the debtor was an officer, director, partner, or managing executive of a corporation, partnership, sole proprietorship, or was a self-employed professional within the two years immediately preceding the commencement of this case, or in which the debtor owned 5% or more of the voting or equity securities within the two years immediately preceding the commencement of this case.

Information as stated should be listed here.

This information gives the trustee a general overview of the debtor's business activities.

b. If the debtor is a partnership, list the names and address of all businesses in which the debtor was a partner or owned 5% or more of the voting securities, within the two years immediately preceding the commencement of this case.

Information as stated should be listed here.

Again, this information gives the trustee a general overview of the debtor's business activities.

c. If the debtor is a corporation, list the names and addresses of all businesses in which the debtor was a partner or owned 5% or more of the voting securities within the two years immediately preceding the commencement of this case.

Information as stated should be listed here.

Again, this information gives the trustee a general overview of the debtor's business activities.

17. *Books, records, and financial statements:*

a. List all bookkeepers and accountants who within the six years immediately preceding the filing of this bankruptcy case kept or supervised the keeping of books and records of the debtor.

Information as stated should be listed here.

The trustee and/or creditors may find this information useful in an investigation of potential estate assets.

b. List all firms or individuals who within the two years immediately preceding the filing of this bankruptcy case have audited the books of account and records or prepared a financial statement of the debtor.

Information as stated should be listed here.

The trustee and/or creditors may find this information useful in an investigation of potential estate assets.

c. List all firms or individuals who at the time of the commencement of this case were in possession of the books of account and records of the debtor. If any of the books of account and records are not available, explain.

This question is seeking the location of the current financial information of the debtor.

The trustee and/or creditors may find this information useful in an investigation of potential estate assets and/or to confirm the accuracy of the information contained within the schedules.

d. List all financial institutions, creditors, and other parties, including mercantile and trade agencies, to whom a financial statement was issued within the two years immediately preceding the commencement of this case by the debtor.

As stated list the identity and address of persons to whom the debtor has provided financial statements as well as the date the financial statement was issued.

The trustee and/or creditors may find this information useful in an investigation of potential estate assets and/or to confirm the accuracy of the information contained within the schedules and/or to investigate potential concealment of assets.

18. *Inventories:*

a. List the dates of the last two inventories taken of your property, the name of the person who supervised the taking of each inventory, and the dollar amount and basis of each inventory.

Information as stated should be listed here.

The trustee and/or creditors may find this information useful in an investigation of potential estate assets and/or to confirm the accuracy of the information contained within the schedules and/or to investigate potential concealment of assets.

b. List the name and address of the person having possession of the records of each of the two inventories reported in entry a.

Information as stated should be listed here.

The trustee and/or creditors may find this information useful in an investigation of potential estate assets and/or to confirm the accuracy of the information contained within the schedules and/or to investigate potential concealment of assets.

19. *Current partners, officers, directors, and shareholders:*

a. If the debtor is a partnership, list the nature and percentage of partnership interest of each member of the partnership.

b. If the debtor is a corporation, list all officers and directors of the corporation, and each stockholder who directly or indirectly owns, controls, or holds 5% or more of the voting securities of the corporation.

Information as stated should be listed here.

This provides the trustee and/or creditors with the basic composition of the business debtor's members who may be considered insiders.

20. *Former partners, officers, directors, and shareholders.*

a. If the debtor is a partnership, list each member who withdrew from the partnership within one year immediately preceding the commencement of this case.

b. If the debtor is a corporation, list all officers or directors whose relationship with the corporation terminated within one year immediately preceding the commencement of this case.

Information as stated should be listed here.

Again, the trustee shall use this information to determine if insiders exist and if a voidable fraudulent conveyance or preference has been made to the detriment of creditors of the estate.[19]

21. *Withdrawals from a partnership or distributions by a corporation.* If the debtor is a partnership or corporation, list all withdrawals or distributions credited or given to an insider, including compensation in any form, bonuses, loans, stock redemptions, options exercised, and any other perquisite (benefit) during one year immediately preceding the commencement of this case.

Information as stated should be listed here.

Again, the trustee shall use this information to determine if a voidable fraudulent conveyance or preference has been made to the detriment of creditors of the estate.[20]

DISCLOSURE OF COMPENSATION OF ATTORNEY FOR DEBTOR

In this statement, which the attorney signs and submits, the amount of funds received from the debtor for legal services is articulated. See Figure 4-14. Additionally, should funds be owed after the filing of the petition (through a Chapter 13 plan, for example) the amount of remaining fees is also disclosed. Further, the disclosure statement reveals if the attorney has agreed to share any of the fees with any other parties (other than with associates within the law firm). Finally, the disclosure statement states the extent of services to be provided to the debtor (such as whether to file bankruptcy, preparation of the statements and schedules, appearance at the 341 meeting or confirmation meeting, and representation in adversary or contested matters).

NOTICE OF AVAILABLE CHAPTERS

The debtor signs this notice as acknowledgement that he or she has been instructed as to the differences between the various chapters as well as the debtor's eligibility under each chapter. (See Figure 4-15.)

MASTER MAILING LIST

The master mailing list is a listing of the debtor, debtor's attorney, the trustee, the U.S. Trustee, and all creditors along with their addresses. This list is used exclusively for "noticing." Within even the most simple bankruptcy, many events require all parties to be noticed. For example, the Bankruptcy Court notices the 341 First Creditors' Meeting and the deadline within which to file dischargeability complaints. Additionally, both debtors and creditors are required to notice all parties on the master mailing list of motions or applications.

Attorneys of creditors and parties in interest make their appearances in a case can request to be added to the master mailing list to ensure their being noticed and kept aware of all events within a case. Therefore, the master mailing list is always changing. Accordingly, when you are called upon to "notice" a hearing date or motion to all parties on the master mailing list, request an updated master mailing list from the court.

Note: Each Bankruptcy Court has a certain format within which it requires the parties to be listed. For example, some courts require three parties across and ten down on each page while other courts require one across and ten down. These differences are due to the specific method each court uses to notice (i.e., copying the list onto precut mailing adhesives, etc.). Also, some courts require the list to be provided on magnetic tape when the number of creditors is extensive (over 100). Therefore, check with the Bankruptcy Court in your district to determine which format is acceptable.

United States Bankruptcy Court

<u>Central</u> **District of** <u>California</u>

In re _____   Case No. _____
                    Debtor

                                                   Chapter _____Seven_____

DISCLOSURE OF COMPENSATION OF ATTORNEY FOR DEBTOR

1. Pursuant to 11 U.S.C.A. § 329(a) and Bankruptcy Rule 2016(b), I certify that I am the attorney for the above-named debtor(s) and that compensation paid to me within one year before the filing of the petition in bankruptcy, or agreed to be paid to me, for services rendered or to be rendered on behalf of the debtor(s) in contemplation of or in connection with the bankruptcy case is as follows:

   For legal services, I have agreed to accept. . . . . $ ___2,500.00___

   Prior to the filing of this statement I have received . . . . $ ___2,500.00___

   Balance Due. . . . . $ _____0.00_____

   Amount of filing fee remaining to be paid. . . . . $ _____0.00_____

2. The source of the compensation paid to me was:

   ☑ Debtor   ☐ Other (specify)

3. The source of compensation to be paid to me is:

   ☐ Debtor   ☐ Other (specify)

4. ☑ I have not agreed to share the above-disclosed compensation with any other person unless they are members and associates of my law firm.

   ☐ I have agreed to share the above-disclosed compensation with a person or persons who are not members or associates of my law firm. A copy of the agreement, together with a list of the names of the people sharing in the compensation, is attached.

5. In return for the above-disclosed fee, I have agreed to render legal service for all aspects of the bankruptcy case, including:

   a. Analysis of the debtor's financial situation, and rendering advice to the debtor in determining whether to file a petition in bankruptcy;
      Yes

   b. Preparation and filing of any petition, schedules, statement of affairs and plan which may be required;
      Yes

   c. Representation of the debtor at the meeting of creditors and confirmation hearing, and any adjourned hearings thereof;
      Yes

FIGURE 4-14a. Disclosure of Compensation for Attorney (page 1).

In re _____ t _____ Case No. _____
                    Debtor

DISCLOSURE OF COMPENSATION OF ATTORNEY FOR DEBTOR (Continued)

d. Representation of the debtor in adversary proceedings and other contested bankruptcy matters;
    N/A
e. [Other provisions as needed]
    None

6. By agreement with the debtor(s), the above-disclosed fee does not include the following services:
    N/A

CERTIFICATION

I certify that the foregoing is a complete statement of any agreement or arrangement for payment to me for representation of the debtor(s) in this bankruptcy proceeding.

_____
Date

_____
Signature of Attorney

Jeffrey S. Shinbrot
_____
Name of law firm

FIGURE 4-14b. Disclosure of Compensation for Attorney (page 2).

LAW OFFICE OF JEFFREY S. SHINBROT
8929 WILSHIRE BLVD, SUITE 100
BEVERLY HILLS, CA 90211
(310) 659-5444

UNITED STATES BANKRUPTCY COURT FOR THE

_____ DISTRICT OF _____

In re

Debtor(s)

(Set forth here all names including trade names, used by debtor(s) within last 6 years.)

Case No.

Social Security No. _____

NOTICE OF AVAILABLE CHAPTERS

Social Security No. _____

Debtor's Employer's Tax Identification No. _____

(If this form is used for joint petitioners, wherever the word "petitioner" or words referring to petitioners are used they shall be read as if in the plural.)

1. Section 342(b) of 11 U.S. Code ("The Bankruptcy Code") states:
   "Prior to the commencement of a case under this title by an individual whose debts are primarily consumer debts, the clerk shall give written notice to such individual that indicates each chapter of this title under which such individual may proceed."

2. If your debts are primarily consumer ones (as opposed to business debts) and they do not exceed $100,000.00 unsecured or $350,000.00 secured (11 U.S.C. § 109(e)), you are eligible to file under Chapter 13 and to use future income to pay all or a portion of your existing debts.

3. You are also eligible to file under Chapter 11 ($500.00 filing fees) for debt reorganization.

4. You are not eligible to file under Chapter 9.

5. You are eligible to file under Chapter 7 ("straight bankruptcy"), whereby debts are eliminated and your non-exempt assets are liquidated by the trustee for the benefit of your creditors.

6. You may be eligible to file under Chapter 12.

7. All general filing eligibility is subject to 11 U.S.C. §§ 109, 727(a)(8), and (9), and 707(b). **Consult your attorney.**

_____
Court Clerk

I HAVE READ THE ABOVE "NOTICE OF AVAILABLE CHAPTERS"

_____
Debtor

_____
Debtor

CSD-001

FIGURE 4-15. Notice of Available Chapters.

BANKRUPTCY DOC PREP OPERATIONS

Bankruptcy document preparation services ("doc prep") are performed without the supervision of a licensed attorney. The 1994 Amendments to the Bankruptcy Code have added certain criteria specifically for doc prep in the preparation of statements and schedules. Failure to adhere to these criteria may result in substantial articulated penalties.

The new requirements for doc prep services are found in 11 U.S.C. Section 110 and include the following:

1. Doc prep preparer must sign the document and print on the document the preparer's name and address. Failure to comply could result in a fine of $500.

2. Doc prep preparer must place his/her social security number on the document filed with the court. Failure to comply could result in a fine of $500.

3. Doc prep preparer must furnish the debtor with a copy of any document the debtor signs, at the time the debtor signs the document. Failure to comply could result in a fine of $500.

4. A doc prep preparer cannot sign any document on behalf of a debtor. The fine for this is $500 for each document signed.

5. No doc prep preparer or company can use the word "legal" in any advertisement or in any category that includes the word "legal." The fine for this is $500 for each violation.

6. A doc prep preparer cannot accept any court fees from the debtor. The fine for this is also $500.

7. A doc prep preparer must file a statement with the Bankruptcy Court within 10 days of the petition which states all fees received from the debtor within the 12 months before the case. All unpaid fees still owed must also be disclosed. This statement must be signed under the penalty of perjury. If the Court orders the doc prep preparer to turn over excess fees and the doc prep does not, the fine is $500.

8. If a case is dismissed because the doc prep preparer negligently did not file all the statements and schedules or if the doc prep preparer committed fraud a fine may be imposed. The fine could include the following: the debtor's actual damages or the greater of $2,000 or twice the amount paid by the debtor to the doc prep preparer. If a trustee or a creditor makes this request an additional $1,000 may be fined.

Finally, the doc prep preparer can be enjoined by the bankruptcy court to discontinue doc prep services if the doc prep preparer has violated any of the above mentioned items, misrepresented the preparer's experience or education, or has engaged in fraud or deceptive conduct.

CONCLUSION

The information contained in the statements and schedules in each bankruptcy case is different. For example, the debtor's identity, the different creditors, and the financial conduct of each debtor is unique. However, the format of the statements and schedules and the information requested is always the same. Therefore, after a bankruptcy paralegal has compiled statements and schedules for a few debtors the task will take less effort. However, it is always essential for the bankruptcy paralegal to ensure the statements and schedules are as accurate as possible.

REVIEW EXERCISE

Prepare all the initial documentation for the following Chapter 7 case. You work for the Law Office of John Doe which has gotten paid $1000 from these clients as well as the filing fee.

Robert (SSN 111-11-1111) and Laura Petre (SSN 222-22-2222) have a son, Richie, who is 6. They own their home at 1234 Sunnyside Ave., Anytown located in your state. The home is worth about $250,000 and has a mortgage with ABC Mortgage Co. for $175,000. Robert leases a 1995 Corvette from XYZ Leasing Co. for $640/mo. and wants to surrender the car. Laura owns a 1982 Honda Civic worth $1000 and makes car payments to Last National Bank. The balance on the Honda owed to Last National is $200.

Rob and Laura have the following furniture which is valued as stated: living room ($2000), dining room ($1500), master bedroom ($750), second bedroom ($500). They also own the following items: clothing ($1750), wedding rings ($3000), 3 bicycles ($300), television ($750), stereo ($250).

Rob's paycheck from DFG Entertainment every two weeks is $3000. Rob has had this job as a writer for 10 years at the same pay. Each paycheck, the taxes taken out are $500 and union dues are $100. Laura is a homemaker.

Together, they pay the following each month to live: house payment $2500; electricity $200; gas $50; water $50; food $800; insurance (life) $200, (auto) $150; telephone $250; doctor bills $200; Rob's car payment $640; Laura's car payment $100; and Richie's private school $200.

Rob and Laura's other creditors are as follows: Plastic Credit Co., 111 Oak Ave., Anytown, Yourstate for a VISA in the amount of $25,000. Dr. Wellby, 222 Maple Ave., Anytown, Yourstate for medical services in the amount of $15,000. Lou's Finance Co., 333 Cactus Dr., Anytown, Yourstate for a signature loan in the amount of $30,000. Rob and Laura also owe Yourstate taxes for last year in the amount of $500 and the IRS taxes for last year in the amount of $1,000.

They bank at Last National Bank with their checking account (Acct. No. 1234) holding $200 and their savings account (Acct. No. 5678) holding $25. Last month Laura gave her mother, Martha Jones, a gold watch worth $3000 for her birthday. Laura sold Avon last year and made $700 but got out of the business.

ENDNOTES

[1] Caution is advised, however, due to the potential of Rule 9011 sanctions, etc. for filing a bad faith exemption schedule.

[2] A detailed analysis of the priority and categorization of claims of creditors is contained in Chapter 9, "Creditor Status, Priority, and Distribution Rights."

[3] Increased from $2,000 by the 1994 Amendments.

[4] Increased from $2,000 by the 1994 Amendments.

[5] Increased from $900 by the 1994 Amendments.

[6] This section was added in its entirety as a new class of priority claims by the 1994 Amendments.

[7] See detailed analysis of these options in Chapter 10, "Chapter 7 Practice."

[8] See Chapter 8, "Voidable Transfers."

[9] See Chapter 8, "Voidable Transfers."

[10] See Chapter 8, "Voidable Transfers."

[11] See Chapter 8, "Voidable Transfers."

[12] See Chapter 8, "Voidable Transfers."

[13] See Chapter 8, "Voidable Transfers."

[14] See Chapter 8, "Voidable Transfers."

[15] See Chapter 8, "Voidable Transfers."

[16] See Chapter 8, "Voidable Transfers."

[17] See Chapter 8, "Voidable Transfers."

[18] See Chapter 8, "Voidable Transfers."

[19] See Chapter 8, "Voidable Transfers."

[20] See Chapter 8, "Voidable Transfers."

5 *Automatic Stay*

Your supervising attorney asks you to sit in on an initial interview with potential new bankruptcy clients. The husband and wife run a "mom and pop" small, local grocery store and seem to be genuinely nice people. However, the wife looks like she hasn't slept in a week and the husband looks like he might have a heart attack at any given second. It turns out these people have been trying to put out dozens of little "financial fires" all at one time. The store neighborhood has been recently overrun with gang activity which lowered the amount of customers coming in. Consequently, sales have greatly dropped and the clients aren't able to pay their suppliers. The suppliers either call or come into the store every day to get paid. The employees of the store haven't been paid for over two weeks and are all threatening to quit. The city sends notices every day for the clients to clean up the graffiti that appears on the walls outside. The clients took money out of their personal credit cards to make the overhead a few months ago and now they can't make their credit card payments. Collection agents for credit card companies call and harass the clients at least three times a day. Six months ago a customer slipped and fell in the store and is now suing the clients in state court for personal injury. Meanwhile, the IRS has threatened to close the store doors tomorrow since the clients never paid their employee withholding taxes for last year.

Is there a quick way to stop all these "fires" so the clients can get back to the business of running the grocery store and figure out a way to pay these creditors in an orderly manner?

DEFINITION

The *automatic stay* is an immediate injunction against all collection activity against a debtor. The stay is imposed the moment a debtor's petition is filed with the Bankruptcy Court. All further creditor activities, including seizures, trustee's sales, rendering of judgments, repossessions, and garnishments are void or voidable after the stay is in effect.[1] For example, in the case of our mom and pop grocer clients above, no creditors can call or write the debtors to collect. Also, the pending state court personal injury litigation cannot proceed any further. The IRS cannot seize the grocery store by closing it down. All the creditors are enjoined against any type of collection activity by virtue of the automatic stay.

Additionally, the automatic stay is not limited to only affirmative actions. Refusal or failure to take action is also encompassed by the stay of 11 U.S.C. Section 362.[2] For example, suppose a debtor's car had been repossessed immediately before a bankruptcy petition is filed. The repossessing creditor cannot refuse to take action. The automatic stay requires the creditor to return the automobile to the debtor.

The automatic stay not only may but *must* be invoked by a Bankruptcy Court sua sponte to protect the debtor, as well as in the interest of the principle of equal treatment of all creditors.[3] Once the petition is filed the debtor doesn't need to file any motions or pleadings to invoke the automatic stay. The automatic stay effects an immediate freeze of the status quo at the outset of bankruptcy. The automatic stay stops and nullifies most postpetition actions and proceedings against a debtor. This includes actions in a nonbankruptcy forum, either judicial or nonjudicial, as well as most extrajudicial action against the debtor, property of the debtor, or property of the estate.[4]

The automatic stay is one of the fundamental debtor protections provided by the Bankruptcy Code. It gives the debtor a breathing spell from creditors. It stops all collection efforts and harassment. The automatic stay permits the debtor to attempt a repayment or reorganization plan, or simply to be relieved of the financial pressures that led to bankruptcy.[5]

The automatic stay also provides creditors protection. Without it, certain creditors would be able to pursue their own remedies against the debtor's property. This includes state court collection lawsuits. Creditors who acted first would obtain payment of their claims in preference to and to the detriment of other creditors. In other words, those creditors who were first to obtain judgments and receive payment could leave all the rest of the creditors without any payment at all.

Bankruptcy is designed to provide an orderly liquidation procedure under which all creditors of the same priority are treated equally. The priority in which creditors get paid is defined by the Bankruptcy Code. Certain creditors are granted an elevated status in order of payment. This hierarchy of payments is called creditor priority.

For example, recent tax debts are treated better than unsecured debts such as credit cards. A debtor may owe both federal taxes and state taxes. Both of these tax debts are given a priority status. The Bankruptcy Code ensures that both types of tax debts are treated equally rather than one being paid in full while the other remains unpaid. Without the automatic stay, a race of diligency by creditors for the debtor's assets would occur, preventing that orderly and equal distribution contemplated by the Bankruptcy Code.[6]

POLICY

The automatic stay is one of the fundamental debtor protections provided by bankruptcy laws and its essential purpose is twofold: (1) to protect creditors and thereby promote the bankruptcy goal of equal treatment, and (2) to give the debtor a breathing spell.[7]

The automatic stay protects creditors by averting a scramble for the debtor's assets and instead promotes an orderly liquidation procedure wherein all creditors are treated equally.[8] The automatic stay prevents one creditor from rushing to enforce its lien to the detriment of other creditors.[9] One of the primary goals of the automatic stay is to sort out creditors into their respective order of priority untainted by postpetition jockeying for position. The intended effect of the stay is to fix the rights and priorities of creditors as of the time of the petition and to prohibit any further acts to advance those rights and priorities.[10]

In essence, the function of the stay is to protect the bankruptcy estate from being eaten away by creditors' lawsuits and seizures of property before the trustee has had an opportunity to collect all the estate's assets and distribute them equitably among the creditors.[11] The automatic stay is a crucial provision of the Bankruptcy Code since it protects the creditors in a manner consistent with the bankruptcy goal of equal treatment of creditors. The stay ensures that no creditor receives more than its equitable share of the debtor's estate. This equitable treatment requires that all creditors, both public and private, be subject to the automatic stay.[12] Public creditors include the government, such as the Internal Revenue Service. Private creditors are entities dealing directly with the debtor such as credit card companies.

The additional purpose of the automatic stay is to give an insolvent debtor an opportunity to take stock and formulate a plan for repayment and reorganization with protection from a chaotic and uncontrolled scramble for the debtor's assets in a variety of uncoordinated proceedings in different courts.[13]

As in our mom and pop grocer example, these different proceedings include state court litigation for the personal injury claim, Internal Revenue Service proceedings, and potential state law collection activities by the credit card companies and suppliers. The automatic stay permits a debtor-in-possession and its management to have a breathing spell from creditors pursuing their claims and causes of action so that they may concentrate on the debtor's business and rehabilitation effort.[14]

Scope

The filing of a bankruptcy petition operates, with certain specific exceptions, as a stay of all judicial and nonjudicial proceedings against debtors or their property.[15] Judicial proceedings are lawsuits in either state or federal court. Nonjudicial proceedings take place outside of court such as a trustee's sale of real property. The scope of the automatic stay is broad.[16] The automatic stay bars any action that would inevitably have an adverse impact on property of the estate.[17]

The automatic stay is pervasive and automatic. Where the automatic stay exists, the debtor is entitled to rely on it and is not required to continually and repeatedly appear in other courts to claim its protection. Rather, the burden falls upon the creditor to come into bankruptcy court and seek relief.[18] Where the law is uncertain, a creditor should first file a motion with the Bankruptcy Court to determine the applicability of the automatic stay.[19] Creditors who act without Bankruptcy Court approval do so at their own peril.[20] For example, if a creditor continues a state court lawsuit after a debtor has filed bankruptcy, any judgment obtained would not be effective. Moreover, the creditor would be subject to sanctions by the Bankruptcy Court.

Actions on claims or lawsuits that have been or could have been brought before the filing of the petition are, with limited exceptions, stayed through the automatic stay provisions of the Bankruptcy Code.[21] The stay is effective against all entities including governmental units such as the Internal Revenue Service.[22] Further, even nondischargeable and priority claims (unless statutorily excluded) are subject to the stay.[23] While both public and private creditors of the debtor are subject to the automatic stay, even parties who are not creditors of the estate are subject to the automatic stay.[24] Even if a creditor is not listed on the debtor's schedules, the automatic stay is still effective for that creditor.[25]

However, despite the broad reach of the automatic stay, it is not all encompassing. The automatic stay does not prevent creditors from revealing that the debtor has filed for bankruptcy.

For example, a creditor/advertiser superimposed statements over the advertisements on billboards of the debtor. The superimposed statements declared "Beware, This Company Is in Bankruptcy." Notwithstanding the automatic stay, the creditor's statements were allowable. The statements represented the advertiser's unfettered First Amendment protection to expressions of pure speech. [*In re National Service Corp.*, 742 F.2d 859 (5th Cir. 1984); see also, *In re Stonegate Secur. Svcs., Ltd.*, 567 B.R. 1014 (N.D. Ill. 1986) (where a creditor who placed a truck outside the debtor's business with signs stating the debtor was not paying its debts was constitutionally protected under the First Amendment).]

The Bankruptcy Code requires all proceedings to be stayed which could have been brought before the filing. In other words, the debtor's conduct which gives rise to the claim must occur prepetition.[26] Accordingly, proceedings or claims arising postpetition are not subject to the automatic stay since such claims are nondischargeable and there is no compelling reason to stay judicial proceedings based on such postpetition claims.[27] Likewise, postponement notices of trustee's sales are not subject to the stay since it merely maintains the status quo and does not harass the debtor, interfere with the process, or gain any advantage inconsistent with the purposes of the automatic stay.[28] Also, the automatic stay does not encompass contempt proceedings arising out of disobedience of state court orders made prior to the petition.[29] Further, the automatic stay provisions of 11 U.S.C. §362 are inapplicable to suits brought by a debtor.[30]

It should be noted that the automatic stay provisions of 11 U.S.C. §362 protect only the debtor, property of the debtor, or property of the estate. For example, prohibited collection against the debtor might include garnishment of a Chapter 7 debtor's postpetition wages. These postpetition wages are not property of the estate but are property of the debtor. Collection against property of the debtor may also include repossession of property claimed as exempt which is also not property of the estate. Also, collection against assets which the trustee could otherwise liquidate is prohibited since these assets are property of the estate. Generally, the automatic stay does not protect nondebtor parties or their property.[31]

For example, a corporation owned by an individual debtor is not protected by the automatic stay against the IRS.[32] Also, other nondebtor parties such as guarantors, sureties, or corporate affiliates, which are also liable for debts with the debtor are not protected by the automatic stay.[33] The limited exception to excluding guarantors from protections of the automatic stay are co-obligors on consumer debts when the debtor has filed either Chapter 13 or Chapter 12 proceedings.[34] This is called the codebtor stay and is discussed later in this chapter.

However, under 11 U.S.C. §362 the filing of the petition serves as an automatic stay of most actions against a debtor.[35] Proceedings violative of the automatic stay need not be formal.[36] In fact, Congress clearly intended the automatic stay to be quite broad and may well embrace modification of actions against a debtor.[37] An example of a modification would be to seek an amended judgment against a debtor in state court.

SPECIFIC ENUMERATED ACTIONS PROHIBITED BY STAY

Section 362(a) specifically enumerates the type of creditor activity restricted by the automatic stay as follows:

1. *Prohibition of the commencement or continuation of judicial or administrative proceedings against debtors.* This includes the service of process (such as an IRS summons).[38] Judicial proceedings precluded by the automatic stay include ordinary civil suits and such things as eviction proceedings.[39] Administrative proceedings enjoined by the automatic stay include a state's refusal to transfer a liquor license[40] and the state's revoking a debtor's corporate charter for nonpayment of fines.[41] Other proceedings include garnishment of the debtor's wages[42] or the collection of taxes.[43]

2. *Unenforceability of prepetition judgments against debtor or estate property.* Prepetition judgment creditors are restrained from execution and levy against the debtor's property and against the debtor personally. Therefore, even if a creditor has obtained a judgment before the petition, the creditor cannot fulfill the judgment by capturing a debtor's property. For example, a prepetition rent judgment may not be enforced to evict the debtor from possession.[44]

3. *Acts to obtain possession of estate property or exert control over estate property.* The phrase "estate property" is very broad and includes all legal or equitable interest in property of the debtor as of the date of the filing of the petition, regardless of who has title or possession, or whether the property is transferable, leviable, or jointly owned. Accordingly, a landlord may not give a termination notice to a prime tenant when the debtor is a subtenant because this would result in the destruction of the debtor's subtenancy.[45] Likewise, cancellation of an insurance policy violates the stay.[46]

4. *Acts to create, perfect, or enforce liens against the property of the estate.* Under this section no enforcement of any lien against estate property as well as any act to create or perfect any lien against estate property is allowed. Creation of a lien may include putting a mortgage on estate property. Perfection of a lien may include recording a judgment. Enforcement of liens is selling the property secured by the lien to satisfy the lien. For example, property tax liens cannot attach postpetition for real property taxes.[47]

5. *Acts to create, perfect, or enforce prepetition liens against the property of the debtor.* The focus of this section is on the *debtor's property*, as distinguished from the *estate property* referred to in 11 U.S.C. Section 362(a)(4).[48] Once the bankruptcy estate is created, the total of the debtor's property will consist of property acquired postpetition, property that is exempt, or property that is abandoned. This section prohibits lien enforcement activities against debtor's property such as foreclosure sales[49] and postpetition filing of UCC financing statements.[50]

The policy behind this section is to protect a debtor's right to discharge these debts. If no lien exists, these claims are unsecured and are subject to discharge. To allow a creditor to attach a lien to debtor's property would make the claim secured. Secured liens survive bankruptcy.

6. *Any act to collect, assess, or recover a prepetition claim.* In essence, an unsecured prepetition creditor may not affirmatively press the debtor to pay a prepetition debt. For example, a bank cannot apply debtors' postpetition earnings to their prepetition debt, even in accordance with a prepetition voluntary payroll-deducting authorization.[51] A landlord cannot send a letter calling a default on a lease.[52] A creditor cannot send a letter after the petition is filed threatening criminal prosecution unless the debtor pays a previously dishonored check.[53]

Finally, the withholding of services to collect a prepetition debt is also in violation of the stay. For example, a college cannot refuse to issue a diploma or transcript until the prepetition debts are paid,[54] or a medical clinic cannot refuse to provide services unless the debtor pays prepetition bills.[55]

7. *Setoffs of prepetition debts owed to the debtor.* Setoff is where a creditor applies money due to the debtor to pay a different obligation of the debtor. For example, the withholding of Medicare reimbursement to a debtor in an effort to recover prepetition Medicare overpayments is prohibited.[56] Also, the government is precluded from setting off prepetition welfare or social security overpayments against postpetition entitlement to such benefits.[57] Even if a setoff is authorized elsewhere under the Bankruptcy Code, such setoff claim is automatically stayed after the case is commenced. A creditor must request that the stay be terminated to allow setoff.

8. *The commencement or continuation of proceedings before the U.S. Tax Court.* Postpetition, any litigation of tax cases in the Tax Court after a debtor files a bankruptcy petition cannot continue. This includes service of a summons by the IRS since the summons actually commences a tax proceeding.

DURATION

The automatic stay continues against estate property until the property is no longer property of the estate. Assets stop being considered estate property under three conditions. These include if property is abandoned back to the debtor, the property is declared exempt by the debtor, or if the property is sold from the estate. The automatic stay always continues against estate property.

However, the stay of any other act, including acts against the debtor or the debtor's property, has a different duration. The automatic stay against the debtor or the debtor's property continues until the earliest of any of the following three events: (1) the case is dismissed, (2) the case is closed, or (3) a discharge is granted or denied to the debtor. A case may be dismissed either voluntarily by a debtor or involuntarily based upon several reasons. A complete discussion of dismissal is included in Chapter 7. A discharge is the order entered by the Court which relieves a debtor of further personal liability. In essence, discharge makes unsecured debts disappear. Discharge is discussed at length in Chapter 6. Finally, after a bankruptcy case is over the Bankruptcy Court closes its file. This is when a case is closed and the automatic stay also terminates against a debtor or debtor's property.

STATUTORY EXCLUSIONS FROM THE AUTOMATIC STAY

There are 18 statutory exceptions to the automatic stay under 11 U.S.C. Section 362(b). These exceptions generally include criminal actions against a debtor, family law actions against a debtor, certain perfection under the Uniform Commercial Code, a government's police power actions, actions involved in certain commodities transactions, repurchase agreement setoffs, certain actions by the Department of Housing and Urban Development, tax audits or notices, certain acts by landlords, certain negotiable instrument transactions, specific actions by the Secretary of Transportation, certain actions against a debtor who is a school, swap agreement setoffs, and action on postpetition ad valorem taxes. Each of these exceptions to the automatic stay is discussed separately below.

1. *The commencement or continuation of a criminal action or proceeding against the debtor.* Congress did not intend the bankruptcy laws to be a means to hinder or delay criminal proceedings. Federal and state court suits against a debtor for criminal behavior are not enjoined by the automatic stay. Accordingly, such things as murder trials, drug trafficking offenses, criminal contempt proceedings, criminal restitution proceedings,[58] or actions for forfeiture of criminal contraband continue despite the filing of a bankruptcy case.

Attorney for

UNITED STATES BANKRUPTCY COURT
CENTRAL DISTRICT OF CALIFORNIA

In re:

Debtor.

Movant(s),

vs.

Respondent(s)

CHAPTER _____ CASE NUMBER

REFERENCE NUMBER

DATE:
TIME:
CTRM:

Motion for Relief from the Automatic Stay
Under 11 U.S.C. § 362 (Real Property)

1. Movant in the above-captioned matter moves this Court for an Order granting relief from the automatic stay on the grounds set forth below:

2. **Type of Case:**

   a. ☐ A Voluntary Petition under Chapter   ☐ 7   ☐ 11   ☐ 12   ☐ 13 was filed on:

   b. ☐ An Involuntary Petition under Chapter   ☐ 7   ☐ 11 was filed on:

       ☐ An Order of Relief under Chapter   ☐ 7   ☐ 11 was entered on:

   c. ☐ An Order of Conversion to Chapter   ☐ 7   ☐ 11   ☐ 12   ☐ 13 was entered on:

   d. ☐ Other:

3. **Procedural Status:**
   a. ☐ Name of Trustee Appointed *(if any)*:
   b. ☐ Name of Attorney of Record for Trustee *(if any)*:
   c. ☐ *(Optional)* Prior Filing Information: Debtor has previously filed a Bankruptcy Petition on *(specify date)*:
       If known: The prior case was dismissed on *(specify date)*:
   d. ☐ *(If Chapter 13 case):* Chapter 13 Plan was confirmed on *(specify date)*:

(Continued on Next Page)

FIGURE 5-1a. Motion for Relief from the Automatic Stay Under 11 U.S.C. § 362 (Real Property) (page 1).

In re	(SHORT TITLE)	CHAPTER _____ CASE NUMBER:
	Debtor.	

4. Movant alleges the following in support of its Motion:

   a. Debtor lists on Schedule ❑ A-2   ❑ B-1   ❑ B-4   ❑ Not Listed   the following real property which is the subject of this motion:

     (1) Street address of property, including county and state in which located:

     (2) Type of real property (e.g., single family residence, apartment building, commercial, industrial, condominium, unimproved):

     (3) Legal Description of property *(specify)*:   ❑ See Attached Page

     (4) Fair market value of property as set forth in Debtor's Schedules *(specify)*: $ _____

   b. Nature of Debtor's interest in the property (e.g., sole owner, co-owner, lessee, etc.):

   c. Present fair market value of the property: $ _____ *(if applicable)* *(Attach supporting evidence)*

   d. Encumbrances:
     (1) Voluntary encumbrances on the property listed in Schedules or otherwise known to Movant:

	Lender Name	Principal Bal.	Pre-Petition Arrearages		Post-Petition Arrearages	
			Total Amt	No. of Months	Total Amt	No. of Months
1st:						
2nd:						
3rd:						
4th:						
Totals for all Liens:	$		$	---	$	---

     (2) Involuntary encumbrances of record (e.g., tax, mechanic's, judgment and other liens, lis pendens) as listed in Schedules or otherwise known to Movant *(specify, including recording date)*:   ❑ See Attached Page

   e. Status of Movant's Loan:
     (1) Amount of Monthly Payment: $
     (2) Date of Last Payment:
     (3) Date of Default:
     (4) Notice of Default recorded on:
     (5) Notice of Sale published on:
     (6) Foreclosure Sale originally scheduled for:
     (7) Foreclosure Sale currently scheduled for:

FIGURE 5-1b. Motion for Relief from the Automatic Stay Under 11 U.S.C. § 362 (Real Property) (page 2).

In re	(SHORT TITLE)	CHAPTER _____ CASE NUMBER:
	Debtor.	

f. *(If Chapter 13 Case, state the following:)*

    (1) Date of Confirmation Hearing:
    (2) Date of Post-Petition Default:
    (3) Amount of Post-Petition Default:

g. Relief from the automatic stay should be granted because:

    (1) ❑ Movant's interest in the property described above is not adequately protected.

    (2) ❑ Debtor has no equity in the real property described above and such property is not necessary to an effective reorganization.

    (3) ❑ Other cause exists as follows *(specify)*:   ❑ See Attached Page

5. Movant attaches the following supporting evidence pursuant to Local Bankruptcy Rule 112(3)(a):

    a. ❑ Declarations under penalty of perjury, which include any material which would be admissible under Federal Rules of Evidence and about which declarant would be allowed to testify if called as a witness at the hearing.

    b. ❑ Other evidence *(specify)*:   ❑ See Attached Page

6. ❑ *(Optional)* Memorandum of points and authorities upon which the moving party will rely.

7. Total number of attached pages of supporting documentation: _____

WHEREFORE, Movant prays that this Court issue an Order (a copy of the form of which is submitted herewith and has been served) granting the following: ❑ Relief from the automatic stay, or alternatively, for adequate protection

        ❑ Prospective relief and findings under 11 U.S.C. § 109(g)

        ❑ Attorney's fees and/or sanctions as requested in the supporting Declaration(s) and Order

Dated: Respectfully submitted,

                                   _____

                                   Firm Name

                                   By: _____

                                   Name: _____

                                      Attorney for Movant

FIGURE 5-1c. Motion for Relief from the Automatic Stay Under 11 U.S.C. § 362 (Real Property) (page 3).

2. *The commencement or continuation of an action to establish paternity, to establish or modify alimony or support, or to collect alimony or support from nonestate property.* The 1994 Amendments added the establishment of paternity as well as the establishment or modification of alimony or support. The policy in excluding these matters is to avoid the bankruptcy court from becoming too entangled with domestic relations disputes. Further, the collection of support from nonestate property does not diminish the goals of the Bankruptcy Code. These types of support are not discharged and there is no reason why an action for such collection should be automatically stayed. In support collection actions no other creditors of the estate are adversely affected.

3. *Any act to perfect, to maintain, or to continue the perfection of an interest in property allowed under other sections of the Bankruptcy Code.* Such actions must be accomplished within the time periods set forth in those specific code sections. This section allows certain actions taken during bankruptcy proceedings under the Uniform Commercial Code. These actions allow a creditor to maintain its secured position as it was at the commencement of the case. These actions include the filing of a continuation statement and the filing of a financing statement. The steps taken by a secured creditor to ensure continued perfection merely maintain the status quo and do not improve the position of the secured creditor.

For example, a U.C.C.-1 statement (a financing statement) is allowed to be recorded within ten days after the debtor receives possession of the collateral. This ten-day period is still allowed, even if a bankruptcy has been filed in the interim. Accordingly, this exception merely reinforces postpetition perfection authorized under other code sections [see 11 U.S.C. §§ 546 and 547].[59]

4. *The commencement or continuation of an action by a governmental unit to enforce its police or regulatory powers.* This section should be narrowly construed to apply to the enforcement laws affecting health, welfare, morals, and safety. This section does not permit the continuation of governmental actions to protect its pecuniary (money) interest in property of the debtor or the estate.[60]

Some examples of a governmental "police power" exception to the automatic stay are:

> The state industrial commission may adjudicate a workers' compensation claim.[61]
>
> The SEC can obtain an order appointing a receiver for violations of the antifraud provisions of the federal securities laws.[62]
>
> A state Board of Medical Quality Assurance may revoke a medical license due to malpractice.[63]
>
> The Department of Labor can enforce the Fair Labor Standards Act.[64]

Note both prepetition governmental actions as well as postpetition activities are encompassed within this exception to the automatic stay. Governmental actions that merely seek to fix damages for violation of any police or regulatory laws are not stayed.[65] However, the enforcement of these money judgments will be stayed.

5. *The enforcement of a nonmonetary judgment obtained by a governmental unit in enforcing its police or regulatory powers.* Note: The judgment must be nonmonetary. In contrast, a state court injunction that requires the debtor to remedy a past environmental harm is not stayed when there is no attempt to collect a money judgment, but only to correct the potential for future harm to the environment.[66]

Penn Terra Ltd. v. Dept. of Environ. Resources
733 F.2d 267 (3rd Cir. 1984)

Garth, J. This case demonstrates the difficulty encountered when two governmental policies—one federal and one state—come into arguable conflict. On the one hand, the federally created bankruptcy policy requires that the assets of a debtor be preserved and protected, so that in time they may be equitably distributed to all creditors without unfair preference. On the other hand, the environmental policies of the Commonwealth of Pennsylvania require those within its jurisdiction to preserve and protect natural resources and to rectify damage to the environment which they have caused. The potential conflict between these two policies is presented in this case, in which the Commonwealth has attempted to force a company which has petitioned in bankruptcy to correct violations of state antipollution laws, even though this action would have the effect of depleting assets which would otherwise be available to repay debts owed to general creditors.

* * *

The facts in this case are largely undisputed. Penn Terra Limited was the operator of coal surface mines in Armonstrong County in western Pennsylvania. The Commonwealth's Department of Environmental Resources (hereafter "DER") found that Penn Terra was operating its mines in violation of various state environmental protection statutes.[67] In February 1981, DER served Penn Terra with a total of 36 citations, both against the corporation and against Harvey Taylor, the president of Penn Terra, for these violations. Penn Terra apparently never contested that these violations existed. On November 9, 1981, DER and Mr. Taylor entered into a consent order and agreement to rectify these infractions and thus place Penn Terra in compliance with the state statutes. The consent agreement listed the violations and established a schedule for corrective measures to be taken. Penn Terra, however, apparently did not comply with that schedule.

On March 15, 1982, Penn Terra filed a petition for bankruptcy under Chapter 7 of the Bankruptcy Code, having previously ceased all operations. In its schedule of assets, Penn Terra listed total property worth $14,000. Of this $13,500 was designated as "certificates of deposit with DER," which Penn Terra had furnished as bonds for the backfilling operation. The schedule further noted that the cost of reclamation, as required under the consent agreement, would greatly exceed the market and book value of those bonds. The total amount of debts listed was $550,000.

On April 14, 1982, DER brought an equitable action in the Commonwealth Court of Pennsylvania, seeking a preliminary injunction against Penn Terra and Harvey Taylor to correct the violations of the state statutes and to enforce the terms of the consent order. DER apparently did not receive a notice of Penn Terra's bankruptcy petition until April 29, 1982. A hearing was conducted on DER's application in Commonwealth Court on May 24, 1982, as previously scheduled; Harvey Taylor appeared but Penn Terra did not, nor did the Trustee. After taking testimony, the Commonwealth Court granted injunctive relief to DER.

On May 28, 1982, Penn Terra filed a Petition for Contempt in the Bankruptcy Court against DER and two of its attorneys for proceeding with the Commonwealth Court hearing. Penn Terra contended that this proceeding violated the automatic stay provisions of 11 U.S.C. §362(a). DER responded that the proceedings and the resulting injunction fell within the exception to the automatic stay which exempts actions by governmental units performed pursuant to the police power of the government, 11 U.S.C. §§362(b)(4)-(5).

The Bankruptcy Court found that the actions by DER were, in its opinion, actions to enforce a money judgment, which do not fall within the exception to §362(a). The Bankruptcy Court opined that, given the "obvious insolvency" of the debtor, DER's pursuit of its action in state court has resulted in the entry of a "meaningless order." * * * On appeal, the district court affirmed the Bankruptcy Court's injunction. * * *

The crux of this case depends on an interpretation of 11 U.S.C. §362 which provides in pertinent part:
* * *

(b) The filing of a petition under section 301, 302, or 303 of this title does not operate as a stay—
* * *

(4) under subsection (a)(1) of this section, of the commencement or continuation of an action or proceeding by a governmental unit to enforce such governmental unit's police or regulatory power;

(5) under subsection (a)(2) of this section, of the enforcement of a judgment, other than a money judgment, obtained in an action or proceeding by a governmental unit to enforce such governmental unit's police or regulatory power.

The general policy behind [§362(a)] is to grant complete, immediate, albeit temporary relief to the debtor from creditors, and also to prevent dissipation of the debtor's assets before orderly distribution to creditors can be effected. * * * Subsections 362(b)(4) & (5), however, return to the States with one hand some of what was taken away by the other. The purpose of this exception is also explained in the legislative history of the Code:

Paragraph (4) excepts commencement or continuation of actions and proceedings by governmental units to enforce police or regulatory powers. Thus where a government unit is suing a debtor to prevent or stop violation of fraud, environmental protection, consumer protection, safety, or similar police or regulatory laws, or attempting to fix damages for violation for such law, the action or proceeding is not stayed under the automatic stay.
* * *

Subsection 362(b)(5), however, creates a further "exception to the exception," in that actions to enforce money judgments are affected by the automatic stay, even if they otherwise were in furtherance of the State's police powers. As the legislative history explains:

Paragraph (5) makes clear that the exception extends to permit an injunction and enforcement of an injunction, and to permit the entry of a money judgment, but does not extend to permit enforcement of a money judgment. Since assets of the debtor are in the possession and control of the Bankruptcy Court, and since they constitute a fund out of which all creditors are entitled to share, enforcement by a government unit of a money judgment would give it preferential treatment to the detriment of all other creditors.
* * *

Turning now to the specific issues in this case, it first is clear to us that the actions taken by DER in obtaining and attempting to enforce the Commonwealth Court's injunction fall squarely within Pennsylvania's police and regulatory powers. DER seeks to force Penn Terra to rectify harmful environmental hazards. No more obvious exercise of the State's power to protect the health, safety, and welfare of the public can be imagined. Indeed, both the Senate and House committee reports on the Bankruptcy Reform Act explicitly acknowledge environmental protection as a part of the State's police power.

Having found that DER's action constitutes an exercise of the Commonwealth's police power, the dispositive issue in this case is whether the Commonwealth Court injunction ordering Penn Terra to perform reclamation work is in fact an attempt to enforce a money judgment. * * *

[A] money judgment is an order entered by the court ... [which] consists of only two elements: (1) an identification of the parties for and against whom judgment is being entered, and (2) a definite and certain designation of the amount which plaintiff is owed by defendant. * * *

Quite separate from the entry of a money judgment, however, is a proceeding to enforce that money judgment. The paradigm for such a proceeding is when, having obtained a judgment for a sum certain, a plaintiff attempts to seize property of the defendant in order to satisfy that judgment. It is this seizure of a defendant-debtor's property, to satisfy the judgment obtained by a plaintiff-creditor, which is proscribed by subsection 362(b)(5).

At least as a matter of form, it is clear to us that the proceeding initiated by DER in Commonwealth Court was not to enforce a money judgment. Indeed, it could not have resulted even in the mere entry of a money judgment. DER brought its action in equity to compel the performance of certain remedial acts by Penn Terra. It did not seek payment of compensation to the Commonwealth's coffers, and the injunction actually issued by the Commonwealth Court did not direct such payment. This proceeding, therefore, could never have resulted in the adjudication of a liability for a sum certain, an essential element of a money judgment. Since this action was in form and substance, not one to obtain a money judgment, it follows that it could not be one to enforce the payment of such judgment.

* * *

[A]n important factor in identifying a proceeding as one to enforce a money judgment is whether the remedy would compensate for past wrongful acts resulting in injuries already suffered, or protect against potential future harm. Thus, it is unlikely that any action which seeks to prevent culpable conduct in futuro will, in normal course, manifest itself as an action for a money judgment, or one to enforce a money judgment. This is consistent with our earlier observations, since a traditional money judgment requires liquidated damages, i.e. a sum certain, and one cannot liquidate damages which have not yet been suffered due to conduct not yet committed. Nor can one calculate such a sum with any certainty. Indeed the very nature of injunctive relief is that it addresses injuries which may not be compensated by money.

* * *

Were we to find that any order which requires the expenditure of money is a "money judgment," then the exception to section 362 for government police action, which should be construed broadly, would instead be narrowed into virtual nonexistence. Yet we cannot ignore the fundamental fact that, in contemporary times, almost everything costs something. An injunction which does not compel some expenditure or loss of monies may often be an effective nullity.

* * *

We believe that the inquiry is more properly focused on the nature of the injuries which the challenged remedy is intended to redress—including whether plaintiff seeks compensation for past damages or prevention of future harm—in order to reach the ultimate conclusion as to whether these injuries are traditionally rectified by a money judgment and its enforcement. Here, the Commonwealth Court injunction was, neither in form nor substance, the type of remedy traditionally associated with the conventional money judgment. It was not intended to provide compensation for past injuries. It was not reducible to a sum certain. No monies were sought by the Commonwealth as a creditor or obligee. The Commonwealth was not seeking a traditional form of damages in tort or contract, and the mere payment of money, without more, even if it could be estimated, could not satisfy the Commonwealth Court's direction to complete the backfilling, to update erosion plans, to seal mine openings, to spread topsoil, and to implement plans for erosion and sedimentation control. Rather, the Commonwealth Court's injunction was meant to prevent future harm to, and to restore, the environment. Indeed, examining the state order, it is clear that erosion control, backfilling, and reseeding were additionally meant to preserve the soil conditions from further deterioration (as well as to rectify a safety hazard).

* * * [W]e decline to equate DER's actions which are those of a governmental unit enforcing the Commonwealth's police power, with those affected by the automatic stay of Section 352(a). We therefore conclude that the suit brought by DER to compel Penn Terra to remedy environmental hazards was properly brought as an equitable action to prevent future harm, and did not constitute an action to enforce a money judgment. The automatic stay provision of 11 U.S.C. Section 362 is therefore inapplicable.
Reversed.

6. *Setoff by a commodity broker, forward contract merchant, stockbroker, financial institution, or securities clearing agency of any mutual debt and claim in connection with commodity contracts that constitutes a setoff of a claim against the debtor for a margin payment.* This exception applies to all setoffs of mutual debts and claims for commodity transactions. The purpose of this exception is to facilitate the administration of liquidations of commodity brokers where market conditions require swift action.

7. *The setoff by a repo participant in connection with a repurchase agreement of a claim against the debtor for a margin payment.* A repurchase agreement, commonly called a "repo," is a transaction where one party sells a security to a second party but agrees to buy the security back at a later date (or upon demand) at a specified higher price. Repos are used in a variety of contexts in the financial markets. For example, dealers in government securities "repo out" securities in their inventories as an inexpensive means of financing those inventories. Again, this statutory exception to the automatic stay is designed to facilitate the prompt closing out of repurchase agreements and to minimize losses of nondebtor participants in such contracts.

8. *The commencement by HUD to foreclose on property of five or more living units.* This exception applies to actions by the Secretary of Housing and Urban Development to foreclose or take possession of property with a loan insured under the National Housing Act. The property must consist of five or more living units. This exception to the automatic stay is limited to "the commencement of any action." Therefore, if a HUD foreclosure was initiated prepetition, then such action would be stayed. Only the commencement of such foreclosure action is permitted after the petition is filed.

9. *An audit by the government to determine tax liability, the issuance of a notice of tax deficiency, a demand for tax returns, or the making of an assessment and issuance of a notice and demand for payment of such an assessment.* This exception to the automatic stay was modified substantially by the 1994 Amendments to include audits, demands for tax returns, allowance of tax assessments, as well as notices and demands for payment of such assessments. However, demands for payment of assessments are limited to two situations. First, the tax liens must be nondischargeable. Next, the property secured by the tax lien must be transferred out of the estate, such as through abandonment by the trustee.

10. *Any act by a landlord to obtain possession of nonresidential real property that has terminated prepetition by the expiration of the terms within the lease.* This applied only to nonresidential leases, such as an office lease. Also, the lease must have terminated before the bankruptcy was filed. A lease that terminates by its own terms before bankruptcy is not property of the estate.[68] Therefore, the automatic stay does not apply.

11. *The presentment of a negotiable instrument and giving notice and protesting dishonor of such an instrument.* Presentment, under UCC law, is a demand for acceptance or payment made upon the maker, acceptor, drawee, or other payor by or on behalf of the holder of a negotiable instrument (such as a check). Notice of dishonor is an oral or written communication to any person liable on the instrument that identifies the instrument and states that it has been dishonored (i.e., notice of a "bounced" check). These types of communications are excepted from the automatic stay.

12. *In Chapter 11 cases, 90 days postpetition, any commencement or conclusion of an action by the Secretary of Transportation to foreclose upon a ship of fleet.* This exception applies to foreclosures on mortgages or a security interest in or relating to a vessel held by the Secretary of Transportation. This exception also applies only once 90 days have lapsed since the filing of the petition. Finally, this exception is applicable only in Chapter 11 cases.

13. *In Chapter 11 cases, 90 days postpetition, any commencement or conclusion of an action by the Secretary of Commerce to foreclose upon a fishing facility.* This exception applies to foreclosures of preferred ship or fleet mortgages in a fishing facility held by the Secretary of Commerce. This exception also applies only once 90 days have elapsed since the filing of the petition. Finally, this exception is applicable only in Chapter 11 cases.

14. *Any action by an accrediting agency regarding the accreditation status of the debtor as an educational institution.* This section deals with a debtor that is a school. This section excepts from the automatic stay all actions by accrediting agencies regarding the accreditation status of a debtor as an educational institution. This section eliminates the delays experienced by accrediting agencies in changing the accreditation status of an educational institution that has filed for bankruptcy relief.

15. *Any action by a state licensing body regarding the licensure of the debtor as an education institution.* Again, this section only applies to debtors that are schools. This section excepts from the automatic stay all actions by state licensing bodies in connection with the licensing of a debtor as an educational institution. This section eliminates the delays experienced by licensing bodies in changing the licensed status of an educational institution that has filed for bankruptcy relief.

16. *Any action by the Secretary of Education or by a guaranty agency regarding the eligibility of the debtor to participate in programs under the Higher Education Act.* Again, this section only applies to debtors that are schools. This section relates to the eligibility of educational institutions who have filed bankruptcy to participate in financial assistance programs (offer financial aid to their students).

17. *The setoff of a swap participant under any swap agreement.* Swap agreements involve transactions concerning interest rates and foreign currency rates. Corporations, financial institutions, and governmental entities enter into swap agreements to minimize borrowing costs and to hedge against fluctuations in interest rates and in foreign exchange rates. Parties to swap agreements enter into a number of such agreements, since fluctuations in the rates can be expected to occur in both directions during the period of the agreement. At the end of the term, the net of the fluctuations is calculated and the amounts are setoff against each other. In this section, the automatic stay does not apply to disturb the end result anticipated in these types of swap agreements.

18. *The creation or perfection of a statutory lien for postpetition real property taxes.* This exception was added in its entirety by the 1994 Amendments. Such exception allows real property taxes that become due postpetition to acquire a lien status against the property.

STAY RELIEF

Creditors have the right to request relief from the automatic stay pursuant to 11 U.S.C. §362(d). In essence, stay relief terminates, dissolves, or modifies the automatic injunction against further activity by such creditor. If stay relief is granted the creditor may then pursue its collection or litigation activities against the debtor, despite the continuance of the bankruptcy.

Stay relief litigation is among the most common of all bankruptcy proceedings. Requests for relief from the stay are "contested matters" under F.R.Bankr.P. 9014 and 4001(a).[69] Stay relief is requested by a motion and opposed by a response. Any creditor and other party in interest has standing to bring a stay relief motion. The necessary respondents are the debtor and the trustee if one has been appointed.[70] There are no time limits on bringing a stay relief motion. The statutory basis for jurisdiction of stay relief motions are 28 U.S.C. Section 157(b)(2)(G) and 28 U.S.C. Section 1334. An example of a motion for relief from stay is presented in Figure 5-1.

Throughout stay relief litigation, the most common issue is valuation of property. This usually takes the form of the battle of the appraisers. When representing debtors, a paralegal should remember to request formal court approval for the employment of such professionals before any services are performed.

The criteria for stay relief fall within the discrete ambit of 11 U.S.C. §362(d)(1), (2), or (3). Each of the three sections within 11 U.S.C. §362(d) is disjunctive.[71] This means a creditor need prevail on only one of the three tests to obtain stay relief.

Cause and Lack of Adequate Protection

Under 11 U.S.C. §362(d)(1), the stay may be lifted based upon "cause, including the lack of adequate protection."

"Adequate protection" is also a term of art within the context of 11 U.S.C. §362(d)(1). The classic method of demonstrating lack of adequate protection is to prove that the underlying collateral is depreciating. This means that the property that is secured by a creditor's lien is declining in value. Along with the decline in value, the debtor has not offered to make payments to compensate the creditor for the depreciated amounts. The policy in granting stay relief due to lack of adequate protection is to prevent a secured creditor from helplessly waiting out the bankruptcy process while its underlying secured property continues to decrease in value.

However, adequate protection does not include a secured creditor's right to compensation for the delay caused by the automatic stay in foreclosure on their collateral.[72] It is crucial to demonstrate that the property's value is decreasing, not mere postponement due to the bankruptcy proceedings. Likewise, an undersecured creditor (a creditor whose claim is more than the value of the property) is not entitled to interest on its collateral during the stay to assure adequate protection.[73]

The existence of an "equity cushion" is a classic form of adequate protection for a secured debt. An equity cushion is the difference between the value of the property and the amount of a secured creditor's lien. An equity cushion justifies restraining a secured creditor from lien enforcement.[74] An equity cushion, standing alone, can provide adequate protection, even though not a single mortgage payment has been made during the bankruptcy.[75]

The existence of junior lienholders is not considered in determining whether the interest of a senior lienholder has an "equity cushion" and is therefore adequately protected.[76] A typical example of a junior lienholder is a second mortgage on real property. To calculate whether the first mortgage holder has an equity cushion, the second mortgage is not included at all. Instead, only the amount of the first mortgage claim is subtracted from the value of the property.

Adequate protection may be provided through the debtor paying secured creditors for any decreases in the property's value. This is proving adequate protection against depreciation of the property. A secured creditor's claim is calculated at the time the petition is filed. Thereafter, the creditor will be granted stay relief based upon lack of adequate protection if the debtor does not propose to make payments to compensate for any decline in the value of the property that occurred since the filing of the bankruptcy and that is likely to occur in the foreseeable future.[77]

For example, stay relief was appropriate when the secured creditor proved that the value of the collateral (equipment) had diminished by $15,000 since the petition date. The equipment was also decreasing in value at the present time. Additionally, the equipment would continue to decrease as the debtor used the equipment in the lawn care/landscaping business (especially with the lawn care season in progress). [See *In re Planned Systems, Inc.*, 78 B.R. 852 (Bankr. S.D. Ohio 1987).]

Cash payments to a secured creditor may also demonstrate sufficient adequate protection. However, the debtor's ability to make such payments is often problematic, which results in stay relief under Section 362(d)(1) (lack of adequate protection.) Often a debtor is not able to obtain credit or generate funds through operation of its business to allow adequate protection payments to a secured creditor.

For example, a Chapter 11 debtor was not allowed an extension of time to make adequate protection payments where it was unbelievable that the debtor, who envisioned developing a large dinner theatre complex costing millions of dollars, was unable to raise $2,500 for adequate protection within a short time frame. [See *In re Ritz Theatres, Inc.*, 69 B.R. 299 (Bankr. M.D. Fla. 1987).]

Further, additional or replacement liens can serve to provide adequate protection. Additional liens mean the debtor gives the secured creditor more liens against the property. Replacement liens mean the debtor gives the creditor a lien against different property. Again, however, the identification of unencumbered assets to provide any value for such additional or replacement liens is often a struggle for a debtor. For example, a debtor's offer of replacement liens on future nonexistent crops was held to be insufficient to constitute adequate protection. [See *In re Lundell Farms*, 86 B.R. 582 (Bankr. W.D. Wis. 1988).]

United Sav. Ass'n v. Timbers of Inwood Forest
108 S.Ct. 626 (1988)

Scalia, J. * * * On June 29, 1982, respondent Timbers of Inwood Forest Associates, Ltd., executed a note in the principal amount of $4,100,000. Petitioner is the holder of the note as well as of a security interest created the same day in an apartment project owned by respondent in Houston, Texas. The security interest included an assignment of rents from the project. On March 4, 1985, respondent filed a voluntary petition under Chapter 11 of the Bankruptcy Code, 11 U.S.C. Section 101 *et seq.* in the United States Bankruptcy Court for the Southern District of Texas.

On March 18, 1985, petitioner moved for relief from the automatic stay of enforcement of liens triggered by the petition, see 11 U.S.C. Section 362(a), on the ground that there was lack of "adequate protection" of its interest within the meaning of 11 U.S.C. Section 362(d)(1). At a hearing before the Bankruptcy Court, it was established that the respondent owed petitioner, $4,366,388.77, and evidence was presented that the value of the collateral was somewhere between $2,540,000 and $4,240,000. The collateral was appreciating in value, but only very slightly. It was therefore undisputed that petitioner was an undersecured creditor.

* * *

We granted certiorari to determine whether undersecured creditors are entitled to compensation under 11 U.S.C. Section 362(d)(1) for the delay caused by the automatic stay in foreclosing on their collateral.

* * *

The phrase "adequate protection" in paragraph (1) of [Section 362(d)(1)] is given further content by Section 361 of the Code, which reads in relevant part as follows:

When adequate protection is required under section 362 ... of this title of an interest of an entity in property, such adequate protection may be provided by—

(1) requiring the trustee to make a cash payment or periodic cash payments to such entity, to the extent that the stay under section 362 of this title ... results in a decrease in the value of such entity's interest in such property;

(2) providing to such entity an additional or replacement lien to the extent that the stay ... results in a decrease in the value of such entity's interest in such property; or

(3) granting such other relief ... as will result in the realization by such entity of the indubitable equivalent of such entity's interest in such property.

It is common that the "interest in property" referred to by Section 362(d)(1) includes the right of a secured creditor to have the security applied in payment of the debt upon completion of the reorganization; and that the interest is not adequately protection if the security is depreciating during the term of the stay. * * * The crux of the present dispute is petitioner asserts, and the respondent denies, that the phrase "interest in property" also includes the secured party's right (suspended by the stay) to take immediate possession of the defaulted security, and apply it in payment of the debt. If that right is embraced by the term, it is obviously not adequately protected unless the secured party is reimbursed for the use of the proceeds he is deprived of during the term of the stay.

* * * The phrase "value of such creditor's interest" in Section 506(a) means "the value of the collateral." ... We think the phrase "value of such entity's interest" in Sections 361(1) and (2), when applied to secured creditors, means the same.

Even more important for our purposes than Section 506's use of terminology is its substantive effect of denying undersecured creditors postpetition interest on their claims—just as it denies oversecured creditors postpetition interest to the extent that such interest, when added to the principal amount of the claim will exceed the value of the collateral. * * *

[P]etitioner's interpretation of Section 362(d)(1) makes nonsense of Section 362(d)(2). On petitioner's theory, the undersecured creditor's inability to take immediate possession of his collateral is always "cause" for conditioning the stay (upon the payment of market rate interest) under Section 362(d)(1), since there is, within the meaning of that paragraph, "lack of adequate protection of an interest in property." But Section 362(d)(2) expressly provides a different standard for relief from a stay "of an act against property," which of course includes taking possession of collateral. It provides that the court shall grant relief "if ...(A) the debtor does not have an equity in such property (i.e. the creditor is undersecured); and (B) such property is not necessary to an effective reorganization." By applying the "adequate protection of an interest in property" provision of Section 362(d)(1) to the alleged "interest" in the earning power of the collateral, petitioner creates the strange consequence that Section 362 entitles the secured creditor to relief from the stay (1) if he is undersecured (and thus not eligible for interest under Section 506(b)), or (2) if he is undersecured and his collateral "is not necessary to an effective reorganization." This renders Section 362(d)(2) a practical nullity and a theoretical absurdity. * * *

Section 362(d)(2) also belies petitioner's contention that undersecured creditors will face inordinate and extortionate delay if they are denied compensation for interest lost during the stay as part of "adequate protection" under Section 362(d)(1). Once the movant under Section 362(d)(2) establishes that he is an undersecured creditor, it is the burden of the debtor to establish that the collateral at issue is "necessary to an effective reorganization." See Section 362(g). What this requires is not merely a showing that if there is conceivably to be an effective reorganization, this property will be needed for it; but that the property is essential for an effective reorganization *that is in prospect.* (emphasis in original). This means, as many lower courts, including the en banc court in this case, have properly said, that there must be "a reasonable possibility of a successful reorganization within a reasonable time."

* * * The Fifth Circuit correctly held that the undersecured petitioner is not entitled to interest on its collateral during the stay to assure adequate protection under 11 U.S.C. Section 362(d)(1).

Affirmed.

"Cause" under 11 U.S.C. Section 362(d)(1) is often asserted to be a debtor's bad faith. The conditions common in bad faith cases are: (1) it is a one-asset case, (2) a secured creditor's lien exists on the real property, (3) the debtor has no employees except principals, (4) the debtor has little or no cash flow, (5) the debtor has no available source of income to sustain a plan or make adequate protection payments, (6) the debtor has few unsecured creditors, (7) the unsecured creditors' claims are small, (8) the real property has been posted for foreclosure, (9) arrearages exist on the secured debt, and (10) the debtor has been unsuccessful in stopping the foreclosure.[78]

Findings of lack of good faith in bankruptcy proceedings based upon these recurring but nonexclusive patterns are through a combination of such factors rather than any one element.[79] Further, "bad faith" must be analyzed on a case-by-case basis depending on the facts and underlying circumstances of the specific debtor. In fact, some courts have held that invocation of the Bankruptcy Court's jurisdiction and the protection afforded by the automatic stay on the eve of foreclosure was not only proper but necessary to stave off foreclosing creditors in order to effectuate the reorganization of a viable entity.[80]

An example of bad faith sufficient to justify relief from the stay is as follows. Prepetition, debtor repeatedly violated state environmental orders and court rulings. The principal of the debtor surrounded the financial status of both himself and the debtor in mystery. The debtor also supplied the court with fictitious figures in an attempt to preserve the stay. The court found the debtor acted in bad faith and granted the secured creditor stay relief.

Another example of bad faith is when a Chapter 11 debtor acquired property postpetition. The debtor corporation was created on the eve of bankruptcy. The debtor's sole business was to hold numerous parcels of real property. The debtor was created to take care of difficult creditors of a nondebtor entity. The debtor had no employees, no priority wage claims, no unsecured claims, no trade claims, and no personal property. The debtor also had no liabilities (beyond the moving secured party) except for a minimal amount of real property taxes and administrative expenses created by the Chapter 11 filing. Accordingly, the debtor had nothing to lose by the bankruptcy filing. Any property transferred to the debtor postpetition outside the ordinary course of business of the debtor and without court approval was presumptively done in bad faith. [See *In re Oklahoma P.A.C. First Ltd. Partnership*, 122 B.R. 394 (Dist. Ariz. 1990).]

"Cause" also may be demonstrated by creditors to justify modification of the automatic stay to allow continuation of ongoing litigation outside the Bankruptcy Court. Often the litigation consists of personal injury or breach of contract suits. The Bankruptcy Court often will modify the automatic stay in such cases. This allows the litigation to continue in order to liquidate such creditor's claim but prevents the creditor from enforcing any judgment. Liquidating a claim merely means determining how much a debtor owes. After the claim is reduced to a sum certain, the creditor must then participate in the ongoing bankruptcy proceedings in order to collect. A creditor's responsibilities in a bankruptcy case are discussed in Chapter 9 of this text.

Lack of Equity and Inability to Reorganize

Under the separate provision of 11 U.S.C. §362(d)(2), stay relief may be granted if there is no equity in the property *and* the debtor is unable to effectively reorganize. Both prongs of 11 U.S.C. §362(d)(2) must be met.

Equity, in the context of stay relief, is the difference between the property value and the total amount of the liens against such property.[81] Note that, while junior liens may not be relevant in determining whether there is an "equity cushion" and thus adequate protection under 11 U.S.C. §362(d)(1), such junior liens are relevant in the "equity" analysis of 11 U.S.C. §362(d)(2).

Suppose, for example, a debtor had a first mortgage on his home in the amount of $100,000. Also, a second mortgage existed in the amount of $75,000. The home is worth $150,000. An equity cushion under subsection (d)(1) for purposes of adequate protection exists. The equity cushion available to the first mortgage would be $50,000. However, no equity under subsection (d)(2) exists. Under 11 U.S.C. Section 362(d)(2), equity would be the value of the property minus all liens, both senior and junior. Here, the amount of all liens less the value of the property is a negative $25,000. Therefore, no equity is present.

Stewart v. Gurley
745 F.2d 1194 (9th Cir. 1984)

Per Curiam. * * * On December 24, 1980, Gurley executed two trust deeds for an eleven unit apartment complex naming James P. Stewart as beneficiary. The trust deeds were executed to secure payment of promissory notes totalling $202,500. Gurley executed a third trust deed securing a $70,000 debt to the Bank of Newport, and a fourth trust deed securing a $150,000 debt to Norma Gurley. Gurley became delinquent on his payments to Stewart. On December 14, 1982, Stewart recorded a notice of default and election to sell. Stewart then initiated foreclosure proceedings but the proceedings were automatically stayed when Gurley filed for bankruptcy under Chapter 11.

On February 14, 1983, Stewart filed a complaint in Bankruptcy Court for relief from the automatic stay pursuant to 11 U.S.C. §362(d). Significantly, the junior trust deed holders, the Bank of Newport and Norma Gurley, did not seek relief from the automatic stay. Stewart alleged that Gurley lacked equity in the encumbered apartment complex because the total amount of the four liens exceeded the market value of the property and the property was not necessary to an effective reorganization of Gurley's business. Under 11 U.S.C. §362(d)(2) a party in interest is entitled to relief from the automatic stay of any acts against the property if "(A) the debtor does not have any equity in such property; and (B) such property is not necessary to an effective reorganization." * * *

The Bankruptcy Court concluded that Gurley lacked equity in the property because the property's market value did not exceed $300,000 while the four liens against it amount to over $400,000. Gurley argues that only the liens of secured creditors seeking relief from the automatic stay should be subtracted from the value of the property to determine whether the debtor has equity. Because Gurley's indebtedness to Stewart is approximately $210,000 and the property is valued at over $270,000, Gurley argues that he does have equity in the property.
   * * *

The language of the statute simply refers to the debtor's "equity," which has been defined as "the amount or value of a property above the *total* liens or charges." *In re Faires,* 34 B.R. 549 (Bankr.W.D.Wash. 1983) [quoting *Black's Law Dictionary,* 484 (5th ed. 1979) (emphasis added)]. The statute does not refer to the debtor's equity as against the only plaintiff-lienholder seeking to lift the stay or persons holding liens senior to that of the plaintiff-lienholder.

Affirmed.

The remaining prong of 11 U.S.C. Section 362(d)(2) requires a showing that the collateral at issue is "necessary to an effective reorganization." This requires not merely a showing that if there is conceivably to be an effective reorganization, the property will be needed for it.[82] It must be demonstrated that the property is essential for an effective reorganization *that is in prospect.*[83] There must be a reasonable possibility of a successful reorganization within a reasonable time.[84] *Necessary* property is property that will contribute to a plan of reorganization.[85]

Note: 11 U.S.C. Section 362(d)(2) is generally effective in Chapter 7 cases if there is no equity. Chapter 7 is a liquidation bankruptcy with *no* reorganization prospects. In Chapter 7, if a creditor can establish that the value of the property is less than all liens, the second prong is automatically shown since there is never a reasonable prospect to reorganize in Chapter 7.

Single-Asset Real Estate

Under the 1994 Amendments a new provision, 11 U.S.C. §362(d)(3), was added to provide creditors with a third basis upon which to request stay relief. Note: 11 U.S.C. §362(d)(3) applies only to cases that are considered "single-asset real estate" debtors. Single-asset real estate is defined as real property of a single property or project other than residential property with less than four units. This real property must generate substantially all of the income of the debtor. Also, the debtor must conduct no substantial business activity other than that of operating the real property. Finally, the amount of secured debt must be no more than $4,000,000.[86]

Under this section of stay relief, a creditor requesting stay relief must be a secured creditor upon the property. (The secured creditor cannot be a claim secured by a judgment or by an unmatured statutory lien). Further, to defeat this stay relief section the debtor must file a reasonable plan of reorganization within 90 days of the petition date. Note that a Chapter 11 debtor is usually given the first 120 days after the petition to file its plan. Otherwise, to defeat stay relief under this section the debtor must make monthly payments to each secured creditor on the property in an amount equal to fair market interest.

The later defense section is problematic since usually secured creditors are receiving most, if not all, of the rents collected from the property during the course of the bankruptcy. The rent received by secured creditors is called cash collateral.[87] This newly created stay relief section does not address whether such cash collateral payments to the secured creditors constitute the "payments" required as a second line of defense of the debtor. Additionally, substantial evidentiary issues will arise regarding "the fair market interest" that dictates the payment amount.

This new section was designed to address bankruptcies for enterprises such as shopping centers, malls, and office buildings.[88] Before this amendment the secured creditors' rights with respect to single-asset debtors were substantially limited. However, this section is notably confined to Chapter 11 cases.

STAY RELIEF BURDEN OF PROOF

The party requesting relief from the automatic stay has the burden of proof on the issue of the debtor's equity in the property under 11 U.S.C. Section 362(g). The party requesting stay relief is the creditor. Therefore, the creditor must prove the value of the property, usually through appraisals. The creditor must also prove the amount of its lien as well as any other junior liens on the property. The party opposing stay relief is usually the debtor. The debtor has the burden of proof on all other issues (including lack of "cause," adequate protection, that the property is necessary to an effective reorganization, etc.) A paralegal in a firm representing creditors should be able to recommend a variety of appraisers. This would include appraisers for either residential or commercial real property as well as appraisers for personal property, such as automobiles. Appraisers employed by creditors do not need prior Bankruptcy Court approval. A paralegal in a firm representing debtors has greater duties. The issues to be proven in defense of stay relief motions may include how much a property is depreciating. Therefore, appraisers must again be employed. However, a debtor's employment of these professionals requires Bankruptcy Court approval. Chapter 12 of this text discusses employment applications for these professionals. Also, the issue of whether a reasonable plan is in prospect is a mini version of a confirmation hearing. Confirmation is also treated in Chapter 12 of this text.

HEARING ON STAY RELIEF MOTIONS

11 U.S.C. Section 362(e) of the Bankruptcy Code provides that a preliminary hearing on a motion to lift the automatic stay must conclude within 30 days

from when the motion is filed. After the initial 30 days for a preliminary hearing, a final hearing to *conclude* the stay relief motion must be held within 30 days.[89] As can be seen, the Bankruptcy Code intends that stay relief motions be determined in a swift manner. The only exception to the limits on these hearing deadlines is through consent of the parties. Even with consent of the parties the Bankruptcy Court must find that any extension beyond the 60 day ultimate deadline is required by compelling circumstances.

This section was modified to achieve the speedy conclusion of hearings on the automatic stay. This reduces the time and cost of bankruptcy proceedings by preventing unjustified or unwarranted postponements of final action.

EXPEDITED STAY RELIEF

The Court is enabled to grant stay relief with an expedited hearing when it is necessary to prevent irreparable damage to the interest of an entity in property.[90] For example, emergency relief was granted when the debtor's shopping center was a public hazard and needed immediate structural repairs.[91]

CODEBTOR STAY

Additionally, Chapter 12 and Chapter 13 provide special protection for certain individuals who are obligated on debts along with debtors, even though such individuals have not filed bankruptcy themselves. This extension of the automatic stay is called the *codebtor stay*. The codebtor stay exists only for the benefit of *individual* codebtors of *consumer* debts.[92] The purpose of the codebtor stay is to relieve pressure on family members or relatives who cosigned consumer debts for a debtor.[93]

Since only individual codebtors are given relief under the codebtor stay, corporations or partnerships also liable on debts are not protected by the codebtor stay. *Consumer debts* are debts incurred primarily for a personal, family, or household purpose [11 U.S.C. Section 101(8)]. Examples of consumer debts are balances due on household furniture, family cars, jewelry, etc. Therefore, the codebtor stay does not protect co-obligors on business debts.[94] Business debts excluded from the codebtor stay include debt for as office furniture, commercial vehicles (such as a moving truck for a Chapter 13 debtor in the moving business), and unsecured signature loans used to fund business operations.

The codebtor stay prevents a creditor from taking any action against any individual who is liable on a consumer debt with the debtor. This includes the commencement or continuation of a state court lawsuit to collect the debt from the codebtor. The codebtor stay is automatic in Chapter 13 cases, the same as the automatic stay of 11 U.S.C. Section 362. The codebtor stay applies upon the filing of the Chapter 13 or Chapter 12 case, without regard to notice. Once a creditor requests relief from the codebtor stay, it automatically terminates after 20 days unless the debtor or the codebtor specifically objects.[95] A creditor may request relief from the codebtor stay in three specific situations:

1. *The codebtor received the consideration from which the creditor's claim arose* (as opposed to the debtor receiving the consideration).[96] Consideration is the thing given by the creditor in exchange for the debt incurred by the debtor and codebtor. Note that to seek stay relief under this section the codebtor must receive the consideration, not the debtor.

For example, if a debtor cosigned on a loan for her mother in order for the mother to purchase a mink stole, the mother has received the consideration (i.e., the coat). Note: If the mother cosigns in order that the debtor may purchase a mink coat, then the debtor has received the consideration and the codebtor stay will not be terminated. Also, if both the debtor and the codebtor share in the benefits, the codebtor stay will not be terminated.[97] For example, debtor and her mother cosign on the obligation for the mink coat and then share the coat. The codebtor stay will remain in place in this situation as well.

2. *The Chapter 13 plan filed by the debtor does not propose full payment of the cosigned obligation.*[98] A plan is the document submitted by the debtor which outlines the amounts and method where creditors get paid. In this section if the obligation is not paid through the Chapter 13 plan then relief from the codebtor stay may be granted. In other words, the obligation is not provided for (i.e., paid through) the Chapter 13 plan. Using our preceding example, the mink coat loan (whether the debtor or her mother uses such coat) is not included in the debtor's proposed plan. Accordingly, the codebtor stay will be terminated upon request of the creditor to collect the balance of the claim from the cosignor.

3. *The creditor can show irreparable harm by the continuation of the codebtor stay.*[99] "Irreparable harm" has been shown where the codebtor's financial condition is shaky, such as where the codebtor has lost her job. Also, irreparable harm includes if the codebtor appears ready to leave the jurisdiction, such as if the mother is ready to move to Canada. Further, when the value of the underlying collateral is shown to be deteriorating or the codebtor herself files bankruptcy, irreparable harm exists.

Under this section to show irreparable harm, the creditor must show something more than mere delay in collection from the codebtor. The creditor must show specific proof that the likelihood of collection from the codebtor is impaired. In other words, a creditor will not prevail if it can only show that collection of the debt is stalled but must prove that collection may not occur at all if the stay is not lifted.

Generally, request for relief from the codebtor stay does not need to be delayed while the debtor is making payments under her confirmed plan. In other words, the creditor may seek relief from the codebtor stay and at the same time receive payments by the debtor under the plan. Therefore, even if the debtor's plan pays the creditor in part or in full, relief from the codebtor stay is appropriate if there is irreparable harm or the codebtor has received the consideration.

The procedure for seeking relief from the codebtor stay is found in F.R.Bankr.P. 4001. Such request is a contested matter initiated by filing a motion (and fee) under F.R.Bankr.P. 9014. The burden of proof to establish the grounds for relief from the codebtor stay is on the creditor.[100] If no relief is sought or granted from the codebtor stay, it continues until the case is closed, dismissed, or converted to Chapter 7 or Chapter 11.

VIOLATIONS OF THE AUTOMATIC STAY

Under 11 U.S.C. 362(h) an individual injured by any willful violation of the stay is entitled to recover actual damages, including attorney's fees and costs. In appropriate circumstances an injured debtor may also recover punitive damages. Punitive damages are designed to punish the wrongdoer. Punitive damages are not based on how much the debtor was financially harmed. Rather, any award of punitive damages may be substantial in order to achieve a reprimand to the offending creditor, depending on the circumstances. It is a willful violation of the stay when a creditor violates the stay with knowledge that the bankruptcy petition has been filed. A creditor violates the automatic stay when it performs any conduct which is prohibited by the stay of 11 U.S.C. Section 362(a), discussed above. Willfulness for purposes of stay violations does not require that the creditor intended to violate the automatic stay. A creditor must merely intend to perform the acts which violated the stay.

For example, to be in violation, a creditor merely must intend to repossess a debtor's vehicle and not specifically intend to violate the stay provisions of 11 U.S.C. Section 362(a). A creditor's good faith belief that he or she is not violating the stay does not determine whether an action is willful.[101]

Willful violations of the stay occur, for purposes of assessing costs, fees, and damages, when a creditor acts deliberately and with knowledge of the bankruptcy proceedings. Generally, an award of punitive damages requires not only a finding of willful violation of the stay, but also a finding of appropriate circumstances, such as egregious, intentional misconduct on the violator's part.[102]

An example of willful violation of the stay is that creditors stated they thought the bankruptcy case had been dismissed, yet they also admit they knew of a second Chapter 13 case at the time of their foreclosure action.[103] Also, the IRS willfully violated the automatic stay, for purposes of imposing sanctions, by filing a notice of federal income tax lien postpetition with knowledge of the Chapter 13 debtor's bankruptcy filing.[104] Further, a landlord violated the automatic stay by filing an unlawful detainer action seeking possession of the property which the Chapter 11 debtor held as sublessee when the landlord knew of the petition and ignored specific warnings that the automatic stay would have to be lifted first.[105]

Debtors are entitled to be compensated for costs and expenses incurred by them as a direct result of a creditor's willful, knowing violation of the automatic stay. [See *In re Tyson*, 145 B.R. 91 (M.D. Fla. 1992) (IRS had sanctions imposed upon it for violating stay).] Punitive damages also may be imposed against anyone due to a willful violation of the automatic stay. For example, punitive damages were awarded against a creditor when it continued to file motions in state court postpetition,[106] and the court canceled a note and mortgage as a penalty for a creditor's willful stay violation.[107]

The procedure for initiating relief from a party's violation of the stay is not an adversary but a contested matter (F.R.Bankr.P. 9014). Accordingly, the request is a "motion for damages for violation of the stay" and brought within the general administrative case of the bankruptcy.

CONCLUSION

Whether a paralegal's duties include representation of either debtors or creditors, the powerful tool provided by the automatic stay must be understood. Also, all acts included or excluded from the automatic stay must be recognized by any bankruptcy paralegal as well as the consequences for violation of the automatic stay. Finally, the procedures and deadlines within stay relief litigation are essential knowledge for the bankruptcy paralegal.

REVIEW QUESTIONS

1. What is the automatic stay?
2. Name five (5) actions specifically prohibited by the automatic stay. Name five (5) actions specifically excluded from the automatic stay.

3. What is the duration of the automatic stay against estate property? What is the duration of the automatic stay against the debtor or property of the debtor?

4. How does a creditor request the automatic stay not apply to it? What are the three standards to make any such request?

5. What is the codebtor stay? What is the criteria for the codebtor stay? What bankruptcy chapter cases does the codebtor stay apply to?

6. On what basis can a creditor request the codebtor stay not apply to it?

7. What is it called when a creditor performs conduct which is prohibited by the automatic stay? What are the standards? What are the penalties?

ENDNOTES

[1]Violations of stay are void, not voidable. *Ellis v. Consolidated Diesel Elec. Corp.*, 894 F.2d 371 (10th Cir. 1990); *In re 48th St. Steakhouse*, 835 F.2d 427 (2nd Cir. 1987), cert. denied, 845 U.S. 1035 (1988); *Borg-Warner Acceptance Corp. v. Hall*, 685 F.2d 1306 (11th Cir. 1982); *Schwartz v. U.S.*, 954 F.2d 569 (9th Cir. 1992). But see *Sikes v. Global Marine, Inc.*, 881 F.2d 176 (5th Cir. 1989) (violations of the automatic stay are voidable and not automatically void).

[2]*In re Dembek*, 64 B.R. 745 (Bankr. N.D. Ohio 1986).

[3]*In re Clark*, 69 B.R. 885 (Bankr. E.D. Pa. 1987).

[4]*ICC v. Holmes Transp., Inc.*, 931 F.2d 984 (1st Cir. 1991).

[5]House Report (Reform Act of 1978), HR Rep No. 595, 95th Cong., 1st Sess. 3340-341 (1977).

[6]*Id.*

[7]*In re H & H Beverage Distributors*, 850 F.2d 165 (3rd Cir. 1988).

[8]*Farley v. Henson*, 2 F.3d 273 (8th Cir. 1993).

[9]*In re Ahlers*, 794 F2d 388 (8th Cir. 1986).

[10]*In re Paul*, 67 B.R. 342 (Bankr. Mass. 1986).

[11]*In re Nelson*, 994 F.2d 42 (1st Cir. 1993).

[12]*In re Parr Meadows Racing Assoc.*, 880 F.2d 1540 (2nd Cir. 1989).

[13]*Accredited Associates, Inc. v. Shottenefeld*, 162 Ga.App. 575, 292 S.E.2d 417 (1982).

[14]*In re Ionosphere Clubs, Inc.*, 105 B.R. 773 (Bankr. S.D. N.Y. 1989).

[15]*Matter of Cash Currency Exchange, Inc.*, 762 F.2d 542 (7th Cir. 1985).

[16]See *In re Elsinore Shore Assoc.*, 66 B.R. 723 (Bankr. D. N.J. 1986); *SBA v. Rinehart*, 887 F.2d 165 (8th Cir. 1989); *In re Bialac*, 712 F.2d 426 (9th Cir. 1983).

[17]*In re Prudential Lines, Inc.*, 119 B.R. 430 (S.D. N.Y. 1990).

[18]*In re Littke*, 105 B.R. 905 (Bankr. N.D. Ind. 1989).

[19]*Birk v. Simmons*, 108 B.R. 657 (Bankr. S.D. Ill. 1988).

[20]*Id.*

[21]*N.L.R.B. v. Bildisco*, 104 S.Ct. 1188 (1984).

[22]*In re Fuller*, 134 B.R. 945 (9th Cir.BAP 1992).

[23]*In re Miller*, 98 B.R. 110 (Bankr. N.D. Ga. 1989).

[24]*In re Claussen,* 118 B.R. 1009 (Bankr. D. S.D. 1990).

[25]*In re Johnson,* 138 B.R. 352 (Bankr. D. R.I. 1992).

[26]*Matter of M. Frenville Co., Inc.,* 744 F.2d 332 (3rd Cir. 1984).

[27]*Id.*

[28]*Matter of Roach,* 660 F.2d 1316 (9th Cir. 1981).

[29]*In re Dumas,* 19 B.R. 676 (9th Cir. BAP 1982).

[30]*Matrin-Trigona v. Champion Fed. Sav.,* 892 F.2d 575 (7th Cir. 1989).

[31]See *Austin v. Unarco Ind., Inc.,* 705 F.2d 1 (1st Cir. 1983); *Otoe County Nat. Bank v. W & P Trucking, Inc.,* 754 F.2d 881 (10th Cir. 1985).

[32]*In re Spencer,* 123 B.R. 858 (Bankr. N.D. Cal. 1991).

[33]*In re Advanced Ribbons and Office Products, Inc.,* 125 B.R. 259 (9th Cir. BAP 1991); *In re Rohnert Park Auto Parts, Inc.,* 113 B.R. 610 (9th Cir. BAP 1990).

[34]See generally, 11 U.S.C. §1301.

[35]*In re Smith Corset Shops, Inc.,* 696 F.2d 971 (1st Cir. 1982) (automatic stay prevents eviction actions).

[36]*In re Farmers Markets, Inc.,* 792 F.2d 1400 (9th Cir. 1986).

[37]*In re Stringer,* 847 F.2d 549 (9th Cir. 1988).

[38]*In re Pyramid Restaurant Equipment Co.,* 24 B.R. 455 (Bankr. W.D. N.Y. 1982).

[39]*In re Butler,* 14 B.R. 532 (S.D. N.Y. 1981).

[40]*In re Farmers Markets, Inc.,* 792 F.2d 1400 (9th Cir. 1986).

[41]*In re Jesus Loves You, Inc.,* 40 B.R. 42 (Bankr. M.D. Fla. 1984).

[42]*In re Elder,* 12 B.R. 491 (Bankr. M.D. Ga. 1981).

[43]*Bostwick v. U.S.,* 521 F.2d 741 (8th Cir. 1975).

[44]*In re Lewis,* 15 B.R. 643 (Bankr. E.D. Pa. 1981).

[45]*In re 48th Street Steakhouse, Inc.,* 835 F.2d 427 (2nd Cir. 1987), cert. denied, 485 U.S. 1035 (1988).

[46]*In re Big Squaw Mountain Corp.,* 122 B.R. 831 (Dist. Me. 1990).

[47]*Equibank v. Wheeling-Pittsburgh Steel Corp.,* 884 F.2d 80 (3rd Cir. 1989).

[48] As noted earlier, once the estate is created via commencement of the case, no interest in estate property remains in the debtor.

[49]*In re Murray,* 5 B.R. 732 (Bankr. D. Md. 1980).

[50]*In re Munsey Corp,* 10 B.R. 864 (Bankr. E.D. Pa. 1981).

[51]*In re Hellums,* 772 F.2d 379 (7th Cir. 1985).

[52]*In re Hub of Military Circle, Inc.,* 13 B.R. 288 (Bankr. E.D. Va. 1981).

[53]*In re Almodovar,* 35 B.R. 289 (Bankr. P.R. 1983).

[54]*In re Gustafosn,* 934 F.2d 216 (9th Cir. 1991).

[55]*In re Olson,* 38 B.R. 515 (Bankr. N.D. Iowa 1984).

[56]*In re University Medical Center,* 973 F.2d 1065 (3rd Cir. 1992).

[57]*In re Hagan,* 41 B.R. 122 (Bankr. D. R.I. 1984)

[58]See generally, *In re Altchek,* 124 B.R. 944 (Bankr. S.D. N.Y. 1991); *In re Newton,* 15 B.R. 708 (Bankr. N.D. Ga. 1981); *In re Ryan,* 15 B.R. 514 (Bankr. Md. 1981).

[59]*In re Fiorillo & Co.,* 19 B.R. 21 (Bankr. S.D. N.Y. 1982).

[60]*Missouri v. U.S. Bankruptcy Court for E. D.,* 647 F.2d 768 (8th Cir. 1981) cert. denied, 454 U.S. 1162 (1982).

[61]*In re Mansfield Tire & Rubber Co.*, 660 F.2d 1108 (6th Cir. 1981).

[62]*SEC v. First Financial Group*, 645 F.2d 429 (5th Cir. 1981).

[63]*In re Thomassen*, 15 B.R. 907 (9th Cir. BAP 1981).

[64]*In re Marchall*, 6 B.C.D.2d 698 (S.D. Ga. 1980).

[65]See generally, *In re D.M. Garber, Inc.*, 13 B.R. 962 (Bankr. N.D. Tex. 1981).

[66]*Penn Terra, Ltd. v. Dept. of Environmental Resources*, 733 F.2d 267 (3rd Cir. 1984).

[67][T]he violations complained of by DER included: mining of a bonded area, failure to maintain adequate backfilling equipment, failure to maintain adequate erosion and sedimentation controls, failure to pump pit water accumulations, failure to treat mine drainage properly, storage of top strata over gas lines, and failure to seal a deep mine pit.

The consent agreement required Penn Terra to complete all backfilling by operating one D-8 bulldozer or its equivalent, and one tractor scraper for eight hours a day, five days a week until reclamation of the mines was completed. * * *

[68]*In re Cohoes Industrial Terminal, Inc.*, 62 B.R. 369 (Bankr. S.D. N.Y. 1986) aff'd 70 B.R. 214 (S.D. N.Y. 1986) aff'd 831 F.2d 283 (2nd Cir. 1987).

[69]See Chapter 13, "Bankruptcy Procedure and Discovery."

[70]Check local rules for notice requirements in relation to stay relief motions.

[71]*Nazareth Nat. Bank v. Trina-Dee, Inc.*, 731 F.2d 170 (3rd Cir. 1984).

[72]*United Sav. Ass'n v. Timbers of Inwood Forest*, 484 U.S. 365, 108 S.Ct. 626 (1988).

[73]*Id.*

[74]*In re Mellor*, 734 F.2d 1396, 1400 (9th Cir. 1984). (A 20% equity cushion is sufficient adequate protection for a secured creditor.)

[75]*Id.*

[76]*Id.*

[77]*In re Wolksy*, 46 B.R. 262 (Bankr. D. N.D. 1984).

[78]*In re Little Creek Development Company*, 779 F.2d 1068 (5th Cir. 1986).

[79]*In re Arnold*, 806 F.2d 937 (9th Cir. 1986).

[80]*In re Beach Club*, 22 Bankr. 597 (Bankr. N.D. Cal. 1982).

[81]*Stewart v. Gurley*, 745 F.2d 1194 (9th Cir. 1984).

[82]*United Sav. Ass'n v. Timbers of Inwood Forest*, 484 U.S. 365, 108 S.Ct. 626 (1988).

[83]*Id.*

[84]*Id.*

[85]*In re Air Beds, Inc.*, 92 B.R. 419 (9th Cir. BAP 1988).

[86]11 U.S.C. §101(51).

[87]See Chapter 12, "Chapter 11 Practice," for a discussion on cash collateral.

[88]See Congressional Record Statements, 140 Cong. Rec. E2101 (Oct. 6, 1994).

[89]11 U.S.C. Section 362(e) was substantially modified by the 1994 Amendments.

[90]11 U.S.C. Section 362(f).

[91]*In re Montgomery Mall Ltd. Partnership*, 704 F.2d 1173 (10th Cir. 1983), cert. denied 464 U.S. 830 (1983).

[92]11 U.S.C. Section 1301(1).

[93]*In re SFW, Inc.*, 83 B.R. 27 (Bankr. S.D. Cal. 1988).

[94]*Id.*

[95]11 U.S.C. Section 1301(d).

[96]11 U.S.C. Section 1301(c)(1).

[97]*In re Rhodes*, 85 B.R. 64 (Bankr. N.D. Ill 1988).

[98]11 U.S.C. Section 1301(c)(2).

[99]11 U.S.C. Section 1301(c)(3).

[100]*In re Burton*, 4 B.R. 608 (Bankr. W.D. Va. 1980).

[101]*In re Lansdale Family Restaurants, Inc.*, 977 F.2d 826 (3rd Cir. 1992).

[102]*In re Knaus*, 889 F.2d 773 (8th Cir. 1989).

[103]*In re Taylor*, 884 F.2d 478 (9th Cir. 1989).

[104]*In re Pinkstaff*, 974 F.2d 113 (9th Cir. 1992).

[105]*In re Johnston Environmental Corp. v. Knight*, 991 F.2d 613 (9th Cir. 1993).

[106]*In re Bloom*, 875 F.2d 224 (9th Cir. 1989).

[107]*Hubbard v. Fleet Mortgage*, 810 F.2d 778 (8th Cir. 1987).

6 *Discharge*

A con man tricked you into investing $10,000 in precious Nigerian gems. The promised return of $1 million never materialized, and your $10,000 investment disappeared. You took swift action and sued the con man in state court. After many months of litigation and a two-week trial, you won the judgment. The judge specifically said you were defrauded. However, right after the judgment, the con man filed bankruptcy. Can he get away with this? Is there anything you can do?

INTRODUCTION

Discharge is the ultimate goal of every debtor filing bankruptcy. Discharge is the relief from personal liability on obligations or debts. In essence, when a discharge is received, the debtor is no longer legally bound to pay the debt. However, fully secured debts are not discharged since liens survive bankruptcy. [See *Nobelman v. American Sav. Bank*, 113 S.Ct. 2106 (1993).] Therefore, the secured creditor may recover the secured property if payment default exists, but may not proceed to collect any deficiency judgment against a debtor personally.

While discharge is the prized objective of debtors, the Bankruptcy Code provides certain limitations or safeguards on the extent of discharge. As a legal assistant, you will have close contact with the client and become familiar with the circumstances under which the debts arose. Therefore, you may be called upon to recognize certain dischargeability problems and voice your concerns to the supervising attorney.

Discharge is provided in Chapter 7,[1] Chapter 11,[2] and Chapter 13.[3] The discharge available to Chapter 13 debtors is greater than Chapter 7 in order to encourage reorganization and thus repayment of even a portion of the debts. Chapter 11 discharge limits individual debtors in substantially the same manner as individual debtors are treated within Chapter 7.[4]

Generally, the Bankruptcy Code interposes these discharge limits as safeguards to prevent debtor misconduct or for protection of basic public policy concerns. For example, a debtor who is untruthful in revealing all assets, tries to hide assets, or tries to escape paying child support should not expect discharge. The major discharge limitations are found within §727 and §523.

DENIAL OF DISCHARGE

Under 11 U.S.C. §727 a debtor may be denied discharge for *all* obligations. Accordingly, denial of discharge under §727 is severe. The safeguards within §727 include:

- Transferring property in order to defraud creditors.[5]
- Concealing or destroying records and books of debtor's finances.[6]
- Lying under oath in the bankruptcy case or withholding documents from the trustee.[7]
- Not being able to justify a debtor's loss of property.[8]
- Purposefully refusing to obey Court orders[9]

As can be seen, these restrictions keep a debtor "honest" and discourage any foulplay, which would allow debtors to keep assets that should otherwise go to the creditors.

Examples of when the court applied U.S.C. §727 to completely deny a debtors' discharge include when the debtor established a trust to shelter funds just prior to filing bankruptcy when those funds would have otherwise been distributed to the creditors. [See *In re Chastant*, 873 F.2d 89 (5th Cir. 1989).] Also, in *In re Couch*, 54 B.R. 682 (Bankr.E.D.Ark. 1985) the debtor intentionally failed to list on his statements and schedules certain ownership interest in stock and was denied discharged. When a debtor concealed assets discharge was also denied entirely. [See *In re Cycle Accounting Services*, 43 B.R. 264 (Bankr.E.D.Tenn. 1984).]

Debtor's "amnesia" or failure to explain loss of assets was the basis for denial of discharge in *In re Dolin*, 799 F.2d 251 (6th Cir. 1986), where the debtor's cocaine addiction and compulsive gambling were held to be unsatisfactory explanations for the loss of his assets. Even property that is acquired after the petition is filed and that is considered part of the bankruptcy estate must be properly reported to the court. [See *In re Jackson*, 141 B.R. 702 (Bankr. Ariz. 1992), where the court revoked the debtor's discharge since she did not report and surrender a house she inherited after her petition date because such property is considered estate property.]

Additionally, corporations and partnerships are not allowed discharges under Chapter 7.[10] These business entities are allowed discharge under Chapter 11, but only if they continue to conduct business. This encourages businesses to reorganize and thus allows the employees to keep their jobs. However, straight liquidation under Chapter 7 does not fulfill this policy of continued employment. Accordingly, once a corporate Chapter 7 debtor's assets have been liquidated, for all intents and purposes, the corporation ceases to exist.

Discharge is also denied to Chapter 7 debtors when they have already received a discharge within the prior six years. The prior discharge could arise from a previous Chapter 7, 11, 13, or 12 case.[11] This is to discourage "serial filers," or those who choose to file one bankruptcy after another. To live in perpetual bankruptcy does not fulfill the Bankruptcy Code's fundamental policy of a "fresh start."

NONDISCHARGEABILITY OF CERTAIN OBLIGATIONS

In addition to safeguards that entirely deny a debtor's discharge, the Bankruptcy Code also prevents certain particular obligations from being discharged within §523. These obligations are termed *nondischargeable* debts. Even if a debtor has one debt that is nondischargeable, all other debts may be completely discharged. Again, the Code inserts these safeguards to prevent debtor misconduct and to protect public policy interests.

Nondischargeable debts due to public policy include:

- Spousal or child support[12] and property settlement under a divorce decree[13] in order to provide for continued obligations to the family.

- Recent tax obligations or penalties for fraudulent tax returns or no tax returns filed whatsoever,[14] or governmental fines or penalties,[15] in order that the government may maintain fiscal stability.

- Recent student loans[16] to otherwise avoid a chill on the availability of student loans.

- Certain obligations incurred involving the FDIC[17] in response to the many recently failed savings and loans.

Additional obligations that are not dischargeable due to public policy under Section 523 have been added by the 1994 Amendments. These include any payment of an order of restitution under federal criminal code,[18] debts incurred in order to pay otherwise nondischargeable taxes,[19] and homeowners' association dues.[20]

Alimony/Support/Property Settlement

Often the tension in spousal/child support cases arises from 11 U.S.C. Section 523(a)(5) of the Code's language that support obligations "in the nature of alimony" are nondischargeable. The Bankruptcy Court is not held to the label of "support" or "alimony" within a divorce decree to ascertain if the obligation is "in the nature of alimony."[21]

For example, in *In re Raff*, 93 B.R. 41 (Bankr.S.D.N.Y. 1988) the court held the wife's 25% interest in her debtor/husband's medical degree was in the nature of alimony, rather than a property settlement, and was thus nondischargeable.

Accordingly, complexities arise when the court is called upon to distinguish between spousal/child maintenance and marital property division. *In re Campbell*, 74 B.R. 805 (Bankr. M.D. Fla. 1987) provides a six-part test to assist in this distinction as follows:

1. Whether the obligation is subject to contingencies, such as death or remarriage.
2. Whether payments are intended to balance the disparate income of the parties.
3. Whether the obligation is payable in installments or in one lump sum.
4. Whether there are minor children requiring support.
5. The respective health and level of education of the spouse.
6. Whether, in fact, there was a need for support at the time of the circumstances of a particular case.

A further example of a nondischargeable "alimony" debt, rather than property settlement, is as follows: Under a divorce decree a debtor owed to his former spouse monthly interest payments on a remaining $270,000 lump sum payment. The obligation was held to be nondischargeable support under 11 U.S.C. Section 523(a)(5). At the time of the divorce decree, the wife was not working, yet the debtor had income of $70,000 per year and had a net worth of $200,000. Additionally, the exwife had a long history of diabetes and attendant medical costs. At the time of the divorce decree, the parties came to an agreement based upon the debtor's repeated assurances that he would take care of her. Further, the exwife used the payments from the debtor to pay rent, food, entertainment, medical expenses, and car expenses. The Bankruptcy Court found that the obligations to the exwife were in the nature of support and therefore nondischargeable. [See *Bereziak v. Bereziak,* 160 B.R. 533 (E.D. Pa. 1993).]

Compare the preceding facts with the following: A debtor had an obligation under a divorce agreement to make mortgage payments on the marital residence for 12 years. The obligation was to continue notwithstanding the exwife's remarriage and would also become a debt owed to the exwife's probate estate should she die before the 12 years had expired. Further, at the time of the agreement the parties understood that the exwife and children would not reside in the home since she would be pursuing a legal education. Accordingly, the Bankruptcy Court found the debt to not be in the nature of support and therefore dischargeable. [See *In re Bedingfield,* 42 B.R. 641 (S.D.Ga. 1983).]

The 1994 Amendments have added 11 U.S.C. Section 523(a)(15) to provide greater protection for support obligations owed to a former spouse or child of a debtor in bankruptcy. Under 11 U.S.C. Section 523(a)(15), property settlement in a divorce decree is nondischargeable. The exceptions or defenses to this section require either that the debtor does not have the ability to pay such property settlement debts from income or property that is reasonably necessary for the debtor's own maintenance or support (or a dependent of the debtor), or the payment would not allow the debtor to continue in the operation of his or her business. An additional defense is that the discharge of such debt would result in a benefit to the debtor that outweighs the detrimental consequences to an exspouse or child.

This new section was added to ensure that a debtor could not use the protection of a bankruptcy filing to avoid legitimate marital and child support obligations. In some instances, divorcing spouses have agreed to make payments of marital debts, holding the other spouse harmless from those debts, in exchange for a reduction in alimony payments. In other cases, spouses have agreed to lower alimony based upon a larger property settlement. If such "hold harmless" and property settlement obligations are not found to be "in the nature of alimony or support," they are dischargeable under 11 U.S.C. Section 523(a)(5). Thereafter, the nondebtor exspouse would be saddled with substantial debt and little or no alimony or support. 11 U.S.C. Section 523(a)(15) makes such property settlement obligations nondischargeable in cases where the debtor has the ability to pay them and the detriment to the nondebtor exspouse from their nonpayment outweighs the benefit to the debtor of discharging such debts.

In short, the debt will remain dischargeable if paying the debt would reduce the debtor's income below that necessary for the support of the debtor and the debtor's dependents. The debt will also be discharged if the benefit to the debtor of discharging it outweighs the harm to the obligee ex-spouse.

For example, suppose a nondebtor spouse would suffer little detriment from the debtor's nonpayment of an obligation required to be paid under a hold harmless agreement. Perhaps the obligation could not be collected from the nondebtor spouse or perhaps the nondebtor spouse could easily pay the obligation. Under these circumstances the obligation would be discharged.

The benefits of the debtor's discharge should be sacrificed only if there would be substantial detriment to the nondebtor spouse that outweighs the debtor's need for a fresh start.

Taxes

In Chapter 7 cases, several criteria must be met in order to discharge taxes. First, the petition must not be filed within three years of the tax due date. Under Sections 523(a)(1) and 507(a)(7), income tax obligations of the debtor are not dischargeable if the last date on which a tax return could have been filed falls within three years of the date of the filing of the bankruptcy petition. Conversely, if the debtor files for bankruptcy after the three-year period, the debt is dischargeable.[22]

For example, for 1985 the debtor's tax return was due April 15, 1986. Debtor filed bankruptcy on April 4, 1989. The petition date was within three years of when the taxes were due. Accordingly, the taxes are nondischargeable. This is regardless of whether the debtor actually filed his 1985 tax return earlier than the due date of April 15, 1986.

The date a tax is last due is the date the return is due, including extensions, and not the date the return is actually filed. Accordingly, tax liability is made nondischargeable when a debtor applies for and receives extensions to file tax returns that extend the filing date to within the three-year period immediately before bankruptcy.

For example, debtors were granted an automatic extension for filing their 1986 tax returns that extended the due date to August 15, 1987. Debtors filed Chapter 7 on June 12, 1990. The petition date in this case was within three years of the extension date and not within three years of the initial due date (April 15, 1987). Accordingly, the 1986 taxes were due within three years of the bankruptcy petition and are therefore nondischargeable.

Further, if the return is filed late, the petition date must not be within two years of the actual date the late return was filed. Also, the petition cannot be filed within 240 days of a tax assessment. Tax assessment is when the taxing authority determines the amount of taxes owed and formally charges for those taxes through a notice of tax assessment to the taxpayer.

The preceding time frames are in addition to the requirement that the returns must, indeed, be filed and that the returns cannot be fraudulent. For example, if a return is filed via the IRS' filing of a substitute income tax return (i.e., "dummy" return) and the debtor never files a return, such taxes are nondischargeable.[23]

Further, in *In re Harris*, 49 B.R. 223 (Bankr.W.D.Va. 1985) the court rejected the debtor's argument that no fraud could exist since the debtor was high on heroin when he completed his tax return, and found the tax obligation was nondischargeable.

Finally, taxes allegedly owed by a Chapter 7 debtor to the government are discharged when the tax obligations were not assessed within 240 days prior to the commencement of the Chapter 7 case. Assessment made before 240 days of the petition date makes Section 523(a) provisions dealing with exceptions to discharge of tax obligations inapplicable. [See *In re King*, 96 B.R. 356 (Bankr. MD.Fla. 1989).]

Governmental Fines/Penalties

To be nondischargeable under Section 523(a)(7), a debt must be (1) for a fine, penalty, or forfeiture, (2) payable to and for the benefit of a governmental unit, and (3) other than compensation for actual pecuniary loss.[24] A government's pecuniary loss is actual monetary loss.

For example, the following have been declared nondischargeable under this "governmental fine/penalty" section:

- Court costs imposed as a part of condition of probation upon the conviction of a criminal drug charge.[25]

- An obligation to the state on a fine for violation of environmental protection laws.[26]

- A restitution obligation imposed following conviction of vehicular homicide and vehicular assault (even though such restitution is payable to and for the benefit of the victim since restitution orders operate to promote penal and rehabilitative interests of the state).[27]

- A civil contempt penalty imposed against the debtor by a state court for the debtor's refusal to surrender custody of children in violation of court order.[28]

- Restitution as a condition for probation for welfare fraud.[29]

- Monetary sanctions due to the Florida State Bar Association (for lawyers) imposed as a result of disciplinary proceedings brought against a debtor.[30]

Student Loans

To be nondischargeable, student loans must be guaranteed, at least in part, by a governmental unit and first become due within seven years of the petition date. Note: 11 U.S.C. Section 523(a)(8) does not refer to a "student debtor." Accordingly, educational loans that are cosigned by Chapter 7 debtors for the benefit of their children's education may also be nondischargeable.[31]

Also, a debtor's government-backed student loan first becomes due when the first installment was due.[32] Usually student loans are not due when they are first made. Rather, the first installment is delayed at least until the student has finished school. Also, the seven-year prepetition initial due date of the student loan excludes any suspension of the repayment period.[33] Accordingly, any suspension of the original repayment date,[34] any deferment granted for the repayment of the loan,[35] or even a new consolidation of the loan[36] potentially may enlarge the seven-year prepetition due date necessary for discharge.

However, the Bankruptcy Code may allow the discharge of student loans even when the seven-year rule has not been met if the debtor can show adequate hardship.[37] Hardship sufficient to discharge a student loan must be extreme. [See *In re Andrews*, 661 F.2d 702 (8th Cir. 1981), where the Court would not grant a hardship discharge unless the debtor could prove he could not repay the loan without sacrificing his minimum standard of living.]

Also, a twist to student loan dischargeability exists in Chapter 13 cases. In a Chapter 13 case, the discharge takes place only after all payments have been made under the plan. Note: Chapter 13 plans continue for at least three years and may last up to five years. Accordingly, to qualify for a discharge of the student loan seven-year time limit, the student loan must become due in only four years (in a three-year plan) or in as little as two years (in a five-year plan) before the debtor files for Chapter 13. In essence, the length of the Chapter 13 plan is subtracted from the seven-year period. What remains is the number of years necessary for a student loan to become due prior to the petition.

Caution is advised when pursuing a discharge of student loans in this manner. A Chapter 13 debtor may be subject to a student loan creditor's bad faith allegations since the debt would otherwise be nondischargeable under Chapter 7.[38] Bad faith allegations could result in the Chapter 13 case being dismissed in its entirety.

Debts Incurred to Pay Otherwise Nondischargeable Taxes

The 1994 Amendments included Section 523(a)(14), which states that debts incurred to pay a tax to the United States that would be nondischargeable under 11 U.S.C. Section 523(a)(1) are also nondischargeable. Accordingly, all loans which are used to pay Federal taxes are nondischargeable. This will preclude individuals from using their credit line advances on credit cards to pay their federal taxes and thereafter discharge the credit card obligations.

Homeowners' Association Dues

The 1994 Amendments included Section 523(a)(16) to except from discharge fees that become due to a condominium, cooperative, or similar membership association and that become due after the filing of a petition. However, such exception is only to the extent that the fee is payable for the time during which the debtor either lived in or received rent for the condominium or cooperative unit. Except to the extent that the debt is nondischargeable under this section, obligations to pay such fees would be dischargeable.[39]

Nondischargeable debts due to "wrongdoing" of a debtor include incurring the debt through fraud,[40] misconduct of a fiduciary,[41] and willful and malicious injuries.[42] Additionally, the Code was amended recently to exclude from discharge, injuries caused by a debtor while DUI.[43]

DUI Injuries

Death and personal injury caused while debtors are operating a motor vehicle while intoxicated or on drugs implicates both the public policy prohibitions against DUI as well as "wrongdoing" on debtors' behalf. Congress enacted 11 U.S.C. Section 523(a)(9) because of a concern with drunk driving on the highways.[44] To prevail under this section, a creditor must show that (1) the debtor was legally intoxicated under state (or other applicable) law and (2) liability resulted from the operation of a motor vehicle. Note: A motorboat is a "motor vehicle" under this Code section. Accordingly, intoxicated operation of boats and aircraft resulting in personal injury or death are included as nondischargeable obligations.[45]

Fraud

There are three separate nondischargeable fraud claims under 11 U.S.C. §523. The first is obtaining property or money through false representations. 11 U.S.C. Section 523(a)(2)(A) prevents a discharge of a debt incurred:

> for money, property, services, or an extension, renewal, or refinancing of credit, to the extent obtained by—
>> false pretenses, a false representation, or actual fraud, other than a statement respecting the debtor's or an insider's financial condition.

A creditor must prove the following allegations to except a debt from discharge pursuant to 11 U.S.C. §523(a)(2)(A):

1. The debtor made a false representation of fact.
2. The fact was material.
3. The debtor made the representation knowing it was false.
4. The debtor made the representation with the intent that the creditor act in reliance on the representation.
5. The creditor relied on the representation.
6. The creditor's reliance was justified; and
7. The reliance caused damage to the creditor.

[See *In re Dunston*, 117 B.R. 632, 637 (Bankr.D.Colo 1990).] Note: Intent to deceive sufficient for an 11 U.S.C. §523(a)(2)(A) claim is difficult to prove but may be inferred from surrounding circumstances.[46]

Additionally, a mere failure to fulfill a promise to pay for goods on credit is not fraudulent so as to make the debt nondischargeable. Fraudulent intent necessary to render a debt nondischargeable under 11 U.S.C. Section 523(a)(2)(A) must exist at the inception of the debt.[47] However, when a debtor purchases goods on credit and does not intend to pay for the goods or knows he or she is unable to comply with the requirements of the contract, the debt will be nondischargeable.[48]

For example, when a debtor procured a loan he told his creditors from the outset that he needed the loan because he was in financial trouble. The creditors did not inquire about the possibility of using debtor's retirement account for security until after they had already agreed to make the loan. Also, the debtor had recently paid off another loan that required a greater monthly payment. Accordingly, the debtor genuinely believed he could pay this loan as promised. Therefore, the debt was not procured through fraud or false pretenses and the debt was dischargeable. [See *In re Austin*, 73 B.R. 937 (Bankr. W.D. La. 1987).]

Matter of Allison
960 F.2d 481 (5th Cir. 1992)

Politz, C.J. * * * Roberts sold certain immovable property in New Orleans to the Allisons. The contract to sell the two residences called for credit sales, secured by second mortgages covering 80% of the purchase prices. The Allisons defaulted on the notes prior to taking bankruptcy. Citing 11

U.S.C. Section 523(a)(2)(A), Roberts maintains that their debt to her should not be discharged in bankruptcy because Allisons obtained her property through false pretenses, false representations, or actual fraud.

In the interim contract the Allisons agreed to limit the first, or primary mortgages on the properties to a maximum of 20% of the purchase price, thus assuring that Roberts would be fully secured for the credit portion. Prior to closing, counsel for the Allisons mailed copies of the proposed deeds and mortgages to George Blue, Roberts' attorney who was also her son-in-law. Blue promptly responded by calling for a revision of the instruments to include language which would "require that limit be placed on original and refinancing of 1st mortgage of 20% of value since we are financing 80% on 2nd." The documents produced by the Allisons' attorney at closing did not contain this language.

After hearing the testimony of those present at the closing, the Bankruptcy Court found that Blue refused to consummate the sales without the first mortgage limitations. Dean Allison agreed to the addition of the clauses. Apparently the clauses could not be added immediately because the secretary for Allison's counsel was at lunch. It was agreed that the clauses would be added upon her return and before the instruments were recorded. Thus assured, Roberts signed the deeds conveying her property to the Allisons. The limiting language was never added; in its place was an incomprehensible, meaningless provision.

On the very day that Dean Allison represented that the first mortgages would not exceed 20% of the market value he executed first mortgages for at least four times that amount, effectively negating Roberts' secured position. Roberts did not discover this until after the Allisons defaulted in payment and it became necessary for her to secure a judgment against them in state court for the unpaid balance. * * *

The discharge exception provided by 11 U.S.C. Section 523 does not discharge a debt for money, property, services, or an extension, renewal or refinancing of credit, to the extent obtained by—

> (A) false pretenses, false representation, or actual fraud, other than a statement respecting the debtor's or an insider's financial condition.

Section 523(a)(2)(A) contemplates fraud involving "moral turpitude or intentional wrong; fraud implied in law which may exist without imputation of bad faith or immorality, is insufficient." The misrepresentations must have been (1) knowing and fraudulent falsehoods, (2) describing past or current facts, (3) that were relied upon by the other party. (citations omitted). It is undisputed that the Allisons received "property", specifically real estate, from Roberts.

As to the first requirement, the Bankruptcy Court made the factual determination that Dean Allison effected an intentional and purposeful de-ception by feigning agreement to the first mortgage limit in order to get Roberts to sign the deeds of conveyance when, in fact, he had already made or was in the process of making arrangements for the first mortgage indebtedness far in excess of that limit... Dean Allison's statements were knowing and fraudulent within the meaning of section 523(a)(2)(A).

The second requirement is that the misrepresentations be of past or current acts; a promise to perform acts in the future is not considered a qualifying misrepresentation merely because the promise is subsequently breached. (citations omitted). A debtor's misrepresentations of his intentions, however, may constitute a false representation within the meaning of the dischargeability provision if, when the representation is made, the debtor has no intention of performing as promised... Dean Allison misrepresented the current fact of his future intention regarding the mortgages.

* * *

[Finally,] we need only ask whether Roberts, in signing the deeds conveying her property, in fact relied upon Dean Allison's representation that the first mortgages would not exceed 20% of the purchase price, thus leaving Roberts adequately secured on the 80% credit portion of the purchase price. After hearing the testimony of those present at the closing of the sales, the Bankruptcy Court found that Roberts' attorney refused to proceed with the closing without a limitation on the first mortgages as agreed to in the contract to sell, the initial agreement on the transactions. That assurance was forthcoming from Dean Allison. Roberts relied on that assurance in signing the deeds conveying her property on a credit basis. The requisite reliance for section 523(a)(2)(A) purposes exists. We therefore reinstate the ruling of the Bankruptcy Court that Dean Allison's debt is not dischargeable in bankruptcy.

The debtor's prepetition use of credit cards often raises dischargeability issues. For example, the debtor's continued use of a credit card after revocation of the card is patently nondischargeable under 11 U.S.C. Section 523(a)(2)(A).[49] However, with respect to prerevocation charges, the card issuer must prove that the debt was incurred through actual fraud. To determine fraudulent intent, the following factors are considered:

1. The length of time between charges made and the filing of the bankruptcy.
2. Whether an attorney had been consulted concerning the filing of a bankruptcy before the charges were made.
3. The number of charges made.
4. The amount of the charges.
5. The financial condition of the debtor at the time the charges were made.

6. Whether the charges were above the credit limit of the account.

7. Whether the debtor made multiple charges on the same day.

8. Whether the debtor was employed.

9. The debtor's prospects for employment.

10. The financial sophistication of the debtor.

11. Whether there was a sudden change in the debtor's buying habits.

12. Whether the purchases were made for luxuries or necessities.

[See *In re Dougherty*, 84 B.R. 653 (9th Cir. BAP 1988).]

Under Section 523(a)(2)(B) obtaining property or money through a false financial statement is nondischargeable. The elements that establish nondischargeability under this section are (1) the existence of a statement in writing concerning a debtor's financial condition, (2) that the statement is materially false, (3) that the statement is made with an intent to deceive, and (4) upon which the creditor reasonably relied. [See *Bonnett v. National Bank of Petersburg*, 73 B.R. 715 (C.D. Ill. 1987).] A material falsity in a financial statement can be premised upon inclusion of false information or upon omission of information about the debtor's financial condition, including concealment or understatement of material liabilities.

For example, a debtor made a substantial omission in a financial statement submitted to a vendor of a pizza restaurant when he represented that the current value of his interest in a trust was $230,000. However, the debtor was subject to distributions from the trust only over five years and the maximum trust fund money available at the time was $90,000. Therefore, the debtor's intent to deceive was inferred from the fact that nowhere on the document did it appear that there was any limitation on the debtor's access to the money held in trust. [See *In re Pretner*, 110 B.R. 942 (Dist. Colo. 1990).]

Finally, the Code presumes there is fraud when a debtor purchases luxury items on credit for over $1,000 within 60 days before bankruptcy or takes a cash advance of over $1,000 within 60 days before bankruptcy. What constitutes "luxury" for purposes of this section depends on the facts and circumstances of each case.[50] For example, items that were considered luxury goods were debts to gambling casinos,[51] designer perfume, lotion, handbags, cosmetics, and stuffed animals purchased as Christmas gifts,[52] and credit card debt for floral arrangements (incurred shortly prepetition).[53]

Meanwhile, items that were *not* considered luxury goods were groceries, gasoline, cigarettes, toiletries, car repairs, shoes, prescriptions, eyeglasses, and lumber;[54] a used van (debtor had a large family and traded in the old vehicle to make the purchase);[55] and a purchase of collector "Barbie" dolls and accessories (while irresponsible and foolish, the debtor did not intend to file bankruptcy at the time she ordered the items but filed bankruptcy on the advice of her attorney only after her husband informed her that he was filing bankruptcy; the debtor intended to make monthly payments for the dolls when she put them on her charge account).[56]

Fiduciary Defalcation

Under 11 U.S.C. Section 523(a)(4), debts incurred for fraud or defalcation while acting in a fiduciary capacity, embezzlement, or larceny are also nondischargeable. Three elements are required under this section. First, the debtor must have been acting in a fiduciary capacity. Next, there must exist an express trust status regarding the property at issue. Finally, the debtor must have breached the relationship by at least defalcation of funds.[57]

To determine whether a trust exists to establish a fiduciary capacity, state law determine whether a trust relationship exists. However, the question of who is a fiduciary is one of federal law.[58] Further, this section requires an express trust, not an equitable or implied trust. A technical or express trust requires a declaration of trust, a clearly defined trust res, and an intent to create a trust relationship.[59] A trust res is the body of the trust or that property which is held within the trust.

Defalcation does not require that a misappropriation be intentional, only that the funds were used for a purpose other than the purpose for which the trust was created.[60] Defalcation is a willful neglect of duty, even if not accompanied by fraud or embezzlement.[61]

For example, a debtor committed defalcation when he directed, while an officer of a corporation, the transfer of $200,000 to himself with no loan agreements, promissory notes, or security agreements provided in connection with these advances. No portion of such funds was ever repaid and no corporate purpose was furthered by the transfers. Accordingly, such debt was nondischargeable as fiduciary defalcation. [See *In re Moreno*, 892 F.2d 417 (5th Cir. 1990).]

Willful and Malicious

Under 11 U.S.C. Section 523(a)(6), willful and malicious injury by the debtor to another entity or to the property of another entity is also nondischargeable. This section seeks to protect persons and their property from intentional and unpermitted contacts such as assault or battery.[62]

However, reckless conduct is insufficient under 11 U.S.C. Section 523(a)(6). Instead, subjective intent to do the wrongful act is required. Subjective intent is where the debtor himself intended to perform the wrongful act. Yet, specific intent to harm the individual actually injured by the wrongful conduct is not required. Debtors must know or expect, or should have known, that their conduct was certain or almost certain to cause harm. Also, when the debtor consciously disregarded his duty, without just cause or excuse, in the manner that he should have known presented a risk of harm was present satisfies the intent element. Finally, the intent element of 11 U.S.C. Section 523(a)(6) is shown if the debtor was willing to risk the creditor's loss due to the prospect of personal benefit.[63]

Some examples of nondischargeable claims based upon assault and battery under 11 U.S.C. Section 523(a)(6) include a debtor's intentional shooting of the plaintiff,[64] a 4- to 5-minute beating in a crowded bar,[65] a debtor's assault with a knife on the creditor (despite defense of PMS),[66] and a debtor (who was a judge) kissing the court reporter (after the court reporter made it clear that he did not share the debtor's affections and would be harmed by the unwarranted kiss, debtor kissed court reporter anyway, despite judge's knowledge his kiss would be unwelcome).[67]

Additionally, the tort of conversion meets the requirements of 11 U.S.C. Section 523(a)(6). Conversion is when the debtor intentionally transfers property to one who is not entitled to it without authorization or approval of the person who is actually entitled to the property.[68] For example, a debtor sold a stamp collection of someone else's and took off with the funds. This misappropriation is conversion and is nondischargeable under 11 U.S.C. Section 523(a)(6). [See *In re Hyers,* 70 B.R. 764 (Bankr. M.D. Fla. 1987).]

Debts Omitted from Schedules

Creditors not included within a debtor's statements and schedules present particular hazards, even if unintentionally omitted. These unlisted claims are called unscheduled debts. Creditors who neither are listed by the debtor in the schedules of creditors filed with the court nor have otherwise learned of the bankruptcy case within a limited period of time may have their claims excepted from discharge under 11 U.S.C. Section 523(a)(3). Under Subsection (A), debts of unscheduled creditors who are not scheduled in time to file a timely proof of claim are excepted from discharge unless the creditor had notice or actual knowledge of the case in time to do so.

However, an unscheduled creditor with actual notice of a pending bankruptcy case has a duty to inquire as to certain deadlines. A creditor's actual knowledge means that somehow the creditor knew of the pending bankruptcy case, even if the creditor was omitted from the schedules. This may include the debtor actually telling the creditor about the bankruptcy. A creditor's duty to investigate deadlines or bar dates includes: (1) filing objections to discharge of the debtor or dischargeability of certain debts and (2) the deadlines for filing proofs of claims.[69] Therefore, a creditor's knowledge of the pending bankruptcy case is sufficient to bar its claim, even if unscheduled when the creditor, which takes no action even if the creditor never received an official notice of the case.

Note: Subsection (A) applies when the unscheduled creditor is not made aware of the case in time to file a timely proof of claim. In a no-asset Chapter 7 case, no bar date is usually set for filing proofs of claims.[70] Accordingly, in this scenario it is technically never too late to file a timely proof of claim. Therefore, some courts hold that an unscheduled creditor in a no-asset Chapter 7 case (in which no bar date has been set for filing proofs of claims) cannot take advantage of the exception provided by 11 U.S.C. Section 523(a)(3)(A). [See *Beezley v. California Land Title Co.*, 994 F.2d 1433 (9th Cir. 1993).]

11 U.S.C. Section 523(a)(3) is one of the most misunderstood exceptions to discharge. The court in *Beezley* stated that dischargeability is unaffected by scheduling a debt when a Chapter 7 case is a no-asset case and no bar dates for filing proofs of claim were set. The court reasoned that if the omitted debt is of a type covered by 11 U.S.C. Section 523(a)(3)(A), it has already been discharged by 11 U.S.C. Section 727. However, in Chapter 7 cases with no assets or bar dates, the date to file proofs of claims is never set and thus Section 523(a)(3)(A) is not triggered since it is never too late to permit timely filing of a proof of claim.

The distinction between 11 U.S.C. Section 523(a)(3)(A) and Section 523(a)(3)(B) is whether the debt arises from some intentional wrongdoing specified in 11 U.S.C. Section 523(a)(2), (4), or (6). Therefore, all debts not arising from fraud, fiduciary misconduct, or the commission of a malicious tort fall within 11 U.S.C. Section 523(a)(3)(A). All debts within subsection (A) are discharged despite lack of scheduling in a no-asset, no-bar-date case.

Meanwhile, subsection (B) of 11 U.S.C. Section 523(a)(3) pertains solely to such debts arising from intentional wrongdoing including fraud, fiduciary defalcation, or willful and malicious torts. To trigger Subsection (B), a creditor must demonstrate that the debt falls within either 11 U.S.C. Section 523(a)(2), (a)(4), or (a)(6).

Additionally, Section 523(a)(3)(B) provides a special rule for three types of nondischargeable debts (namely, fraud/false financial statement, fiduciary defalcation, and willful/malicious conduct). For these types of claims, the debts are nondischargeable if they are not listed and the creditor does not have knowledge of the case in time to file a proof of claim or a complaint to determine dischargeability. Again, even unscheduled debts arising under fraud, fiduciary defalcation, or willful/malicious conduct will be discharged if the creditor had actual notice of the bankruptcy case in time to file a dischargeability complaint.[71]

Prior Bankruptcies

Debts affected by a prior bankruptcy where the global discharge of 11 U.S.C. Section 727 was denied (or waived) are also excepted from discharge in any later bankruptcies under 11 U.S.C. Section 523(a)(10). In short, debts existing at the beginning of a case wherein a debtor is denied discharge under 11 U.S.C. Section 727 can never be discharged in any bankruptcy case filed any time later.

Likewise, a determination of nondischargeability of a debt in an initial case under Section 523 also has the same effect in any subsequent bankruptcy case. In other words, if a debt was declared nondischargeable [under Section 523(a)(2), (4), (5), (6), (9), (13), (14), (15), or (16)], then the debt is forever barred from being discharged in subsequent cases.

However, if the debtor merely "jumps the gun" and waits only four years since the last bankruptcy (instead of the requisite six), the denial of discharge in the premature case will not preclude the discharge of the debts in any later case. Also, if a case is dismissed, the dismissal does not bar a later discharge of the debts that were dischargeable in the dismissed initial bankruptcy case.

PLAINTIFFS IN NONDISCHARGEABILITY ACTIONS

Creditors are the appropriate plaintiffs in dischargeability actions based upon Section 523(a)(2) (fraud/false financial statement), 523(a)(4) (fiduciary defalcation), 523(a)(6) (willful and malicious conduct), or 523(a)(15) (property settlement under divorce). The burden on all other nondischargeability sections is upon the debtor to bring and resolve the dischargeability of the claims.

For example, suppose a debtor never brought a dischargeability action regarding a student loan. After the bankruptcy was over, if the student loan creditor believed the debt had not been discharged it could attempt to collect, including a state court collection action. Of course, the debtor could raise the discharge as a defense in the state court collection action. However, in order to have the Bankruptcy Court resolve the matter, the debtor must institute the dischargeability action during the course of the bankruptcy.[72]

Procedural Aspects of Nondischargeability Actions

Deadlines. In Chapter 7, 11, and 12 cases, a creditor's bar date for complaints to determine dischargeability of Sections (2), (4), (6), and (15) of 11 U.S.C. Section 523(a) is 60 days after the first date set for the 341 First Creditors'

Meeting under F.R.Bankr.P. 4007(c) and 4004(a). Likewise, in a Chapter 7 case, complaints objecting to discharge (11 U.S.C. Section 727) also must be filed within 60 days of the first date set for the 341 First Creditors' Meeting.

Procedure. Requests to determine dischargeability of a claim (11 U.S.C. Section 523) or debtor's discharge (11 U.S.C. Section 727) must be filed by complaint. This is filed as an adversary proceeding. [F.R.Bankr.P. 7001.] A summons must be issued by the Bankruptcy Clerk's office and the summons and complaint must be served on the defendants. The adversary proceeding itself will be subject to the discovery rules of Bankruptcy Procedure. [See F.R.Bankr.P. 7026-7037 (incorporating F.R.Civ.P. 26-37).][73]

In Re Williamson
15 F.3d 1037 (11th Cir. 1994)

Per Curiam: * * * Joe Williamson filed a voluntary petition for bankruptcy under 11 U.S.C. Chapter 11 on November 14, 1991. Durham filed an Adversary Proceeding to determine dischargeability of a debt under 11 U.S.C. Section 523(a)(2)(A) on March 5, 1992, sixteen days after the sixty day period specified in 11 U.S.C. Section 523(c). Williamson filed a motion to dismiss based on Rule 4007 of the Bankruptcy Rules of Civil Procedure which provides that "a complaint to determine the dischargeability of any debtor pursuant to Section 523(c) of the Code shall be filed not later than 60 days following the first date set for the meeting of creditors held pursuant to Section 341(a)." On September 21, 1992 the bankruptcy court dismissed Durham's complaint on the basis that it was not timely filed.

* * * Durham presents four issues on appeal: (1) whether the filing was timely due to an affirmative statement in the initial Bankruptcy Notice that the filing deadline was "to be set;" (2) whether the failure of the clerk to give a thirty day notice of the dischargeability complaint deadline pursuant to Rule 4007 ("the court shall give all creditors not less than 30 days notice of the time so fixed in the manner provided in Rule 2002") stays the sixty day limit: (3) whether this lack of notice is a violation of its Fifth amendment right of due process; and (4) whether principles of equity demand that its Complaint be heard on the merits.

The fact that the notice stated that the deadline was "to be set" does not relieve Durham of its duty to file within the time prescribed by Rule 4007. In a similar case, the Fifth Circuit held that the creditor was on notice of the time limit even though the clerk left the space for the deadline to file objections to dischargeability blank and the clerk's office gave subsequent assurances that no deadline had been set. *Neeley v. Murchin-*

son, 815 F.2d 345 (5th Cir. 1987). . . Durham acted unreasonably in waiting for subsequent notice instead of following the clear requirements of Rule 4007.

* * * A holding that the language of 4007(c) about notice gives a creditor the right to such official notice before he is under a duty to make inquiries to protect his own rights would conflict with the language of 11 U.S.C. Section 523, which makes actual notice sufficient to impose a duty-to-inquire on the creditor. (citations omitted)...

Durham had actual notice of the bankruptcy proceeding. Even though the initial notice said the filing deadline was "to be set," Durham was on notice of the proceeding and the requirements of Rule 4007. The sixty day deadline applies regardless of the thirty day notice if the creditor has actual notice of a bankruptcy proceeding and sufficient time to file a dischargeability complaint. This is not a case where the creditor relied on an incorrect date given by the court. This conflict could have been easily avoided by Durham by filing within the sixty day period. Durham could very easily have determined the outside deadline itself. It was unreasonable to rely on future information.

This case does not present a due process violation. Durham received actual written notice of the proceeding. This was sufficient to put Durham on notice of the pending action. (citations omitted). Durham does not argue that it was unaware of the pending action, only that it should have received additional notice. The Fifth Amendment does not require such additional notice.

The equities in this case do not justify the disregard of the time provisions in the Bankruptcy Code. "The time specifications set out in the Bankruptcy Code are sufficiently clear to have placed an obligation on creditor [Durham] to follow the case and to take the timely action necessary to pursue [its] claim." (citations omitted). The difference between no notice from the clerk and the "to be set" notice in this case does not justify different treatment. In both cases the creditor was on actual notice of the pending action. Durham could have protected itself by simply filing within the sixty day period set forth in Rule 4007. It was Durham's inaction and not any action by Morrison or the court that caused the filing to be late. Any harm to Durham could have been avoided by simply following Rule 4007.

The Bankruptcy Court properly dismissed Durham's Adversary Proceeding as not timely filed. The decision of the Bankruptcy Court is hereby affirmed.

Burden of Proof. The objecting creditor must prove the nondischargeability of its claim by a preponderance of the evidence. [See *Grogan v. Garner,* 498 U.S. 279 (1991).]

SANCTIONS AVAILABLE TO DEBTOR

The Bankruptcy Court is required to award costs and reasonable attorney's fees to a debtor who successfully defends a fraud dischargeability case based on consumer debt. [11 U.S.C. Section 523(d).] These sanctions are mandatory unless the position of the creditor is found to be substantially justified or unless the awarding of the fees would be clearly inequitable. *Consumer debt* is debt incurred by an individual primarily for a personal, family, or household purposes.[74] Therefore, when a creditor fails to present any colorable claim on the issue of intent to defraud, then sanctions in the way of attorney's fees and costs are appropriate.[75] The purpose of the sanction provision of 11 U.S.C. Section 523(d) is to discourage creditors from initiating meritless nondischargeability litigation in the hopes of obtaining a settlement from an honest debtor anxious to save attorney's fees. Such practices impair the debtor's fresh start.

APPLICABILITY OF SECTION 523 TO CHAPTERS 7, 11, AND 13

All of 11 U.S.C. Section 523 applies to Chapter 7 cases. In Chapter 11 cases "the confirmation of a plan does not discharge an individual debtor from any debt excepted from discharge under Section 523 of this title." [11 U.S.C. Section 1141.] Therefore, all of Section 523 applies to all individual Chapter 11 debtors but not corporate or partnership Chapter 11 debtors.

Finally, Chapter 13 has a "superdischarge" provision within 11 U.S.C. Section 1328(a). This provision allows only a select number of the Section 523 exceptions to apply in Chapter 13. The exceptions to discharge in Chapter 13 therefore are Section 523(a)(5) (support/maintenance), Section 523(a)(8) (student loans), and Section 523(a)(9) (DUI injuries). However, note that Chapter 13 also excepts from discharge restitution or criminal fines included in a debtor's criminal sentence. [11 U.S.C. Section 1328(a)(3).]

EFFECT OF DISCHARGE

11 U.S.C. Section 524(a)(1) provides that a discharge voids a judgment to the extent that it is a determination of personal liability of the debtor. Once the discharge order is entered an injunction is placed on any action to collect the debt as a personal liability of the debtor. Therefore, the effect of a discharge is to interpose a permanent injunction against debt collection.

A willful violation of the permanent injunction may, in appropriate circumstances, lead to an award of sanctions against the creditor. The term "willful" means a deliberate and intentional act done with the knowledge that the act violates a discharge injunction.[76] Also, the debtor's attorney's fees may be assessed against a creditor that willfully disobeys the discharge injunction.[77]

The injunction is to give complete effect to the discharge and to eliminate any doubt concerning the effect of the discharge as a total prohibition on debt collection efforts. The injunction covers any act to collect, such as dunning by telephone or letter, or indirectly through friends, relatives, or employers, harassment, threats of repossession, and the like. This is intended to ensure that, once a debt is discharged, the debtor will not be pressured in any way to repay it.[78]

CONCLUSION

A bankruptcy paralegal must be able to recognize the conduct which would completely prevent a debtor's discharge as well as certain particular debts which are nondischargeable under the various bankruptcy chapters. Also, a paralegal's duties may include the drafting and service of any dischargeability complaints and/or answers. A paralegal has substantial responsibilities in dischargeability litigation to obtain facts to prove/disprove all the elements of an action brought under 11 U.S.C. Section 523. Therefore, the knowledge of the elements within the different types of nondischargeability actions is crucial. Finally, the paralegal should recognize the importance and effect of a debtor's ultimate discharge.

REVIEW QUESTIONS

1. What is a discharge?

2. In Chapter 7 cases, under what circumstances could a debtor be denied discharge completely?

3. What are the exceptions to discharge of individual debts in Chapter 7 bankruptcy cases?

4. What are the exceptions to discharge of individual debts in Chapter 13 bankruptcy cases?

5. In what situations does a creditor request that a debt not be discharged? What are the deadlines for these creditors? In what form is the request made? Under what circumstances does a debtor request the court to find a debt dischargeable?

6. If a debtor wins a dischargeability matter, can he collect his attorney's fees from the creditor? Under what circumstances?

7. If a creditor has a state court judgment against a Chapter 7 debtor for fraud, does it matter in dischargeability litigation? Why?

8. What is the effect of a discharge order?

ENDNOTES

[1] 11 U.S.C. §727

[2] 11 U.S.C. §1141/

[3] 11 U.S.C. §1328

[4] See §1141(d)(2), which incorporates §523 restrictions, and §1141(d)(3)(C), which incorporates the restrictions within §727(a).

[5] §727(a)(2)

[6] §727(a)(3)

[7] §727(a)(4)

[8] §727(a)(5)

[9] §727(a)(6).

[10] §727(a)(1)

[11] §§727(a)(8), (9).

[12] §523(a)(5)

[13] 11 U.S.C. Section 523(a)(15).

[14] §523(a)(1)

[15] 11 U.S.C. Section 523(a)(7).

[16] §523(a)(8)

[17] §§523(a)(11), (12)

[18] 11 U.S.C. Section 523(a)(13).

[19] 11 U.S.C. Section 523(a)(14).

[20] 11 U.S.C. Section 523(a)(16).

[21] *In re Palm v. Palm,* 142 B.R. 976 (Dist. Wyo. 1991).

[22] *In re Molina,* 99 B.R. 792 (S.D. Ohio 1988).

[23] *In re Rench,* 129 B.R. 649 (Bankr. D. Kan. 1991).

[24] *In re Hollis,* 810 F.2d 106 (6th Cir. 1987).

[25] *In re Hollis,* 810 F.2d 106 (6th Cir. 1987).

[26] *In re Carracino,* Bankr.L.R. 70816 (Dist. N.J. 1985).

[27] *Steiger v. Clark County,* 159 B.R. 907 (9th Cir. BAP 1993).

[28] *In re Gedeon,* 31 B.R. 942 (Dist. Colo. 1983).

[29] *In re Pellegrino,* 42 B.R. 129 (Bankr. D. Conn. 1984).

[30] *The Florida Bar v. Cillo,* 159 B.R. 340 (Bankr. M.D. Fla. 1993).

[31] *In re Pelkowski,* 990 F.2d 737 (3rd Cir. 1993).

[32]*In re Nunn*, 788 F.2d 617 (9th Cir. 1986).

[33]11 U.S.C. Section 523(a)(8)(A).

[34]*In re Eckles*, 52 B.R. 433 (E.D. Wis. 1985).

[35]*In re Rahlf*, 95 B.R. 572 (Bankr. N.D. Ill. 1988).

[36]*In re Saburah*, 136 B.R. 246 (Bankr. C.D. Cal. 1992).

[37]§523(a)(8)(B)

[38]See *In re Ali*, 33 B.R. 890 (Bankr. D. Kan. 1983); *In re Hawkins*, 33 B.R. 908 (Bankr. S.D. N.Y. 1983).

[39]See *Matter of Rosteck*, 899 F.2d 694 (7th Cir. 1990).

[40]§523(a)(2)

[41]§523(a)(4)

[42]§523(a)(6)

[43]§523(a)(9)

[44]See *State Farm Mut. Auto. Ins. Co. v. Mahlman*, 136 B.R. 723 (Bankr. S.D. Ohio 1992).

[45]*In re Williams*, 101 B.R. 356 (Bankr. S.D. Fla. 1989) aff'd 111 B.R. 361 (S.D. Fla. 1989).

[46]*In re Hulquist*, 101 B.R. 180 (9th Cir. BAP 1989).

[47]*In re Fontana*, 92 B.R. 559 (Bankr. M.D. Ga. 1988).

[48]*In re Faulk*, 69 B.R. 743 (Bankr. N.D. Ind. 1986).

[49]*In re Dougherty*, 84 B.R. 653 (9th Cir. BAP 1988).

[50]*In re Faulk*, 69 B.R. 743 (Bankr. N.D. Ind. 1986).

[51]*Trump Plaza Assoc. v. Poskanzer*, 143 B.R. 991 (Bankr. D. N.J. 1992).

[52]*In re Williams*, 106 B.R. 87 (Bankr. E.D. N.C. 1989).

[53]*In re Barthol*, 75 B.R. 305 (Bankr. S.D. Ohio 1987).

[54]*In re Tondreau*, 117 B.R. 397 (Bankr. N.D. Ind. 1990).

[55]*In re Davis*, 56 B.R. 120 (Bankr. D. Mont. 1985).

[56]*Sears Roebuck & Co. v. Johannsen*, 160 B.R. 328 (Bankr. W.D. Wis. 1993).

[57]*In re Boshell*, 108 B.R. 780 (Bankr. N.D. Ala. 1989).

[58]*In re Schnitz*, 52 B.R. 951 (W.D. Mo. 1985).

[59]*In re Boshell*, 108 B.R. 780 (Bankr. N.D. Ala. 1989).

[60]*Id.*

[61]*In re Moreno*, 892 F.2d 417 (5th Cir. 1990).

[62]*In re Price*, 123 B.R. 42 (Bankr. N.D. Ill. 1991).

[63]*In re Keller*, 106 B.R. 639 (9th Cir. BAP 1989).

[64]*In re Morton*, 100 B.R. 607 (Bankr. N.D. Ga. 1989).

[65]*In re Martinez*, 110 B.R. 353 (Bankr. N.D. Ill. 1990).

[66]*In re Irvin*, 31 B.R. 251 (Bankr. D. Colo. 1983).

[67]*In re Miera*, 926 F.2d 741 (8th Cir. 1991).

[68]*Vulcan Coals, Inc. v. Howard*, 946 F.2d 1226 (6th Cir. 1991).

[69]*In re Price*, 79 B.R. 888 (9th Cir. BAP 1987) aff'd 871 F.2d 97 (9th Cir. 1989).

[70]F.R.Bankr.P. 2002(e).

[71]*Briley v. Hidalgo*, 981 F.2d 246 (5th Cir. 1993).

[72]If the matter arises once his bankruptcy case is closed, a debtor may also request the case be re-opened to litigate the dischargeability matter before the Bankruptcy Court. Reopening a case is discussed in Chapter 10 of this text.

[73]See also Chapter 13, "Bankruptcy Procedure and Discovery."

[74]11 U.S.C. Section 101(8).

[75]*In re Carmen*, 723 F.2d 16 (6th Cir. 1983).

[76]*In re Leber*, 134 B.R. 911 (Bankr. N.D. Ill. 1991).

[77]*In re Wasp*, 137 B.R. 71 (Bankr. M.D. Fla. 1992).

[78]H.R. Rep. No. 595, 95th Cong., 1st Sess. 363-65 (1977); S. Rep. No. 989, 95th Cong., 2nd Sess. 80 (1978).

7 *Dismissal/Conversion*

Three weeks ago you prepared the emergency Chapter 13 filing for a nice couple to save their house from being foreclosed on and their car from being repossessed. The Bankruptcy Court threw their case out yesterday because their plan wasn't filed in time. The car company came and repossessed their car in the middle of the night last night. A foreclosure on their house is scheduled for tomorrow. How could this have been avoided?

INTRODUCTION

Dismissal of a bankruptcy case is the removal of the case from bankruptcy jurisdiction. Dismissal removes further case administration within the Bankruptcy Court. Additionally, the automatic stay is no longer in effect upon dismissal of the case. Once the case is dismissed, the creditors may pursue their state law rights and remedies.

Conversion of a bankruptcy case is the changing (voluntarily or involuntarily) of the chapter of the case. For example, a Chapter 11 reorganization case may "convert" to a liquidating Chapter 7 case. Likewise, a consumer reorganization case (Chapter 13) may also convert to Chapter 7. Also, Chapter 7 cases may "convert" to either Chapter 11, 12, or 13 if they otherwise meet the eligibility requirements.

Dismissal and/or conversion may be *voluntary* (with the consent of the debtor) or *involuntary* (brought by a creditor, U.S. Trustee, or by the Bankruptcy Court itself). A debtor may wish to voluntarily dismiss its case if the reason for the bankruptcy has been resolved. For example, settlement with major creditors may have occurred during bankruptcy, an appeal of a state court action may have been won, or the property sought to be saved through bankruptcy has been foreclosed upon after stay relief was granted. Debtors may wish to voluntarily convert their case if they find themselves ineligible for the chapter originally filed under, or if reorganization proves to be either impossible or more advantageous under a different chapter.

Creditors may wish to dismiss a bankruptcy case so they may immediately proceed against the debtor without the restraints of the automatic stay. Creditors may wish a case to be converted if it will result in a greater ultimate distribution to them. For example, a creditor may wish a Chapter 11 case be converted to Chapter 7 liquidation to reduce the accruing expenses of the Chapter 11 which diminish any potential distribution to creditors.

A case may be dismissed or converted in essentially three ways. The first manner in which a case is dismissed or converted is based upon an administrative deficiency. This is where some procedural defect causes the dismissal or conversion, such as the debtor's lack of appearance at the 341 First Creditors' Meeting or a debtor's failure to file schedules. The next way a case could be dismissed or converted is brought about by a creditor's request to the Bankruptcy Court. Finally, a case may be dismissed or converted upon a debtor's own request.

ADMINISTRATIVE DISMISSAL

Dismissal of a bankruptcy case is most frequently brought about due to the debtor's failure to comply with a Bankruptcy Code or Rule requirement or lack of compliance with the Court's or trustee's requirements. This may range from paying certain fees to a debtor's failure to timely file reports of its business activities. The Court is empowered, usually through the local rules of the district, to dismiss cases based upon such failures. In most instances but not always, the Court shall notify debtors of the impending dismissal to allow them time to cure the deficiency.

For example, the Bankruptcy Court may send an Order to Show Cause why a case should not be converted or dismissed based upon a Chapter 11 corporate debtor's failure to appear in the case through counsel. At the hearing on the OSC, the debtor must either be represented by an attorney or the Bankruptcy Court will either dismiss the case entirely, or convert the Chapter 11 to Chapter 7.

The U.S. Trustee's Office files formal motions to dismiss or convert with the Court for any failure to file documents or make payments. Requests for dismissal from the U.S. Trustee's Office will allow an opportunity for a hearing on such matters. The most common motions to dismiss or convert filed by the U.S. Trustee's Office are based upon a Chapter 11 debtor's failure to file its monthly financial statements, failure to pay the required U.S. Trustee's quarterly fees, or failure to file a Chapter 11 plan in a prompt manner.

Also, the Chapter 13 trustee may object to certain plan provisions of a debtor or require that the debtor demonstrate certain confirmation issues. These objections and requirements are noted within the Court minute entries or within notices to the debtor. These objections and requirements usually come with specific deadlines for the debtor. If the debtor fails to remedy the objection or comply with the trustee's requirements a request for automatic dismissal will be filed with the Court without further hearing. A common example is when the Chapter 13 trustee requires the debtor to file all delinquent tax returns by a certain date. If the debtor does not bring his tax filings current and send a copy to the Chapter 13 trustee within the deadline, the case may be dismissed or converted.

Court Dismissals

The Bankruptcy Court may also dismiss or convert a case *sua sponte*.[1] Often a bankruptcy is filed in an emergency situation. These "emergency filings" invoke the automatic stay and stop pending foreclosure sales, garnishment of wages, tax seizures, sheriff's levies, and similar collection activity. It is not uncommon for the local rules to allow the debtor to file an emergency filing and include only a select number of all the required initial documents. Universally, the required emergency filing documentation includes the petition, master mailing list, and often the list of the top 20 unsecured creditors. (Check with the local rules in your district to ascertain whether emergency filings are permitted and, if so, which documents must be filed.)

When a limited number of documents is initially filed, local rules also state the deadline after the emergency filing by which the remaining statements and schedules must be filed (e.g., all remaining schedules must be filed within 15 days of the petition date). Should the debtor fail to submit the remaining documents within the deadline, the Court may automatically dismiss the case without advance notice to the debtor.

Additionally, pro se debtors (debtors representing themselves) may request of the Bankruptcy Court to pay the filing fee in installments. If granted, a schedule for the remaining payments is provided to the debtor. Again, should the debtor fail to make the installment payments to the Court on schedule, the Court may automatically dismiss the case without any advance notice to the debtor.

Often a Chapter 13 plan is not filed with the initial statements and schedules. Analysis of the plan, along with negotiations with creditors, may take place after the filing of the initial petition. Local rules also govern when the Chapter 13 plan must be filed by the debtor. Again, the deadline is usually short with the plan being due 15 days from the petition date. Should a Chapter 13 debtor fail to file a plan in a timely manner, the Court may automatically dismiss the case without advance notice to the debtor.

Regardless of which chapter relief is sought under, a debtor is required to attend the First Creditors' Meeting. [11 U.S.C. Section 341(a).] These meetings are often called 341 Meetings. At the 341 Meetings, creditors as well as the trustee or U.S. Trustee are allowed to question the debtor. The debtor is placed under oath and answers the questions regarding jurisdictional matters and whether the debtor may file bankruptcy in that district. Questions may also concern the statements and schedules filed with the Court and whether there are available assets. Other issues which may be raised at the 341 Meeting may include a debtor's concealment of assets, a debtor's eligibility under particular Chapters, or issues relating to a particular creditor's obligation such as reaffirmation.

Should a debtor fail to attend the 341 First Creditors' Meeting, the Court will automatically dismiss the case. Note: In some districts the trustee or U.S. Trustee may suggest a continuance of the 341 meeting upon the debtor's nonappearance. This allows the debtor another opportunity to appear. Whether such continuances are regularly provided or strictly prohibited is a matter of local practice. A legal assistant must ascertain the flexibility of the Trustee's Office on continuances of 341 First Creditors' Meetings in his/her area.

United States Trustee's Office Dismissals

One of the prominent functions of the United States Trustee's Office is to ensure the smooth administration of Chapter 11 cases. The policy of this function is to protect creditors of the estate from unnecessary delays when a debtor is acting as the trustee in Chapter 11 cases which is called a debtor-in-possession. In this respect, the U.S. Trustee's Office plays an active role in requesting dismissal of cases for deficiencies within a Chapter 11 case.

At the outset, the U.S. Trustee's Office requires the debtor-in-possession to supply certain detailed information to the U.S. Trustee's Office.[2] This is in addition to the information contained within the debtor's statements and schedules filed with the Court. Additionally, in some districts, the debtor-in-possession is required to physically attend an "initial interview" with a representative of the U.S. Trustee's Office. These interview are before the 341 Meeting and are much less formal. At the interview with the U.S. Trustee's Office the debtor is orally examined in addition to supplying the specific detailed written information regarding the business. Should a debtor-in-possession fail to supply the U.S. Trustee's Office with all the relevant information requested in a timely manner or fail to attend the initial interview, the U.S. Trustee's Office will request the Court to dismiss the case.

Throughout the course of a Chapter 11 case, monthly financial reports are required to be filed with the Court by the debtor. Copies of these reports must be supplied to the U.S. Trustee's Office. Should a debtor-in-possession fail to file the monthly financial reports, the U.S. Trustee's Office will formally request the Court to dismiss the case.

Also, in a Chapter 11 case until a plan is confirmed, the debtor is required to make quarterly fee payments to the U.S. Trustee's Office. The amount of such payments is on a sliding scale but is no less than $250 per quarter.[3] Should a debtor fail to timely make the quarterly fee payments, the U.S. Trustee's Office will formally request the Court to dismiss the case.

A key function of the U.S. Trustee's Office's in fulfilling its duty to oversee the administration of Chapter 11 cases is to ensure that a plan and disclosure statement are timely filed by the debtor. A Chapter 11 plan and disclosure statement are formal documents filed with the Bankruptcy Court and propose the manner in which creditors are to be paid in a case.[4] The purpose of the U.S. Trustees' oversight in the timely filing of these documents is to prevent any undue delay in Chapter 11 cases. Any substantial and unexplained delay in the filing of the plan and disclosure statement, usually any delay past four months, will bring about a formal request from the U.S. Trustee's Office to dismiss the case.

As already noted, the requests by the U.S. Trustee's Office to the Court for dismissal are formal requests. Such requests are brought about by motion with notice to the debtor and all parties on the master mailing list. A hearing is held on U.S. Trustee's motions to dismiss or convert. Any deficiency pointed out by the U.S. Trustee's Office presumably may be cured by the time of the hearing. In other words, the debtor pays the delinquent fees or brings the back monthly reports current. Also, the debtor may negotiate an agreement with the U.S. Trustee's Office as to when a plan and disclosure statement shall be filed.

Chapter 13 Trustee's Dismissals

A Chapter 13 trustee's duties are substantially administrative in nature. In essence, the Chapter 13 trustee ensures that the debtor's case is progressing without undue delay and that the proposed plan is one with potential. Accordingly, the Chapter 13 trustee often plays a critical role in requesting dismissal of Chapter 13 cases due to failure of the debtors to file certain information and/or make timely payments as outlined in the Chapter 13 plan. A debtor is required to make monthly payments from the inception of the case, even before the Chapter 13 plan is confirmed.

At the outset the Chapter 13 trustee will make objections regarding the debtor's proposed plan. These objections may include requirements that the debtor prove current income, the feasibility of any plan payment increases (prove where and how the additional funds will be coming from), or filing of all tax returns. Usually, the Chapter 13 trustee allows the debtor a certain time within which to make proof to the U.S. Trustee's Office or the trustee will recommend automatic dismissal to the Court. Note: Recommendations for dismissal by a Chapter 13 trustee are commonly acted upon without hesitation by the Court. The Chapter 13 trustee acts on behalf of all the creditors in a bankruptcy case. Further, Chapter 13 trustees usually handle exclusively Chapter 13 cases, yet hundreds of them at once. The Bankruptcy Court recognizes the chapter trustee's unique position as well as expertise in determining the trustee's dismissal or conversion requests.

Within his or her administrative duties, the Chapter 13 trustee is responsible for collecting and distributing all plan payments. The Chapter 13 trustee collects the plan payments from the debtor and issues checks to the creditors according to the manner outlined in the debtor's confirmed plan. Should the debtor fall behind in the plan payments, the Chapter 13 trustee makes a formal request to the Court for dismissal. This request is made by motion, noticed to all creditors on the master mailing list, and an opportunity for a hearing is provided. Presumably, the debtor is allowed to catch up on the missed plan payments before the hearing to prevent dismissal or conversion.

Often a Chapter 13 debtor is in business as a sole proprietor. A sole proprietor is an individual conducting business without a corporation or partnership structure. In these circumstances, the debtor is required to supply the Chapter 13 trustee's office with monthly business operating reports. These reports outline the income and expenses of the business for each month. Failure to supply such reports in a timely fashion will result in the trustee's request to the Court for dismissal.

Accordingly, as can been seen, the possibilities for dismissal based upon administrative deficiencies alone are enormous. However, the deficiencies themselves are not insurmountable. Most often, it is a legal assistant's duty to ensure that such details as all filing requirements, fees, and reports are maintained on a continuous basis. Preventing the possibility of dismissal based upon one if not many of these administrative deficiencies by regular reminders to the debtors will avert the potential dismissal of a case.

DISMISSAL DUE TO LACK OF ELIGIBILITY

Debtors who do not qualify for bankruptcy protection under 11 U.S.C. Section 109 shall have their case dismissed or converted. As discussed in detail in Chapter 3 of this text, the basic eligibility requirements are as follows:

Chapter 7 is available to all "persons" (excluding banks, credit unions, etc.). [11 U.S.C. §109(b).]

Chapter 9 is available to "municipalities." [11 U.S.C. §109(c).]

Chapter 11 is available to all those who qualify as Chapter 7 debtors (except stock brokers, railroads, etc.). [11 U.S.C. §109(d).]

Chapter 12 is available to "family farmers" with regular annual income. [11 U.S.C. §109(f).]

Chapter 13 is available to individuals with regular income, with debt caps of $250,000 unsecured and $750,000 secured (noncontingent, liquidated). [11 U.S.C. §109(e).]

If a debtor does not qualify as an entity entitled to file a specific chapter under 11 U.S.C. Section 109 then the case shall be dismissed or converted. For example, banks and railroads which file for Chapter 7 or corporations which file for Chapter 13 must be dismissed or converted. The eligibility of each specific Chapter is discussed in Chapter 3.

Also, if a debtor files a second bankruptcy case within six months of an initial case, the second bankruptcy may also be dismissed under 11 U.S.C. Section 109(g). Debtors who file successive bankruptcy cases are often known as *serial filers*. However, the ineligibility requirements of 11 U.S.C. Section 109(g) apply to only two kinds of debtors. To be ineligible under 11 U.S.C. Section 109(g) a debtor must be either an individual or a family farmer. This section is inapplicable to business entity debtors such as corporations or partnerships.

In essence, an individual or family farmer debtor may be ineligible for a second bankruptcy if it is filed within 180 days of the dismissal of a previous bankruptcy. In short, a second bankruptcy cannot be filed on the heels of a dismissed first bankruptcy. However, ineligibility under 11 U.S.C. Section 109(g) requires more than just shortness of time between the filings. Either one of the two remaining options for disqualification under Section 109(g) must be shown.

The two ineligibility requirements for previously dismissed cases are as follows: (1) The previous case was dismissed for willful failure of the debtor to abide by orders of the court or appear in proper prosecution of the case, or (2) the case was dismissed upon the debtor's voluntary request to dismiss after a stay request had been filed in the initial case.

Willful Failure/Lack of Prosecution

The policy of 11 U.S.C. Section 109(g)(1) (willful failure/lack of prosecution) is to prevent a debtor's willful actions done to delay proceedings to the prejudice of creditors.[5] In essence, the purpose of this provision is to prevent abuse of the Bankruptcy Code through successive bankruptcy filings of the debtor.

Under this section, the debtor's conduct is willful when it is intentional, knowing, and voluntary. This is opposed to conduct that is accidental or beyond the debtor's control. Willful failure to do a required act necessarily involves that the person had notice of his or her responsibility and intentionally disregarded it or demonstrated plain indifference.[6]

Willful failure of a debtor has been held to include:

- Debtor habitually used cocaine during his first bankruptcy, wherein the debtor failed to attend the first creditors' meeting.[7]

- Debtor ignored warnings of the U.S. Trustee and demonstrated plain indifference to the bankruptcy time requirements for filing documents.[8]

- The plan in the second bankruptcy was similar to the plan in the first bankruptcy, which the Court ordered the debtor to amend since it was not feasible; yet debtor failed to amend the plan.[9]

- The debtor's failure to pay a secured creditor $10,000/month, as ordered in the prior case.[10]

- A Chapter 11 debtor's failure to file a financial statement by a date set in the prior case (considered in conjunction with other delays of debtor).[11]

A successive bankruptcy case will not be dismissed for debtors' failure, due to ignorance, to obey local rules when it cannot be shown that they acted in a willful manner when they violated the local rule.[12] Successive cases are also not dismissed under this section when the failure was beyond the control of the debtor.[13] Failure beyond the control of a debtor may include failure to make plan payments due to reduced income because of the debtor's medical condition,[14] or where "technical problems" such as an inexperienced courier and an inexperienced attorney led to failure to file schedules and plan, which ultimately caused the dismissal,[15] or where debtors become unemployed after the plan is filed and therefore have no funds to make payments.[16]

Voluntary Dismissal after Stay Relief Request

The second ineligibility criteria of 11 U.S.C. Section 109(g) is intended to address situations in which a debtor files a second bankruptcy case to stop a foreclosure. After a creditor seeks relief from the automatic stay in the first case, the debtor voluntarily dismisses the first bankruptcy. Next, the debtor then refiles a second bankruptcy before the creditor can complete an attempt to foreclose upon the property.[17] Under 11 U.S.C. Section 109(g)(2) a debtor is ineligible for the second bankruptcy since the first was voluntarily dismissed once the creditor requested stay relief. The second bankruptcy will therefore be dismissed.

This section does not apply to any kind of involuntary dismissal of prior cases such as when a creditor requests and obtains dismissal of the initial case. Instead, a connection must exist between the request for relief and the debtor's request for voluntary dismissal. For example, a creditor's motion to dismiss based upon 11 U.S.C. §109(g)(2) was denied when in the prior case the debtor voluntarily surrendered the property that was subject to the stay relief motion. In the debtor's second bankruptcy a completely different creditor requested dismissal of the case based on 11 U.S.C. §109(g)(2). However, the creditor in the second bankruptcy never filed a motion for stay relief in the first case. [See *In re Copman*, 161 B.R. 821 (Bankr. E.D. Mo. 1993).]

In essence, a debtor's request for voluntary dismissal must follow the relief from stay request to be disqualified under 11 U.S.C. Section 109(g)(2). This is true even if the actual order of dismissal is not entered until after such motion for relief has been filed.[18] For example, a debtor may orally request the Bankruptcy Court to dismiss her case at a hearing. Perhaps the order granting dismissal is not entered by the Bankruptcy Court for a week. In the interim, a creditor files a motion for relief from the automatic stay. However, this series of events does not make the debtor ineligible for a second bankruptcy under 11 U.S.C. Section 109(g)(2) since the request for dismissal was made before the stay relief motion. It is also important to note that the stay relief motion need not be either litigated or granted in the first case, merely filed.

CREDITOR REQUESTED DISMISSAL

Chapter 7

Under 11 U.S.C. §707(a), cause for dismissal of a Chapter 7 proceeding includes but is not limited to unreasonable delay by the debtor that is prejudicial to creditors and failure of the debtor to pay certain fees or file required documents. The most important criterion for dismissal is prejudice to creditors. The debtor's failure to account honestly for assets constitutes "cause" which is prejudicial to creditors.[19] For example, when a case involves the debtor's extensive looting and laundering of assets, false financial statements, and fraud, dismissal is justified if it does not delay creditors.[20]

Fraud or misrepresentation by the debtor will also constitute cause to grant a creditor's motion to dismiss. For example, tax fraud, embezzlement, and corporate misconduct are determinative of whether a Chapter 7 case should be dismissed.[21] Also, a debtor's failure to read the petition containing false statements before signing it is still a false statement and the debtor should not receive the benefits of discharge.[22]

Lack of good faith constitutes "cause" for dismissal of a Chapter 7 case. Such a case could include concealed or misrepresented assets and/or sources of income, excessive and continued expenditures, lavish lifestyles, and an intent to avoid a large single debt.[23] Bad faith is also demonstrated where the case is really a two-party dispute. A two-party dispute is where a case is predominantly a dispute between the debtor and a single creditor.[24] Bad faith is also when the debtor continues to earn a substantial annual income that could pay a portion of unsecured debts.[25]

Bad faith also must be considered in a debtor's prepetition planning activities. Prepetition planning is when the debtor knows he is going to file bankruptcy and tries to shield as many assets as possible that is provided under the Bankruptcy Code. Prepetition planning may consist of a debtor simply filing a declaration of homestead before he files bankruptcy. However, prepetition planning may also be considered excessive where the debtor transforms a fortune in assets into exempt property which would otherwise be available to creditors.

Whether the debtor used excessive prepetition bankruptcy planning sufficient to justify dismissal must be considered on a case-by-case basis. [See *In re Campbell*, 124 B.R. 462 (Bankr. W.D. Pa. 1991) (dismissal appropriate where debtor used clever prepetition planning to place all of his assets outside the reach of his creditors); *contra In re Latimer*, 28 B.R. 354 (Bankr. E.D. Pa. 1988) (debtor's manipulation of property to maximize exemptions does not constitute cause for dismissal).

Also, a Chapter 7 case filed within six years of a previous discharge will be dismissed. A discharge for a Chapter 7 individual is not available until six years have passed from any previous discharge. [11 U.S.C. Section 727(a)(8).] The debtor in the second case has no legitimate reason to obtain the relief provided by the automatic stay. Therefore, the second Chapter 7 is dismissed.

Chapter 13

Chapter 13 cases may also be dismissed for lack of good faith.[26] Numerous factors have been adopted as a guideline to determine good faith, including:

- The amounts of proposed payments and debtor's surplus.
- The debtor's employment history, ability to earn, and likelihood of future increases in income.

- The probable or expected duration of the plan.
- The accuracy of the plan's statement of debts, expenses, and percentage of repayment of unsecured debt and whether any inaccuracies are an attempt to mislead by the debtor.
- The extent of preferential treatment between classes of creditors.
- The extent to which secured claims are modified.
- The type of debt to be discharged and whether any such debt is nondischargeable in Chapter 7.
- The existence of special circumstances, such as inordinate medical expenses.
- The frequency with which a debtor has sought relief under bankruptcy.
- The motivation and sincerity of the debtor in seeking Chapter 13.
- The burden the plan's administration would place upon the trustee.

[See *In re Warren*, 89 B.R. 87 (9th Cir. BAP 1988).]

For example, a debtor initially files Chapter 7 and one of the few debts he attempts to discharge is found nondischargeable in Chapter 7. Consequently, the debtor converts to Chapter 13 and proposes a repayment plan for 0% repayment to all unsecured creditors (including the otherwise nondischargeable debt). This is "bad faith" and the case may be subject to dismissal. [See *In re Caldwell*, 895 F.2d 1123 (6th Cir. 1990) ("veiled" Chapter 7 plan is bad faith).] Would the case still be dismissed if the repayment provided 100%? What about 50%? 10%?

Chapter 11

Creditor dismissal of a Chapter 11 case for "cause" is governed by 11 U.S.C. §1112(b). Dismissal of a Chapter 11 case must be at the request of a party in interest or U.S. Trustee, and must have notice and a hearing. "Cause" under 11 U.S.C. Section 1112(b) is enumerated in the ten nonexclusive categories itemized in such section. These include:

1. *Continuing loss to or diminution of the estate and absence of a reasonable likelihood of rehabilitation.* Diminution of the estate is when the property of the estate is being eroded away or is depreciating. An example is when postpetition property taxes attach to real property of the estate and thereby leave less and less equity for creditors. Absence of a reasonable likelihood of rehabilitation is when it appears the debtor will be unable to propose a plan to pay back its creditors.

2. *Inability to effectuate a plan.* This is where the debtor does not have the means to fulfill any type of reasonable repayment to its creditors.

3. *Unreasonable delay by the debtor that is prejudicial to creditors.* This is where the debtor has not promptly filed its proposed plan to repay the creditors and the creditors are suffering, such as when the property is depreciating while the Chapter 11 is pending.

4. *Failure to propose a plan within any time fixed by the court.* The Bankruptcy Court often sets a deadline for Chapter 11 debtors to file a plan of reorganization. When a debtor fails to file a plan by this deadline dismissal is justified.

5. *Denial of confirmation of every proposed plan and denial of a request for additional time to file another plan.* This is when a debtor has filed a plan but it is not approved by the Bankruptcy Court. Also in this section the debtor is not allowed by the Bankruptcy Court any more time to get a new plan on file.

6. *Revocation of an order confirming plan.* When the Bankruptcy Court approves a plan it is called confirmation of the plan. Once the plan is confirmed a creditor may request the confirmation order be revoked. A request for revocation must be made within six months of the confirmation order. Also, a creditor must show that the plan was only confirmed through a debtor's fraud.

7. *Inability to effectuate substantial consummation of a confirmed plan.* Under this section the debtor's plan has already been confirmed. However, the confirmed plan simply does not work or the debtor has not performed the repayment as proposed in the plan.

8. *Material default by the debtor with respect to a confirmed plan.* Under this section the debtor's plan has already been confirmed. However, the debtor has failed to perform the things proposed in the plan.

9. *Termination of a plan by conditions specified in the plan.*

10. *Failure to pay any Court fees.*

Further, it is appropriate to dismiss a Chapter 11 case for "cause" if it appears that the petition was filed in bad faith.[27] Findings of lack of good faith in proceedings based upon 11 U.S.C. Section 1112(b) include certain repeating but nonexclusive factors.[28] These factors include:

1. Debtor has one asset.

2. The secured creditors' liens encumber this asset.

3. There are few, or no, employees.

4. There is little cash flow or available income.

5. There are few, if any, unsecured creditors with small claims.

6. The property has been scheduled for foreclosure.

7. There are allegations of wrongdoing by the debtor or its principals.

8. The case is a "new debtor syndrome."

New debtor syndrome simply means that the debtor is a new legal entity specifically created in order to file for bankruptcy. Such entities can include corporations and limited partnerships. After its creation, usually just prior to bankruptcy, all assets are transferred to the new entity. Usually these transferred assets have foreclosures scheduled for the immediate future. After the assets are transferred to the new entity, it files bankruptcy to invoke the automatic stay. The reason to create such a new entity is ostensibly to protect the remaining assets of the person who created the new entity and transferred the assets into the new entity. However, New Debtor Syndrome Chapter 11 cases are routinely dismissed based upon bad faith.

SUBSTANTIAL ABUSE FILING

A Chapter 7 bankruptcy may be dismissed for substantial abuse of the Bankruptcy Code under 11 U.S.C. Section 707(b). Only the Court, on its own initiative, or the U.S. Trustee's Office may bring such a motion to dismiss.[29] Creditors and parties in interest do not have the right to bring a motion for dismissal based upon substantial abuse under 11 U.S.C. Section 707(b).[30] Of course, the U.S. Trustee's Office may make such motion at the suggestion of a creditor or party in interest.

To dismiss a Chapter 7 case for substantial abuse under 11 U.S.C. Section 707(b), the Court must find that the debtor's debts are primarily consumer debts and that the relief sought is a substantial abuse of the bankruptcy process.[31] Note that Section 707(b) applies only to cases filed by individuals.

Consumer debts are defined as debts incurred by an individual primarily for personal, family, or household purposes.[32] Consumer debts include such things as credit cards, utilities, insurance, dental work, jewelry, magazines, and appliance repairs.[33] Mortgage debts are also considered consumer debts for purposes of 11 U.S.C. Section 707(b).[34]

"Primarily" consumer debts under 11 U.S.C. Section 707(b) means "for the most part"—in other words, when more than half of the dollar amount owed is consumer debt.[35] Therefore, a mathematical calculation of the total amount of debt listed in the schedules and the percentage of the debt that is considered "consumer debt" is necessary.

To determine "substantial abuse," the Courts generally look to see whether the debtor has the ability to fund a Chapter 13 plan.[36] Dismissal under 11 U.S.C. Section 707(b) does not require that the debtor has displayed "egregious behavior," but rather the mere ability to fund a Chapter 13 plan through excess income is sufficient to dismiss a Chapter 7 case.

For example, a debtor had obligations that were exclusively consumer debts. The debtor was a professional with proven earning ability of over $96,000 per year, which was expected to continue at such amount. The debtor's statement of monthly expenditures was highly inflated (i.e., $500 per month for food, $450 per month for car expenses, $200 per month for recreation, $300 per month paid to his wife to answer the telephone). Accordingly, after eliminating the inflated expenses, the debtor had an excess of $1,000 per month of income over his expenses. The total unsecured debts amounted to only $37,000. Accordingly, almost all unsecured debt could be paid in full through a Chapter 13 plan within three years. Therefore, the case was dismissed under Section 707(b) as substantial abuse. [See *In re Kress*, 57 B.R. 874 (Dist. N.D. 1985).]

U.S. Trustee v. Harris
960 F.2d 74 (8th Cir. 1992)

Friedman: * * *In April 1990, the appellants, Ronald and Rhonda Harris ("the Harrises") filed a petition for a liquidating bankruptcy under Chapter 7 of the Bankruptcy Act, 11 U.S.C. Sections 701-766. The debtors' schedule showed unsecured debts of $9,735, assets other than real property of $7,295, net monthly income of $2,249 and monthly expenses of $1,973.

The U.S. Trustee ("Trustee") moved to dismiss the petition under Section 707(b) which permits the Bankruptcy Court to dismiss a Chapter 7 proceeding if it finds that granting a discharge "would be a substantial abuse of the provisions of this chapter." * * *

Section 707(b) provides, in relevant part:

The court, on its own motion or on a motion by the United States Trustee ... may dismiss a case filed by an individual debtor under this chapter whose debts are primarily consumer debts if it finds that the granting of relief would be a substantial abuse of the provisions of this chapter.

In [*In re Walton*, 866 F.2d 981 (8th Cir. 1989)] we considered the meaning of "substantial abuse" under Section 707(b). Walton had urged that we equate "substantial abuse" with "bad faith." We rejected this "cramped interpretation" because it "would drastically reduce the Bankruptcy Courts' ability to dismiss cases filed by debtors who are not dishonest, but who are also not needy."

The debtor's ability to pay his debts when due as determined by his ability to fund a Chapter 13 plan is the primary factor to be considered in determining whether granting relief would be substantial abuse ... We find this approach fully in keeping with Congress's intent in enacting Section 707(b) ... This is not to say that inability to pay will shield a debtor from section 707(b) dismissal where bad faith is otherwise shown. But a finding that a debtor is able to pay his debts, standing alone, supports a conclusion of substantial abuse.

* * *

The District Court correctly rejected, as clearly erroneous, a number of the Bankruptcy Court's findings upon which it based its conclusion that the Harrises would be able to repay only 56 percent of their unsecured debt over three years. For example, the Bankruptcy Court *sua sponte* increased the Harrises' monthly food expenses by $200, failed to consider Ronald Harris' wage increase of $60 per month, and overstated the Harrises' monthly child care expense. On the basis of these adjustments, the District Court determined that the Harrises would have a disposable income of $421.25 which would enable them "to pay approximately 156 percent of their unsecured debt over three years," rather than the $152 per month upon which the Bankruptcy Court based its determinations.

* * *

In *Walton,* we held that the debtor's ability to pay, out of future income, 68 percent of unsecured debt within three years supported the determination of "substantial abuse." In the present case, the District Court, after readjusting the Harrises' income and expense figures to reflect the record, concluded that the Harrises' income in excess of expenses would enable them to pay 156 percent of their unsecured debt within three years. *A fortiori,* permitting the Harrises to discharge their unsecured debts through a Chapter 7 liquidating bankruptcy would constitute "substantial abuse" of that Chapter.

* * *

The judgment of the District Court, reversing the order of the Bankruptcy Court and remanding the case with instructions to dismiss the debtors' petition, is affirmed.

VOLUNTARY DISMISSAL

Chapter 7 Cases

A debtor does not have an absolute right to dismissal of a Chapter 7 case.[37] The debtor's asserted ability to pay creditors does not constitute adequate cause for dismissal when dismissal results in prejudice to creditors.[38] Dismissal of a Chapter 7 case on motion of the debtor is within the discretion of the Court, and a debtor's motion ought not be granted when prejudice to creditors would result.[39]

Moreover, a mere change of heart on the part of the debtors does not provide sufficient basis to dismiss their voluntary petition under Chapter 7. This is true especially when the motion to dismiss is filed very late in the case by the debtors. During the bankruptcy the debtors have languished under the protective umbrella of the automatic stay while their creditors have been prevented from being paid or pursuing their state law remedies.[40]

Also, settlement of previously pending lawsuits may not establish cause for dismissal of a Chapter 7. Dismissal in this case is not justified when the debtor's scheduled liabilities, even omitting the lawsuit creditor, far exceed the debtor's scheduled assets. This would force all the other creditors to pursue their claims in state court.[41] In essence, dismissal would allow only payment to the lawsuit the debtor settled and leave the rest of the creditors unpaid.

Under 11 U.S.C. Section 707(a), a policy exists of not dismissing a voluntary case on the motion of the debtor unless it can be shown that dismissal would be in the best interest of the debtor and the estate. It is not in the best interest of the estate if the debtor's assets would produce a substantial dividend for creditors if the Chapter 7 case were to continue.[42]

Suppose the trustee has filed objections to a debtor's claim of exemptions. If the trustee prevails on his objections these nonexempt assets would provide a payment to unsecured creditors. In such a case, a debtor's motion to voluntarily dismiss will be denied.

Also, a debtor's motion to dismiss so she can convert nonexempt assets into exempt assets and then refile bankruptcy will be denied. For example, a debtor requested dismissal of her Chapter 7 case. She intended to dismiss the case and file a homestead declaration. This would allow her to claim an exemption on her home. After she filed the necessary homestead declaration the debtor intended to then refile a new bankruptcy. The homestead exemption would leave no distribution to unsecured creditors and the debtor's motion to dismiss was denied.[43]

Voluntary dismissal of a proceeding that causes "some plain legal prejudice" to creditors should be denied unless all creditors affirmatively consent. In deciding whether a debtor should be allowed to voluntarily dismiss a voluntary bankruptcy case, the Court determines whether this high degree of prejudice exists. The Court determines whether the creditor's prejudice is outweighed by the articulated prejudice to the debtor if dismissal is denied.[44] Plain legal prejudice may include the creditors' expenses in pursuing their state court rights against the debtor if the bankruptcy is dismissed.

Some examples of where a debtor's voluntary motion to dismiss a Chapter 7 case was denied are as follows:

- Trustee was successful in recovering a preferential transfer that yielded assets for distribution, and the debtor thereafter filed a motion to dismiss, which was denied.[45]
- The debtor engaged in fraudulent conduct, then requested that the case be dismissed once such conduct was discovered (motion denied).[46]
- Lack of adequate prebankruptcy exemption planning that, in hindsight, made the filing of the petition seem improvident was held to be insufficient cause for dismissal.[47]
- The debtor mistakenly believed all her assets would be exempt when she filed was held to be insufficient cause for dismissal.[48]

Chapter 13 Cases

A Chapter 13 debtor may voluntarily, and without any notice or hearing to creditors, convert the Chapter 13 to a Chapter 7 or dismiss the bankruptcy altogether if no conversion has taken place. [11 U.S.C. Section 1307(a), (b).] The rationale for allowing a Chapter 13 debtor to dismiss such case without restrictions is to avoid any violation of the Thirteenth Amendment's prohibition against slavery. Postpetition earnings are property of the estate in Chapter 13 cases. Therefore, to deny a Chapter 13 debtor's request to dismiss would amount to holding the debtor captive in slavery.

Chapter 11 Cases

Under 11 U.S.C. Section 1112(a) a debtor-in-possession has an absolute right to convert the Chapter 11 case to a case under Chapter 7.[49] This right extends neither to a Chapter 11 debtor where a trustee has been appointed nor to a Chapter 11 case where the plan has been confirmed.[50]

EFFECT OF DISMISSAL

To the extent possible, dismissal of a bankruptcy case returns all parties and property to the place they were before the petition was filed. Dismissal of a case reinstates proceedings that were suspended by the intervening bankruptcy case such as state court lawsuits or pending foreclosures. Additionally, dismissal reinstates transfers avoided during the course of the bankruptcy. Dismissal makes liens which were voided during the bankruptcy valid again. Dismissal vacates all orders, judgements, or transfers as a result of the avoidance of a transfer. Additionally, dismissal returns property of the estate to whoever had the property before the bankruptcy was filed. Of course, the Bankruptcy Court may order a different result and/or retain jurisdiction for sufficient cause.

The basic purpose of the dismissal provisions of 11 U.S.C. Section 349 is to undo the bankruptcy case, as far as practicable, and to restore all property rights back to the position where they were at the time the initial bankruptcy petition was filed. In essence, dismissal of a bankruptcy action puts all creditors in the same position they were in on the date the petition was filed. An exception to this "undoing" of the bankruptcy is the undoing of sales of estate property to a good faith purchaser.

For example, a dismissal order vacates a Chapter 13 debtor's confirmed plan order,[51] reinstates avoided transfers to creditors,[52] and allows the IRS to calculate penalties and interest from the original prepetition date forward (penalties and interest were previously suspended by the original filing).[53]

When a bankruptcy case is dismissed, the automatic stay also disappears.[54] This means that all creditors can contact the debtor for collection, pursue lawsuits, garnish the debtor's wages, foreclose on property, and perform all the other acts prohibited by 11 U.S.C. Section 362 during bankruptcy.

CONVERSION

Conceptually, there are essentially three directions a bankruptcy case may convert. There are two basic types of bankruptcy cases, liquidation and reorganization. The first course of conversion is from a reorganization case to a liquidation case. This would be either a Chapter 11 or a Chapter 13 case being converted to a case under Chapter 7. A Chapter 11 case may convert to a Chapter 7 case if there simply is nothing left of the estate to reorganize. Estate assets may disappear during a Chapter 11 from creditors obtaining relief from the automatic stay and foreclosing on property. Estate assets may also dwindle during a Chapter 11 from ongoing expenses such as postpetition taxes or attorney's fees. Also, a Chapter 11 case may be converted to Chapter 7 if reorganization of any remaining assets proves to be impossible.

A Chapter 13 reorganization case may also convert to Chapter 7. This type of conversion is usually voluntary on the part of the debtor. Conversion of Chapter 13 to a Chapter 7 may occur when the proposed Chapter 13 plan is no longer workable, such as when the debtor loses his job. Conversion also may be advisable when the Chapter 13 plan has paid in full all the debts which would not otherwise go away in a Chapter 7. For example, a Chapter 13 plan made distributions in full to all priority creditors in two years. Priority creditors are not discharged in Chapter 7. In this situation, after the two years it may be advisable for the Chapter 13 debtor to convert to Chapter 7 and discharge all remaining debts.

The next course of conversion is from a liquidation case to a reorganization case. Conversion from Chapter 7 to Chapter 11 usually only takes place if some asset has been recovered which can be reorganized. For example, a Chapter 7 trustee was successful in recovering a partially completed real estate development project. If the case is converted to Chapter 11, the debtor would be able to propose a plan to repay creditors, such as finishing and selling the project.

Conversion from Chapter 7 to Chapter 13 usually only occurs voluntarily by the debtor. The debtor must be eligible for Chapter 13, including that the debtor is an individual and does not exceed the debt limits. Imagine if the Bankruptcy Court is to dismiss a Chapter 7 case based on substantial abuse under 11 U.S.C. Section 707(b) since the debtor has disposable income. The debtor could convert the case to Chapter 13 and pay his debts in an orderly manner over time rather than fighting off various state court lawsuits.

The final conversion path is from one reorganization case to another. Conversion from Chapter 11 to Chapter 13 is often a practical solution for individuals who meet the debt requirements. In Chapter 13 the creditors do not vote on any plan. Therefore, it is much easier to confirm a proposed plan over the objection of a hostile creditor.

Conversion from Chapter 13 to Chapter 11 also may be advantageous to many debtors. In Chapter 13 a debtor must begin making monthly plan payments at the outset of the case. Often a debtor is an entrepreneur or is on commissions and has difficulty producing income on a monthly basis. In this sense, Chapter 11 allows a debtor flexibility to propose a plan with a more creative payment schedule. Also, often debtors find that they are ineligible for Chapter 13 since they exceed the debt limits. In such cases Chapter 11 provides an alternate avenue for reorganization.

CONCLUSION

A paralegal can easily prevent involuntary dismissal of a bankruptcy based upon some administrative failure through diligent calendaring of deadlines and ongoing obligations the debtor must perform and simple reminders. Also, it is imperative that the paralegal be aware of the potential for dismissal or conversion requested by a creditor and what justifies dismissal or conversion under those circumstances. Finally, it is essential that the bankruptcy paralegal be familiar with the alternatives present in converting from one bankruptcy chapter to another.

REVIEW QUESTIONS

1. What is dismissal of a bankruptcy case? What is conversion?

2. What are the three primary manners in which a bankruptcy case may be dismissed? Give examples of each manner.

3. Upon what grounds would a U.S. Trustee's office typically move for dismissal or conversion of a Chapter 11 case?

4. What are some typical grounds a Chapter 13 Trustee would move for dismissal of a Chapter 13 case?

5. What are some of the elements for bad faith in a Chapter 13 case? What are some of the elements for bad faith in a Chapter 11 case? What is the new debtor syndrome?

6. When would a Chapter 7 debtor not be allowed to voluntarily dismiss a case?

7. Describe the eligibility requirements under 11 U.S.C. Section 109(g).

8. Describe the rationale for conversion from a reorganization case to a liquidation case. From a liquidation case to a reorganization case. From one type of reorganization case to another type of reorganization case.

ENDNOTES

[1] *Sua sponte* is where the Bankruptcy Court takes action on a matter by its own initiative.

[2] The contents of such information and examples of some pertinent U.S. Trustee's information sheets are more fully covered within Chapter 12, "Chapter 11 Practice."

[3] Again, the scale of the quarterly U.S. Trustee's fees is dealt with in greater detail within Chapter 12, "Chapter 11 Practice."

[4] The Chapter 11 plan and disclosure statement are discussed in detail in Chapter 12 of this text ("Chapter 11, Practice").

[5] *In re Krattiger,* 52 B.R. 383 (W.D. Wis. 1985).

[6] *In re Correa,* 58 B.R. 88 (Bankr. N.D. Ill. 1986).

[7] *Id.*

[8] *In re Welling,* 102 B.R. 720 (Bankr. S.D. Iowa 1989).

[9] *In re Jones,* 105 B.R. 1007 (N.D. Ala. 1989).

[10] *In re Nugelt, Inc.,* 142 B.R. 661 (Bankr. D. Del. 1992).

[11] *In re Kattiger,* 52 B.R. 383 (W.D. Wis. 1985).

[12] *In re Hollis,* 150 B.R. 145 (Bankr. D. Md. 1993).

[13] *In re Haggerty,* 57 B.R. 384 (S.D. Miss. 1986).

[14] *In re Bradley,* 152 B.R. 74 (E.D. La. 1993).

[15] *In re Burgart,* 141 B.R. 90 (W.D. Pa. 1992).

[16] *In re Howard,* 134 B.R. 225 (Bankr. E.D. Ky. 1991).

[17]*In re Patton,* 49 B.R. 587 (Bankr. M.D. Ga. 1985).

[18]*In re Hicks,* 138 B.R. 505 (Bankr. D. Md. 1992).

[19]*In re Schwartz,* 58 B.R. 923 (Bankr. S.D. N.Y. 1986).

[20]*In re Mathis Ins. Agency, Inc.,* 50 B.R. 482 (Bankr. E.D. Ark. 1985).

[21]*In re Micro Brokers, Inc.,* 59 B.R. 498 (Bankr. E.D. N.Y. 1985).

[22]*In re Kimball,* 19 B.R. 300 (Bankr. D. Me. 1982).

[23]*In re Zick,* 931 F.2d 1124 (6th Cir. 1991).

[24]*In re Hammonds,* 139 B.R. 535 (Bankr. D. Colo. 1992).

[25]*In re Johnson,* 137 B.R. 22 (Bankr. E.D. Ky. 1991).

[26]*In re Loya,* 123 B.R. 338 (9th Cir. BAP 1991).

[27]*In re Thirtieth Place,* Inc., 30 Bankr. 503 (9th Cir. BAP 1983).

[28]*In re Arnold,* 806 F.2d 937, 939 (9th Cir. 1986); *In re Stolrow's Inc.,* 84 Bankr. 167, 171 (9th Cir. BAP 1988); *In re Little Creek Dev. Co.,* 779 F.2d 1068, 1072-1073 (5th Cir. 1986).

[29]See *In re Keebler,* 106 B.R. 662 (Bankr. D. Hawaii 1989); *In re Clark,* 927 F.2d 793 (4th Cir. 1991).

[30]*In re Young,* 92 B.R. 782 (Bankr. N.D. Ill. 1988); *In re Frisch,* 76 B.R. 801 (Dist. Colo. 1987).

[31]*In re Woodhall,* 104 B.R. 544 (Bankr. M.D. Ga. 1989).

[32]*In re Wegner,* 91 B.R. 854 (Bankr. D. Minn. 1988).

[33]*In re Struggs,* C.C.H. Bankr. L. Reporter Para. 71704.

[34]*In re Kelly,* 57 B.R. 536 (Bankr. D. Arizona. 1986).

[35]*Id.*

[36]See *In re Andrus,* 94 B.R. 76 (Bankr. W.D. Pa. 1988); *In re Woodhall,* 104 B.R. 544 (Bankr. N.D. Ga. 1989).

[37]*In re Klein,* 39 B.R. 530 (Bankr. E.D. N.Y. 1984); *In re Martin,* 30 B.R. 24 (Bankr. E.D. N.C. 1983).

[38]*In re Williams,* 15 B.R. 655 (E.D. Mo. 1980).

[39]*In re Baylies,* 114 B.R. 324 (Bankr. D. D.C. 1990).

[40]*In re Pagnotta,* 22 B.R. 521 (Bankr. Md. 1982).

[41]*In re MacDonald,* 73 B.R. 254 (Bankr. N.D. Ohio 1987).

[42]*In re St. Laurent,* 17 B.R. 768 (Bankr. D. Me. 1982).

[43]*In re Hall,* 15 B.R. 913 (9th Cir. BAP. 1981).

[44]*In re Geller,* 74 B.R. 685 (Bankr. E.D. Pa. 1987).

[45]*In re Green,* 49 B.R. 7 (Bankr. W.D. Ky. 1984).

[46]*In re Jennings,* 31 B.R. 378 (Bankr. S.D. Ohio 1983).

[47]*In re Carroll,* 24 B.R. 83 (Bankr. N.D. Ohio 1982).

[48]*In re St. Laurent,* 17 B.R. 768 (Bankr. D. Me. 1982).

[49]*In re Texas Extrusion Corp.,* 844 F.2d 1142 (5th Cir. 1988).

[50]*In re T.S.P. Industries, Inc.,* 120 B.R. 107 (Bankr. N.D. Ill. 1990).

[51]*In re Nash,* 765 F.2d 1410 (9th Cir. 1985).

[52]*In re Mel-O-Gold, Inc.,* 88 B.R. 205 (Bankr. S.D. Iowa 1988).

[53]*In re Whitmore,* 154 B.R. 314 (Dist. Nev. 1993).

[54]*Norton v. Hoxie State Bank,* 61 B.R. 258 (Dist. Kan. 1986).

8

Voidable Transfers

You got repaid the $5,000 you loaned to your cousin the day before he filed bankruptcy. What a relief! Now, you've just been served a summons and complaint by the trustee in your cousin's case. You are the defendant and the trustee wants the $5,000 back from you. You weren't trying to cheat anyone. In fact, you didn't even know your cousin was going to file bankruptcy. Can the trustee do this? Will he win?

Your father-in-law gives you his lakefront vacation property in Tahoe as a present when you graduate from the legal assistants' program in your business college. Congratulations! Of course, your father-in-law keeps the keys to the property and uses it as often as, if not more than, before he "gave" it to you. Nine months later your father-in-law files bankruptcy. You are served with a summons and complaint by the trustee in your father-in-law's case. The trustee either wants the Tahoe property back from you or he wants what the property is worth. Again, can the trustee do this? Will he win?

INTRODUCTION

Voidable transfers under the Bankruptcy Code are transactions that may be "undone" by the trustee. Such transactions may be as simple as the debtor's giving money to others or as elaborate as the debtor's placing multiple liens on property. They may even take place involuntarily, where the creditor acts to take property or place liens on the property without the consent of the debtor. In each case, such transfers must reduce the debtor's property that would otherwise be available to creditors of the estate.

DUTIES OF LEGAL ASSISTANTS IN VOIDANCE ACTIONS

Legal assistants play a vital role in all aspects of voidable transaction matters. Initially, a legal assistant commonly has the duty to interact with the debtor in compiling the initial statements and schedules. Within the statements and schedules are a variety of questions regarding transactions and transfers that would reveal any possible voidable transfers. Therefore, the legal assistant will be the first alerted if a transaction appears to be a voidable transfer. Thereafter, the legal assistant must alert the supervising attorney. This will allow the attorney to structure further prepetition planning, consensual voiding of the transfer, or to obtain Court authorization, as the case may be.

Moreover, when a legal assistant's firm represents debtors, often the legal assistant will be the key person interfacing with the debtors. Debtors often are vaguely aware that some of their property may be at risk. Consequently, the legal assistant will be asked such questions as "Is it okay for me to sell my BMW to my sister for a dollar before I file for bankruptcy?" While this is a legal question, the legal assistant should admonish the debtor to take no action until speaking with the supervising attorney. Thereafter, it is crucial that the supervising attorney be alerted as to the potential voidable transaction the debtor is considering.

Note: Not only is the transfer itself at risk. The debtor's claim to any exemption upon the transferred property would be eliminated. [11 U.S.C. Section 522(g).] Also, the debtor's entire discharge may be denied based upon the debtor's fraudulent transfer of property. [See 11 U.S.C. Section 727(a)(2).]

Even when representing the trustee or a creditor, the legal assistant's duty often is to analyze the debtor's statements and schedules filed with the Court. The legal assistant must recognize and alert the supervising attorney as to any potential voidable transfers.

When potential voidable transfers are apparent on the statements and schedules, a firm representing either creditors or the trustee will often request the legal assistant to prepare questions to be asked of the debtor regarding the transactions at the First Creditors' Meeting. [11 U.S.C. Section 341.] The legal assistant may also be asked to prepare questions regarding the transfer at subsequent 2004 Debtor's Examinations. Therefore, a legal assistant must know what the key elements are to a voidable transfer and where this information can be found on bankruptcy statements and schedules.

Finally, once a voidable transfer action has been filed in a case, the legal assistant's role is crucial. Such actions are adversary proceedings which are mini-lawsuits within a bankruptcy case. Accordingly, the legal assistant's duties will include the calendaring of critical dates, such as response dates, discovery deadlines, etc. The legal assistant plays an active role in preparing and propounding or responding to discovery requests. This may include preparation of interrogatories, requests for production, requests for admissions, or compiling the F.R.Bankr.P. 26 disclosure documents. Additionally, legal assistants should be prepared to compile questions for depositions of either the debtor, transferee, or creditor. Legal assistants are often requested to digest deposition transcripts to discover facts to prove or disprove each element of a voidance action. Further, legal assistants help prepare trial notebooks.

The avoidance actions in bankruptcy often involve an enormous amount of discovery and therefore a vast number of documents. It is a legal assistant's duty to analyze and assemble these documents obtained through discovery. Thus, the legal assistant's tasks in voidance actions begin at the initiation of the case (through the statements and schedules) and continue throughout the winding evidentiary trail that most voidable transfer adversary matters take. Accordingly, legal assistants should familiarize themselves with the various types of voidance actions, as well as with the elements and defenses of each.

PREFERENCES

A trustee may void a transaction as a preference under 11 U.S.C. Section 547. To qualify as a preference, the transfer must be something that is debtor's property or that could have been property of the bankruptcy estate. Further, the transfer must be made to a person to whom the debtor owed before the transaction. Additionally, the transfer must take place within 90 days before the bankruptcy petition was filed (or one year before the petition was filed if the creditor is an "insider," discussed in detail later in the chapter). Finally, the transfer must allow the receiving creditor to obtain more than the creditor would have received in a Chapter 7 case if the transfer had not occurred.

For example, a debtor owns a vintage 1965 Corvette worth approximately $10,000. The debtor also owes money to ABC Financing ($500), Haste Credit Card ($750), and the debtor's brother ($1,000). Two months before debtor files bankruptcy, ABC has been calling the debtor every night and sending letters every day. ABC is also threatening to bring a state court lawsuit and garnish the debtor's wages if not paid. The debtor is thoroughly harassed by ABC and gives ABC the Corvette.

This transaction is a preference and can be voided or "undone" by the trustee once the petition is filed. The transfer in this case is the debtor's giving ABC his car. The car would otherwise be the property of the estate available for distribution to all the debtor's creditors.[1] Further, the debtor owed ABC money before the transfer was made (antecedent debt). The transfer was made 60 days before the petition was filed, well within the 90-day reach-back period. Finally, ABC was allowed to receive $10,000 due to this transaction instead of the $500, which is the most it could have received as a distribution in the debtor's case if the car had not be transferred.

Would it matter if ABC had not been harassing the debtor, but the debtor transferred the car because he believed ABC would keep extending him credit? No. Motive is immaterial in preference actions and the transfer could still be voided by the trustee as long as all the other elements are met.

Would it matter if the debtor gave the car to his brother because he did not want his brother to be "stiffed" or discharged in bankruptcy? No. Again, motive is irrelevant. What if the debtor gave the car to his brother six months before bankruptcy? Six months is outside the 90-day reach-back period. However, relatives, such as a brother, are considered "insiders" and therefore the reach-back period is extended to one year. Accordingly, the transfer would still be voidable by the trustee.

Would it make a difference if the debtor did not actually give the car to either ABC or his brother, but instead gave either of them a lien on the car? No. Providing a lien to an unsecured creditor is elevating their status to secured. Any lien would reduce the amount available for distribution to other creditors if the lien had not been placed upon the car.

Would it make a difference if the debtor did not agree to give the car to ABC? Instead, ABC obtained judgment and had the sheriff levy the car and obtained possession of the car in that manner. No. The transfer need not be voluntary for the transaction to be voided. Here, the debtor did not consent to the transfer, making it an "involuntary" transfer. However, the transaction is still voidable since it does not matter whether the transfer is voluntary or involuntary.

Policy of Voidable Transfers

There are two policy goals to voiding preferences under the Bankruptcy Code. [11 U.S.C. Section 547.] These policy themes support the prime bankruptcy policy of equal distribution among similar creditors. Also, preferential voidances reduce the incentive of creditors to rush to dismember a financially unstable debtor prior to the bankruptcy filing.[2]

The first of these goals in bankruptcy reflects the policy of an orderly distribution of assets of a troubled debtor. This orderly distribution allows a systematic and balanced payment of creditors. This bankruptcy policy is in direct conflict with state law collection rights of creditors. The state law rights allow the first creditor to pursue collection against the debtor the first right against the debtor's property. This bankruptcy policy of preferences attempts to discourage unusual efforts at debt collection by creditors during the period immediately before the petition is filed.

For example, assume one credit card company either constantly calls demanding payment from the debtor or files a lawsuit in state court before all other credit cards and ultimately obtains payment. The other credit cards were not as aggressive in contact with the debtor or as fast in filing their state court suits for recovery. Under the preference laws of the Bankruptcy Code, the amounts recovered by the aggressive creditor may be recovered and distributed among all similar creditors, even if the other creditors were not as forceful in collection prior to the bankruptcy filing.

The second goal in the bankruptcy preference context is to obtain equality of distribution for similarly situated creditors. This is not to say that all creditors must be treated equally. Note the unequal treatment of various creditors mandated by the distribution priority scheme of 11 U.S.C. Section 726 in Chapter 9 of this text. Rather, voiding preferential transfers allows equality for creditors of a similar type, e.g., two competing unsecured creditors.

This second policy of preferences within bankruptcy allows the restructure of transactions that occur over a defined period prior to bankruptcy. This levels the overall treatment received by the same type of creditors. For example, prior to her bankruptcy filing, assume a debtor pays in full only one of her credit cards (possibly based upon such credit card's promise to allow the debtor to continue to use the card after she files bankruptcy). Additionally, the debtor allows the other credit cards to remain unpaid. The preference laws of bankruptcy permit such a prepetition payment to be recovered from the preferred creditor. The recovered proceeds are distributed equally among all the credit cards.

In essence, the Bankruptcy Code policy of equality of distribution among similar creditors is fostered by 11 U.S.C. Section 547 preferential voidance powers. A trustee is permitted to void certain prepetition preferences and thereby prevent a debtor from favoring one creditor over others by transferring property shortly before filing bankruptcy.[3] Additionally, the purpose of the preferential transfer rule is to return parties to the position they would have been in had it not been for a premature raid on the debtor's assets.[4]

Therefore, the purposes of the Bankruptcy Code voidance powers are:

1. To promote the prime bankruptcy policy of equality of distribution among creditors by ensuring that all creditors of the same class will receive the same pro rata share (proportionate share) of the debtor's estate.

2. To discourage creditors from attempting to outmaneuver each other in an effort to carve up the estate of a financially unstable debtor.[5] This allows the debtor to work out financial difficulties in an atmosphere conducive to cooperation.[6]

Elements of Preferential Transfer Actions

Under 11 U.S.C. Section 547(b), the basic elements of a preference are:

1. A transfer of property,
2. Of the debtor,
3. To or for the benefit of a creditor,
4. On account of an antecedent debt,
5. Made while the debtor was insolvent, with insolvency presumed during the 90 days prepetition,
6. Made either:
    a. within 90 days of the bankruptcy filing, or
    b. within 91 days and one year of the filing if the creditor was an insider, and
7. Enabling the creditor to receive more than it would in a Chapter 7 case if the transfer had not been made.[7]

Generally, the debtor's or creditor's motive with respect to a preference is irrelevant. The purpose of the transfer does not affect whether it qualifies as a voidable preference because it is the effect of the transaction, rather than the debtor's or creditor's intent, that is controlling.[8]

Transfer of Property. At initial glance, a transfer of property may appear as obvious as in this classic example: D owes money to C. D makes full payment of the amount owed by delivering cash to C. The transfer in this case is the delivery of the cash, which constitutes property. However, a transfer of property may be much more inclusive than this simple illustration.

Transfer is defined as every mode—direct or indirect, absolute or conditional, voluntary or involuntary—of disposing of or parting with property or with an interest in property, including retention of title as a security interest and foreclosure of the debtor's equity of redemption.[9] This definition is intended to broadly encompass all forms of conveying property interest. In fact the conveyance by the debtor need not be voluntary, which further demonstrates that the motive or intent is irrelevant, with the focus rather on the effect of the transaction.

Some forms of involuntary transfer that have been held to be preferential include:

> Repossession of a debtor's property.[10]
>
> Attachment or imposition of judicial liens upon debtor's property.[11]
>
> Garnishment liens.[12]
>
> Execution and levy upon a debtor's property.[13]
>
> Seizure of a debtor's property.[14]

Other forms of "transfer of property," not as apparent as in the original example, include:[15]

> A transfer of a check (upon the date the check is honored by the bank rather than the date of delivery of the check).[16]
>
> Recording a mortgage with an assignment of rents clause.[17]
>
> The debtor's pledge of his assets in exchange for the issuance of letters of credit.[18]

Accordingly, from these examples it is apparent that a "transfer of property" extends beyond the simple delivery of cash to a creditor. In fact, a transfer of property broadly includes all forms of conveying property interests, even transfers of "mere possession."[19]

Property of the Debtor. The subject matter of the transfer must be a property interest of the debtor. *Property of the debtor* subject to preference avoidance is property that would have been part of the bankruptcy estate had it not been transferred before the bankruptcy was filed.[20] "Transfers," for preference purposes, are determined under federal law. However, "property" and "interests in property" are creatures of state law.[21]

Property of the estate under 11 U.S.C. Section 541 includes all legal or equitable interests of the debtor in property. Accordingly, "property of the debtor" for preference actions is equivalent to property of the estate.[22] Therefore, a transfer of property of the debtor includes the giving or conveying of anything of value that has debt-paying or debt-securing power, even property with intangible value.[23] Intangible means something that cannot be touched, such as accounts receivable.

A transfer is voidable only if property or interest in the property belongs to a debtor. Therefore, the use of another's property to repay a creditor is not subject to preferential voidance.[24] For example, if a supplier is paid from assets of a nondebtor general contractor, then the funds do not constitute property of the debtor and are thus not recoverable under 11 U.S.C. Section 547.[25]

The complexity in determining whether a transfer is "property of the debtor" often arises in the doctrine of "earmarked funds." Basically, earmarked funds is where a debtor physically receives funds from a third party specifically for the purpose of payment to a certain creditor. However, to overcome avoidance as a preference, earmarked funds must be advanced to the debtor with the specific purpose of payment to such creditor. An agreement must exist that directs the debtor to use the funds to pay the specified creditor. The debtor must lack control of the funds. Also, the overall transaction must not result in reducing the estate.[26]

To or For the Benefit of a Creditor. The recipient or beneficiary of the transfer must be the debtor's creditor. The term "creditor" includes only holders of prepetition claims against the debtor.[27] If the recipient is a creditor of another entity closely connected to the debtor (such as a creditor of a corporate debtor's president), it is not sufficient to make a transfer preferential.[28]

However, a transfer may be preferential as to a creditor even if another entity actually received the property transferred. The key is whether the transfer benefits the creditor. An example of such a transfer is a debtor's payment on a first mortgage. Such payment increases the value of the second mortgagee's interest in the collateral since more equity exists if the second mortgage were to foreclose.[29] Another example of this "indirect benefit" doctrine is a voidable preference to a guarantor or co-obligor of the debtor. When the creditor is paid by the debtor this payment discharges the guarantor's or co-obligor's obligation to the creditor.[30] Therefore, the co-obligor indirectly benefits from the transfer through its eliminated obligation.

In relation to the "indirect benefit" doctrine, prior to the 1994 Amendments several cases allowed trustees to recapture payments made to noninsider creditors a full year prior to the bankruptcy filing if an insider benefited from the transfer in some way. [See generally *In re V.N. Deprizio Construction Co.*, 974 F.2d 1186 (7th Cir. 1989).] The creditor was not an insider in such cases but rather a lending institution, such as a bank. However, the courts reasoned that the repayment benefited a corporate insider of the debtor, namely an officer who signed a personal guarantee. Accordingly, the noninsider transferee (i.e., the bank) was liable for returning the transfer to the estate as if the transferee were an insider as well. These transfers included regular repayment installments made by the debtor to the bank within the year before filing the petition.

The 1994 amendment to 11 U.S.C. Section 550(c) states that if a transfer made within a year prepetition is voided under Section 547(b), the transferee (the one receiving payment) must be an insider. Accordingly, the 1994 legislation specifically overruled the *Deprezio* line of decisions and clarified that noninsider transferees are not subject to the preference provisions beyond the 90-day preference period. The legislative aim was to encourage commercial lenders and landlords to extend credit to smaller business entities.[31]

Other nonexclusive examples of "creditors of the debtor" are as follows:

> Victim of the debtor's bad check passing paid under criminal restitution order.[32]
>
> Supplier of minks to a Chapter 7 debtor since the debtor had to either return the minks or pay for the merchandise.[33]
>
> Investor of $2.3 million in debt when the debtor did not use the funds to purchase stock as represented.[34]
>
> Landlords.[35]
>
> Return of consignment goods to consignee.[36]

Therefore, asset or interest transfers made to third parties in exchange for payment of a debtor's obligations are transferees "to or for the benefit of a creditor" within the meaning of 11 U.S.C. Section 547.

On Account of an Antecedent Debt. Although antecedent debt is not defined in the Code, it is a preexisting or prior debt. In essence, the debt must precede the transfer.[37] To determine whether payments are made on account of antecedent debts, one must first determine when the debt was incurred. A debt is incurred on the date on which a debtor first becomes legally bound to pay.[38] A debt is "antecedent" for preference purposes when a debtor becomes legally bound to pay before the transfer is made.[39]

Debts are incurred upon performance giving rise to the debt, not when payment is due. Should performance occur before payment, even when due, such debts are antecedent.[40] Debts arise at the time of performance, or when the debtor becomes legally bound to pay as opposed to later invoicing.[41] Accordingly, debts on installment contracts are incurred on the date the contract is executed and not on the date when the installment becomes due.[42]

Some nonexclusive examples of antecedent debt are as follows:

Federal withholding taxes are due on the date the penalty is imposed, which occurs if payment is not made within three business days of tax-payer's payroll, rather than the date tax returns are due.[43]

When a security interest is given and a lapse occurs prior to recording the security instrument, the obligation is antecedent.[44]

Security interest given to a bank in the debtor's assets on a previously owed loan.[45]

Payment for back rent (since the debtor becomes indebted for rental payment at time rent is due).[46] (Note: Lease payments arise due to lessor's possession, not when lease is signed.)[47]

Payment to corporate officers of previously earned compensation.[48]

Payment of arrears on an insurance policy.[49]

"Check kiting," where subsequently "covered" checks were kited on bank accounts under the debtor's control at other banks.[50]

Restitution obligation to county for welfare fraud conviction.[51]

However, in order to be "antecedent" obligations, debts must arise before the transfer. Should such transfers be made before the debts occur, they are not subject to voidance as preferential transfers. For example, if a debtor makes a payment to a hospital for services to be provided to his wife and baby prior to the provision of such services, such payment is not on account of an antecedent debt and therefore not voidable.[52]

Made While the Debtor Was Insolvent, with Insolvency Presumed During the 90 Days Prepetition. Under 11 U.S.C. Section 547(f), a debtor is presumed to have been insolvent on and during the 90 days immediately prepetition. The issue of insolvency will arise in preference actions against insiders, which transactions may have occurred up to a year before the petition is filed. Also, defendants in preference actions may attempt to rebut the statutory presumption of insolvency by presenting evidence of a debtor's solvency during the 90-day prepetition period.

The standard for calculating insolvency for bankruptcy purposes is when the fair market value of a debtor's liabilities exceeds the fair market value of the debtor's assets.[53] The fair market value of the debtor's assets is determined by estimating what the debtor's assets would realize if sold in a prudent manner in current market conditions.[54] This calculation may also include the debtor's "going concern value" to determine valuation of its assets at the time of the transfer.[55]

Transfer Made Within 90 Days of the Bankruptcy Filing. The 90-day voidance period in bankruptcy preference actions is to be calculated by counting backward 90 days from the filing of the bankruptcy petition rather than by counting forward from the date of the transfer.[56] In computing the preference period, the Federal Rules of Civil Procedure apply. Specifically, F.R.Bankr.P. 9006(a) establishes that the first day is excluded but the last day is included. Accordingly, the Bankruptcy Court will count the day the transfer was made but will exclude the day the petition was filed.[57]

While this point may initially appear trivial, this legal calculation may determine whether certain subject transactions are within the ambit of the 90-day period mandated by the Bankruptcy Code. Consider the following facts: Counting forward from the date of transfer, the 90th day would be on a Sunday, thereby extending the 90-day period to Monday, the day on which the petition was filed. However, counting backward from the petition date, the 90th day is on a Tuesday, one day after the subject transfer.[58]

Additional issues arise when calculating whether a transaction is made within 90 days prepetition. For example, the preference period is measured from the date the involuntary petition is filed, not the date the order for relief is entered.[59] Further, separate but related bankruptcy cases are often substantively consolidated. Substantive consolidation is where two separate bankruptcy cases are treated as one bankruptcy case. In substantive consolidation cases, the petition dates often are not the same date. Accordingly, issues arise as to which petition date must be used to measure the 90-day period.[60]

Transfer Made Within One Year of the Filing If the Creditor Was an Insider. The key issue to determine whether the 90-day preference period may be extended to a full year prepetition is whether the transferee (the one who obtained the transfer) is an "insider." An *insider* is basically a person with a sufficiently close relationship with the debtor that he or she is not dealing at arm's length with the debtor. If the debtor is a corporation, its insiders may include any officer, director, controlling person, or a partnership in which the debtor is a general partner, general partner of the debtor, or relative of the general partner. The crux of the "control" issue is whether the transferee is in a position to exert considerable influence over the affairs of the debtor corporation.[61] Any person that is an officer or director of a corporate debtor is automatically considered to be an insider.[62]

Additionally, the transferee must be an insider at the time of the transfer. This is required even if the transferee is no longer an insider on the date of the petition.[63] When the transfer is arranged while the transferee is in an insider position, it does not matter whether the insider resigned prior to the actual transfer.[64]

Further, "affiliates" of the debtor are also considered insiders for extending the reach-back period of preferences to one year prepetition. For example, individuals who hold more than 20% of the common stock of the debtor at the time of the transfer are affiliates of the debtor as defined in 11 U.S.C. Section 101.[65] A debtor's statements and schedules indicate all shareholders of 20% or more as well as all corporate officers and directors. The statements and schedules also list recent resignations of these parties. This information is vital to determine a person's insider status and therefore whether the reachback period is 90 days or one full year.

Additionally, relatives of debtors may be considered insiders for preference purposes. For example, a debtor's father-in-law may be considered an insider,[66] or the wife of an officer of a Chapter 7 corporate debtor,[67] or a debtor's minor child,[68] or a debtor's grandparents.[69] However, the doctrine of "affinity" to define relative in preference actions is that of relationship by marriage, not mere close relationship.[70] For example, a Chapter 7 debtor's fiance was not considered an insider in *In re Hollar*, 100 B.R. 892 (Bankr. N.D. Ohio 1989).

Finally, in addition to the "controlling party," corporate insiders, relatives, and partners may also be considered insiders for preference periods. For preference purposes, a limited partnership is an insider of its general partners, and the general partners are insiders of the limited partnership.[71] Additionally, a partnership that is the sole shareholder of the debtor corporation as well as the general partners who are officers and directors of the debtor corporation are insiders for purposes of preference actions.

Transfer Enables the Creditor to Receive More Than It Would in a Chapter 7 Case if the Transfer Had Not Been Made. In order to be preferential, the transfer must enable the creditor to receive more than it would have in a Chapter 7 liquidation if the transfer had not been made. This test is often termed the "greater percentage test" of 11 U.S.C. Section 547(b)(5). This test is determined as to the ultimate distribution expected if the case were in Chapter 7, not at the time of the transfer.[72]

Under this requirement if a debtor's liabilities exceed its assets, an unsecured creditor is sure to receive less than 100% of its claim in Chapter 7. If this creditor received 100% of its claim before bankruptcy, then the transfer is preferential.[73] In essence, the Court will look to a hypothetical liquidation as of the bankruptcy filing date and determine whether other creditors holding unsecured claims are prejudiced.[74] This is satisfied if the transferee creditor has an unsecured claim and receives payment within the 90-day period unless the assets of the estate are sufficient to provide a 100% distribution to other creditors.[75]

However, note that, if the transferee is a fully secured creditor at the time of the payment, it receives no more than it would have under Chapter 7. In Chapter 7 secured creditors are either paid in full from the sales proceeds of the secured property or simply given back the property if no equity exists. Therefore, a fully secured creditor cannot receive more than it is entitled to receive in Chapter 7.

Defenses to Preferential Transfer Actions

For a preferential transfer to exist, all the preceding statutory criteria must be proven. However, even if all elements are present, a trustee may not void a transfer if a creditor can demonstrate the existence of one of the statutory defenses that except the transfer from being voidable.[76] While the burden of proving the initial preference case is upon the plaintiff (i.e., the trustee), all the statutory defenses asserted are affirmative defenses. The burden of proof of affirmative defenses falls upon the defendant (i.e., the transferee). Proof of any one of the statutory defenses defeats the trustee's preference action.

In addition to the eight affirmative statutory defenses found in 11 U.S.C. Sections 547(c)(1)–(c)(8), a transferee may also defend the transfers on other grounds. Nonaffirmative defenses include lack of standing, improper jurisdiction, or improper service, or may merely assert a defense to negate one of the elements of the transfer, such as the earmarking doctrine.[77]

The exclusive statutory defenses to preference actions are as follows:

1. Contemporaneous transactions.
2. Ordinary course of business.
3. Enabling loans.
4. Subsequent new value.
5. Floating liens.
6. Statutory liens.
7. Spousal/child support transfers.
8. Consumer debts under $600.

Contemporaneous Transactions. Transfers that are a substantially contemporaneous exchange for new value are not voidable. In essence, this requires that a transfer is given by the debtor at approximately the same time that some new thing of value is given by the creditor. This exception requires that the debtor and creditor *intended* the transfer to be a contemporaneous exchange, *new value* was furnished by the creditor, and the transaction was actually a *substantially contemporaneous* exchange (i.e., transfer was made at approximately same time as new value was provided to the debtor).

The intent of both parties determines whether there has been a contemporaneous exchange. This is the critical starting point. Compare the following factual situations:

> The bank makes a secured cash loan to the debtor, who promises to transfer a mortgage on the debtor's property to the bank in exchange. The mortgage was shortly thereafter signed and recorded. Days later the bankruptcy petition was filed.

In this situation, both parties intended to have the loan secured contemporaneously by the mortgage. Accordingly, the transfer is nonvoidable.[78]

> The bank makes a loan to the debtor on an unsecured basis. That same day, the bank finds out the debtor is having financial problems and then demands property to secure the loan. The debtor complies by delivering property to the bank as collateral. Later that same day, the bankruptcy petition was filed.

In this situation, the transfer of the property does not fall within the contemporaneous exchange exception because at the time of the transfer it was not intended either by the debtor or by the bank to be contemporaneous. Accordingly, this transaction is a voidable preference.[79]

Consider if the bank provided a loan to the debtor and the debtor intended a portion of the loan to be used for interest payments for past debts to the bank. In such a case, the portion of the loan used to make such interest payments is not intended to be contemporaneous. Accordingly, that portion of the loan attributable to the interest payments is voidable as a preference.[80]

The second element to the contemporaneous exchange exception is the requirement that "new value" be provided by the creditor. The Bankruptcy Code defines *new value* as money or money's worth in goods, services, or new credit, or the release of property by the creditor. New value does not include an obligation substituted for an existing obligation.[81]

The following examples have been considered to be "new value":

> Payment to creditor in settlement of lawsuit.[82]
>
> Payment to creditor in release of a lien.[83]

Providing a personal guarantee to allow debtor to obtain a loan otherwise unavailable.[84]

Some examples of transfers that did not constitute new value are:

Creditor's forbearance from exercising its rights.[85]

Payment of an electricity bill for electricity already used.[86]

Payment to the landlord of past due rent in exchange for canceled eviction proceedings.[87]

Promise to continue to do business with the debtor if old bills are paid.[88]

Further, after determining that new value is given, the next step is to determine how much value was involved in the exchange. The value of the new consideration must be compared to the value of the property conveyed in order to render the entire transfer saved by the contemporaneous exchange exception.[89] Accordingly, the creditor must prove specific value of the goods, services, or new credit extended to meet the new value exception.[90]

Finally, the exchange must actually be "substantially contemporaneous." This does not mean that the transfer be made at the exact moment the new value was provided. However, the transfer must occur close to the time the property or funds were given.

For example, a 1½-month delay in recording a car lien was deemed substantially contemporaneous when such registration papers were initially sent to the wrong county.[91] However, a year delay in recording grant deeds on property were not contemporaneous.[92] Nor was a delay of one month before treating reassignments of loans upon the creditor's books considered a contemporaneous.[93]

Ordinary Course of Business. A transfer is not voidable if it was made in the ordinary course of business between the debtor and the transferee. This requires that the debtor incurred its debt and paid this creditor in similar ways in past transactions.[94] Additionally, the transfer must also be according to the ordinary business practices of the industry.[95] Ordinary practices of the industry mean the way in which other companies in the same business as the debtor conduct business. Finally, the transfer is nonvoidable only if the debt repaid was incurred in the ordinary course of the business of the debtor and the transferee.[96] The ordinary course of the business of the debtor focuses on the historic transactions between the debtor and the transferee to see if the same kinds of transactions occurred before.

Matter of Tolona Pizza Products Corp.
3 F.2d 1029 (7th Cir. 1993)

Posner, J.: * * * Tolona, a maker of pizza, issued eight checks to Rose, its sausage supplier, within 90 days before being thrown into bankruptcy by its creditors. The checks, which totaled a shade under $46,000, cleared and as a result Tolona's debts to Rose were paid in full. Tolona's other major trade creditors stand to receive only 13 cents on the dollar under the plan approved by the Bankruptcy Court, if the preferential treatment of Rose is allowed to stand. Tolona, as a debtor-in-possession, brought an adversary proceeding against Rose to recover the eight payments as voidable preferences. * * *

Rose's invoices recited "net 7 days," meaning that payment was due within seven days. For years preceding the preference period, however, Tolona rarely paid within seven days; nor did Rose's other customers. Most paid within 21 days, and if they paid later than 28 or 30 days Rose would usually withhold future shipments until payment was received. Tolona, however, as an old and valued customer (Rose had been selling to it for fifteen years), was permitted to make payments beyond the 21-day period and even beyond the 28-day or 30-day period. The eight payments at issue were made between 12 and 32 days after Rose had invoiced Tolona, for an average of 22 days; but this actually was an improvement. In the 34 months before the preference period, the average time for which Rose's invoices to Tolona were outstanding was 26 days and the longest time was 46 days. Rose consistently treated Tolona with a degree of leniency that made Tolona ... one of a sort of exceptional group of customers of Rose ... falling outside the common industry practice and standards.

It may seem odd that paying a debt late would ever be regarded as a preference to the creditor thus paid belatedly. But it is all relative. A debtor who has entered the preference period—who is therefore only 90 days, or fewer, away from plunging into bankruptcy—is typically unable to pay all his outstanding debts in full as they come due. If he pays one and not the others, as happened here, the payment though late is still a preference to that creditor, and is voidable unless the conditions of section 547(c)(2) are met. One condition is that the payment be in the ordinary course of both the debtor's and the creditor's business. A late payment normally will not be. It will therefore be a voidable preference.

This is not a dryly syllogistic conclusion. The purpose of the preference statute is to prevent the debtor during his slide toward bankruptcy from trying to stave off the evil day by giving preferential treatment to his most importunate creditors, who may sometimes be those who have been waiting the longest to be paid. Unless the favoring of particular creditors is outlawed, the mass of creditors of a shaky firm will be nervous, fearing that one or a few of their number are going to walk away with all the firm's assets; and their fear may precipitate debtors into bankruptcy earlier than is socially desirable. [Citations omitted.]

From this standpoint, however, the most important thing is not that the dealings between the debtor and the allegedly favored creditor conform to some industry norm but that they conform to the norm established by the debtor and the creditor in the period before, preferably well before, the preference period. That condition is satisfied here—if any, Rose treated Tolona more favorably (and hence Tolona treated Rose less preferentially) before the preference period than during it.

But if this is all that the third subsection of 547(c)(2) requires, it might seem to add nothing to the first two subsections, which require that both the debt and payment be within the ordinary course of business of both the debtor and the creditor. For provided these conditions are fulfilled, a "late" payment really isn't late if the parties have established a practice that deviates from the strict terms of their written contract. But we hesitate to conclude that the third subsection, requiring conformity to "ordinary business terms," has no function in the statute. We can think of two functions that it may have. One is evidentiary. [Citations omitted.] If the debtor and creditor dealt on terms that the creditor testifies were normal for them but that are wholly unknown in the industry, this casts some doubt on his (self-serving) testimony. Preferences are disfavored, and subsection C makes them more difficult to prove. The second possible function of the subsection is to allay the concerns of creditors that one or more of their number may have worked out a special deal with the debtor, before the preference period, designed to put that creditor ahead of the others in the event of bankruptcy. It may seem odd that allowing late payments from a debtor would be a way for a creditor to make himself more rather than less assured of repayment. But such a creditor does have an advantage during the preference period, because he can receive late payments then and they will still be in the ordinary course of business for him and his debtor.

* * *

[Therefore] the creditor must show that the payment he received was made in accordance with the ordinary business terms in the industry. But this does not mean that the creditor must establish the existence of some single, uniform set of business terms... Not only is it difficult to identify the industry whose norm shall govern (Is it, here, the sale of sausages to makers of pizza? The sale of sausages to anyone? The sale of anything to makers of pizza?), but there can be great variance in billing practices within an industry. Apparently there is in this industry, whatever exactly "this industry" is; for while it is plain that neither Rose nor its competitors enforce payment within seven days, it is unclear that there is a standard outer limit of forbearance. It seems that 21 days is a goal but that payment as late as 30 days is generally tolerated and that for good customers even longer delays are allowed. The average period between Rose's invoice and Tolona's payment during the preference period was only 22 days, which seems well within the industry norm, whatever exactly it is. The law should not push businessmen to agree upon a single set of billing practices; antitrust objections to one side, the relevant business and financial considerations vary widely among firms on both the buying and the selling side of the market.

We conclude that "ordinary business terms" refers to the range of terms that encompasses the practices in which firms similar in some general way to the creditor in question engage, and that only dealings so idiosyncratic as to fall outside that broad range should be deemed extraordinary and therefore outside the scope of subsection C. (citations omitted). [This] case is within the scope of "ordinary business terms" as just defined. Rose and its competitors pay little or no attention to the terms stated on their invoices, allow most customers to take up to 30 days to pay, and allow certain favored customers to take even more time. There is no single set of terms on which the members of the industry have coalesced; instead there is a broad range and the district judge plausibly situated the dealings between Rose and Tolona within it. These dealings are conceded to have been within the normal course of dealings between the two firms, a course established long before the preference period, and there is no hint either that the dealings were designed to put Rose ahead of other creditors of Tolona or that other creditors of Tolona would have been surprised to learn that Rose had been so forbearing in its dealings with Tolona.

* * *

The judgment reversing the bankruptcy judge and dismissing the adversary proceeding is affirmed.

Enabling Loans. This exception protects from voidance certain purchase money security interests. These security interests must arise from new value extended to the debtor for purposes of acquiring certain property. The property must be described in the underlying security agreement and must actually be purchased by the debtor with the funds furnished by the creditor. For this exception to apply, the debtor must actually use the funds advanced from the creditor to purchase the new collateral. Additionally, the creditor must perfect (record) the purchase money security interest no later than 20 days after the debtor takes possession (physical control or custody) of the collateral.[97] These types of loans are called *enabling loans* since they enable or allow the debtor to acquire new property with the funds advanced.

Subsequent New Value. This exception is also known as the "subsequent advance rule." In this case a preferential transfer may occur initially. However, after the transfer the creditor then makes advances to the debtor before the bankruptcy is filed. In this case, the initial preferential transfer may be set off against those new advances given after the preference was received by the creditor.[98] The rationale for this exception is to induce trade creditors to continue to extend credit and do business with debtors in financial straits.[99]

Floating Liens. Often creditors secure a debtor's obligation with an "after-acquired property" clause within their security agreements. For example, a bank makes a loan to a furniture company and secures the loan with not only the inventory of the company (the furniture) but all after-acquired inventory (furniture the company obtains after the initial loan and security instrument). This allows the company to continue to sell its furniture and obtain new inventory to sell. Meanwhile the bank does not lose any of its security by the sale of the initial inventory since the loan is also secured by the new inventory. These types of "after-acquired property" security interests are known as *floating liens* and are protected to a certain extent from preference actions.

A floating lien is voidable only to the extent that the creditor's position has improved. This is the difference between the outstanding balance of the debt owed and the value of the collateral existing at two specific times. One first looks to the 90th day before bankruptcy to ascertain the position of the creditor. Thereafter, one calculates the position of the creditor on the date of the petition.

For example, in the preceding illustration, on the 90th day before bankruptcy the furniture company held 400 couches secured by the bank's lien. On the bankruptcy date, the furniture company held 500 couches. In this situation, the bank's lien would be voidable to the extent of the value of the additional 100 couches.[100]

Statutory Liens. The sixth exception makes the fixing of a statutory lien nonvoidable as a preference. Moreover, payment to prevent attachment or perfection of a statutory lien may in some jurisdictions also not be voided as a preference.[101] Statutory liens that are nonvoidable include mechanic's and materialman's liens,[102] tax liens,[103] maritime liens,[104] and possibly attorney's liens.[105]

Other liens that are not considered statutory liens under 11 U.S.C. Section 545, which may be voided as preferences, include judicial liens[106] and landlord's liens.[107]

Spousal/Child Support Transfers. The 1994 Amendments added an additional exception to preference exceptions. Under 11 U.S.C. Section

547(c)(7) a transfer that is a payment of a debt to a spouse, former spouse, or child of the debtor in connection with a separation agreement or divorce decree may not be voided as a preference. However, the transfer to the initial (ex)spouse or child must not have been assigned to another entity (such as the exspouse's attorney). Additionally, the liability of the debtor must be "actually in the nature of alimony, maintenance or support." This language parallels the language within the dischargeability exception of 11 U.S.C. Section 523(a)(5) with case law focusing upon the difference between support and property settlement.[108]

Consumer Debts Under $600. The final exception to transfers voidable as preferences is in cases filed by individuals. Those cases must include debts that are primarily consumer debts (i.e., credit cards v. commercial loans). Further the total amount of the property that is transferred must amount to less than $600.[109]

FRAUDULENT CONVEYANCES

A trustee may void a transaction as a fraudulent conveyance under 11 U.S.C. Section 548. To qualify as a fraudulent conveyance, the transfer must be of something that is the debtor's property. The transaction must occur within one year before the bankruptcy petition is filed. Also, the transaction must entail either of the following: (1) the debtor's actual intent to hinder, delay, or defraud creditors, or (2) not enough given in exchange for the transfer (less than reasonably equivalent value).

Before filing bankruptcy a debtor may give away, or transfer, valuable property. A debtor would make these prepetition transfers in order to keep the trustee from collecting and liquidating the property. The property would be saved and the creditors would go unpaid. However, these types of transfers are made with a debtor's intent to hinder, delay, or defraud creditors. Therefore, these types of transfers may be undone by the fraudulent conveyance statute of 11 U.S.C. Section 548.

For example, the debtor owns a vintage 1965 Corvette worth approximately $10,000. Nine months before his bankruptcy, the debtor gives his car to his brother (to whom he owes nothing). The debtor makes this transfer because he knows the trustee would be able to take his car and sell it to pay the creditors. The brother gives nothing for the car.

This transaction is a fraudulent conveyance and is voidable by the trustee under 11 U.S.C. Section 548. The car is the property of the debtor. The transfer took place nine months before the petition was filed, well within the one-year reach-back limit. Also, the debtor intended to delay, hinder, and defraud his creditors by placing the car out of their reach. Accordingly, the trustee may "undo" the transfer of the car and obtain the vehicle to sell. The sales proceeds would be available to all creditors for distribution in Chapter 7.

The "less than reasonably equivalent value" fraudulent conveyance must include any one of the following three additional circumstances:

- At the time of the transfer the debtor was insolvent or became insolvent because of the transfer.
- Due to the transfer the debtor was ultimately left with not enough money to continue to do business.
- Due to the transfer it was believed or intended that the debtor could no longer pay his or her debts as they became due.

Note: In the "less than reasonably equivalent value" fraudulent conveyances, the intent of the debtor is irrelevant. This means the debtor could be innocent of trying to avoid creditors. However, the transaction would still be voidable if not enough was given in exchange and any one of the other three factors is proven.

Would it matter if the debtor was not trying to trick his creditors and the brother paid $2,000 for the car (fabulous deal!) because the debtor had no money whatsoever and needed to buy some food? No. This falls within the second option of voidable preference, "unreasonable equivalent value." While there is no actual intent to defraud the creditors, the $2,000 is an unreasonable amount compared to the value of the car ($10,000). Additionally, the debtor was insolvent at the time of the transfer (the debtor had no funds at all). Accordingly, this transaction is also voidable by the trustee.

Would it matter if the debtor sold the car to XYZ Used cars for $2,000? No. Fraudulent conveyances do not have the "insider" prolonged reach-back period as in preferences. Instead, all transfers are subject to attack if they occur within one year prepetition. Here, XYZ is not an insider but it does not matter.

Policy of Fraudulent Conveyance

The policy of voiding fraudulent conveyances under bankruptcy law, 11 U.S.C. Section 548, is more apparent than that of preferences. Fraudulent conveyances are an infringement of a creditor's right to realize upon the available assets of the debtor. Fraudulent conveyances are transfers that are made with the actual intent to hinder, delay, or defraud creditors or those made without actual intent to defraud but that are deemed to be unfair to other creditors.

Accordingly, the policy behind voiding fraudulent conveyances is to preserve the assets of the estate. This differs from preferential transfer provisions, which are meant to guard all parties by promoting equal distribution of the debtor's estate.[110] The purpose of voiding fraudulent transfers is to prevent a debtor from diminishing, to the detriment of some or all creditors, funds that are generally available for distribution to creditors.[111] Under the fraudulent transfer voidance laws, a trustee is enabled to gather assets of a bankruptcy estate from recent transferees (those to whom a transfer has been made) who took more than their due.[112]

The following is a prime example of the policy of voiding fraudulent transfers. Assume a debtor held vacation property on the beach in Florida without a mortgage. Immediately before the debtor filed bankruptcy, he transferred this beach property to his brother. In this case, a trustee may recover either the property or the value of the property from the debtor's brother. Obviously, the debtor transferred the property to the brother to prevent the property being sold and the sales proceeds being distributed to creditors as estate property. Accordingly, the debtor intended to diminish estate property to the detriment of creditors. Such a transfer is prevented by the bankruptcy fraudulent conveyance laws.

Fraudulent Conveyances Brought Under State or Federal Law

Fraudulent transfer actions may be brought under state fraudulent conveyance laws through 11 U.S.C. Section 544(b). Additionally, fraudulent conveyance actions may be brought directly under federal law, which is 11 U.S.C. Section 548. Complaints to avoid fraudulent conveyances are usually structured in the alternative. This means that a fraudulent conveyance complaint will put all the elements of state law in one count of the complaint and all the elements of federal law under another count of the complaint. This allows the trustee to use the facts of each transfer to fit within one or the other or both state or federal fraudulent conveyance statutes. There are critical differences between bringing such actions under either state or federal laws.

Initially, under federal law 11 U.S.C. Section 548, the trustee may bring an action in his own right, not that of a creditor. Conversely, state law requires the trustee to identify an actual unsecured creditor who could have set aside the transfer outside of bankruptcy. This subjects the trustee to all the defenses that could have been asserted against that creditor.[113] Further, under federal law, transfers subject to fraudulent conveyance actions must occur within one year prior to the petition date. Conversely, under state law, the trustee often is able to probe into fraudulent conveyances that occurred more than one year before the petition (e.g., Arizona law has a three-year statute of limitations on these actions [A.R.S. Section 12-543(3)], and Wisconsin has a six-year statute of limitations [Wis. Stats. Section 893.93(1)(b)].} Finally, state fraudulent conveyance law generally has a more stringent standard of proof than federal law.[114]

Given the variety of state fraudulent conveyance laws available to the trustee under 11 U.S.C. Section 544(b), legal assistants should research the essential elements in their own states. However, most applicable state statutes are modeled after either the Uniform Fraudulent Transfer Act (UFTA) or the Uniform Fraudulent Conveyance Act (UFCA).[115]

Elements of Fraudulent Conveyances Under Federal Law

There are essentially five elements in a fraudulent conveyance suit under federal law (11 U.S.C. Section 548). The trustee must prove:

1. A transfer of the debtor's property,
2. Made within one year before the petition date,
3. Made with either:
   A. "Actual fraud" (the actual intent to hinder, delay, or defraud a creditor of the debtor), or
   B. "Constructive fraud" (for which the debtor received less than reasonable equivalent value in exchange from such transfer), and
      i.   The debtor was insolvent when the transfer was made or rendered insolvent thereby, or
      ii. The debtor was engaged in a business for which the debtor's remaining property represented unreasonably small capital, or
      iii. The debtor intended or believed he would incur debts beyond his ability to repay as they matured.

The first two elements are the same for either actual fraud or constructive fraud suits. Namely, the initial elements are a transfer of debtor's property and the transfer was made within one year before the petition. However, note the difference where a conveyance is made with actual intent to hinder, delay, or defraud creditors. For actual intent cases it is not necessary to show that the debtor was insolvent for the conveyance to be voidable as fraudulent.[116]

Transfer of Debtor's Property. Transfer includes virtually every type of voluntary or involuntary disposition of real or personal property. It includes not only physical transfers of property and transfers of title to property, but also transfers of interests in property, such as granting security interest or incurring liens. *Transfer* is defined as every mode—direct or indirect, absolute or conditional, voluntary or involuntary—of disposing of or parting with property or with an interest in property, including retention of title as a security interest and foreclosure of debtor's equity of redemption.[117]

State law governs when a transfer is perfected against bona fide purchasers for purposes of 11 U.S.C. Section 548. For example, under Alaska law as well as New York law, a deed of trust becomes perfected against subsequent bona fide purchasers when it is recorded.

Made Within One Year Before the Petition Date. The transfer or perfection of such transfer must occur within one year before the petition in order to bring a federal 11 U.S.C. Section 548 action. However, the one-year time period under Section 548 does not constitute a statute of limitations on the trustee's powers to bring suit under other sections, such as an 11 U.S.C. Section 544(b) action based on state law. In the latter, the state fraudulent conveyance law is applied (such as in Florida a four-year statute of limitation is applicable).[118]

"Actual Fraud"—Made with Actual Intent to Hinder, Delay, or Defraud a Creditor of the Debtor. To avoid a transfer under 11 U.S.C. Section 548(a), there must be actual intent to defraud creditors. It is often impractical to demonstrate intent to hinder, delay, or defraud creditors. For example, it is unlikely the debtor will testify that it intended to defraud creditors and thereby jeopardize its discharge. Accordingly, fraudulent intent may be inferred from circumstances surrounding the transfer.

Such circumstantial evidence is often presented as "badges of fraud."[119] Badges of fraud include:

1. When conveyances were made the debtor was indebted to various creditors.
2. Transfers were general and the debtor's entire estate was diminished.
3. No bona fide consideration was present.
4. The transfers were secret and concealed from creditors.
5. Transfers were made to family members or one with close relationships to the debtor.
6. Lawsuits were pending against the debtor when the transfers were made.
7. Transfers were made with an understanding that the property would actually be held in trust for the debtor.[120]

Due to the difficulty in proving intent to defraud, it may be implied from circumstances. However, while a finding of actual fraud may be inferred from such circumstances, the facts supporting such inference must preclude any reasonable conclusion other than that the purpose of the transfer was to defraud the debtor's creditors.[121] Additionally, the trustee must show fraudulent intent on the part of the debtor (or transferor) rather than on the part of the transferee (the one who receives the transfer).

Some examples of fraudulent conveyances are:

- A debtor conveys his house, car, and business stock to his brother with the intent to delay, hinder, and defraud creditors who would have otherwise been able to receive distribution upon the liquidation of such assets.[122]

- A debtor transfers his life insurance policy to his wife one week before bankruptcy without fair consideration.[123]

- A former officer of debtor trucking company is paid sums when such sums are not for consulting services, but payments in fraud of creditors.[124]

- The title to the debtor corporation's Jaguar was transferred to an employee and was a fraudulent transfer when the car was not compensation for employment.[125]

"Constructive Fraud"—Debtor Received Less Than Reasonable Equivalent Value in Exchange from the Transfer. The purpose of 11 U.S.C. Section 548(a)(2) is to establish a test for constructive fraud, as opposed to actual fraud. If the conditions are met, a conclusive presumption of fraud arises. The key issue in constructive fraud cases is whether the debtor received the "reasonably equivalent value" for the transfer.

The concept of "reasonably equivalent value" is whether the debtor received a fair exchange in the marketplace for the goods transferred.[126] In other words, the debtor must receive direct or indirect economic benefit to constitute reasonably equivalent value. Such a determination is factual and depends on the market value of the property transferred and whether the sale was an arm's-length transaction.[127] Further, the date for defining reasonable equivalence is the date of the transfer.[128]

BFP v. Resolution Trust Corp.
114 S.Ct. 1757 (1994)

Scalia, J.: [Petitioner BFP took title to a California home subject to, *inter alia*, a deed of trust in favor of Imperial Savings Association. After Imperial entered a notice of default because its loan was not being serviced, the home was purchased by respondent Osborne for $433,000 at a properly noticed foreclosure sale. BFP soon petitioned for bankruptcy and, acting as a debtor-in-possession, filed a complaint to set aside the sale to Osborne as a fraudulent transfer, claiming that the home was worth over $725,000 when sold and thus was not exchanged for a "reasonably equivalent value" under 11 U.S.C. Section 548(a)(2).]

* * *

Section 548 of the Bankruptcy Code, 11 U.S.C. Section 548, sets forth the powers of a trustee in bankruptcy (or, in a Chapter 11 case, a debtor-in-possession) to void fraudulent transfers. It permits to be set aside not only transfers infected by actual fraud but certain other transfers as well—so-called constructively fraudulent transfers. The constructive fraud provision at issue in this case applies to transfers by insolvent debtors. It permits voidance if the trustee can establish (1) that the debtor had an interest in property; (2) that a transfer of that interest occurred within one year of the filing of the bankruptcy petition; (3) that the debtor was insolvent at the time of the transfer or became insolvent as a result thereof; and (4) that the debtor received "less than a reasonably equivalent value in exchange for such transfer." 11 U.S.C. Section 548(a)(2)(A). It is the last of these four elements that presents the issue in the case before us.

Section 548 applies to any "transfer," which includes "foreclosure of the debtor's equity of redemption." 11 U.S.C. Section 101(54). Of the three critical terms "reasonably equivalent value," only the last is defined: "value" means, for purposes of Section 548, "property, or satisfaction or securing of a ... debt of the debtor," 11 U.S.C. Section 548(d)(2)(A). The question presented here, therefore, is whether the amount of debt (to the first and second lien holders) satisfied at the foreclosure sale (viz., a total of $433,000) is "reasonably equivalent" to the worth of the real estate conveyed. The Courts of Appeals have divided on the meaning of those undefined terms. In *Durrett v. Washington Nat. Ins. Co.,* 621 F.2d 201 (1980), the Fifth Circuit, interpreting a provision of the old Bankruptcy Act analogous to Section 548(a)(2), held that a foreclosure sale that yielded 57 percent of the property's fair market value could be set aside, and indicated in dicta that any such sale of less than 70 percent of fair market value should be invalidated. This "Durett rule" has continued to be applied by some courts under Section 548 of the new Bankruptcy Code. * * * In this case the Ninth Circuit adopted the position that the consideration received at a noncollusive, regularly conducted real estate foreclosure sale constitutes a reasonably equivalent value under Section 548(a)(2)(A). The Court of Appeals acknowledged that it "necessarily parted from the positions taken by the Fifth Circuit in Durett ..."

In contrast to the approach adopted by the Ninth Circuit in the present case, ... Durett refers to fair market value as the benchmark against which determination of reasonably equivalent value is to be measured. In the context of an otherwise lawful mortgage foreclosure sale of real estate, such reference is in our opinion not consistent with the text of the Bankruptcy Code. The term "fair market value," though it is a well-established concept, does not appear in Section 548. * * * Section 548, on the other hand, seemingly goes out of its way to avoid that standard term. It might readily have said "received less than fair market value in exchange for such transfer or obligation," or perhaps "less than a reasonable equivalent of fair market value." Instead, it used the (as far as we are aware) entirely novel phrase "reasonably equivalent value." * * *

[M]arket value, as it is commonly understood, has no applicability in the forced-sale context; indeed it is the very antithesis of forced-sale value. "The market value of ... a piece of property is the price which it might be expected to bring if offered for sale in a fair market; not the price which might be obtained on a sale at public auction or a sale forced by the necessities of the owner, but such a price as would be fixed by negotiation and mutual agreement, after ample time to find a purchaser, as between a vendor who is willing (but not compelled) to sell and a purchaser who desires to buy but is not compelled to take the particular piece of property." In short, "fair market value" presumes market conditions that, by definition, simply do not obtain in the context of a forced sale. (citations omitted).

* * * Market value cannot be the criterion of equivalence in the foreclosure-sale context. The language of Section 548(a)(2)(A) ("received less than a reasonably equivalent value in exchange") requires judicial inquiry into whether the foreclosed property was sold for a price that approximated its worth at the time of the sale. An appraiser's reconstruction of "fair market value" could show what similar property would be worth if it did not have to be sold within the time and manner strictures of state-prescribed foreclosure. But property that must be sold within those strictures is simply worth less. No one would pay as much to own such property as he would pay to own real estate that could be sold at leisure and pursuant to normal marketing techniques. And it is no more realistic to ignore that characteristic of the property (the fact that state foreclosure law permits the mortgagee to sell it at forced sale) than it is to ignore other price-affecting characteristics (such as the fact that state zoning law permits the owner of the neighboring lot to open a gas station). * * *

For the reasons described, we decline to read the phrase "reasonably equivalent value" in Section 548(a)(2) to mean, in its application to mortgage foreclosure sales,either "fair market value" or "fair foreclosure price" (whether calculated as a percentage of fair market value or otherwise). We deem, as the law has always deemed, that a fair proper price, or a "reasonably equivalent value," for foreclosed property, is the price in fact received at the foreclosure sale, so long as all the requirements of the state's foreclosure law have been complied with.

* * *

For the foregoing reasons, the judgment of the Court of Appeals for the Ninth Circuit is affirmed.

In addition to establishing the lack of reasonable equivalent value, the trustee must also establish one of the three statutory criteria to demonstrate constructive fraud. These three criteria are as follows:

1. The debtor was insolvent at the time of the transfer or became insolvent because of the transfer.
2. The transfer left the debtor's business with unreasonably small capital.
3. The debtor intended/believed he or she would incur debts beyond his or her ability to pay at the time of the transfer.

As in preference litigation, *insolvency* means that the sum of a debtor's obligations must be greater than the fair valuation of the debtor's assets.[129] Additionally, the date of insolvency is calculated as of the date of the transfer.[130]

Unreasonably small capitalization, as used in fraudulent conveyance actions, is not the equivalent of insolvency. This term encompasses difficulties that are short of insolvency but that are likely to lead to insolvency in the future.[131] An example of a transfer that leads a business debtor to become undercapitalized is as follows: A corporate debtor gave payments and promissory notes to its president prepetition. Meanwhile the debtor's financial condition was precarious even before the transfer and the business thereafter incurred substantial debt. After the transfer, the business was left unable to meet its financial obligations as they became due and was placed in further financial straits in order to meet the financial obligations to the president under the transfer. In short, the promissory note given to the president placed additional debt on the debtor. The combination of the payments and promissory notes transferred to the president left the business without sufficient capital to continue to do business. Accordingly, when the debtor filed for bankruptcy, the transfer to the president was a voidable fraudulent conveyance under Section 548(a)(2)(B)(ii). [See *In re Joshua Slocum, Ltd.*, 103 B.R. 610 (Bankr. E.D. Pa. 1989), aff'd 121 B.R. 442 (Dist. E.D. Pa.).]

Also, in addition to proving unreasonably equivalent value, the trustee may also show the transferor's (debtor's) intent or belief that the transfer would lead to its inability to pay its debts as they mature.[132]

An example of a case that allows the trustee to void the transfer as a fraudulent conveyance is as follows: Prior to bankruptcy, the shareholders of the company knew the debtor was economically instable. However, the shareholders allowed some of the stock to be transferred and thereafter placed the proceeds into escrow for ultimate distribution to the shareholders as dividends. This resulted in the immediate inability of the debtor to pay the debts (i.e., the checking account was immediately overdrawn). The trustee was able to prove that the shareholders believed that the debtor would incur debts beyond its ability to pay at the time of the transfer. Accordingly, the transfer was voidable as a fraudulent conveyance. [See *In re Suburban Motor Freight, Inc.*, 124 B.R. 984 (Bankr. S.D. Ohio 1990).]

The Bankruptcy Code has statutory provisions that allow a trustee to bring a voidable fraudulent conveyance action against partners of a debtor partnership.[133] The transfer of a partnership debtor to a general partner made within one year prepetition may be voided if the debtor was insolvent at the time of the transfer or became insolvent because of the transfer. A partnership is deemed insolvent if the sum of the partnership debt is greater than the fair value of the partnership property plus any amounts of each general partner's assets that are in excess of each general partner's nonpartnership debts. (Note: General partners are liable for partnership debts after all assets of the general partnership are exhausted.)

Under the Bankruptcy Code, a transfer for fraudulent conveyance purposes is deemed to have been made when such transfer is "perfected" against a subsequent bona fide purchaser. This means that the transaction cannot be undone by some third party stepping in and claiming rights to the property.

The distinction of a transfer being made at the time of perfection is important since it may delay the time that a transfer is deemed to have occurred. This may bring the transaction within the one-year reach-back period of the fraudulent conveyance statutes. Therefore, the crucial issue is not when the transfer occurred, but rather when such transfer was perfected.

Additionally, the issue of when a transfer is perfected against a subsequent bona fide purchaser is determined by state law rather than by bankruptcy law.[134] Accordingly, it is important in the analysis of the timing of the "transfer" to determine the applicable laws of the state within your jurisdiction. For example, in New York and Alaska a transfer of real property is perfected only when the deed is recorded. In Arkansas, a transfer of real property is perfected at the time the mortgages are signed.

Each element of a fraudulent conveyance for federal bankruptcy purposes is measured not when the transfer actually took place but when such transfer is deemed to have been perfected. This includes elements of whether the debtor was insolvent, what the debtor's intentions or beliefs were, and whether reasonably equivalent value is provided. Accordingly, a delay that may be caused between the actual transfer and the date of perfection may cause the transaction to fall within the one-year statute of limitations of 11 U.S.C. Section 548.

Consider the following: A deed is executed when a debtor is solvent but not recorded (perfected) until a later date. At the later date on which the deed was recorded, the debtor had since become insolvent. The "perfection" date is the "transfer" date under this scenario. Accordingly, the court will deem the debtor insolvent at the time of the perfection date and the transaction will be voidable as a fraudulent conveyance. [See *In re Brown Iron & Metal, Inc.,* 28 B.R. 426 (Bankr. E.D. Tenn. 1983).]

Finally, should the debtor conceal transfers but continue to use the property, the transaction will likely be deemed to have taken place at the time when the trustee learned of such transfer.[135] This is to prevent debtors from successfully concealing fraudulent transfers in the hopes that the trustee will never discovery them or simply discover the transfers after the statute of limitations has expired.

Defenses to Fraudulent Conveyance Actions

A defendant in a fraudulent conveyance action may assert all the defenses such as sovereign immunity (governmental agency),[136] res judicata or collateral estoppel (issue already determined by other court),[137] improper service, lack of jurisdiction, expiration of statute of limitations, etc.

Also, the defendant in a fraudulent conveyance action may assert as an affirmative statutory defense its status as a good faith transferee who takes the property for value. In such a defense, transferees may fall within three categories: (1) those who give reasonably equivalent value in good faith; (2) those who give some value, although not reasonably equivalent value, in good faith; and (3) those who give either no value or value but not in good faith. Parties seeking to establish that they are good faith transferees have the burden of demonstrating that they are entitled to this status.[138]

The initial inquiry is whether the transferee (one who receives the transfer) has good faith. Initially, if a transferee has knowledge of a debtor's fraudulent purposes, then the transferee does not accept the transfer in good faith.[139] Additionally, transferees who have knowledge of a debtor's insolvency or have knowledge sufficient to put them on notice of the debtor's possible insolvency shall have difficulty demonstrating their good faith.[140] For example, transactions known by the transferee to be out of the usual and ordinary course of business tend to negate any finding of good faith.

Under 11 U.S.C. Section 548(c), the transferee may get a lien in the property recovered by the trustee to the extent that the transferee gives value in good faith. However, since bona fide purchasers get a lien only to the extent of the value they transferred, any excess over that value belongs to the trustee. For example, a purchaser of a debtor's car is entitled to a lien against the car to the extent he gave value in good faith, even if the transfer is voidable.[141] Therefore, if a defendant purchased a debtor's car for $5,000 without any knowledge of the debtor's financial difficulties, the defendant maintains a lien against the car for $5,000. However, the car may ultimately be recovered by the trustee and sold. If the trustee sells the car for $7,500, then the defendant will get only $5,000 with the remainder distributed to the debtor's creditors.

Additionally, a defendant may also retain a lien against the property for improvements made in good faith after the fraudulent conveyance.[142] Improvements means additions or renovations which increase the value of the property. For example, presume the purchaser of the car in the example puts in a new stereo and paints the car after the transfer and still has no knowledge of the debtor's financial straits. These "improvements" allow the trustee to sell the car for $10,000 instead of $7,500. Accordingly, the purchaser will retain a lien for the initial value ($5,000) plus the improvement value ($2,500), with the remainder being distributed to creditors of the estate.

Finally, transferees will receive no lien, even if value is given, if they cannot show good faith.[143] Instead, the transferees must return the property and are left with only an unsecured claim against the estate for value given. In our example, the purchaser knew the debtor was going to file bankruptcy due to his financial problems. Therefore, the purchaser would have to return the vehicle and would only thereafter be able to file a proof of claim as an unsecured creditor.

POSTPETITION TRANSFERS

A trustee may void a transaction as a postpetition unauthorized transfer under 11 U.S.C. Section 549. To qualify as a unauthorized postpetition transfer, the transfer must be something that is the debtor's property. Also, the transfer must occur after the bankruptcy petition is filed. Finally, the transfer was never authorized by the Court or the Bankruptcy Code.

For example, the debtor owns a vintage 1965 Corvette worth approximately $10,000. The debtor files bankruptcy and still owns the car. After he files, the debtor realizes the car is subject to sale by the trustee and therefore gives it to his brother.

This transaction is a voidable postpetition transfer under 11 U.S.C. Section 549. The car is the debtor's property. The transfer occurred after the petition was filed and was never authorized.

Would it make a difference if, again, the debtor realized the car was subject to sale by the trustee? However, this time the debtor requests the Court for authorization to sell the car to his brother for $10,500. (The brother has always loved this car and the debtor is in fear that the trustee will not sell it for as much as it is worth.) The Court approves the sale with all sales proceeds to be turned over to the trustee after the debtor keeps all exemptible amounts.

This transaction is not voidable by the trustee. While the transaction takes place postpetition, formal court approval was sought and obtained by the debtor. Accordingly, this transfer would overcome any voidance suit by the trustee.

Elements of Unauthorized Postpetition Transfers

All postpetition transfers of property of the estate that are unauthorized by the Code or by a bankruptcy judge are subject to voidance by a bankruptcy trustee under 11 U.S.C. Section 549. However, such transfers must be property of the estate and must occur after the filing of the debtor's bankruptcy petition. An example is a debtor's converting estate funds by depositing them in a private account and thereafter making payments from the account to other individuals.[144]

Defenses to Postpetition Transfer Actions

The Bankruptcy Code specifically empowers the Bankruptcy Court to grant the debtor prior permission to pay prepetition claims. For example, payment of prepetition wages to a debtor's employees may take place only upon the debtor's request and formal approval by the Bankruptcy Court.[145] Formal Court approval for a postpetition transfer defeats any action for recovery of the property. 11 U.S.C. Section 549 also permits transfers that are otherwise authorized by the Bankruptcy Code. This includes payments made in the ordinary course of a debtor's ongoing business that are authorized under 11 U.S.C. Section 363. To qualify as "ordinary course" payments, such payments must be consistent with ordinary day-to-day operations, as well as industrywide practices of the debtor's business.[146]

Otherwise, 11 U.S.C. Section 549 allows for two statutory exceptions to overcome postpetition transfers. Initially, in an involuntary case before an order of relief has been entered (the "gap" period), a transfer may not be voided to the extent value is provided for the transfer. In this gap period, it does not matter whether the transferee had knowledge or notice that an involuntary case had been filed.

The second defense for a postpetition transfer applies to voluntary cases. In a voluntary case a transferee of real estate may overcome a postpetition voidable transfer action by showing that a copy of the bankruptcy petition had not been recorded in the county where the real estate is located. Further, the transferee must show it was a good faith purchaser without knowledge of the commencement of the bankruptcy. In essence, the transferee must show it had neither actual nor constructive knowledge of the bankruptcy.[147] Finally, the transferee must show that it purchased the property for the present fair equivalent value.

Any purchase for less than present fair equivalent value makes the purchase voidable. However, the purchaser retains a lien against the real estate in the amount of the present value given.[148]

COLLECTION OF VOIDABLE TRANSFERS

Transferee liabilities under 11 U.S.C. Sections 547, 548, and 549 are governed generally under 11 U.S.C. Section 550. Under 11 U.S.C. Section 550, the trustee and an individual debtor have the option of seeking recovery of either the actual property involved in a voidable transfer *or* its value.[149] To the extent an individual debtor claims that the potentially recovered property is exempt, the trustee ordinarily will allow the debtor to exercise the trustee's voiding powers. This will shift the expense of voidance to the debtor who is the principal beneficiary.

The initial transferee and any other entity for whose benefit the voidable transfer was made must show good faith if the property is recovered in order to be given a lien on the property. However, an immediate transferee and subsequent transferees (called subtransferees, those to whom the property is transferred by the initial transferee) may defeat liability of a voidable transfer by showing each of the following elements: (1) taking for value (includes satisfaction/security of either present or antecedent debt); (2) taking in good faith; and (3) taking without actual knowledge of the voidability of the transfer. To be in good faith, the value must have a reasonable equivalency to the value of the property transferred.

As soon as any subtransferee obtains immunity by satisfying all three prerequisites, all subsequent subtransferees qualify for immunity against the trustee's voidability actions on the basis of good faith alone. This means that, even if the subtransferees do not give value or find out the transfer was voidable after it was made, they are not subject to voidability claims by the trustee. Note: If a subtransferee is aware of the voidability of a transfer when it was made, then the subtransferee cannot acquire the property in good faith.

In any case, neither a trustee nor a debtor can recover both the value of the property *and* the property itself. Accordingly, regardless of the number of transferees subject to liability, a trustee is limited to recovery of either the property transferred or its value.[150]

AUTHORITY TO BRING VOIDABLE TRANSFER ACTIONS

The authority to bring voidable transfer actions such as preference actions under 11 U.S.C. Section 547, fraudulent conveyance actions under 11 U.S.C.

Section 548, or postpetition transfer actions under 11 U.S.C. Section 549, is governed by 11 U.S.C. Section 544. This Code section is known as the trustee's "strong-arm" statute. The trustee has three separate rights and powers under the strong-arm clause. First, the trustee has the rights of a creditor on a simple contract with a judicial lien on the property of the debtor as of the date of the petition. Next, the trustee has the rights of a creditor with a writ of execution against the property of the debtor unsatisfied as of the date of the petition. Third, the trustee has the rights of a bona fide purchaser of the real property of the debtor as of the date of the petition. Therefore, under 11 U.S.C. Section 544 the trustee is empowered to bring voidable transfer actions.

However, in Chapter 11 cases where no trustee is appointed and the debtor is acting as the debtor-in-possession, the debtor is empowered by 11 U.S.C. Section 1107 to act as the trustee to pursue preference or fraudulent conveyance actions. Also, the commencement of litigation by the trustee or debtor-in-possession on behalf of the bankruptcy estate is permissive and not mandatory. Therefore, the trustee or debtor-in-possession has a substantial degree of discretion to sue or not to sue.

In essence, only the trustee or debtor-in-possession can bring any voidance actions. The filing of a debtor's petition transforms the state law rights of the creditors seeking recovery of the debtor's assets transferred.[151] Individual creditors lack authority to institute voidance actions.[152]

The rationale for this exclusive standing is that it is the trustee who should weigh the merits of the action, the likelihood of success, the litigation cost to the estate, and the ultimate net benefit to the estate, not individual creditors.[153] The trustee acts as a fiduciary for the benefit of all creditors of the estate and is in a unique position to determine if voidance actions are globally merited. The trustee is able to make this determination without bias toward either the debtor or the transferees. Voidance actions are brought by the trustee in the name of the bankruptcy estate as the real party in interest.

However, there are exceptions to the trustee's exclusive power to bring voidance actions. An official creditors' committee has implied authority to bring an action on behalf of the estate with approval of the Bankruptcy Court.[154] In order for an official committee to receive Court authority to initiate the action, the committee must demonstrate the trustee or DIP's unjustifiable failure to employ the statutory arsenal of voiding powers or otherwise show an abuse of discretion in not suing.[155] A prime example of when an official committee is allowed to initiate voidance actions is when the debtor is acting as debtor-in-possession and refuses to bring voidance actions against friends or family members.

Another example of exceptions to the trustee's exclusive powers arises in Chapter 13 cases. However, the ability of Chapter 13 debtors to bring voidance actions is not as established as the ability of the trustee or a debtor-in-possession. Some jurisdictions allow the Chapter 13 debtor to bring fraudulent conveyance actions under 11 U.S.C. Section 548.[156] This often occurs when a Chapter 13 debtor is attempting to void the transfer of a residence which is claimed as exempt under Section 522(h). [See *In re Willis*, 48 B.R. 295 (Dist. S.D. Tex. 1985) and *In re Wheeler*, 34 B.R. 818 (Bankr. N.D. Ala. 1983).] However, some jurisdictions hold that the Chapter 13 debtor has standing to bring fraudulent conveyance actions without resorting to the exempt status of the property under 11 U.S.C. Section 522. [See *In re Carr*, 34 B.R. 653 (Bankr. Conn. 1983) aff'd 40 B.R. 1007 (Dist. Conn).]

Standing to initiate a preference action in Chapter 13 also is not as clear-cut. For example, some courts do not allow a Chapter 13 debtor to initiate a preference action under 11 U.S.C. Section 547 and allow only the Chapter 13 trustee to bring such actions. [See *Hill v. Fidelity Fin. Svcs.*, 152 B.R. 204 (Bankr. S.D. Ohio 1993).] Meanwhile other courts do not allow the Chapter 13 trustee to bring preference actions under 11 U.S.C. Section 547 over the objection of the Chapter 13 debtor. [See *In re Ciavarella*, 28 B.R. 823 (Bankr. S.D. N.Y. 1983) (reasoning that since Chapter 13 trustee's rights and duties are administrative in nature and the Chapter 13 debtor alone controls whether or not he remains in Chapter 13).]

In essence, the ability of a debtor in Chapter 13 to initiate voidance actions will depend on the stare decisis of a paralegal's jurisdiction. A legal assistant representing either debtors or creditors must identify the standing of a Chapter 13 debtor in his or her jurisdiction. As a practical matter, it is advisable for the legal assistant to research the issue of Chapter 13 debtor standing to bring voidance actions for the jurisdiction where the legal assistant will be practicing.

STATUTES OF LIMITATIONS ON VOIDABLE TRANSFER ACTIONS

Statutes of limitations are deadlines. In voidance actions there are two different types of deadlines. The first of these statutes of limitations is the lapse of time from the date of the transaction to the petition. The other statute of limitations is the deadline measured from the petition to the date within which a voidable lawsuit must be filed. For sake of ease the first type will be termed the "reach-back" statute of limitations (the lapse of time from the transaction to the petition) and the second type will be called the "follow-through" statute of limitations (the deadline from the petition and the date within which suit must be filed).

The reach-back statutes of limitations for each of the statutory voidable transfer causes (11 U.S.C. Sections 547, 548, and 549) are discussed at length in each section. However, a summary of such reach-back statute of limitations is as follows:

1. Preference actions (11 U.S.C. Section 547) may be brought for transactions occurring 90 days prepetition (or one year prepetition if the transferee is an insider).

2. Fraudulent conveyance actions (11 U.S.C. Section 548) may be brought if the transaction occurred within one year before the petition was filed.

3. For postpetition voidance actions (11 U.S.C. Section 549), the transaction must occur after the petition has been filed.

Prepetition transfers subject to voidance are preferences and fraudulent conveyances. The follow-through statutes of limitations (or deadline from the petition to the date within which the trustee must file suit) on these prepetition transfers are governed exclusively by 11 U.S.C. Section 546.[157] Under 11 U.S.C. Section 546(a)(1), two different statutes of limitations exist within which to file a prepetition voidance action. Generally, these may be thought of as the "two-year rule" or the "one-year from a trustee rule."

The first of these statutes of limitations (the two-year rule) requires a voidance action to be brought within two years after the order for relief has been entered. In voluntary cases the order for relief is entered when the petition is filed. In involuntary cases the Bankruptcy Court actually enters an order for relief. Therefore, under this first follow-through statute of limitations under 11 U.S.C. Section 546(a)(1), a voidance action must be filed within two years of the petition date.

The second statute of limitations (the one-year from a trustee rule) available under 11 U.S.C. Section 546(a)(1) is one year after the appointment of the first trustee, regardless of the Chapter of the case. If the follow-through statute of limitations uses the appointment date of the trustee, then a trustee must be appointed within two years of the petition date. Also note that the one-year time limit is from the appointment of the *first* trustee, and not from the appointment of any successor trustee.

For example, ABC Corporation files Chapter 11 on January 1, 1995. Under the two-year rule, the deadline to file any prepetition voidance actions is December 31, 1997. However, suppose the Chapter 11 is ultimately converted to Chapter 7 on December 15, 1997. A Chapter 7 Trustee is appointed on December 30, 1997. In this case the Chapter 7 Trustee has the opportunity to file voidance suits up until December 30, 1998. The trustee's appointment was before two years lapsed in the initial case. In essence, the statute of limitations is lengthened when a case is converted and a trustee appointed. However, in our example if a trustee is not appointed within the first two years of the case then he is barred from initiating any voidance actions.

Once a debtor has filed bankruptcy, any state law statute of limitations is tolled (i.e., prolonged) by federal law. 11 U.S.C. Section 546(a). For example, in Georgia there is a 12-month state law statute of limitations to file claims against counties. However, once the debtor files bankruptcy (presumably within the 12-month period), the trustee is empowered to bring action within two years of the filing of the petition. Accordingly, a federal voidance action may add an extra two years to the state law 12-month limit. [See *In re Maytag Sales & Service, Inc.*, 23 B.R. 384 (Bankr. N.D. Ga. 1982).]

Postpetition voidable transfers under 11 U.S.C. Section 549 are not governed by 11 U.S.C. Section 546.[158] However, 11 U.S.C. Section 549 contains its own specific follow-through statute of limitations in 11 U.S.C. Sections 549(d)(1) and (2). The follow-through deadline within which to bring suit in a postpetition transfer is the *earlier* of (1) two years after the date of the transfer or (2) at the time the case is closed or dismissed.

CONCLUSION

There are essentially three types of transactions which may be undone in the bankruptcy arena. These include preferential transfers, fraudulent conveyances, and unauthorized postpetition transfers. A legal assistant plays an essential role in any actions brought under these three distinct Bankruptcy Code sections. A legal assistant's duties regarding these transfers may begin at the inception of the case and can continue throughout litigation of these types of adversary matters. Therefore, a legal assistant's knowledge of the different types of voidable transfers as well as the elements of each is warranted.

REVIEW QUESTIONS

1. What is a preferential transfer? What is a fraudulent conveyance? What is an unauthorized postpetition transfer?
2. What are the elements of each of the three voidable transfers indicated above?
3. What are the affirmative defenses to a preferential transfer?
4. What are the affirmative defenses to a fraudulent conveyance?
5. What are the defenses to an unauthorized postpetition transfer?
6. Who has standing to bring each of these three actions?

7. What are the two types of statutes of limitations regarding these voidable transfers? Describe each statute of limitations in the context of each of the three voidable actions.

ENDNOTES

[1] Federal exemptions allow a debtor only $2,400 equity in a vehicle. After the trustee sells the car, this would allow the remaining $7,600 to be distributed to all creditors.

[2] *In re Smith*, 966 F.2d 1527 (7th Cir. 1992) cert. dismissed, 113 S.Ct. 683 (1992).

[3] *Begier v. IRS*, 496 U.S. 53 (1990).

[4] *In re Spada*, 903 F.2d 971 (3rd Cir. 1990).

[5] *In re Barefoot*, 952 F.2d 795 (4th Cir. 1991).

[6] *Id.*

[7] *Union Bank v. Wolas (In re ZZZZ Best Company, Inc.)*, 112 S.Ct. 527 (1991).

[8] *Matter of T.B. Westex Foods, Inc.*, 950 F.2d 1187 (5th Cir. 1992); *In re Interior Wood Products Co.*, 986 F.2d 228 (8th Cir. 1993).

[9] 11 U.S.C. Section 101(58).

[10] *In re Dakota Country Store Foods, Inc.*, 107 B.R. 977 (Bankr. D. S.D. 1989) (repossession of grocery store); *In re Pearson Industries, Inc.*, 142 B.R. 831 (Bankr. C.D. Ill. 1992).

[11] *In re Omni Development Svcs. Inc.*, 31 B.R. 482 (Bankr. S.D. Fla. 1983); *In re Lassiter*, 42 B.R. 631 (Bankr. E.D. Mo. 1984).

[12] *In re Riverfront Food & Beverage Corp.*, 29 B.R. 846 (Bankr. E.D. Mo. 1983). See also *In re Da-Sota Elevator Co.*, 135 B.R. 873 (D. N.D. 1991) (where service of garnishment summons created a lien and therefore service was transfer rather than payment).

[13] *In re McMahon*, 70 B.R. 290 (Bankr. N.D. N.Y. 1987).

[14] *In re Veteran Plate Glass Co.*, 71 B.R. 74 (Bankr. N.D. Ohio 1987).

[15] This list is merely illustrative and is noninclusive of every form of transfer.

[16] *Barnhill v. Johnson*, 112 S.Ct. 1386 (1992).

[17] *In re Financial Center Associates of East Meadow, L.P.*, 140 B.R. 829 (Bankr. E.D. N.Y. 1992).

[18] *In re Lease-A-Fleet, Inc.*, 141 B.R. 853 (Bankr. E.D. Pa. 1992).

[19] *In re Pearson Industries, Inc.*, 142 B.R. 831 (Bankr. C.D. Ill. 1992).

[20] *Begier v. IRS*, 496 U.S. 53 (1990) (where debtor's payment of withholding taxes to IRS was held not to be preferential since the transfer was considered a transfer of funds held in trust for the government, rather than a transfer of property of the estate).

[21] *Barnhill v. Johnson*, 112 S.Ct. 1386 (1992).

[22] *In re Bellanca Aircraft Corp.*, 850 F.2d 1275 (8th Cir. 1988).

[23] *In re Trejo*, 44 B.R. 539 (Bankr. E.D. Cal. 1984).

[24] *Brown v. First National Bank of Little Rock*, 748 F.2d 490 (8th Cir. 1984).

[25] *In re Flooring Concepts, Inc.*, 37 B.R. 957 (9th Cir. BAP 1984).

[26] Generally see *Coral Petroleum, Inc. v. Banque Paribas-London*, 797 F.2d 1351 (5th Cir. 1986); *In re Chase & Sanborn Corp.*, 848 F.2d 1196 (11th Cir. 1988); *Bonded Financial Svcs., Inc. v. European American Bank*, 838 F.2d 890 (7th Cir. 1988); *In re Bohlen Enterprises, Ltd.*, 859 F.2d 561 (8th Cir. 1988).

[27]11 U.S.C. Section 101(10).

[28]*In re Evans Potato Co.,* 12 B.C.D. 518 (Bankr. S.D. Ohio 1984).

[29]*In re Prescott,* 805 F.2d 719 (7th Cir. 1986).

[30]*In re Newberry Corp. v. Fireman's Fund Ins. Co.,* 106 B.R. 186 (Bankr. D. Ariz. 1989).

[31]140 Cong. Rec. Section 14461 (Oct. 6, 1994).

[32]*Zimmerman v. Itano Farms, Inc.,* 144 B.R. 490 (Bankr. D. Idaho 1992).

[33]*In re Fisher,* 100 B.R. 351 (Bankr. S.D. Ohio 1989).

[34]*In re Cohen,* 875 F.2d 850 (5th Cir. 1989).

[35]*In re Villa Roel, Inc.,* 57 B.R. 879 (Bankr. D. D.C. 1985).

[36]*In re Castle Tire Center, Inc.,* 56 B.R. 180 (Bankr. W.D. Pa. 1986).

[37]*In re Mobley,* 15 B.R. 573 (Bankr. S.D. Ohio 1981).

[38]*In re Wathen's Elevators, Inc.,* 37 B.R. 870 (Bankr. W.D. Ky. 1984).

[39]*In re Fonda Group, Inc.,* 108 B.R. 956 (Bankr. D. N.J. 1989).

[40]*In re Minnesota Utility Contracting, Inc.,* 101 B.R. 72 (Bankr. D. Minn. 1989) aff'd in part, rev'd in part, and remanded 101 B.R. 414.

[41]*In re Transpacific Carriers Corp.,* 50 B.R. 649 (Bankr. S.D. N.Y. 1985) aff'd 113 B.R. 139.

[42]*In re Pippin,* 46 B.R. 281 (Bankr. W.D. La. 1984).

[43]*In re American International Airways, Inc.,* 83 B.R. 324 (Bankr. E.D. Pa. 1988) aff'd 878 F.2d 762, aff'd 496 U.S. 53.

[44]*In re Drewes,* 139 B.R. 472 (Bankr. D. N.D. 1991) (mortgage granted to brother yet not recorded until ten months later is antecedent debt); *In re South Atlantic Packers Assoc.,* 30 B.R. 836 (Bankr. D. S.C. 1983) (six-month lapse between creation of creditor's security interest and perfection amounts to antecedent debt).

[45]*In re Aerco Metals, Inc.,* 60 B.R. 77 (Bankr. N.D. Tex. 1985).

[46]*In re Durant's Rental Center, Inc.,* 116 B.R. 362 (Bankr. D. Conn. 1990).

[47]*In re Coco,* 67 B.R. 365 (Bankr. S.D. N.Y. 1986).

[48]*Total Technical Svcs., Inc. v. Whitworth,* 150 B.R. 893 (Bankr. D. Del. 1993).

[49]*In re Dick Henley, Inc.,* 45 B.R. 693 (Bankr. M.D. La. 1985).

[50]*McLemore v. Third National Bank,* 123 B.R. 801 (Bankr. M.D. Tenn. 1991) aff'd 136 B.R. 727 (6th Cir.).

[51]*In re Hackney,* 83 B.R. 20 (Bankr. N.D. Cal. 1988).

[52]*In re Mobley,* 15 B.R. 573 (Bankr. S.D. Ohio 1981).

[53]*In re Grove Peacock Plaza, Ltd.,* 142 B.R. 506 (Bankr. S.D. Fla. 1992).

[54]*In re Lease-A-Fleet, Inc.,* 141 B.R. 853 (Bankr. E.D. Pa. 1992).

[55]*In re Tennessee Chemical Co.,* 143 B.R. 468 (Bankr. E.D. Tenn. 1992).

[56]*In re Nelson,* 959 F.2d 1260 (3rd Cir. 1992).

[57]*In re Hogg,* 35 B.R. 292 (Bankr. D. S.D. 1983).

[58]*Id.*

[59]*In re Cavalier Homes of Georgia, Inc.,* 102 B.R. 878 (Bankr. M.D. Ga. 1989).

[60]See *In re Baker & Getty Financial Svcs., Inc.,* 974 F.2d 712 (6th Cir. 1992); *In re Evans Temple Church of God in Christ & Community Center, Inc.,* 55 B.R. 976 (Bankr. N.D. Ohio 1986).

[61]*In re Trans Air, Inc.,* 103 B.R. 322 (Bankr. S.D. Fla. 1988) aff'd 104 B.R. 477.

[62]*In re Babcock Dairy Co.,* 70 B.R. 657 (Bankr. N.D. Ohio 1986).

[63]*In re F & S Cent. Mfg. Corp.*, 53 B.R. 842 (Bankr. E.D. N.Y. 1985).

[64]*Dent v. Martin*, 104 B.R. 477 (Dist. S.D. Fla. 1989); *In re Davenport*, 64 B.R. 411 (Bankr. M.D. Fla. 1986).

[65]*Roost v. Timber Components, Inc.*, 139 B.R. 520 (Bankr. D. Or. 1992); *In re Captain's Paradise, Inc.*, 29 B.R. 516 (Bankr. S.D. Fla. 1983) (owners of 33% of stock).

[66]*In re Winn*, 127 B.R. 697 (Bankr. N.D. Fla. 1991).

[67]*In re Trans Air, Inc.*, 78 B.R. 351 (Bankr. S.D. Fla. 1987).

[68]*In re Harris*, 7 B.R. 456 (Bankr. S.D. Fla. 1980).

[69]*In re Aldridge*, 94 B.R. 589 (Bankr. W.D. Mo. 1988).

[70]*In re Standard Stores, Inc.*, 124 B.R. 318 (Bankr. C.D. Cal. 1991).

[71]*Sender v. C & R Co.*, 149 B.R. 941 (Dist. Colo. 1992).

[72]*Neuger v. United States*, 801 F.2d 819 (6th Cir. 1986).

[73]*In re Lease-A-Fleet, Inc.*, 141 B.R. 853 (Bankr. E.D. Pa. 1992).

[74]*In re Grove Peacock Plaza, Ltd.*, 142 B.R. 506 (Bankr. S.D. Fla 1992).

[75]*Id.*

[76]*In re Cockreham*, 84 B.R. 757 (Dist. Wyo. 1988).

[77]*In re Gabill Corp.*, 135 B.R. 101 (Bankr. N.D. Ill. 1991).

[78]*Dean v. Davis*, 242 U.S. 438 (1917).

[79]*National City Bank of New York v. Hotchiss*, 231 U.S. 50 (1913).

[80]*Cambridge Meridian Group, Inc./Weingarten v. Connecticut Nat'l. Bank*, 140 B.R. 14 (Dist. Mass. 1991) rev'd. on other grounds 890 F.2d 792 (1st Cir.).

[81]*In re Duffy*, 3 B.R. 263 (Bankr. S.D. N.Y. 1980).

[82]*In re Diethorn*, 893 F.2d 648 (3rd Cir. 1990).

[83]*In re E.R. Fegert, Inc.*, 88 B.R. 258 (9th Cir. BAP 1988), aff'd 887 F.2d 955 (9th Cir.).

[84]*In re Kumar Bavishi & Assoc.*, 906 F.2d 942 (3rd Cir. 1990).

[85]*In re Air Conditioning, Inc.*, 845 F.2d 293 (11th Cir. 1988) cert. denied 488 U.S. 933.

[86]*Keydata Corp. v. Boston Edison Co.*, 37 B.R. 324 (Bankr. D. Mass. 1983).

[87]*In re Advertising Assoc.*, 95 B.R. 849 (Bankr. S.D. Fla. 1989).

[88]*In re Robinson Bros. Drilling, Inc.*, 877 F.2d 32 (10th Cir. 1989).

[89]*In re Spada*, 903 F.2d 917 (3rd Cir. 1990).

[90]*In re Jet Florida Systems, Inc.*, 861 F.2d 1555 (5th Cir. 1988).

[91]*In re Martella*, 22 B.R. 649 (Bankr. Colo. 1982).

[92]*In re Chenich*, 100 B.R. 512 (9th Cir. BAP 1987).

[93]*In re Express Liquors, Inc.*, 65 B.R. 952 (Dist. Md. 1986).

[94]*In re Energy Cooperative, Inc.*, 832 F.2d 997 (7th Cir. 1987).

[95]*Yurika Foods Corp. v. United Parcel Svcs.*, 888 F.2d 42 (6th Cir. 1989).

[96]*In re Fulghum Construction Co.*, 872 F.2d 739 (6th Cir. 1989).

[97]Prior to the 1994 Amendments, the deadline within which to perfect was ten days.

[98]*In re Wingspread Corp.*, 120 B.R. 8 (Bankr. S.D. N.Y. 1990).

[99]*In re Gold Coast Seed Co.*, 30 B.R. 551 (9th Cir. BAP 1983).

[100]See generally *In re Melon Produce, Inc.*, 976 F.2d 71 (1st Cir. 1992); *In re American Ambulance Svcs., Inc.*, 46 B.R. 658 (Bankr. S.D. Cal. 1985).

[101]*In re White*, 46 B.R. 843 (Bankr. E.D. Tenn. 1986), contra *In re Nucorp Energy, Inc.*, 902 F.2d 729 (9th Cir. 1990).

[102]*In re APC Constr., Inc.*, 132 B.R. 690 (Dist. Vt. 1991).

[103]*In re Debmar Corp.*, 21 B.R. 858 (Bankr. S.D. Fla. 1982).

[104]*In re Bay State Yacht Sales, Inc.*, 117 B.R. 16 (Bankr. D. Mass. 1990).

[105]*In re Territo*, 35 B.R. 343 (Bankr. E.D. N.Y. 1983).

[106]*In re Ottawa Cartage, Inc.*, 55 B.R. 371 (Bankr. D. N.D. Ill. 1985).

[107]*In re Teasley*, 29 B.R. 314 (Bankr. W.D. Ky. 1983).

[108]See generally *In re Williams*, 703 F.2d 1055 (8th Cir. 1983).

[109]See 11 U.S.C. Section 547(c)(8).

[110]*In re United Energy Corp.*, 944 F.2d 589 (9th Cir. 1991).

[111]*In re Chase & Sanborn Corp.*, 813 F.2d 1177 (11 Cir. 1987).

[112]*In re Rosenberg*, 69 B.R. 3 (Bankr. E.D. N.Y. 1986).

[113]*In re McDowell*, 87 B.R. 554 (Bankr. S.D. Ill. 1988).

[114]*In re Brasby*, 109 B.R. 113 (Bankr. E.D. Pa. 1990).

[115]UFTA states include Alabama, Arizona, Arkansas, California, Colorado, Connecticut, Florida, Hawaii, Idaho, Illinois, Maine, Minnesota, Montana, Nebraska, Nevada, New Hampshire, New Jersey, New Mexico, North Dakota, Ohio, Oklahoma, Oregon, Rhode Island, South Dakota, Texas, Utah, Washington, West Virginia, and Wisconsin.

UFCA states and territories include Delaware, Maryland, Massachusetts, Michigan, New York, Pennsylvania, Tennessee, Virgin Islands, and Wyoming.

[116]*In re Vaniman International, Inc.*, 22 B.R. 166 (Bankr. E.D. N.Y. 1982).

[117]See 11 U.S.C. Section 101(54).

[118]*Crews v. Carwile*, 138 B.R. 106 (Bankr. M.D. Fla. 1992).

[119]*Jackson v. Star Sprinkler Corp.*, 575 F.2d 1223 (8th Cir. 1978).

[120]*In re Sergio, Inc.*, 16 B.R. 898 (Dist. Haw. 1981).

[121]*In re Missionary Baptist Foundation, Inc.*, 24 B.R. 973 (Bankr. N.D. Tex. 1982).

[122]*In re McDonald*, 16 B.R. 618 (Bankr. S.D. Fla. 1981).

[123]*In re Kuhns*, 101 B.R. 243 (Bankr. D. Mont. 1989).

[124]*In re Silver Wheel Freightlines, Inc.*, 64 B.R. 563 (Bankr. D. Or. 1986).

[125]*In re Landbank Equity Corp.*, 83 B.R. 362 (Dist. E.D. Va. 1987).

[126]*In re Ozark Restaurant Equipment Co.*, 850 F.2d 342 (8th Cir. 1988).

[127]*In re Morris Communications N.C., Inc.*, 914 F.2d 458 (4th Cir. 1990).

[128]*Id.*

[129]*In re Goodman Industries, Inc.*, 21 B.R. 512 (Bankr. D. Mass. 1982).

[130]*In re Nacol*, 36 B.R. 566 (Bankr. M.D. Fla. 1983).

[131]*In re Vadnais Lumber Supply, Inc.*, 100 B.R. 127 (Bankr. D. Mass. 1989).

[132]11 U.S.C. Section 548(a)(2)(B)(iii).

[133]11 U.S.C. Section 548(b).

[134]*In re Emerald Oil Co.*, 807 F.2d 1234 (5th Cir. 1987).

[135]*In re Kauffman*, 675 F.2d 127 (7th Cir. 1981).

[136]*In re T & D Management Co.*, 40 B.R. 781 (Bankr. D. Utah 1984).

[137]*Oliver v. Kolody*, 142 B.R. 486 (Bankr. M.D. Fla. 1992).

[138]*In re Health Gourmet, Inc.*, 29 B.R. 673 (Bankr. D. Mass. 1983).

[139]*In re Conador Diamond Corp.*, 76 B.R. 342 (Bankr. S.D. N.Y. 1987).

[140]See *Id.*; *In re Anchorage Marina, Inc.*, 93 B.R. 686 (Dist. N.D. 1988).

[141]*In re Nacol*, 36 B.R. 566 (Bankr. M.D. Fla. 1983).

[142]*In re Morris Communications N.C., Inc.*, 75 B.R. 619 (Bankr. W.D. N.C. 1987).

[143]*In re Roco Corp.*, 701 F.2d 978 (1st Cir. 1983).

[144]*In re Dietz*, 69 B.R. 637 (9th Cir. BAP 1988) aff'd 914 F.2d 161 (9th Cir. 1990).

[145]*In re Quality Interiors, Inc.*, 127 B.R. 391 (Bankr. N.D. Ohio 1991).

[146]*Habinger, Inc. v. Metropolitan Cosmetic & Reconstructive Surgical Clinic, P.A.*, 124 B.R. 784 (Dist. Minn. 1990).

[147]*In re Wingo*, 89 B.R. 54 (9th Cir. BAP 1988).

[148]*In re Powers*, 88 B.R. 294 (Bankr. D. Nev. 1988).

[149]*In re Rice*, 83 B.R. 8 (Bankr. 9th Cir. 1987).

[150]*In re Computer Universe, Inc.*, 58 B.R. 28 (Bankr. M.D. Fla. 1986).

[151]*Delgado Oil Co. v. Torres*, 785 F.2d 857 (10th Cir. 1986).

[152]*In re V. Savino Oil & Heating Co.*, 91 B.R. 655 (Bankr. E.D. N.Y. 1988).

[153]*In re Feldhahn*, 92 B.R. 834 (Bankr. S.D. Iowa 1988).

[154]*In re V. Savino Oil & Heating Co.*, 91 B.R. 655 (Bankr. E.D. N.Y. 1988).

[155]*Id.*

[156]*In re Ottaviano*, 68 B.R. 238 (Bankr. D. Conn. 1986).

[157]*In re Railroad Reorganization Estate, Inc.*, 133 B.R. 578 (Dist. Del. 1991).

[158]*In re Majesto Electro Industries, Ltd.*, 71 B.R. 84 (Bankr. M.D. Pa. 1987).

9

Creditor Status, Priority, and Distribution Rights

Your spouse works at Q-Mart, a large department store chain. Today is payday and he should get a paycheck for two weeks wages. Also, today is his 5-year anniversary with Q-Mart and he should get an extra $1,000 in his Q-Mart employee benefit plan. You have a television and VCR on lay-away at Q-Mart and have paid down $750 on the balance. Also, you discover that you were overbilled, and overpaid, $200 on your Q-Mart credit card last month. Yesterday, Q-Mart filed Chapter 11.

You and your spouse are creditors. However, Q-Mart has hundreds of creditors. Where do you stand in that long line of creditors to get paid? Will you get paid first or will you get paid last?

INTRODUCTION

A *creditor* is defined in the Bankruptcy Code as any entity that has a claim against the debtor that arose before the petition, as well as certain claims that arise after the petition.[1] "Claim" is defined very broadly as:

> Either any right to payment, whether or not such right is reduced to judgment, liquidated, unliquidated, fixed, contingent, matured, unmatured, disputed, undisputed, legal, equitable, secured, or unsecured.

Or a right to an equitable remedy for breach of performance if such breach gives rise to a right to payment, whether or not such right to an equitable remedy is reduced to judgment, fixed, contingent, matured, unmatured, disputed, undisputed, secured, or unsecured.[2]

In bankruptcy, creditors can typically be divided into four basic categories: (1) secured creditors, (2) priority claim creditors, (3) general unsecured creditors, and (4) debtor's interest, such as shareholder's interests in a corporate debtor. This chapter will analyze the classification of claims into each of these categories as well as the "allowability" of all claims. Additionally, the requirements of creditors to file proofs of claim and deadlines to file proofs of claims, as well as the failure or untimeliness in filing a proof of claim shall be discussed.

Generally all bankruptcy cases follow a payment distribution hierarchy. This payment distribution hierarchy establishes the order in which creditors get paid according to their status. The hierarchy of payment is as follows: first, payment of secured creditors' claims upon a particular property. Next, if funds exist in excess of the secured creditors' claims upon a property, priority claim holders are paid. Then, if funds still remain available from the sale of the property (after payment of all secured claims upon the property and payment of all priority claims), general unsecured creditors are paid. Finally, should funds still remain from any sale of the property, they are distributed to the debtor (or equity holders, such as shareholders).

This chapter provides a detailed analysis of the general distribution schedule of 11 U.S.C. Section 726 which is followed in all chapters. Additionally, the distribution schedule of untimely proof of claims will be discussed.

SECURED CREDITORS

A *secured creditor* is any creditor holding a valid, perfected lien on collateral that is property of the estate. There are generally three types of liens in bankruptcy cases: consensual, statutory, and judicial.

Consensual liens are liens or encumbrances created by agreements between the debtor and the creditor. State law governs whether a lien is created and if the lien is perfected. Most states have adopted the Uniform Commercial Code (U.C.C.), which governs lien creation and perfection on personal property. Otherwise, state law must be referenced concerning perfection on real property, such as through mortgages or deeds of trust.

Statutory liens are essentially all liens created by either federal or state statute. For example, a federal tax lien can exist upon either real or personal property and is governed by the Internal Revenue Code. Real property tax liens (ad valorem taxes) exist through governing state law. Additionally, mechanic's liens or materialman's liens also exist by nature of state law. Note: Most statutory liens are involuntary.

Finally, *judicial liens* arise from perfected judgments. Judicial liens may exist upon either real or personal property. Again, state law governs whether a judgment is perfected against either real or personal property. For example, under California state law, a judgment recorded in the County Recorder's office operates to perfect such judgment against all the debtor's real property in such county.

All secured property with excess equity (value above and beyond the amount of liens upon the property) shall be sold by the trustee (or debtor-in-possession).[3] All secured property that holds no equity for the estate (such as property with value that is above liens but that is consumed by a debtor's exemptions[4]) shall be abandoned from the estate.[5] Further, all secured property with no equity whatsoever (the amount of liens upon the property exceed the value of the property) will likely be foreclosed upon by the secured creditor(s) after obtaining relief from the automatic stay.[6] Finally, should any secured property remain in the estate, the trustee is required to dispose of such property under 11 U.S.C. Section 725 prior to final distribution of the estate. The purpose of 11 U.S.C. Section 725 is to ensure that the secured collateral is returned to the proper secured creditor.

"Pro Rata" Distribution

Payment of claims within a particular class is governed by 11 U.S.C. Section 726(b). In the event the estate is unable to fully satisfy each claimant in a particular category, distributions should be made pro rata among each of the claims that hold equal status. Pro rata means in equal proportion. This does not necessarily mean in equal amounts. If one claim is very large and another quite small, an equal payment to both would not be in proportion to the underlying amount of the claim.

For example, sufficient funds exist only to completely pay creditors holding priority administrative expenses with $2,000 remaining. Assume the case is a voluntary bankruptcy (and therefore there are no "gap" priority creditors). After payment of all administrative priority claims, prepetition wages are entitled next to distribution. However, five individuals have filed timely proofs of claim, each claiming the maximum $4,000 as a priority. In this case, each of the wage-priority claimants receives a "pro rata" share of what remains of the estate funds. In essence, each former employee receives $400 ($2,000 divided by five equal claimants). Each claimant receives 10% of his or her claim.

However, assume there were two former employees. Employee A files a proof of claim for $3,000 and employee B (who quit after not getting her first paycheck) filed a proof of claim for $1,000. Employee A receives $1,500 (50% of his claim) and employee B receives $500 (50% of her claim). These distributions, based upon an equal percentage of the available funds provided to each claim, are termed "pro rata."

PRIORITY CREDITORS

After creditors holding liens have been provided for, the payment distribution of estate assets begins with certain claims that are granted statutory "priority." Priority claims are given preferred status in repayment depending upon the hierarchy of their priority classification.

In essence, distribution of estate assets under 11 U.S.C. Section 726 allows for payment of certain unsecured creditors granted priority. Whether a creditor is granted priority status depends upon whether the claim falls within a category under 11 U.S.C. Section 507. All priority claims are paid in the order specified within 11 U.S.C. Section 507 to the extent funds exist. For example, if the trustee has collected $10,000 beyond all secured claims upon a property, the trustee will first distribute such funds to priority claimants in 11 U.S.C. Section 507(a)(1), next to priority claimants in 11 U.S.C. Section 507(a)(2), etc., until the funds run out.

The classification and order of such claims provided a priority status within 11 U.S.C. Section 507 are as follows:

1. *First to administrative expenses allowed under 11 U.S.C. Section 503(b), as well as to any fees and charges assessed against the estate by the Bankruptcy Court (i.e., filing fees, copy costs, noticing costs, etc.).* The administrative expenses referred to consist of actual and necessary postpetition costs of preserving the bankruptcy estate. Examples are postpetition wages of the debtor's employees, postpetition lease of the debtor's premises, as well as postpetition normal operating costs of running a Chapter 11 business. Administrative expenses entitled to first priority status also include postpetition taxes incurred by the estate.[7] Additionally, administrative expenses given priority are compensation and reimbursement of professionals hired by the estate.[8] This would include the debtor's attorney, trustee's attorney, Official Committee's attorney, examiners, accountants, auctioneers, realtors, property managers, etc.

Priority administrative claims also include expenses incurred by creditors that file an involuntary petition against the debtor (such as the filing fee and the creditor's attorney's fees incurred in filing such involuntary petition). Also, the necessary expenses of creditors who recover any property that was transferred or concealed by the debtor are provided priority administrative status. All necessary expenses of creditors in connection with prosecution of a criminal offense relating to the case or the business or property of the debtor are priority administrative expenses.

Further, any creditor or unofficial committee that makes a substantial contribution in a Chapter 11 case may receive priority administrative status for their actual and necessary expenses. Additionally, the expenses and compensation of a prepetition custodian are granted priority administrative expense status as long as such services benefitted the estate. Also, a member of an official committee may receive administrative priority status if the expenses incurred are in the performance of the duties of such committee. Administrative expense priority is also granted to professional attorneys or accountants of those creditors allowed administrative expense priority as indicated above, as long as such services are actual and necessary as well as reasonable. Reasonable compensation for the services of an indenture trustee who makes a substantial contribution in a Chapter 11 case is also provided administrative priority status. Finally, witnesses' fees and mileage expenses are administrative expenses that are entitled to priority status.

Note: If a case is initially filed as a reorganization case (i.e., Chapters 11, 12, or 13) and later converts to Chapter 7, all administrative costs of the Chapter 7 case are paid before the administrative expenses incurred prior to the conversion. In essence, administrative fees of the Chapter 11 case such as the debtor's attorney's fees, will be subordinated to the administrative fees of the Chapter 7 case, such as the trustee's fees or the trustee's attorney's fees. [See generally 11 U.S.C. Section 726(b); *In re Energy Cooperative, Inc.*, 13 B.D.C. 1150 (Bankr. N.D. Ill. 1985) (Chapter 11 attorney's fee award subject to disgorgement in converted case); *In re Vernon Sand & Gravel, Inc.*, 109 B.R. 255 (Bankr. N.D. Ohio 1989) (same).]

2. The second tier of priority status is "gap" creditor's claims. In an involuntary case, claims that arise after the petition but before an order for relief is filed and that are in the ordinary course of the debtor's business or financial affairs are given second priority status. Therefore, these "gap" creditors are in line behind the administrative expense claims.

3. The third tier of priority claims is prepetition earnings (or wages) of employees of a debtor. The restriction on such earnings is that the earnings must be earned within 90 days of the petition date (or the date the debtor stopped its business). Wages entitled to third-position priority status are no more than $4,000[9] per individual (or per corporate employee).

These earnings may be wages, salaries, or commissions, including vacation, severance, and sick leave pay earned by an individual. Further, these earnings may be sales commissions earned by an individual or corporation (with one employee) acting as an independent contractor for the debtor, as long as in the previous year the independent contractor received at least 75% of its earnings from the debtor.[10]

4. The fourth tier of priority is given to claims for contributions to employee benefit plans. However, the restrictions upon such claims are that the claims must arise from services provided to the debtor within six months of the petition date (or the date the debtor ceased business). Further, for each employee benefit plan, priority status is given only to the number of employees covered by such plan multiplied by $4,000. Finally, deducted from this amount are all amounts paid to such employees as third-priority claimants, as well as all amounts paid by the estate through other employee benefit plans.

5. The fifth tier of priority claims includes grain producers or U.S. fishermen who hold claims against a debtor that operates a grain storage facility or a fish produce, storage, or processing facility. Again, the extent of such priority claims for grain producers or fishermen is $4,000 per individual.[11]

6. The sixth-priority tier includes all consumer "lay-away" claims. These claims arise from the prepetition deposit of money in connection with the purchase, lease, or rental of property, or the purchase of services, for personal, family, or household use of such individuals, which were not delivered or provided. Note: The amount of any one "lay-away" priority claim cannot exceed $1,800.[12]

For example, a buyer deposited $2,000 earnest money with a homebuilder to purchase a new home. The homebuilder thereafter filed bankruptcy. The buyer is entitled to a sixth-priority claim in the homebuilder's bankruptcy case up to the amount of $1,800. (The remaining $200 is treated as an unsecured claim.) [See *In re James R. Corbitt Co.*, 48 B.R. 937 (Bankr. E.D. Va. 1985).]

7. The seventh tier of priority claims is prepetition support payments owed to an exspouse or child. Such claims must be actually "in the nature of alimony, maintenance or support." Further, the support payments must not have been assigned to another party, either voluntarily or involuntarily.[13]

8. The eighth-position priority claims are certain types of taxes. Income taxes are given priority status if all three of the following conditions are met: (a) The tax returns must be due within three years of the petition date. (b) The taxes must be assessed within 240 days of the petition date.[14] (c) Other than taxes that are nondischargeable (i.e., not filed, untimely filed—within two years of the petition date, or fraudulently filed), taxes that are assessable postpetition.

Property taxes are also given eighth-position priority. However, such property taxes must be assessed prepetition and last payable one year prepetition. Additionally, taxes for which the debtor is liable to collect or withhold (i.e., trust fund taxes) are also provided priority in eighth position. Note: It does not matter how old these taxes are. An example is an employee's withholding taxes. Any amount of income tax or social security tax that a debtor should have withheld from an employee is treated as an eighth-position priority claim.

Excise taxes for transactions occurring prepetition when the return is due within three years of the petition date are also provided priority status at the eighth level. Customs duty (within one to four years) and tax penalties relating to actual pecuniary loss are also included as tax priority claims.

9. Finally, claims entitled to ninth-priority status include those based upon any commitment by the debtor to the FDIC to maintain the capital of an insured depository institution.

UNSECURED CREDITORS

If after all secured creditors and all priority creditors have been paid, funds still remain, the general unsecured creditors have an opportunity to participate in distribution. As one can well imagine, the general unsecured creditors normally do not receive 100% of their claims through distribution since they are, in essence, at the back of the line. In fact, it is not uncommon for the general unsecured claimants to receive nothing whatsoever after all the secured claims and all the priority claims have had an opportunity to "gnash upon the carcass" of the debtor's estate.

Timely Filed Proofs of Claim

To be eligible for distribution as a general unsecured creditor, a creditor must timely file a proof of claim. (See below for deadlines within which to file proofs of claim.)

Tardily filed

However, even if a proof of claim is not timely filed, a claim still may be entitled to distribution. If a creditor holds a claim and did not have notice or actual knowledge of the case in time to file a proof of claim before the deadline, the creditor may still file a tardy proof of claim. If such tardy proof of claim is filed with adequate time to permit payment, then the creditor is entitled to distribution.[15] The policy underlying this exception to timely filed proofs of claim is that it would be unfair to penalize the creditor by subordinating its claim where the untimely filing is not the result of the creditor's failure to act.

However, if a general unsecured creditor does have knowledge of the debtor's filing of a petition, yet fails to file a timely proof of claim, then the re-payment hierarchy of such claim will be lowered. In fact, the untimely filed proof of claim of general unsecured creditors[16] gets paid only after all the other general unsecured creditors have received distribution in full. In essence, late filed proofs of claim force the creditor to get in line behind all the rest of the general unsecured creditors. The penalty imposed by subordinating late claims to the other claims of unsecured general creditors is justified since the tardy filing is due to the creditor's failure to act.

PUNITIVE-TYPE DEBTS

Next in the distribution food chain are allowed claims (secured or unsecured) for any prepetition fine, penalty, forfeiture, or for multiple, exemplary, or punitive damages, to the extent that such claims are not compensation for ac-tual pecuniary loss suffered by the claimant. Examples of punitive-type debts that are in the distribution line behind even untimely filed general unsecured creditors are: treble damages awarded to creditors on their RICO claims against a debtor,[17] penalties on real property taxes,[18] employer tax penalties,[19] and punitive damages for fraud claims.[20]

POSTPETITION INTEREST

The general rule is that unsecured creditors are not entitled to postpetition in-terest upon their allowable claims.[21] However, an exception to this rule exists in the distribution scheme of 11 U.S.C. Section 726(a)(5) which allows for post-petition interest from any surplus that exists in the estate. The purpose of this exception is to prevent debtors from abusing the bankruptcy process to delay payments and avoid interest on obligations when, at the time of the filing of the petition, the debtor was actually solvent.[22]

An award of postpetition interest under 11 U.S.C. Section 726 may be al-lowed in only three exceptional cases: (1) where the debtor proves to be sol-vent; (2) where collateral produces income after the filing of the petition; and (3) where collateral is sufficient to pay interest as well as the principal of the claim.[23] As a matter of substantive law, if the debtor's assets are sufficient to pay all indebtedness, 11 U.S.C. Section 726(a)(5) requires interest earned since the date of filing to be paid before any surplus is returned to the debtor.[24]

However, note the conflict among the Circuits as to the appropriate rate of interest to be paid under this section. For example, some courts deem that the federal judgment rate established by 28 U.S.C. Section 1961 is the appropriate rate.[25] Other courts hold the state law legal rate of interest applies.[26] Still other courts hold that the interest rate within the creditor's contract is the appropriate rate of interest.[27]

SURPLUS TO DEBTOR

The last level of distribution of any surplus after payment of all the preceding debts is to the debtor. Accordingly, the surplus of assets remaining unclaimed after payment of all timely presented debts should be returned to the debtor.[28] If the debtor is a corporation and its corporate existence has been terminated, then the surplus should be distributed to the shareholders of the defunct corporation.[29]

SUPERPRIORITY CREDITORS

11 U.S.C. Section 507(b) grants the highest priority among priority claims to certain creditors for whom adequate protection was provided but subsequently proved to be inadequate. Adequate protection relates to creditors with claims secured by the property of the estate in the context of reorganizational cases. Cash collateral cannot be used without the consent of parties with secured interest in such cash collateral (or court approval). Accordingly, adequate protection is offered by the debtor to the creditor in order to be allowed to use the cash collateral. These adequate protection offers take the form of monthly payments with any resulting deficiency accorded priority status above all other priority debts. In other words, the parties agree that the secured creditor will be granted "superpriority" in order to allow the debtor to continue to use the cash collateral.

However, to be deemed superpriority, two requisites must be met. First, the claim must otherwise be allowable as an administrative expense. This is usually accomplished since such a claim constitutes an "actual, necessary cost or expense" of preserving the estate.[30] Second, the adequate protection provided must be insufficient. To the extent that the adequate protection is insufficient, the creditor's claim has priority over all other priority debts.

For example, a debtor offers ABC Mortgage Company adequate protection in the form of monthly payments of $1,000 for the use of all the rental income from an apartment complex. Debtor makes the first few payments, but then defaults. Thereafter, an earthquake destroys most of the apartment complex.

In this case, the adequate protection failed in two ways. First, the adequate protection monthly payments were not made. Next, unexpected diminution in value of the collateral also made adequate protection fail. Accordingly, under 11 U.S.C. Section 507(b) ABC would be entitled to superpriority status for all unpaid adequate protection monthly payments as well as the damage incurred in the earthquake. These claims of ABC will be paid before any other priority creditor, including administrative expenses.

SUPER SUPERPRIORITY CREDITORS

Certain claims are allowed a "super superpriority" status. In essence, not only are these claims elevated above all other priority claims (i.e., administrative expenses, etc.), they are first in line to be paid even over superpriority claims (arising from adequate protection deficiencies discussed above).

In essence, if a trustee or debtor-in-possession is unable to obtain unsecured postpetition credit by granting the lender an administrative expense priority, the court may approve new credit or debt with priority over all administrative expense claims, including any superpriority claims arising from the failure of adequate protection.[31]

FILING PROOFS OF CLAIM

Generally, for its claim or interest to be allowed, an unsecured creditor must file a proof of claim and an equity security holder must file a proof of interest. [F.R.Bankr.P. 3002.] However, if a creditor fails to file a proof of claim, one may be filed for the creditor by a codebtor, surety/guarantor, the debtor, or the trustee. [11 U.S.C. Section 501(b), (c); F.R.Bankr.P. 3004.] The debtor is allowed to file a proof of claim on behalf of a creditor (after the first 341 First Creditors' Meeting) in order to reduce the debtor's postbankruptcy liability for a debt that possibly is nondischargeable.

In a Chapter 7, 12, or 13 case, a proof of claim must be filed within 90 days after the *first date set* for the 341 First Creditors' Meeting. [F.R.Bankr.P. 3002.] In Chapter 11 cases, the court fixes a bar date that operates as a deadline for the filing of proofs of claim or interest. [F.R.Bankr.P. 3003(c)(3), 2002(a)(8).] The Court orders notice of this bar date to be sent to all parties. Claims in Chapter

11 cases that are listed in the schedules filed by the debtor are deemed automatically filed unless the claim or interest is scheduled as contingent, unliquidated, or disputed. [11 U.S.C. Section 1111(a); F.R.Bankr.P. 3003(b)(1).]

A secured creditor may file a proof of claim. However, if it does not, its lien on the collateral securing the claim remains intact.[32] However, as a practical matter, a prudent secured creditor files a proof of claim nonetheless.

ALLOWANCE OF CLAIM

Unless a party in interest objects, a proof of claim that has been filed will be allowed by the Bankruptcy Court and will serve as the basis for distribution. In other words, if no objection to a proof of claim is filed, the proof of claim establishes prima facie evidence of the allowability, amount, and characterization (priority, unsecured, etc.) of such claim.

However, a claim for any of the following is not allowable in bankruptcy:

- Claims that are unenforceable due to a valid defense under any applicable law or agreement, such as the statute of limitations or failure of consideration, are not allowable.[33]
- Claims for postpetition interest on unsecured claims are not allowed except as provided under 11 U.S.C. Section 726(a)(5).[34]
- Claims for property taxes are not allowed above the value of the property.[35]
- Claims for an insider's or an attorney's services to the debtor are allowable only to the extent that the claims are reasonable.[36]
- Support or maintenance payments that become due postpetition are not allowed.[37]
- Any excessive claims by a landlord for the termination of a lease are disallowed.[38]
- Excessive claims against an employer for the breach of an employment contract are not allowed.[39]
- Claims for disallowance of a federal employment tax credit caused by the late payment of state unemployment insurance taxes are not allowable.[40]
- Any claim by a transferee of a voidable transfer is not allowable unless the transferee returns the property or pays its value.[41]
- All untimely proofs of claims (not otherwise provided for in 11 U.S.C. Section 726 or in the F.R.Bankr.P.) are disallowed.[42]

Allowed Secured Claims

Under 11 U.S.C. Section 506(a) there are three possible types of allowed secured claims: (1) oversecured claims, (2) fully secured claims, and (3) undersecured claims. In essence, a creditor is "secured" to the extent of the fair market value of the underlying collateral.[43] The remainder of the creditor's claim is unsecured.[44]

Oversecured claims are those in which the value of the underlying property exceeds the amount of the claim. For example, the debtor owns a commercial building with a fair market value of $500,000. ABC Mortgage holds a duly perfected, first-position deed of trust on the commercial building in the amount of $250,000. Accordingly, ABC is an oversecured creditor.

Under 11 U.S.C. Section 506(b) the allowable secured claim of an oversecured claim is the full amount of principal *plus* prepetition accrued interest *plus* postpetition accrued interest up until payoff[45] *plus* reasonable attorneys' fees and costs.[46]

Fully secured claims are those in which the value of the underlying property equals the amount of the claim. For example, the debtor owns a commercial building with a fair market value of $500,000. ABC Mortgage holds a duly perfected, first-position deed of trust on the commercial building in the amount of $500,000. Accordingly, ABC is a fully secured creditor.

Under 11 U.S.C. Section 506(b) the allowable secured claim of a fully secured claim is only the full amount of the principal. No additional interest or attorney's fees and costs may be included.

Undersecured claims are those in which the value of the underlying property is less than the amount of the claim. For example, the debtor owns a commercial building with a fair market value of $500,000. ABC Mortgage holds a duly perfected, first-position deed of trust upon the commercial building in the amount of $750,000. Accordingly, ABC is an undersecured creditor.

Under Section 506(a) the allowable secured claim of an undersecured claim is only the amount of the claim that equals the value of the property. In this case ABC's allowable secured claim would be for $500,000. All the rest of ABC's claim (the remaining $250,000) is considered an unsecured claim.

Note: All claims that are subject to setoff under 11 U.S.C. Section 553 are also treated in the same manner as secured claims, depending upon the value of the property against which setoff is asserted.[47]

For example, the debtor has a checking account at Third National Bank of Iowa. Debtor also owes Third National Bank on an unsecured signature loan in the amount of $1,000, which was in default at the time the debtor filed bankruptcy. Accordingly, Third National Bank may have setoff rights under 11 U.S.C. Section 553.

If the debtor has $1,500 in its checking account as of the petition date, Third National Bank's allowed setoff claim may include the principal amount owed ($1,000) plus pre- and postpetition interest, plus any reasonable attorney's fees (analogous to oversecured claims).

However, if the checking account held only $1,000 as of the petition date, Third National Bank's setoff claim would amount to only the principal balance ($1,000) and not include interest or attorney's fees (analogous to fully secured claims).

Finally, if the debtor's account held only $500 as of the petition date, Third National Bank's setoff claim would amount to only $500, with the remainder being treated as an unsecured claim (analogous to undersecured claims).

CONCLUSION

The Bankruptcy Code specifies the order in which creditors are to be paid. Creditors are ranked according to their status as secured or unsecured. Secured creditors are paid first. Certain unsecured creditors are then paid if they qualify as priority claimants. Then other unsecured claims are paid. Creditors must recognize their responsibilities in filing proofs of claim to receive distribution.

REVIEW QUESTIONS

1. What are the four basic types of creditors?
2. List the payment hierarchy of 11 U.S.C. Section 726.
3. List priority claims in the order of priority. Describe each.
4. What are the deadlines for a creditor to file a proof of claim? What are the consequences for filing a late proof of claim or no proof of claim whatsoever?
5. When are secured claims allowed postpetition interest?
6. What are the three types of secured claims? Describe each.
7. Is postpetition interest ever given to unsecured claims?
8. Using the example at the beginning of this chapter, list each type of claim you and your spouse would be entitled to and the hierarchy of payment.

ENDNOTES

[1]11 U.S.C. Section 101(9).

[2]11 U.S.C. Section 101(14).

[3]11 U.S.C. Section 363.

[4]The proceeds from a trustee's sale of estate property are first used to extinguish any valid liens on properties, with the remaining proceeds then to be distributed to the debtor to the extent that the debtor has claimed exemptions in such funds. Finally, any excess is used to satisfy claims against the estate in accordance with Section 726. [See *In re Lambdin*, 33 B.R. 11 (Bankr. M.D. Tenn. 1983).]

[5]11 U.S.C. Section 554.

[6]11 U.S.C. Section 362(d).

[7]11 U.S.C. Section 503(b)(1)(B). See also *U.S. v. Friendship College, Inc.*, 737 F.2d 430 (4th Cir. 1984).

[8]Compensation and reimbursement must be awarded under 11 U.S.C. Section 330(a).

[9]Increased from $2,000 by the 1994 Amendments.

[10]The "sales commission" provision was added in its entirety through the 1994 Amendments.

[11]Raised from $2,000 per individual through the 1994 Amendments.

[12]Increased from $900 by the 1994 Amendments.

[13]This priority category was included in its entirety through the 1994 Amendments.

[14]The 240-day assessment is tolled to a certain degree if an offer in compromise is made in between the assessment date and the petition date. [See 11 U.S.C. Section 507(a)(8)(A)(ii).]

[15]11 U.S.C. Section 726(a)(2)(C).

[16]With knowledge of the bankruptcy proceeding.

[17]*In re Comstock Financial Services, Inc.*, 111 B.R. 849 (Bankr. C.D. Cal. 1990).

[18]*In re Parr Meadows Assoc.*, 880 F.2d 1540 (2nd Cir. 1989).

[19]*In re R.G. Fisher Constructors*, 116 F.R. 726 (Bankr. E.D. Cal. 1990).

[20]*In Re Kroh*, 88 B.R. 972 (Bankr. W.D. Mo. 1988).

[21]11 U.S.C. Section 502(b)(2).

[22]*In re Kentucky Lumber Co.*, 860 F.2d 674 (6th Cir. 1988).

[23]*Id.*

[24]*In re Wilson*, 56 B.R. 693 (Bankr. M.D. Ala. 1986).

[25]*In re Laymon*, 117 B.R. 856 (Bankr. W.D. Tex. 1990) rev'd on other grounds 985 F.2d 72 (5th Cir. 1991) cert. denied 113 S.Ct. 832 (1992)

[26]*In re Adcom, Inc.*, 89 B.R. 2 (Bankr. D. Mass. 1988).

[27]*In re A & L Properties*, 96 B.R. 287 (Dist. C.D. Cal. 1988).

[28]*Hendrie v. Lowmaster*, 152 F.2d 83 (6th Cir. 1945).

[29]*Id.*

[30]*In re California Devices, Inc.*, 126 B.R. 82 (Bankr. N.D. Cal. 1991).

[31]*In re Dubose*, 7 C.B.C.2nd 169 (Bankr. N.D. Ohio 1982).

[32]11 U.S.C. Section 506(d)(2).

[33]11 U.S.C. Section 502(b)(1).

[34]11 U.S.C. Section 502(b)(2).

[35]11 U.S.C. Section 502(b)(3).

[36]11 U.S.C. Section 502(b)(4).

[37]11 U.S.C. Section 502(b)(5).

[38]See 11 U.S.C. Section 502(b)(6) for formula to calculate allowable lease termination claims.

[39]11 U.S.C. Section 502(b)(7).

[40]11 U.S.C. Section 502(b)(8).

[41]11 U.S.C. Section 502(d).

[42]The last "untimely proof of claims" provision was added by the 1994 Amendments.

[43]11 U.S.C. Section 506(a).

[44]An undersecured creditor is entitled to surrender or waive its security and prove its entire claim as an unsecured one. [See *United Sav. Assoc. v. Timbers of Inwood Forest Associates, Ltd.*, 484 U.S. 356 (1988).]

[45]*U.S. v. Ron Pair Enterprises, Inc.*, 109 S.Ct. 1026 (1989).

[46]Attorney's fees and costs are included only if the underlying contract and lien documents between the parties provide for such. [See *In re Lane Poultry of Carolina, Inc.*, 63 B.R. 745 (Bankr. M.D. N.C. 1986).] However, an oversecured statutory lien may also be entitled to reasonable attorney's fees and costs. [See *In re Provincetown-Boston Airline, Inc.*, 67 B.R. 66 (Bankr. M.D. Fla. 1986).]

[47]11 U.S.C. Section 506.

10 *Chapter 7 Practice*

As a paralegal, you are reviewing the statements and schedules for accuracy with Chapter 7 clients. The clients ask what is going to happen once the bankruptcy is filed? Do they have to go to court? Does a creditor's judgment against them go away? Can they keep the furniture they bought but haven't finished paying for? When is the bankruptcy going to be over?

A paralegal deals most closely with the Chapter 7 client. Consequently, the paralegal fields most of the common questions and concerns of Chapter 7 debtors. Familiarity with the procedure and tools available in Chapter 7 is essential for any paralegal in the bankruptcy field.

INTRODUCTION

Chapter 7 is the most prevalent bankruptcy filed throughout the country. It is imperative that a legal assistant understand all the parties involved, their roles and duties, and the deadlines associated with each party's rights. In general, the Chapter 7 case will include a debtor, the trustee, and an assortment of creditors. A broad overview of the parties was provided earlier in this text. However, this chapter provides in-depth details regarding the specific role each party plays as well as his or her responsibilities, duties, and rights. Also, the bar dates are provided within which parties must act in order to preserve their substantive rights.

Whether representing debtors, creditors, or trustees, a legal assistant will need to be familiar with the responsibilities of each party in order to prepare and file or analyze the documents and pleadings on behalf of the party represented. Also, it will be a legal assistant's duty to calendar all deadlines for such things as dischargeability complaints, exemption objection deadlines, proof of claim deadlines, as well as all response deadlines to such matters.

DEBTOR'S ROLE

Eligibility

Chapter 7 relief is available to almost all types of debtors, including individuals and businesses, such as sole proprietorships, partnerships, and corporations. Husbands and wives may file a joint petition.[1] However, such joint petitioners must be legally married to file a joint petition (cohabitation is insufficient).[2]

Note: Governmental units, railroads, domestic insurance companies, banks, savings and loan associations, and credit unions may not liquidate under Chapter 7.

Additional restrictions on eligibility are involved if a debtor had previously filed bankruptcy. Under 11 U.S.C. Section 109(g) a six-month bar to filing bankruptcy is imposed upon a debtor if the previous case was dismissed due to a debtor's willful failure to obey court orders or prosecute its case.[3] Also, a debtor is not allowed a Chapter 7 discharge if a previous discharge had been granted in a case commenced within six years of the present petition date.[4]

Voluntary v. Involuntary

In a voluntary case, a petition for a Chapter 7 case must be filed by the debtor with the office of the Clerk of the Bankruptcy Court. Petitioners must reside[5] in the United States and also must show that their residences[6] are within the district where the petitions are filed for the greater part of 180 days before the petition.[7] Note: Venue is also proper in a district where there is a pending bankruptcy case of the debtor's affiliate, general partner, or partnership.[8]

The Chapter 7 petition must be accompanied by a $160 filing fee.[9] Individual debtors who are unable to pay the filing fee all at once may apply for permission to pay the filing fee in installments. Such application must be made by formal request and filed with the petition. The application should set forth the proposed payment terms.[10] The number of installments cannot exceed four, and the final payment must not be made later than 120 days after the petition is filed.[11] Note, the filing fee must be paid in full before the debtor may pay an attorney or any other person who renders services to the debtor in connection with the case.[12] Finally, there is no provision for waiver of the filing fee imposed in order to file a bankruptcy petition. In essence, bankruptcy petitions cannot be filed in forma pauperis (28 U.S.C. Section 1915 is inapplicable), which creates a situation wherein a person can truly be too poor to file bankruptcy.

An involuntary Chapter 7 petition may be commenced against anyone except a farmer or a nonprofit corporation.[13] Note: An involuntary petition cannot be commenced against a husband and wife as a joint case.[14] An involuntary case is initiated by the filing of an involuntary petition by three secured or unsecured creditors owed in the aggregate of at least $10,000[15] of noncontingent unsecured (or undersecured) debt. The debt must not be subject to a "bona fide dispute." Further, an involuntary Chapter 7 petition may be commenced by any single creditor if the debtor has less than 12 creditors as long as the single creditor holds at least $10,000 in claims. Further, if the involuntary debtor is a partnership, any general partner may commence an involuntary case.

Once the involuntary petition is filed, the Bankruptcy Clerk issues a summons, which must be served upon the debtor.[16] Service under the Bankruptcy Rules may be done by first class mail; personal service is not required.[17] The involuntary petition must allege only that the debtor is generally not paying its debts as they become due or that, within 120 days prior to the involuntary petition, a receiver was appointed to take charge of the property of the debtor to enforce a lien against such property.[18]

If an answer or response is filed by the debtor, an evidentiary hearing is held.[19] If a hearing is to be held, discovery is allowed. However, discovery is limited to the issue of nonpayment of debts when due and whether a bona fide dispute exists. Involuntary petition hearings are intended to be single-issue proceedings. Therefore, counterclaims against a petitioning creditor are not allowed unless it is to defeat the petition.[20]

After the hearing, the court must either enter the order for relief, dismiss the petition, or enter other appropriate orders.[21] If a petition is dismissed, the court may assess fees and costs against any and all petitioners, as well as both actual and punitive damages.[22] This sanction imposed on creditors who file a meritless involuntary petition is designed to discourage abuse of the involuntary provisions of the code.

The period before the entry of the order for relief and after the involuntary petition is filed is called a *gap period*. During the gap period the debtor may continue to operate any business it has, as well as use, acquire, or dispose of any property unless the court restricts such actions.[23] For example, during the gap period an involuntary debtor that operates a landscape business may continue to use its equipment, buy new equipment, or even sell its existing equipment. However, a party may request the appointment of an interim trustee in an involuntary Chapter 7 even before the entry of the order for relief. Appointment of an interim trustee may be necessary to preserve property of the estate and to ensure no diminution of the estate.[24]

Duties

Basically, a Chapter 7 debtor's duties are to file its lists of articulated statements and schedules,[25] cooperate with the trustee,[26] surrender all property of the estate to the trustee, including any books or records relating to estate property,[27] appear and be examined under oath at the 341 First Creditors' Meeting,[28] and appear at the discharge hearing.[29]

In a voluntary case, the debtor must file a master mailing list with the petition.[30] Local rules provide the form of the master mailing list required in the district. In an involuntary case, the debtor must file a master mailing list within 15 days of the order for relief.[31]

Schedules

Within 15 days of the petition date (in a voluntary case) and within 15 days of the order for relief (in an involuntary case), the debtor must file the schedule of assets and liabilities, which includes all liabilities and all property of the debtor. During these same times debtors must also file a schedule of current income and expenses, a schedule of executory contracts and unexpired leases, and a statement of financial affairs. The official form for debtors not engaged in business is No. 7 and the official form for debtors engaged in business is No. 8.[32]

A debtor must also file a list of property acquired within 180 days from the date of the petition. This list of postpetition property must be filed within 10 days of the receipt of such property.[33] This is because certain postpetition property also becomes part of the bankruptcy estate. For example, inherited money, divorce settlement amounts, and life insurance benefits all become estate property. [11 U.S.C. §541(a)(5).]

An individual Chapter 7 debtor must file a statement of intent pursuant to 11 U.S.C. Section 521. This statement indicates the debtor's intention regarding secured debts (i.e., reaffirm, surrender, redeem).[34] This 11 U.S.C. Section 521 statement must be served on the trustee and all creditors on the statement at the time it is filed. This statement must be filed and served either within 30 days of the petition date or by the 341 First Creditors' Meeting.

Finally, all statements and schedules filed must be amended if the debtor later learns they are inaccurate.[35] All petitions, lists, schedules, statements, and amendments thereto must be verified or contain an unsworn declaration under the penalty of perjury.[36] If the statements and schedules are inaccurate, yet sworn to be accurate by the debtor, the debtor is subject to denial of discharge or dismissal of the case and may even be subject to criminal penalties of five years in prison, $5,000, or both. [18 U.S.C. Section 152.]

DEBTOR'S RIGHTS

Automatic Stay

The petition invokes the automatic stay of 11 U.S.C. Section 326. The automatic stay serves as an injunction against all entities and individuals from any action that may directly or indirectly interfere with the administration of the estate.[37] The automatic stay protects the estate property as well as actions against the debtor and the debtor's property. In essence, the automatic stay provides Chapter 7 debtors a breathing spell from all their creditors.[38]

Claim Exemptions

Individual debtors are allowed to claim certain property as exempt. Under either 11 U.S.C. Section 522 or state law,[39] the debtor is entitled to retain certain property to prevent the debtor from becoming destitute. A schedule of claimed exemptions is usually filed with the debtor's statements and schedules. The bar date for any objections to a debtor's claimed exemptions is 30 days from the conclusion of the 341 First Creditors' Meeting. This deadline is last 341 Meeting, including all continuances. Additionally, if the debtor later amends the list of claimed exemptions, the bar date is 30 days from when the amended list is filed. Once the time period for objecting to the claimed exemptions has elapsed,[40] all further claims are forever barred and the property is unconditionally exempt. [See *Taylor v. Freeland*, 112 S.Ct. 1644 (1992).]

Avoid Liens on Exempt Property

The debtor may avoid a nonpurchase money, nonpossessory, security interest in personal property (household goods, jewelry, books, tools of trade, health aids, etc.) to the extent the lien impairs an exemption interest. [11 U.S.C. Section 522(f)(2).] Any waiver of exemption rights by a debtor is not enforceable.[41] In other words, the debtor may avoid certain liens on household goods that are claimed as exempt. Lien avoidance is only available if the debt did not arise from the purchase of the household goods. Lien avoidance is also only available if the creditor does have possession of the property. All creditors whose liens are avoided under 11 U.S.C. Section 522(f) are converted to unsecured creditors. A debtor may also avoid a judicial lien that impairs an exemption of either personal or real property.[42] A sample of a motion to avoid a lien on debtor's personal property is shown in Figure 10-1.

The 1994 Amendments to the Bankruptcy Code resolved conflict among the jurisdictions by defining "impair an exemption" in 11 U.S.C. Section 522(f). In essence, a judicial lien is completely avoided if any one of the following three conditions is met: Debtor has equity in the property that either consumes the entire exemption, consumes only a portion of the allowed exemption, or if no equity exists at all but the debtor is still entitled to an exemption upon the property.[43]

Avoid Transfers to Protect Exemptions

A debtor has a right to avoid transfers such as statutory liens (11 U.S.C. Section 545), preferences (11 U.S.C. Section 547), fraudulent conveyances (11 U.S.C. Section 548), postpetition transfers (11 U.S.C. Section 549), as well as liens securing penalties [11 U.S.C. Section 724(a)]. However, to invoke this right, the trustee must first have a right to avoid such liens and must refuse to exercise it. Further, the property recoverable (or freed from such lien) must be exemptible by the debtor. [11 U.S.C. Section 522(h).][44]

Free from Discrimination

The discharge of 11 U.S.C. Section 524 provides broad protection against post-discharge collection efforts on the part of creditors. Additionally, the Bankruptcy Code provides a debtor with protection against discriminatory treatment from entities other than creditors under 11 U.S.C. Section 525.

Discrimination based upon a debtor's filing for bankruptcy, insolvency, or nonpayment of discharged debts would seriously affect the "fresh start" policy of the Bankruptcy Code. Accordingly, 11 U.S.C. Section 525 prohibits discrimination by a governmental entity with respect to a license, permit, charter, franchise, or other similar grant. Discrimination by the government is also prohibited with respect to employment based solely on the fact that the person was a debtor in bankruptcy, was insolvent either before or during bankruptcy, or has not paid debts that were discharged in bankruptcy.

Examples of governmental discriminatory acts that are prohibited are:

- A state university cannot withhold a debtor's transcripts.[45]
- The government cannot deny a contract bid based upon the debtor's prior bankruptcy filing.[46]

FOR COURT USE ONLY

UNITED STATES BANKRUPTCY COURT
CENTRAL DISTRICT OF CALIFORNIA

In re:

CHAPTER _____ CASE NUMBER

Debtor.

(No Hearing Required)

NOTICE OF MOTION AND MOTION TO AVOID LIEN
UNDER 11 U.S.C. § 522(f) (PERSONAL PROPERTY)
(Creditor Name: _____)

(Insert Name of Creditor holding Lien to be Avoided)

1. TO THE CREDITOR, CREDITOR'S ATTORNEY AND OTHER INTERESTED PARTIES:

2. NOTICE IS HEREBY GIVEN that the Debtor hereby moves this Court for an Order, without a hearing, avoiding a lien on the grounds set forth below.

3. **Deadline for Opposition Papers:**
Pursuant to Local Bankruptcy Rule 111(7)(a), any party objecting to Debtor's Motion may file and serve a written objection and request a hearing on this Motion. If you fail to file a written response within twenty (20) days of the date of service of this Notice, the Court may treat such failure as a waiver of your right to oppose this Motion and may grant the requested relief.

4. **Type of Case:**

   a. ❑ A Voluntary Petition under Chapter ❑ 7 ❑ 11 ❑ 12 ❑ 13 was filed on:

   b. ❑ An Involuntary Petition under Chapter ❑ 7 ❑ 11 was filed on:

   ❑ An Order of Relief under Chapter ❑ 7 ❑ 11 was entered on:

   c. ❑ An Order of Conversion to Chapter ❑ 7 ❑ 11 ❑ 12 ❑ 13 was entered on:

   d. ❑ Other:

5. **Procedural Status:**

   a. ❑ Name of Trustee Appointed *(if any):*

   b. ❑ Name of Attorney of Record for Trustee *(if any):*

(Continued on Next Page)

FIGURE 10-1a. Motion to Avoid Lien (page 1).

In re	(SHORT TITLE)		CHAPTER _____ CASE NUMBER:
		Debtor.	

6. Debtor claims an exemption in the subject personal property under:

   a. ☐ California Code of Civil Procedure § _____ (Homestead): Exemption amount claimed on Schedules: $ _____

   b. ☐ California Code of Civil Procedure § _____ Exemption amount claimed on Schedules: $ _____

   c. ☐ Other Statute *(specify)*:

   d. ☐ Other Statute *(specify)*:

7. Debtor's entitlement to an exemption is impaired by a non-judicial lien, the details of which are as follows:

   a. On *(specify date)*: _____, Debtor obtained a consumer loan from Respondent in the principal amount of *(specify amount)*: $

   b. As security for said loan, Debtor gave Respondent a security interest in certain personal property in Debtor's possession

   c. The loan was neither obtained nor used for the purpose of buying the personal property described in Paragraph (b) above

   d. The current balance due on the loan is *(specify amount)*: $

8. On Schedule C, Debtor claimed an exemption in said personal property.

9. Debtor alleges that the fair market value of each individual item of the personal property claimed exempt is set forth in a declaration attached hereto. *(Attach Debtor's declaration to this motion)*

10. Debtor attaches the following documents in support of the motion (as appropriate):

    a. ☐ Schedule C listing all exemptions claimed by Debtor(s)

    b. ☐ Loan agreement

    c. ☐ Security agreement

    d. ☐ Declaration of Fair Market Value

    e. ☐ Other *(specify)*:

    f. ☐ Other *(specify)*:

    g. ☐ Other *(specify)*:

11. Total number of attached pages of supporting documentation: _____

12. Debtor declares under penalty of perjury under the laws of the United States of America that the foregoing is true and correct and that this motion was executed on the following date at _____, California.

WHEREFORE, Debtor prays that this Court issue an Order (a copy of the form of which is submitted herewith and has been served) avoiding the subject lien.

Dated: _____

Debtor's Signature

Dated: _____

Law Firm Name

By: _____

Name: _____

Attorney for Debtor

FIGURE 10-1b. Motion to Avoid Lien (page 2).

In re	(SHORT TITLE)		CHAPTER _____ CASE NUMBER:
		Debtor.	

PROOF OF SERVICE BY MAIL

STATE OF CALIFORNIA
COUNTY OF _____

I am employed in the above County, State of California. I am over the age of 18 and not a party to the within action. My business address is as follows:

On _____, I served the foregoing document described as: NOTICE OF MOTION AND MOTION TO AVOID LIEN UNDER 11 U.S.C. § 522(f) (PERSONAL PROPERTY) on the interested parties at their last known address in this action by placing a true and correct copy thereof in a sealed envelope with postage thereon fully prepaid in the United States Mail at _____, California, addressed as follows:

(IMPORTANT NOTE: Compliance with F.R.B.P. 7004(b)(3) and California Code of Civil Procedure, Section 416.10 is required for service upon corporations. Service must be made upon an officer or other agent of the corporation authorized to accept service of process.)

❑   Addresses continued on attached page

I declare under penalty of perjury under the laws of the United States of America that the foregoing is true and correct.

Dated:

_____   _____
Type Name   *Signature*

FIGURE 10-1c. Motion to Avoid Lien (page 3).

- A county cannot refuse to renew a building contractor's certificate of competency based upon failure to pay discharged debts.[47]

Further, discrimination in employment by a private entity is also prohibited.[48] Note that, within the private sector, the discrimination prohibition is limited only to individual debtors. The prohibition against discrimination is further limited to actions by the employer regarding the debtor's employment. Governmental agencies are forbidden to discriminate regarding hiring, termination, and discrimination in employment. However, the discrimination ban of private employers does not include the actual hiring of debtors. In order for discrimination by a private employer to exist, there must already be an employer-employee relationship between the parties.[49]

In essence, the prohibition of discrimination for private employers is therefore limited to terminating a debtor employee or refusing advances to such an employee based upon the debtor's insolvency, the filing of the bankruptcy, or the nonpayment of discharged debts. [11 U.S.C. Section 525(b).]

However, there is no prohibition against consideration of the debtor's future financial responsibility. This is not considered discrimination under 11 U.S.C. Section 525. For example, a state loan agency may properly deny a debtor's loan application on the basis of unsound future financial ability.[50]

The remedy available for a debtor when discrimination occurs is to request the court to order injunctive relief, such as ordering the state to remove license restrictions.[51] Injunctive relief is requested through an adversary proceeding pursuant to F.R.Bankr.P. 7001(7). Further, the debtor's right to collect damages may also be appropriate. If private discrimination is tied to efforts to collect a discharged debt, this may also be sanctionable under 11 U.S.C. Section 525.

Abandonment

The debtor may request that the trustee be compelled to abandon certain property from the estate under 11 U.S.C. Section 554. Once abandoned, the property revests in the debtor. To be granted the request, the debtor must show that the property is burdensome to the estate or that the property is of inconsequential value and benefit to the estate.[52]

Discharge

This is the most significant benefit afforded a Chapter 7 debtor. Discharge is the tool that makes debtors not liable on obligations. A discharge in Chapter 7 is the primary objective in filing bankruptcy. Note: Only individuals are entitled to discharge under Chapter 7 (or husbands and wives filing joint petitions). Discharge is the means wherein a debtor obtains a "fresh start." A discharge essentially acts to release the debtor from any further liability or obligation to pay unsecured prepetition debts. Discharge releases all personal liability of debtors on prepetition judgments.[53] Further, all unliquidated, contingent, and unmatured claims that existed as of the petition date are discharged. An example of these types of debts would be if a debtor were responsible for a car accident and was without insurance, yet the injured parties did not file suit against the debtor prepetition. The discharge also acts as an injunction against continuation or commencement of any act or proceeding to enforce a discharged debt. [11 U.S.C. Section 524(a).]

However, note that certain exceptions to the comprehensive discharge exist based upon a debtor's misconduct. In short, a discharge will be denied altogether under 11 U.S.C. Section 727 as follows:

1. If the debtor transfers, removes, destroys, mutilates, or conceals property in order to hinder, delay, or defraud creditors or an officer of the estate.

2. If the debtor has concealed, destroyed, mutilated, falsified, or failed to keep or preserve any records.

3. If the debtor knowingly and fraudulently makes a false oath, presents a false claim, attempts to bribe someone in connection with the case, or withholds records from the trustee.

4. If the debtor fails to satisfactorily explain any loss of estate assets.

5. If the debtor refuses to obey any Court orders (other than refusal to testify regarding privileged information or based upon a debtor's privilege against self-incrimination).[54]

Also, certain specific debts may be excepted from discharge even if all other debts are discharged. Such nondischargeable debts under 11 U.S.C. Section 523 are certain taxes, claims based on fraud, certain claims not listed in debtor's schedules, claims based upon fiduciary defalcation, embezzlement or larceny, spousal/child support, willful and malicious injury claims, certain student loans, claims arising from personal injury or wrongful death caused while a debtor was DUI, federal restitution claims, loans used to pay taxes, certain property settlement claims in divorce, certain homeowners' association dues, etc.[55]

However, once a discharge is granted, it can later be revoked. If a creditor or the trustee discovers that the debtor's discharge was obtained through fraud or if the debtor acquired estate property and failed to report or surrender the property to the trustee, then a creditor or the trustee may request that the debtor's discharge be revoked. Note: A request to revoke a discharge must be made within one year after the discharge was granted or before the case is closed.[56]

Reaffirmation

Regardless of the debtor's right to a discharge, the Bankruptcy Code allows a voluntary reaffirmation of a debt, provided both the debtor and the creditor agree. [11 U.S.C. Section 524(c).] Reaffirmation has the effect of making the debtor legally liable on both the secured portion of the debt and any unsecured deficiency.

Reaffirmation agreements must be made before the debtor is granted a discharge. Reaffirmation agreements must include certain specific conspicuous language. This language must state that the agreement may be rescinded by the debtor at any time prior to discharge or within 60 days after the agreement is filed with the court, whichever occurs later. The language must also state how a debtor rescinds, which is by giving notice of rescission to the holder of the claim. The specific conspicuous language included within the reaffirmation agreement, must advise the debtor that such agreement is not required under bankruptcy law, under nonbankruptcy law, or under any other agreement not in accordance with the provisions of 11 U.S.C. Section 524(c).

Reaffirmation agreements must be filed with the Bankruptcy Court. Reaffirmation agreements must include a declaration (or affidavit) of the debtor's attorney stating that the agreement represents a fully informed and voluntary agreement by the debtor. The declaration must state that the agreement does not impose an undue hardship on the debtor (or dependent), and that the attorney fully advised the debtor as to the legal effect and consequences of reaffirmation agreements and defaults therein.[57]

In cases where debtors are not represented by counsel, the Bankruptcy Court must approve a reaffirmation agreement. To give approval, the Court must determine that the reaffirmation agreement will not impose an undue hardship on the debtor (or dependent) and that the agreement is in the best interest of the debtor.

A legal assistant will usually participate actively in negotiating reaffirmation agreements on behalf of either the debtor or a creditor. Reaffirmation agreements are generally not advisable for a debtor since they subject a debtor to deficiency judgments which would otherwise be dischargeable.

For example, the debtor financed a truck through XYZ Finance (secured creditor upon the truck). The debtor filed Chapter 7. XYZ Financing wants the debtor to "reaffirm" the debt with XYZ. If the debtor does not reaffirm the debt, the only remedy XYZ retains after discharge is to repossess the truck should the debtor default on any of the payments. If the debtor reaffirms the debt, XYZ is entitled to repossess the truck upon any default *plus* obtain a deficiency judgment against the debtor for all amounts of sales costs of the vehicle and for the difference between the sales price and the amount remaining on the loan.

However, what if the debtor was behind on his payments to XYZ for three months? Reaffirmation agreements allow debtors and creditors to come to mutually agreeable terms as to the repayment. For example, in this instance, it may be advisable for the debtor to reaffirm the obligation to XYZ in exchange for XYZ's allowing the debtor to make up the three payments by putting three extra payments at the end of the note or allowing the debtor to make half payments (in addition to the original payments) for the first six months.

To induce debtors to reaffirm, some creditors offer the debtor a reduced amount of the debt owed. This reduced amount often equals the present value of the secured property. Thereafter, the debtors are allowed to pay this reduced amount in installment payments (over time) with interest. For example, ABC appliance sold a microwave to the debtor two years ago for $1,500. At the time the debtor filed bankruptcy, she still owed $500 on the microwave. The microwave was then worth about $150. ABC voluntarily reduced its claim and offered to allow the debtor to reaffirm the debt in the amount of $150 payable over time with interest.

Note: Secured creditors do not have to reduce their claim and allow installment payments. (See "Redemption" immediately following.) However, in practical terms, the creditor may be willing to accept these types of repayment arrangements, rather than invest time and funds in attempting to repossess and then sell used collateral.

In essence, reaffirmation agreements are whatever can be negotiated (with the preceding restrictions). A legal assistant plays a vital role in the reaffirmation negotiating process. (Note: Often the same secured creditors appear in case after case, such as Montgomery Ward, Sears, GMAC, etc.). Accordingly, put on your negotiator's cap and get the best deal you can for your client.

Redemption

Under 11 U.S.C. Section 722 debtors are allowed to retain certain household and consumer goods from secured creditors. A debtor may redeem consumer personal property classified as exempt under 11 U.S.C. Section 522 or abandoned under 11 U.S.C. Section 544 by paying the amount of the allowed claim secured by the lien. In essence, a debtor makes a "lump sum" payment to the secured creditor for the value of the property. The effect is to retain the property free of the underlying liens.

The right to redemption is not conditioned upon the consent of the lienholder; so the debtor may retain the property despite the objections of the creditor. However, relief through redemption under 11 U.S.C. Section 722 is specifically limited to individuals and is not available to corporate or partnership debtors.

The policy of the redemption section of the Code is to prevent creditors with security interests in household and personal goods from using the threat of repossession to extract more than they would have otherwise been capable of gaining through actual foreclosure or repossession. Often, these items have little value on the open marketplace, but their replacement cost to the debtors is quite high. Without redemption, creditors could seek reaffirmations of the entire debt by threatening to repossess these household items from debtors. The redemption section allows debtors to retain their necessary property and avoid the high replacement costs. Note: The redemption rights of a debtor cannot be waived before or after a bankruptcy.[58]

To redeem personal property from a lien under 11 U.S.C. Section 722, four requirements must be met:

1. Both the property subject to the lien and the underlying debt must be consumer-related.
2. The debt secured by the lien must be dischargeable in bankruptcy.
3. The property must be exempted under 11 U.S.C. Section 522 or abandoned under 11 U.S.C. Section 544.
4. The debtor must pay the lienholder the amount of the allowed secured claim.

Consumer-related property is tangible personal property intended primarily for personal, family, or household use. Note: The right of redemption does not extend to intangible property, such as stocks and bonds, or to real property. Also, the lien must be a consumer debt. *Consumer debt* is debt incurred by an individual primarily for a personal, family, or household purpose.

Further, to redeem property, the underlying debt must be dischargeable in bankruptcy. Note: If the creditor does not take the proper steps to object to dischargeability within the time restrictions of 11 U.S.C. Section 523, then the debt will be dischargeable and the property may be redeemed.

Additionally, the secured property to be redeemed must be either claimed as exempt or abandoned from the estate. For purposes of redemption, exemptions of secured property are still limited in dollar value to the extent as provided in 11 U.S.C. Section 522 (or by state law in states that have "opted out" of the federal exemption scheme). Abandonment applies to any property of the estate. Therefore, it provides an alternate means for a debtor to redeem property that is not exemptible under 11 U.S.C. Section 522 or property for which all exemptions have been exhausted. The effect of abandonment is to remove specific property from the estate and return it to the debtor.

The "allowed secured claim" under 11 U.S.C. Section 506 equals the value of the property of undersecured creditors. Therefore, secured creditors will receive in redemption the value of the property or the amount of their liens, whichever is less.

Valuation of property for redemption purposes (and thus the allowed secured claim amount) is the "fair market value" of the property. Factors to determine this valuation include the point in time at which the valuation occurs, the age and physical condition of the property, the prevailing price dictated by market demand, and the market and circumstances under which the property would be sold. In essence, the wholesale market value or forced-sale/liquidation value is the best approximation of the value of the property.[59]

Finally, redemption under 11 U.S.C. Section 722 is available only upon payment in full of the allowed amount of the secured claim (i.e., the "value" of the property.) However, note that redemption does not allow the involuntary imposition of installment payments. The value of the allowed secured claim must be paid promptly after valuation in one lump sum.[60]

In Re Carroll
11 B.R. 725 (9th Cir.BAP 1981)

Katz, J.: Under the facts in this case the Arizona Bank held a valid security interest in a pickup truck owned by the debtors herein and valued at $2,400.00. In the court below the debtors applied for a redemption of the truck in installment payments. On January 1, 1981, Judge Maggiore ordered that a redemption under 11 U.S.C. Section 722 can be made in installment payments. (citations omitted).

11 U.S.C. Section 722 provides:

> An individual debtor may, whether or not the debtor has waived the right to redeem under this section, redeem tangible personal property intended primarily for personal, family, or household use, from a lien securing a dischargeable consumer debt, if such property is exempted under Section 522 of this title or has been abandoned under Section 554 of this title, *by paying the holder of such lien the amount of the allowed secured claim of such holder that is secured by such lien.* (emphasis in original).

After reviewing Section 722 and the applicable legislative history this court finds that a redemption must be made through a lump sum payment. (citations omitted). To hold otherwise would frustrate the clear meaning of the section.

Reversed.

Timing and Procedure—Redemption

If the parties are in agreement, the debtor needs to pay the creditor only the amount of the allowed secured claim. However, if there is a dispute as to whether the property may be redeemed, the debtor must file a motion to redeem property. [F.R.Bankr.P. 6008.] The procedure is treated as a contested matter under Rule 9014, which includes an opportunity for the opposing party to respond and be heard.

Surrender

An alternative to either reaffirming an obligation or redeeming an obligation is for the debtor to voluntarily surrender the collateral to the secured creditor. This would allow the debtor to "walk away" entirely from a transaction without being straddled with any ongoing monthly payments. An example of surrender of the collateral being in the best interest of the debtor is when a debtor foolishly enters into a five-year lease for a brand new Jaguar. The monthly payments are approximately $700. The debtor soon discovers that, based upon his salary as a pizza delivery man, he cannot make both the car payment and his house payment. The debtor attempts to return the car to the dealership but discovers he cannot "get out" of his five-year commitment. Surrender of the vehicle to the dealership will enable the debtor to escape from his poor business decision without being burdened with the monthly payment or any deficiency arising from the breach of the lease.

Another example: The debtor tries her hand at the trucking business (sole proprietorship). The debtor purchases an 18-wheeler and tractor. The business never takes off. Now the debtor owes $50,000 more on the truck and tractor than they are worth. She may surrender the property, which would allow her to obtain a "fresh start" without any debt remaining from the truck or tractor.

11 U.S.C. Section 521 and Alternatives Thereto

A debtor is required to file a "Statement of Intent," as prescribed by 11 U.S.C. Section 521. This statement includes secured consumer debts and whether the debtor wishes to reaffirm, redeem, or surrender the collateral. The statement of intent is due within 30 days of the petition date or on the date of the 341 First Creditors' meeting. Further, 45 days after the Statement of Intent is filed, 11 U.S.C. Section 521 dictates that debtors perform on their intention with regard to the property included in the Statement of Intent.

However, note that the Statement of Intent does not alter the debtors' rights in any way. In fact, debtors could change their minds and decide not to reaffirm a debt, regardless of whether they initially listed their intent to reaffirm. Moreover, there is no remedy for creditors for a debtor's nonperformance within the 45-day time limit. A creditor must appear at the 341 First Creditors' Meeting and question the debtor as to intent. After this, should the debtor fail to comply in either reaffirming, redeeming, or surrendering the collateral in an expeditious manner, the creditor may request the trustee's assistance.

Note: Some Bankruptcy Courts do not insist that the debtor's options rest solely within the choices articulated in 11 U.S.C.Section 521 (reaffirmation, redemption, or surrender). In fact, if the debtor is current on monthly payments and remains so, there is no cause to insist that the debtor reaffirm the obligation (thus exposing the debtor to potential deficiency claims).

Reopen Case

Once a discharge is entered and the final distribution is made, if any, a case is thereafter "closed." However, a debtor may request the court to reopen the case once it is closed. The Bankruptcy Court is empowered to reopen a case in order to "administer assets, to accord relief to the debtor, or for other cause." [11 U.S.C. Section 350.]

Often debtors realize that a judicial lien exists upon some of their exempt property long after the bankruptcy case has been closed. For example, if a judicial lien has attached to the debtor's home, the debtors may not be aware of the lien until they attempt to sell their home, which may be years after a bankruptcy case. The Bankruptcy Court has discretion to reopen a case for the filing of a debtor's lien avoidance action.[61]

An additional reason wherein a debtor may seek to have a case reopened is in the arena of dischargeability complaints. Often, the debtor must file a complaint to determine dischargeability of a claim in order to have the matter heard before the Bankruptcy Court. For example, complaints regarding student loans, support, homeowners' dues, etc. are normally filed by the debtor. Often the debtor mistakenly assumes that these obligations have been discharged and acts no further. However, at some later date these claims may come back to haunt the debtor. At that point the debtor may request the court to reopen the case and afford relief to the debtor by determining whether the debts are discharged.

A request to reopen a case is made by a motion. The Bankruptcy Court has discretion whether or not to reopen a case. A fee may be required to reopen a case which is the same amount as the initial filing fee. [28 U.S.C. Section 1930(b).] A trustee is not automatically appointed in a reopened case unless the Court directs.

TRUSTEE

Once discharged, the debtor's participation in the bankruptcy proceedings is minimal, at best. The trustee's job, however, is just beginning. Trustees are fiduciaries of the estate and have substantial responsibilities and duties as well as liabilities. A trustee serves to protect the interests of the creditors.

Appointment

The U.S. Trustee appoints an interim trustee from a panel of private trustees when the petition is filed. If no member of the panel is willing to serve, the U.S. Trustee must serve as the interim trustee in the case. At the 341 First Creditors' Meeting, the interim trustee presides as the hearing officer. Note: The Bankruptcy Judge is not allowed to preside at, or even attend, the 341 Meeting.[62] A permanent trustee is appointed for the case at the 341 Meeting.

Eligibility/Qualifications

The Bankruptcy Code requires that an individual trustee be competent to perform the duties of a trustee and must reside (or have an office) within the district or an adjacent district. The trustee must file a bond with the Bankruptcy Court in favor of the United States ensuring faithful performance of duties.[63]

The Bankruptcy Court may remove a trustee for cause and after notice and hearing. The Court may remove a trustee appointed by the U.S. Trustee's Office, but not the U.S. Trustee herself. The U.S. Trustee is an appointee of the United States Attorney General and may be removed only by the Attorney General.[64]

Role/Capacity

Once appointed, the trustee becomes the only representative of the estate with the capacity to sue or be sued.[65] Accordingly, the trustee may prosecute or defend pending actions by or against the debtor, or actions on behalf of the estate before any tribunal.[66] Further, the trustee may waive the attorney–client privilege of a corporate debtor, even regarding prebankruptcy communications.[67] The trustee also has the benefit of any defenses available to the debtor as against any entity, including the statute of limitations, usury, and other personal defenses. Even if the debtor waives a defense, the trustee still has the benefit of the defense.

Duties

Generally, the trustee is entrusted with the collection, preservation, and liquidation of nonexempt assets and the subsequent distribution to creditors. Once assets are collected, the trustee must deposit the funds in federally insured depositories. Additionally, the trustee must manage or operate estate property within the guidelines of federal law as well as in compliance with state and local laws. The following are the statutorily enumerated duties of the trustee under 11 U.S.C. Section 704.

1. Collect and reduce to money the property of the estate for which such trustee serves and close the estate as expeditiously as is compatible with the best interests of parties in interest of the estate.

2. Be accountable for all property received.

3. Ensure that the debtor shall perform his or her intention as specified in 11 U.S.C. Section 521(2)(B).

4. Investigate the financial affairs of the debtor.

5. If a purpose would be served, examine proofs of claims and object to the allowance of any improper claim.

6. If advisable, oppose the discharge of the debtor.

7. Unless the Court orders otherwise, furnish such information concerning the estate and the estate's administration as is requested by a party in interest.

8. If the business of the debtor is authorized to be operated, file with the Court and with any governmental unit charged with responsibility for collection or determination of any tax arising out of such operation, periodic reports and summaries of the operation of such business, including a statement of receipts and disbursements, and such other information as the Court requires.

9. Make a final report and file a final account of the administration of the estate with the Court.

10. File a complete inventory within 30 days after qualifying and file a notice of the petition in every county where the debtor has real estate.

11. The trustee is given substantial statutory powers to accomplish the task of collection of assets.

Other Powers

Aside from the preceding broad collection and the avoidance powers granted the trustee, other powers are conferred upon the trustee in Chapter 7, which contemplate the collection and disbursement process.

For example, a trustee has the power to assume or reject executory contracts or unexpired leases. The trustee is given the power to either assume and retain the unexpired leases and executory contracts for the benefit of the estate, assume and assign them, or reject them. Such contracts or leases can often be of great value to the estate. For example, a lease in a popular shopping center under favorable terms may be assumed by the trustee and thereafter assigned (for a price to the highest bidder). It does not matter if there is a nonassignment clause in the underlying lease agreement between the debtor and the landlord. [11 U.S.C. Section 365.] This would ultimately generate funds for the estate to be disbursed to creditors.

However, to assume and assign, the lease must not be terminated prepetition and the trustee must make a "prompt" cure of any defaults prior to the assumption of the lease. "Prompt" has been held to mean very shortly after assumption.

Additionally, the trustee has the ability to sell property free and clear of all liens and adverse claims. However, a trustee may sell secured property only if the lienholder consents, nonbankruptcy law permits such sale, the sales price is in excess of the liens on the property, or the lienholder can be compelled to accept a money satisfaction of its claim. Usually, a sale of property for less than the total amount of the liens and encumbrances on the property is not allowed since there is no benefit to the estate.

A property that is burdensome to the estate or that is of inconsequential value to the estate may be abandoned by the trustee pursuant to 11 U.S.C. Section 554. As noted, property with liens in excess of its value is usually considered a burden to the estate and will be abandoned by the trustee.[68]

Voiding Powers

The trustee has the power to void or "undo" certain prepetition and postpetition transactions. These voidance powers include voidance of preferential transfers (11 U.S.C. Section 547), voidance of fraudulent conveyances (11

U.S.C. Section 548), and voidance of unauthorized postpetition transfers (11 U.S.C. Section 549).[69]

The trustee also may apply to the Bankruptcy Court for authorization to employ professionals, such as attorneys, to assist in the prosecution of voidance actions. Note: Attorneys must be disinterested parties and apply for Court authorization for employment in order to be compensated. [See generally, 11 U.S.C. Sections 327(a), 327(b), 330(a), and 331.]

Liquidation

Estate assets may consist of real property (such as commercial buildings), personal property (such as automobiles recovered in voidance actions), and intangible assets (such as leasehold interests in commercial retail space). The trustee must liquidate all these assets as expeditiously as possible. As with the employment of attorneys, the trustee also must request Bankruptcy Court authorization to employ professionals such as realtors, auctioneers, etc. to assist in the liquidation of estate assets. Again, such professionals must be disinterested parties and apply for Court authorization for employment in order to be compensated.[70]

Disbursement

Once all property is reduced to cash, the trustee begins the task of disbursement. At this stage, the trustee must take stock of all the proofs of claims filed in the case and determine if objections to any such proofs of claims is appropriate. Note: A trustee may employ professionals, such as attorneys to assist them in representation of any type, including objecting to proofs of claim.[71]

Thereafter, the trustee files a final account with the Court indicating the cash on hand and the proposed distribution to each creditor. The Clerk of the Bankruptcy Court notices this proposed distribution report to all creditors. [F.R.Bankr.P. 2002(f).] A hearing on the final account is held with an opportunity for any interested party to raise objections. Ultimately, an order for distribution is entered, which authorizes the trustee to disburse the funds of the estate.

As articulated in the final account and proposed distribution schedule, the trustee shall make distribution on a pro rata basis to the creditors in the priority provided under 11 U.S.C. Section 726.[72]

After the payment of distributions to the creditors, the creditors are allowed 90 days to receive, deposit, and collect their checks while the estate remains open. [11 U.S.C. Section 347.] Thereafter, the trustee stops payment on uncashed checks and writes a check to the Court for the unclaimed funds. [*Id.*] Finally, after such final distribution the estate is fully administered and the Court enters an order discharging the trustee and closing the case.[73]

Liability/Indemnity

Trustees are fiduciaries and are held accountable as such.[74] For example, trustees may be personally liable for a breach of their fiduciary duty, such as allowing an estate's redemption rights to lapse.[75] However, trustees are immune from liability based on the proper performance of their duties. For example, trustees have immunity from liability based on publication of results of an investigation that alleged fraud of the debtor's former management. [See *Weissman v. Hasset*, 47 B.R. 462 (S.D. N.Y. 1985).]

Compensation

A trustee's compensation in a Chapter 7 case is statutorily fixed and cannot be exceeded. Under the 1994 Amendments, trustees are allowed to receive compensation up to 25 percent of the first $5,000 in disbursement to creditors, 10 percent of additional amounts up to $50,000, 5 percent of additional amounts up to $1 million, and 3 percent of any amounts in excess of $1 million. The trustee is also entitled, separate and apart from compensation, to reimbursement for reasonable and necessary out-of-pocket expenses.[76]

CREDITORS

A creditor has the right to file a proof of claim within the limits set by the rules. Failure to file a timely proof of claim may result in the claim being disallowed. Disallowed claims are not eligible for participation in the distribution made from the estate.[77] The deadline to file proofs of claim is 90 days after the first date set for the 341 First Creditors' Meeting.[78]

Once a proof of claim is filed, a creditor may thereafter withdraw the proof of claim.[79] It is generally accepted that, once a proof of claim is filed, it may be amended.[80] Amended proofs of claims may correct the dollar figure or priority status of a claim. However, amended proofs of claims cannot assert an entirely new claim. This is especially important when an amended proof of claim is filed after the deadline for proofs of claims has elapsed.

Additionally, a creditor may object to the debtor's list of claimed exemptions. The absolute deadline for objections to exemptions is 30 days after the conclusion of the 341 First Creditors' Meeting. [F.R.Bankr.P. 4003(b).] However, if a debtor amends a list of claimed exemptions, then the objection deadline will extend to 30 days after the amendment.

Further, a creditor has a right to file a dischargeability complaint based either upon 11 U.S.C. Section 727 to disallow a debtor's discharge entirely or upon 11 U.S.C. Section 523 to disallow the discharge of such creditor's claim. The deadline for filing objections to discharge under either 11 U.S.C. Section 727 or Section 523 is 60 days after the date first set for the 341 First Creditors' Meeting. The importance of the 60-day absolute deadline cannot be over emphasized. F.R.Bankr.P. 4007 requires that the creditor's complaints under 11 U.S.C. Section 523(c) *must* be filed within this 60-day period or be forever forfeited. Note: The burden to file a dischargeability complaint under 11 U.S.C. Section 523(c) within the deadlines prescribed is upon the creditor asserting fraud, fiduciary defalcation/embezzlement/larceny, willful and malicious injury, or property settlement claims arising from a divorce.

However, note that a frivolously filed dischargeability complaint based upon fraud [Section 523(a)(2)] may subject the creditor to sanctions and possibly punitive damages. [See *In re Carmen,* 723 F.2d 16 (6th Cir. 1983).] (See Chapter 6, "Discharge.")

A creditor is also permitted to request that the automatic stay be terminated, modified, or annulled. Secured creditors usually base their stay relief request upon (1) lack of adequate protection, (2) lack of equity and inability to effectively reorganize, or (3) failure to file a reasonable plan of reorganization in 90 days. (See Chapter 5, "Automatic Stay.")

An unsecured creditor may also request that the stay be terminated, annulled, or modified for "cause" to proceed with eviction proceedings, to liquidate their claims in state court, etc.

Finally, creditors may always request the Chapter 7 case be dismissed (based upon bad faith filing, serial filing, 180-day bar to filing, prior bankruptcy discharge, etc.).[81] Additionally, creditors may also request the U.S. Trustee's Office or the trustee appointed to the case to request of the Court a dismissal based upon the debtor's substantial abuse of the Code. [11 U.S.C. Section 707(b).] However, note that creditors have no standing to make a direct request for dismissal based upon substantial abuse.[82]

GENERAL TIMELINE FOR CHAPTER 7

Day 1:	*Petition filed.*
	a. An order for relief is entered in voluntary cases.
	b. The list of statements, schedules, and master mailing list are due with the petition. [F.R.Bankr.P. 1007.]
Day 20:	*Notice to all creditors* sent by Clerk of the Bankruptcy Court. [F.R.Bankr.P. 2002(n).]
Days 30–40:	*341 First Creditors' Meeting* should be set during this time period. [F.R.Bankr.P. 2003(a).]

Debtors must file their statement of intention regarding consumer debts within 30 days of petition. [Section 521(2)(A).]

Day 60 (approx.) Deadline for the creditor/trustee to file *objections to property claimed as exempt*. [F.R.Bankr.P. 4003(b).] The actual deadline is 30 days after conclusion of 341 First Creditors' Meeting. Accordingly, 30 calendar days from the actual date of the meeting or any continued 341 First Creditors' Meeting(s).

Day 75 (approx.) Deadline for the debtor to *perform on stated intentions* of Section 521 Statement (i.e., surrender, reaffirm, redeem). [11 U.S.C. Section 521(a)(A).] The actual date is 45 days from the date of filing the petition (however, it is impossible most often since issues regarding dischargeability and abandonment are not resolved at the 45-day limit).

Day 90 (approx.) Deadlines for the creditors/trustees *to file dischargeability complaints* under Section 727 or Section 523. [F.R.Bankr.P. 4004(a), 4007(c).] The actual date to be calendared is 60 days after *first date set* for the 341 First Creditors' Meeting (not any continuances of the meeting).

Day 120 (approx.) Deadline for creditors to *file proofs of claim*. [F.R.Bankr.P. 3002(c).] The actual deadline is 90 days after the *first date set* for 341 First Creditors' Meeting (not any continuances of the meeting).

Days 150–160: Hearings are held on discharge complaints and approval of reaffirmation agreements (pro se debtors).

Day 161–Closure of Case: Resolution of discharge complaints, motions to avoid liens [Section 522(f)], trustee's voidance actions, claims litigation, liquidation of estate assets, distribution, final accounting, and closing of the case.

CONCLUSION

Chapter 7 is the least complex and swiftest of all the bankruptcy chapters. Chapter 7 is often referred to as "straight liquidation" and entails the trustee's collection and distribution of estate assets. However, Chapter 7 individual debtors are able to protect some of their assets through exemption and lien avoidance. Likewise, creditors in a Chapter 7 case are also entitled to protect their claims through nondischargeability complaints and by filing proofs of claim if any assets exist. The goal of Chapter 7 is to provide an honest debtor with a fresh start.

REVIEW QUESTIONS

1. What is the primary goal of the debtor in Chapter 7?

2. What are the debtor's responsibilities in Chapter 7?

3. What are the primary responsibilities of a trustee in Chapter 7?

4. What may creditors do in Chapter 7 to protect their rights? What are the deadlines within which creditors must act?

5. What two kinds of liens may be voided by a debtor in Chapter 7? What are the requirements?

6. How is a Chapter 7 case reopened? Give an example of when it is appropriate to reopen a case.

7. How is an involuntary Chapter 7 initiated? What are the requirements and the procedure?

ENDNOTES

[1] 11 U.S.C. Section 302

[2] *In re Malone,* 50 B.R. 2 (Bankr. E.D. Mich. 1985).

[3] 11 U.S.C. Section 109(g). See also Chapter 7, "Dismissal/Conversion."

[4] 11 U.S.C. Section 727(a)(8).

[5] Or have a domicile, or place of business or property.

[6] Or principal place of business or substantial assets.

[7] 28 U.S.C. Section 1408.

[8] *Id.*

[9] 28 U.S.C. Section 1930.

[10] F.R.Bankr.P. 1006(b)(1); Official Form No. 2.

[11] F.R.Bankr.P. 1006(b)(2).

[12] *Id.*

[13] 11 U.S.C. Section 303.

[14] *In re Benny,* 842 F.2d 1147 (9th Cir. 1988).

[15] Increased from $5,000 by the 1994 Amendments.

[16] F.R.Bankr.P. 1010.

[17] F.R.Bankr.P. 7004(b).

[18] 11 U.S.C. Sections 3003(h)(1), (2).

[19] F.R.Bankr.P. 1013(a).

[20] F.R.Bankr.P. 1011(d).

[21] F.R.Bankr.P. 1013(a).

[22] 11 U.S.C. Sections 303(i)(1), (2). See *In re Walden,* 781 F.2d 1121 (5th Cir. 1986).

[23] 11 U.S.C. Section 303(f).

[24]11 U.S.C. Section 303(g).

[25]11 U.S.C. Section 521(1), (2).

[26]11 U.S.C. Section 521(3).

[27]11 U.S.C. Section 521(4).

[28]11 U.S.C. Sections 343, 341.

[29]11 U.S.C. Section 521(5).

[30]F.R.Bankr.P. 1007(a)(1).

[31]F.R.Bankr.P. 1007(a)(2).

[32]Official Forms No. 6-8.

[33]F.R.Bankr.P. 107(h).

[34]Official Form No. *A.

[35]F.R.Bankr.P. 1009.

[36]F.R.Bankr.P. 1008.

[37]11 U.S.C. Section 362.

[38]See Chapter 5, "Automatic Stay," for detailed discussion of the scope and duration of the automatic stay.

[39]State law exemptions apply to all states that have "opted out" of the federal exemption scheme.

[40]Thirty days after the conclusion of the 341 First Creditors' Meeting. [F.R.Bankr.P. 4003(b).]

[41]11 U.S.C. Section 522(e).

[42]In most states judgments attach as liens to a debtor's residence once they are recorded (in the County Recorder's office in the county in which the real property is located).

[43]See Chapter 2, "Infrastructure of a Bankruptcy Case," for a discussion regarding the avoidance of liens on exempt property.

[44]See Chapter 8, "Voidable Transfers," for a detailed analysis of the avoidance of transfers.

[45]*In re Heath,* 3 B.R. 351 (Bankr. N.D. Ill. 1980).

[46]*In re Coleman American Moving Services, Inc.,* 8 B.R. 379 (Bankr. D. Kan. 1980).

[47]*In re Lambillotte,* 25 B.R. 392 (Bankr. M.D. Fla. 1982).

[48]11 U.S.C. Section 525(b).

[49]*In re Madison International, P.C.,* 77 B.R. 678 (Bankr. E.D. Wis. 1987).

[50]*In re Richardson,* 27 B.R. 560 (E.D. Pa. 1982).

[51]*In re Duffey,* 13 B.R. 785 (Bankr. S.D. Ohio 1981).

[52]See Chapter 2, "Infrastructure of a Bankruptcy Case," for detailed discussion of procedure and burden of proof in order to abandon property.

[53]Liens arising from judgments pass through bankruptcy unaffected. Accordingly, the ability to avoid such liens through Section 522(f) and therefore convert such judgments into unsecured dischargeable claims is extensive.

[54]See Chapter 6, "Discharge," for a detailed discussion of denial of discharge under Section 727.

[55]See Chapter 6, "Discharge," for a detailed analysis of each of the Section 523 exceptions to discharge.

[56]See Chapter 6, "Discharge," for discussion regarding revocation of discharge.

[57]Substantially modified by the 1994 Amendments.

[58]H.R. Rep. No. 595, 95th Cong., 1st Sess. 380-81.

[59]*In re McQuinn,* 6 B.R. 899 (Bankr. D. Neb. 1980).

[60]*In re Polk,* 76 B.R. 148 (9th Cir. BAP 1987).

[61]*In re Hawkins,* 727 F.2d 324 (4th Cir. 1984).

[62]11 U.S.C. Section 341(c).

[63]11 U.S.C. Section 322(a).

[64]28 U.S.C. Section 581(d).

[65]11 U.S.C. Sections 323(a), (b).

[66]F.R.Bankr.P. 6009.

[67]*In re O.P.M. Leasing Svcs., Inc.,* 670 F.2d 383 (2nd Cir. 1982).

[68]See Chapter 2, "Infrastructure of a Bankruptcy Case," for a detailed discussion regarding procedural requirements and standards for abandonment.

[69]See Chapter 8, "Voidable Transfers," for a detailed analysis of each of these causes of action.

[70]See generally 11 U.S.C. Sections 327(a), 327(b), 330(a) and 331.

[71]For a detailed discussion of the procedure for claims litigation, see Chapter 9, "Creditor Status, Priority, and Distribution Rights."

[72]A detailed analysis of the priority of payment structure to creditors is included in Chapter 9, "Creditor Status, Priority, and Distribution Rights."

[73]11 U.S.C. Section 350; F.R.Bankr.P. 5009.

[74]11 U.S.C. Section 322(a)(d); F.R.Bankr.P. 2010(d).

[75]*In re Rigden,* 795 F.2d 727 (9th Cir. 1986).

[76]11 U.S.C. Section 330(a)(2).

[77]F.R.Bankr.P. 3002(a), (b).

[78]For the procedural aspects of claims litigation see Chapter 9, "Creditor Status, Priority, and Distribution Rights."

[79]F.R.Bankr.P. 3006.

[80]*In re Gardiner, Inc.,* 68 B.R. 352 (Bankr. M.D. Fla, 1986).

[81]See Chapter 7, "Dismissal/Conversion."

[82]Only the trustee, the U.S. Trustee, or the Court has standing to raise the issue of substantial abuse of the debtor in dismissal proceedings. (For a detailed discussion regarding dismissal procedure and elements, see Chapter 7, "Dismissal/Conversion.")

11 *Chapter 13 Practice*

Your law firm filed an emergency Chapter 13 for a married couple yesterday. Today, the supervising attorney has assigned you to meet with the clients and formulate a Chapter 13 plan. The clients come in with a list of all their creditors, the amount they are behind on their house payment as well as their monthly income and expenses. You are supposed to "crunch the numbers" with your clients to make the Chapter 13 work.

What is a Chapter 13 plan? How does Chapter 13 work? How do all the different kinds of creditors get paid? How do you formulate a Chapter 13 plan?

INTRODUCTION

Chapter 13 bankruptcy cases are commonly known as "wage earner" reorganizations. Chapter 13 is intended as an alternative to liquidation in Chapter 7 cases to allow individuals to reorganize and repay at least some of their debts. As an incentive to choose Chapter 13 and reorganize rather than liquidate, Chapter 13 discharge is greater than that afforded in Chapter 7. Of course, the primary goal of Chapter 13 is to allow the debtor to make a fresh start.[1]

Further, the implicit policy of Chapter 13 serves an important societal goal. Chapter 13 essentially teaches debtors how to live within a fixed budget, make timely payments (i.e., monthly plan payments), and regularly file their taxes. Presumably, once debtors learn and practice these essential objectives for a period of three to five years, they will continue to practice these valuable life lessons once emerged from bankruptcy.

The Chapter 13 proceeding involves a formulation of a plan to pay back certain debts. The plan is confirmed by the Bankruptcy Court. However, unlike a Chapter 11, creditors do not have an opportunity to vote in favor or to reject a Chapter 13 plan. A trustee is appointed in a Chapter 13 case to act as an administrator and disbursing agent for all funds paid into the plan. The procedure for confirming a Chapter 13 plan is relatively quick and usually achieved within one or two months from the petition date. Once the plan payments have been completed (over a three- to five-year period) the debtor obtains a discharge.

The respective parties within a Chapter 13 are the debtor (who is an individual voluntarily seeking Chapter 13 relief), the Chapter 13 trustee (who acts in an administrative capacity rather than to liquidate assets), all the usual prepetition creditors found within Chapter 7 or 11 cases, as well as postpetition creditors. Further, Chapter 13 provides special protection for codebtors, i.e., those obligated on debts with the debtor but not themselves in bankruptcy.

PARTIES: ROLES, DUTIES, AND RIGHTS

Unlike Chapter 7 or Chapter 11, only an individual may qualify as a Chapter 13 debtor. Therefore, no corporations or partnerships may file for Chapter 13 relief. However, a debtor and spouse may file a joint Chapter 13 case. Also, a debtor who is self-employed (i.e., a sole proprietorship) is eligible for Chapter 13.

A Chapter 13 cannot be forced upon an individual, unlike the involuntary petition allowed in both Chapter 7 and Chapter 11. [11 U.S.C. Section 301.] Similarly, a debtor holds an absolute right to dismiss a Chapter 13 case if it has not already been converted from Chapter 7, 11, or 12. [11 U.S.C. Section 1307(b).]

In order to qualify, a Chapter 13 debtor must have "regular income." *Regular income* is defined as income sufficiently stable and regular to enable the individual to make payments under a Chapter 13 plan.[2] Accordingly, Chapter 13 is available to traditional wage earners, proprietors of businesses, farmers, service persons, professionals, retirees, recipients of welfare or disability payments, and others with regular income.

For example, the following sources of income have been deemed "regular income" sufficient to qualify for Chapter 13 eligibility: individuals receiving AFDC,[3] individuals receiving research stipends,[4] farm income of individuals,[5] disability payments,[6] child support payments,[7] welfare payments,[8] unemployment benefits,[9] or even working odd jobs.[10]

Further, a husband and wife may file a joint petition even though one of the spouses is unemployed (i.e., househusband, housewife, domestic engineer). The combination of their joint income is sufficient to meet the "regular income" requirement and therefore qualify them both as Chapter 13 debtors.

An additional limitation for eligibility for Chapter 13 is found in the maximum debt limits. The unsecured, liquidated, noncontingent debts must not exceed $250,000.[11] Further, the secured, liquidated, noncontingent debts must not exceed $750,000.[12] Two issues regarding these debt limits arise in determining eligibility. The first is whether debts are considered noncontingent or liquidated. The second is the depth of litigation required to determine if the debt amounts are within the prescribed range.

Nonliquidated and contingent debts are distinguished from disputed debts in the eligibility analysis. *Nonliquidated obligations* are those that have not been reduced to a sum certain or whose precise sum owed is not easily calculable. For example, a debtor has certain outstanding debts due to an auto accident while driving without insurance. However, the personal injury claims of the victim/creditor have not been reduced to judgment, nor can a bankruptcy court second-guess the extent of damages a jury may award to the creditor. In this instance, the obligation is unliquidated and not included in the total amount of unsecured debt.

A claim will be considered *contingent* if the debtor's obligation to pay does not come into existence until some "triggering" future event. Prime examples of contingent debts are where the debtor is a guarantor or cosigner of obligations. Since the debtor's obligation to pay on such debts does not come into existence until a future event (i.e., default of the primary person obligated on the loan), such debts will be considered contingent and be excluded from the total amount of debts.

Both unliquidated and contingent debts differ from mere disputed debts. In a *disputed debt,* the debtor asserts that the obligation is not owed or the debtor may assert some counterclaim or defense. Unlike unliquidated and contingent debts, disputed debts are included within the debts to determine if the debts exceed the $250,000/$750,000 maximum for eligibility.

Whether a debtor falls within the maximum "cap" of the $250,000/$750,000 limits often depends on the timing and extent of the evaluation of claims. Generally, a debtor's eligibility will be determined as of the petition date. Therefore, some Courts determine eligibility by accepting the characterization (noncontingent and liquidated) and amount of the debt as set forth in the debtor's schedules. This general acceptance is as long as the debtor's schedules have been filed in good faith.[13] Other Courts allow more extensive litigation of the amount and characterization of debt, even if the schedules are prepared in good faith, in order to determine if a Chapter 13 debtor is eligible.[14] Finally, other Courts fully litigate all issues concerning claims allowance that may affect the amount or characterization of a debt.[15] This last method requires a Court's scrutiny of claims at the inception of the case to determine a debtor's eligibility.

A Chapter 13 debtor plays an active role in the bankruptcy proceeding, unlike the Chapter 7 debtor. In fact, the Chapter 13 debtor is given some of the same powers as the Chapter 7 trustee, including the operation of his business or entering into transactions such as the lease or sale of property of the estate. [11 U.S.C. Sections 1304 and 363(c)(3).] These rights are reserved exclusively for the debtor. However, the Chapter 13 debtor's rights to use the estate property are limited the same as any trustee's. [See 11 U.S.C. Section 363.] Most importantly, the Chapter 13 debtor also retains possession of the assets.

Meanwhile, the Chapter 13 debtor enjoys rights and benefits of counsel, the automatic stay, exemptions, lien avoidance on exempt property, nondiscriminatory treatment, and discharge. Note: Certain jurisdictions now require a Chapter 13 debtor's counsel to submit an application to be employed. Debtor's counsels are often paid a portion of their fees and costs "through the plan." Such payment is an administrative expense from estate property. For example, in Arizona an application to be employed must be filed, yet can be combined with the proposed Chapter 13 plan. Accordingly, check with the local rules to ensure that the application is filed if necessary.

Also, the automatic stay in Chapter 13 cases continues until the debtor's discharge. The discharge does not take place until some three to five years postpetition. Accordingly, the debtor's respite from creditor harassment is for a greater period than in Chapter 7 or 11. Moreover, the automatic stay is broadened in Chapter 13 cases to include certain "codebtors." Discussion of the codebtor stay is discussed later in this chapter.

Further, debtors in Chapter 13 may claim any exemptions that would be available to them in a Chapter 7 or 11 case. These include either the exemptions articulated in 11 U.S.C. Section 522 or the state law exemptions if the debtor's state has "opted out."[16]

Chapter 13 contains no specific grant of power to the Chapter 13 debtor to use the strong-arm, avoidance, or recovery powers specified elsewhere in the Code. However, 11 U.S.C. Section 103(a) renders Chapter 5 applicable in Chapter 13 cases. Therefore, some courts have found that a Chapter 13 debtor is the most appropriate party to identify recoverable property. This recovery and voidance of transfers furthers the rehabilitative intent of Chapter 13. Accordingly, in some districts, Chapter 13 debtors may, for example, seek turnover of property under Section 542, such as requiring the turnover of monies paid under an unenforceable reaffirmation agreement in a prior Chapter 7 case,[17] the turnover of funds held by a state court under a prepetition attachment,[18] or the turnover of vehicles to the debtor.[19]

Other courts have held that a Chapter 13 debtor may exercise the strong-arm powers under 11 U.S.C. Section 544 and stand in the shoes of the trustee and assert the trustee's powers granted under 11 U.S.C. Section 544 to avoid fraudulent conveyances.[20] However, other courts hold that Chapter 13 debtors have no 11 U.S.C. Section 544 powers. [See *In re Perry*, 131 B.R. 763 (Bankr. Mass. 1991); *In re Tillery*, 124 B.R. 127 (Bankr. M.D. Fla. 1991); *In re Carter*, 2 B.R. 321 (Bankr. Colo. 1980).]

Further, in some jurisdictions a Chapter 13 debtor may recover preferences under 11 U.S.C. Section 547 with the same powers as a trustee.[21] However, other jurisdictions expressly do not permit the Chapter 13 debtor to recover preferences, reserving this role exclusively for the trustee.[22] Accordingly, research the power of a Chapter 13 debtor in the jurisdiction in which you will be practicing.

Likewise, the jurisdictions are split over whether a Chapter 13 debtor may exercise the voidance powers for fraudulent conveyances under 11 U.S.C. Section 548. [See *In re Reece*, 117 B.R. 480 (Bankr. E.D. Mo. 1990) (in absence of action by the trustee, a Chapter 13 debtor enjoys standing to prosecute adversary complaint to avoid a fraudulent transfer under Section 548). Contra, *In re Houston*, 96 B.R. 717 (Bankr. W.D. Tex. 1989) (Chapter 13 debtor does not have standing to pursue any strong-arm voidance actions).][23]

The Chapter 13 debtor has the use of the voidance and recovery powers for the recovery of exempt property under 11 U.S.C. Section 522(f). In essence, the Chapter 13 debtor may avoid either certain judicial liens on exempt property or certain nonpurchase, nonpossessory liens on property claimed as exempt. [11 U.S.C. Section 522(f).] (See Chapter 10, "Chapter 7 Practice," for discussion of voidance of liens on exemptions.)

While the Chapter 13 debtor enjoys considerable rights, certain duties also accompany the Chapter 13 debtor status. Such duties include filing the initial documentation required in all chapters (i.e., statements and schedules) within 15 days of the petition date. The Chapter 13 debtor is also required to make plan payments to the Chapter 13 trustee within 30 days of the petition date. The Chapter 13 debtor also must file a plan within 15 days of the petition date.[24]

The duties and powers of a Chapter 13 trustee are limited since the trustee's role is somewhat limited. In a Chapter 13 case, the trustee acts more as a supervisor and distributing agent for the payments by the debtor. The Chapter 13 trustee supervises the plan to make sure all the mandatory elements are present and the plan payments are made. The Chapter 13 trustee distributes payments to the creditors according to the confirmed plan.

The Chapter 13 trustee's duties are to be accountable for all property received, to investigate the financial affairs of the debtor, to examine (and object to) proofs of claims, to oppose the debtor's discharge (if appropriate),[25] to furnish information about the estate to parties in interest, to render a final report and final accounting with the court, to appear at hearings regarding valuation of encumbered property or plan confirmation[26] or postconfirmation modification, to assist the debtor in performing under the plan, and to ensure that the debtor makes timely payments under the plan.[27]

Additionally, the trustee is also required to investigate the conduct of the debtor's business and report on such investigations. Such reports outline any discoveries of mismanagement or fraud.[28] However, the Chapter 13 trustee is not required to file periodic reports of the operation of the business; that duty is imposed upon the Chapter 13 debtor.[29] Further, the Chapter 13 trustee is the only representative of the estate. Accordingly, the estate can sue or be sued only through the Chapter 13 trustee.

Also, the Chapter 13 trustee has the responsibility to "advise, other than on legal matters, and assist the debtor in performance under the plan." [11 U.S.C. Section 1302(b)(4).] This duty has been interpreted to require the Chapter 13 trustee to provide financial counseling to the debtor.[30] In fact, in some districts, the Chapter 13 trustee counsels with debtors about money management, family budgeting, and using care in the marketplace.

Moreover, the Chapter 13 trustee is the focal point through which most Chapter 13 activity in a district passes. The most fundamental responsibility of the Chapter 13 trustee is to receive, disburse, and account for payments under Chapter 13 plans. All plans proposed by debtors and debtor's counsel are carefully reviewed by the Chapter 13 trustee. In some districts, the Chapter 13 trustee assists pro se debtors in drafting plans. The Chapter 13 trustee plays an active role at the 341 First Creditors' Meeting. Chapter 13 trustees also have the responsibility to object to or support confirmation of a debtor's plan. Finally, the trustee polices the conversion and dismissal of cases due to failing plans. The trustee provides an essential information link between debtors and creditors during the administration of the Chapter 13 case.

The Chapter 13 trustee possesses the statutory powers, duties, and responsibilities of the strong-arm powers contained in 11 U.S.C. Section 544. Therefore, the Chapter 13 trustee may avoid statutory liens and transfers that are preferential or fraudulent under 11 U.S.C. Sections 545, 547, and 548. Also the Chapter 13 trustee may be permitted to join with the debtor to avoid liens that impair exemptions under 11 U.S.C. Section 522(f). Further, the Chapter 13 trustee may seek conversion or dismissal of a pending case or request modification of a confirmed plan.[31] Lastly, the Chapter 13 trustee has the duty to review the incurring of postpetition debts. Failure to seek the trustee's prior approval of such debts renders the postpetition claims nondischargeable in the Chapter 13 case.[32]

Note: While a Chapter 13 trustee's powers are broad, certain powers are exclusively reserved to the debtor in Chapter 13. Accordingly, the Chapter 13 trustee may not use, sell, or lease property of the estate.[33]

In most districts, the Chapter 13 trustees are appointed as standing trustees to handle all Chapter 13 cases.[34] There are no interim trustees or creditor election rights in Chapter 13 cases. In other words, creditors cannot choose a Chapter 13 trustee. Further, Chapter 13 trustees must fit the eligibility and qualification requirements the same as Chapter 7 trustees. Additionally, the Chapter 13 trustee receives compensation on the basis of a percentage (10%) of money paid into the Chapter 13 plan.[35]

The creditors in Chapter 13 are the same as in Chapter 7 with two exceptions. These are postpetition claims for taxes and postpetition claims for consumer debts (to the extent they are for property or services necessary for the debtor's performance under the plan). These postpetition claims are treated and allowed or disallowed as though they existed prepetition.[36] Therefore, if a creditor extends credit on a postpetition consumer debt without the trustee's approval, and knew—or should have known—that the trustee's approval was practicable yet not obtained, such claim may be disallowed.[37]

The creditor structure for classification in Chapter 13 cases is essentially the same as in any other chapter.[38] In essence, there are three types of claims: secured (oversecured, fully secured, and undersecured), priority, and unsecured. Note, undersecured creditors in Chapter 13 may be forced to go through the 11 U.S.C. Section 506 "strip-down." This bifurcates their claims into secured claims up to the value of the underlying collateral. The remainder of the claim is treated as an unsecured claim and placed in the unsecured class.

One of the fundamental duties of a creditor in Chapter 13 cases is to file its proof of claim. Failure to file a proof of claim will result in disallowance of the claim. [See *In re Owens,* 67 B.R. 418 (Bankr. E.D. Pa. 1987) (where IRS lost its claim for failure to file a proof of claim).] The deadline for creditors to file their proof of claims is 90 days from the *first date set* for the 341 First Creditors' Meeting. [F.R.Bankr.P. 3002(c).] However, as a practical matter cautious creditors should file their proofs of claim as quickly as possible and no later than the confirmation date. This will ensure that the plan analysis will include the appropriate amount and priority of the claim. This makes "feasibility" issues regarding the debtor's plan more apparent. For example, if the proofs of claim filed in a case indicate substantially more priority debt than listed in the debtor's schedules, any underfunding of a plan would be obvious.

Finally, creditors within a Chapter 13 case are allowed to request stay relief, are allowed to object to confirmation of the debtor's proposed plan, and are allowed to retain their liens on property if no affirmative action by the debtor is taken to avoid the liens. However, creditors are not allowed to "vote" on the debtor's plan, unlike creditors in Chapter 11 cases. Additionally, the automatic stay in Chapter 13 cases encompasses nondebtor entities, such as guarantors and cosignors. Accordingly, it may be incumbent upon the creditor to request not only stay relief, but also codebtor stay relief.

Chapter 13 provides a unique "codebtor" stay.[39] This is a limited extension of the automatic stay to nonbankruptcy individuals. In essence, codebtors have not filed bankruptcy. However, the codebtors are obligated, along with the debtor, on certain debts. For example, a cosignor on a loan or guarantor on a debt are codebtors. The codebtor stay exists only for the benefit of *individual* codebtors of *consumer* debts.[40] The purpose of the codebtor stay is to relieve pressure on family members or relatives who cosigned consumer debts for a debtor.[41] Accordingly, the codebtor stay does not protect co-obligors on business debts.[42]

The codebtor stay prevents a creditor from taking any action, including the commencement or continuation of a civil action, against any individual who is liable on a consumer debt with the debtor. In other words, the creditor cannot pursue any codebtor once the bankruptcy is filed. The codebtor stay is automatic in Chapter 13 cases, the same as the automatic stay of 11 U.S.C. Section 362. The codebtor stay starts when the Chapter 13 case is filed. The codebtor stay applies regardless of notice to the creditor.

If a creditor requests relief from the codebtor stay, it automatically terminates after 20 days unless the debtor (or the codebtor) specifically objects to the termination.[43] There are three specific situations wherein a creditor may request relief from the codebtor stay:

1. The codebtor received the consideration from which the creditor's claim arose.[44] For example: A debtor cosigned on a loan for his brother so that the brother could purchase a car, and the brother has received the consideration (i.e., the car). If, on the other hand, the brother cosigns in order that the debtor may purchase a car, then the debtor has received the consideration and the codebtor stay will not be terminated. Also, if both the debtor and the codebtor share in the benefits, the codebtor stay will not be terminated.[45] For example, the debtor and brother cosign an automobile loan, and both use the car to carpool to work, etc. The codebtor stay will remain in place in this situation as well.

2. The Chapter 13 plan filed by the debtor does not propose full payment of the cosigned obligation.[46] In other words, the obligation is not provided for in (i.e., paid through) the Chapter 13 plan. Using our preceding example, the car loan (whether the debtor uses the vehicle or the

brother) is not included in the debtor's proposed plan. Accordingly, the codebtor stay will be terminated upon request of the creditor to collect the balance of the claim from the cosignor.

3. The creditor can show irreparable harm by the continuation of the codebtor stay.[47] *Irreparable harm* has been shown where the codebtor's financial condition is shaky, such as when the codebtor has lost her job. Also, irreparable harm can be shown if the codebtor appears ready to leave the jurisdiction. Also, when the value of the underlying collateral is shown to be deteriorating or the codebtor himself files bankruptcy, irreparable harm may be shown.

To show irreparable harm, the creditor must show something more than mere delay in collection from the comaker. The creditor must show specific proof that the likelihood of collection from the codebtor is impaired.

Relief from the codebtor stay does not need to be deferred while the debtor is making payments under a confirmed plan. In other words, the creditor may seek relief from the codebtor stay and at the same time receive payments from the debtor under the plan.

Matter of Sommersdorf
139 B.R. 700 (Bankr. S.D. Ohio 1991)

Aug, J.: The Debtors filed their Chapter 13 petition on May 24, 1991. . . The Debtors' plan, which provides for 100% payment to Society National Bank ("Society") was confirmed on September 16, 1991.

* * *

The specific issue before the Court is whether the refusal to remove the notation on the non-debtor comaker's credit report constitutes contempt, where the creditor who caused the credit report notation to be made is receiving a 100% payment under Debtor's plan.

The broader related issue of whether this notation on a non-debtor comakers credit report violates the automatic stay of action against the comaker is a serious question for the Chapter 13 practitioner who is often asked by his potential clients: "What effect will the Chapter 13 filing have on a comaker?"

The underlying July 1988 promissory note in favor of Society was signed by the Debtors and by their friend, William Parrish, ("Parrish"), a non-debtor. The loan proceeds were used by the Debtors to purchase a 1987 Oldsmobile Cutlass Ciera.

Subsequent to the Order for Relief, Society transmitted to Trans-Union Corporation ("Trans-Union") and Trans-Union published an entry on the credit report of Parrish reflecting the fact that Society had taken a profit and loss write-off on the account. As a result of the credit report Parrish was unable to obtain a home loan. * * *

Section 362 of the Bankruptcy Code defines the scope of the automatic stay as it pertains to the *Debtor,* by listing the acts that are stayed by the commencement of the case. One of the eight general prohibitions Section 362(a)(6) stays is

> any act to collect, assess, or recover a claim against the debtor that arose before the commencement of the case under this title.

The above paragraph applies to any "act" whether or not the act is related to a "proceedings." (citation omitted). This provision is intended to prevent creditor harassment of the debtor. The conduct prohibited by this provision ranges from that of an informal nature, such as telephone contact or dunning letters, to more formal judicial and administrative proceedings also stayed under Section 362(a)(1). * * *

Pursuant to Section 1301(a) of the Bankruptcy Code, which creates a stay of action against a codebtor,

> ... a creditor may not act, or commence or continue any civil action, to collect all or any part of a consumer debt of the debtor from any individual that is liable on such debt with the debtor ...

On its face and as a whole, the stay created by Section 1301 is not as broad as the stay created by Section 362. But the policies of the two provisions are related and the two provisions must be read together. Section 1301 is designed primarily for the protection of the principal debtor by insulating that individual from indirect pressures exerted by creditors on friends, relatives, and fellow employees of the Chapter 13 debtor. (citations omitted). It operates only as a procedural delay for the creditor who retains all of his substantive rights. And, like Section 362(a)(6), Section 1301(a) prohibits "acts" to collect debts. Therefore, we find that the notation on the non-debtor comaker's credit reports violates the automatic stay of action against the codebtor of Section 1301.
   * * *

However, ... while we find that Society's actions did violate the stay of action against the codebtor created by Section 1301, we do not find the actions of Society to be tantamount to civil contempt. Further, while Section 362(h) states that an individual injured by any willful violation of a stay provided by that section shall recover actual damages, including costs and attorneys' fees, and in appropriate circumstances punitive damages, there is no such similar provision in Section 1301.

It is hereby ordered that Society shall cause the profit and loss write-off notation to be deleted from the non-debtor comaker's credit report and that Society shall cause the corrected credit report to be reissued to the affected parties.

> * * * An award to the Debtors is appropriate [under Section 362 for damages].

The procedure for seeking relief from the codebtor stay is found in F.R.Bankr.P. 4001. The request is a contested matter initiated by filing a motion (and fee) under F.R.Bankr.P. 9014. The burden of proof to establish the grounds for relief from the codebtor stay is on the creditor.[48] If no relief is sought or granted from the codebtor stay, it continues until the case is closed, dismissed, or converted to Chapter 7 or Chapter 11.

CONFIRMATION PROCESS

A legal assistant often assists in the formulation and the drafting of a Chapter 13 plan. A Chapter 13 plan is the document filed with the Bankruptcy Court which proposes the manner and means of repayment to creditors. When representing creditors, the legal assistant will be called upon to analyze any proposed plans in order to draft objections to confirmation. Accordingly, it is vital for legal assistants to be familiar with the mandatory elements of a plan, the items prohibited in a Chapter 13 plan, as well as the provisions that may be permitted under Chapter 13. Further, it is important for the legal assistant to know all the local rules regarding Chapter 13. For example, in the Central District of California the local rules require that the Chapter 13 plan be submitted in a "form" that is provided by local rules. Likewise, in Arizona local rules require a Chapter 13 plan to include an employment application for the debtor's attorney.

A Chapter 13 plan must be filed by the debtor within 15 days of the petition date.[49] Only a debtor may file a Chapter 13 plan.[50] Creditors or the trustee cannot propose a Chapter 13 plan. Once a Chapter 13 plan is proposed, the Bankruptcy Court must hold a hearing on the confirmation.[51] Confirmation is formal Court approval of the plan which binds the debtor and all creditors. The confirmation hearing must be noticed to all creditors at least 25 days before the hearing.[52]

Essentially, there are two kinds of Chapter 13 plans. An *extension plan* proposes to pay 100 percent to all creditors over the life of the plan. A *composition plan* pays less than 100 percent on unsecured debts. A plan may provide for payments over three years or up to a maximum of five years. However, the Bankruptcy Court must approve any plan length over three years. A copy of a Chapter 13 plan appears in Figure 11-1.

Janette Anderson
LAW OFFICES OF JANETTE ANDERSON
420 West Roosevelt Rd.
Phoenix, Arizona 85003-1331
(602) 253-0400
(602) 253-0033 (FAX)

Attorney for Debtor

UNITED STATES BANKRUPTCY COURT

DISTRICT OF ARIZONA

In re:	)	
	)	CASE NO.
	)	
	)	Chapter 13
	)	
Debtor.	)	CHAPTER 13 PLAN
	)	
_____	)	

Debtor proposes the following Chapter 13 Plan:

1. **PROPERTY AND INCOME SUBMITTED TO THE PLAN.** Debtor shall submit the following amounts of property and future income to the Trustee for distribution under the Plan:

   a. **FUTURE EARNINGS OR INCOME.** Debtor shall pay $717.00 per month to the Trustee, on or before the 20th day of each month, commencing November 20, 1994. Debtor is to make her payments to the trustee assigned to her case in the form of a cashier's check or money order payable to the Chapter 13 Trustee.

   b. **OTHER PROPERTY.** Debtor shall pay to the Chapter 13 Trustee the entire proceeds of any income tax refund received for tax years 1994 through 1995 to be applied as supplements to the Plan payments otherwise required.

2. **DURATION.** This Plan shall continue for 48 months from the first payment. If at any time before the end of this period all claims are paid, the Plan shall terminate.

FIGURE 11-1a. Chapter 13 plan (page 1).

3. **CLASSIFICATION AND TREATMENT OF CLAIMS.** Claims shall be classified and paid as set forth below:

a. **ADMINISTRATIVE EXPENSES.**

(1) **Trustee's Fees:** The Trustee shall receive the percentage of each monthly payment made by the Debtor in an amount as may be approved by the U.S. Trustee from time to time, in an amount not to exceed 10%.

(2) **Attorney's Fees:** None.

b. **CLAIMS SECURED BY REAL PROPERTY.**

The following creditors shall retain their security interests in the real property and the Trustee shall have no interest in or claim to the property securing the claim. Regular monthly payments becoming due after the filing of the petition shall be made outside of this Plan. No payment shall be deemed late and the agreement which is the basis for a claim shall not be deemed in default as a result of arrearages cured under this Plan. The estimated arrearages listed below shall be adjusted to reflect the actual arrearage at the time of the confirmation. The arrearage as adjusted, including late charges, shall be cured prior to the commencement of payment on claims listed hereafter. Interest on such payments to cure arrearages shall be at the rate of 10% per annum. Trustee shall pay all funds received after deduction for administrative expenses above.

The estimated arrearages are as follows:

CLAIMANT	SECURITY	ARREARAGE
	Residence	NONE
	Residence	NONE
	Rental Prop.	NONE
	Rental Prop.	NONE

c. **CLAIMS SECURED BY PERSONAL PROPERTY.** The following creditors shall retain their interest in personal property securing their claims. They shall be paid the debt balance plus the interest at the rate provided for under the parties' original contract. Regular monthly payments becoming due after the filing of the petition shall be made outside of this Plan. Upon payment of this amount, their security interests shall be released.

FIGURE 11-1b. Chapter 13 plan (page 2).

Any claims not specifically named in this Plan are presumed to be unsecured claims. Creditors, including but not limited to Sears, Roebuck & Co., Montgomery Ward, Radio Shack and/or J.C. Penney Co., claiming secured status shall serve an objection to the Plan upon Debtor's counsel as required by the court prior to the first scheduled confirmation hearing date. If this case is assigned to Judge _____, objections shall be filed and served no later than 30 days prior to the first scheduled confirmation hearing. If this case is assigned to any of the other judges, objections shall be filed and served no later than 7 days prior to the first scheduled confirmation hearing.

If no objections are filed and served upon Debtor's counsel within the deadline prior to the hearing on the confirmation of the Plan as set forth above, claims not specifically named below will be fully treated as other unsecured claims.

CREDITOR/ SECURITY	BALANCE/ VALUE OF SECURITY	INTEREST RATE	PAID AS: SECURED/ UNSECURED
	$4,000.00	12%	$4,000.00
	$4,000.00		-0-

d. **PRIORITY TAX CLAIMS.**

(1) The following priority tax claims shall be paid in full without postpetition interest. Payments on tax claims shall begin after payment of administrative expenses and any secured claims. All taxes for any year not provided for or paid by the Plan shall be discharged upon completion of the Plan and shall abate even if the Internal Revenue Service or the Arizona Department of Revenue do not file Proofs of Claim or objections to the Plan. Any liens held by the respective tax agencies will be deemed extinguished and are to be released upon completion of this Plan.

Debtor does not have any outstanding tax obligations.

(2) Debtor asserts she has filed all required tax returns through tax year 1993.

e. **UNSECURED CODEBTOR CLAIMS.** Unsecured codebtor claims to the following shall be paid in full by this plan prior to the

FIGURE 11-1c. Chapter 13 plan (page 3).

payment of general unsecured claims pursuant to 11 U.S.C. §362(a) and §1301.

Creditor	Amount

None

f. **EDUCATIONAL LOANS.** Any and all educational loans listed in the Debtor's schedules or for which claims are filed are to be classified as unsecured claims and shall be paid in full prior to general unsecured claims. Any amounts unpaid through this Plan shall <u>not</u> be discharged by these proceedings unless a determination is made after an appropriate hearing that such liability is dischargeable.

Creditor	Amount

None

g. **UNSECURED CLAIMS.** All other claims shall be classified as unsecured with any claims of security interest in property being avoided. Unsecured claims shall be paid the balance of payments under the Plan, pro rata allowed in full satisfaction thereof, except for any disputed or rejected claims. Any amounts unpaid shall be discharged. However, this Plan contemplates 100% payment to unsecured claims. Accordingly, the Plan meets requirements of the Code and achieves Chapter 7 reconciliation.

4. **OBJECTIONS.** Objections by all creditors to the Plan must be received by Debtor's attorney within the time period set forth in paragraph 3(c) above.

5. **LIEN AVOIDANCE.** Debtors hereby elect to avoid the fixing of liens pursuant to §522(b) of the Bankruptcy Code. All secured creditors, except those whose liens are avoidable pursuant to the provisions of §522(b), shall retain their liens until paid as provided for by this Plan.

6. **REJECTION OF CLAIMS - SECURED CREDITORS.** Debtor elects not to assume the lease or contract with creditors named in this paragraph and shall surrender to each creditor the collateral subject to the lien or lease in full satisfaction of any and all claims that each secured or unsecured creditor may have against Debtor arising from the transaction creating creditor's interest in said property.

/ / /

FIGURE 11-1d. Chapter 13 plan (page 4).

Creditor	Amount

None

7. **EXCLUSION OF CREDITORS.** Notwithstanding any other provisions of this Plan, Debtor elects not to assume the existing lease or contract with creditors named in this paragraph. These named creditors shall not be dealt with or provided for by this Plan. Debtor shall surrender all interest in the underlying collateral to the secured creditor as and for full satisfaction and discharge of her obligation on such debt as follows:

Creditor	Collateral
	1992 Baja Boat

8. **EFFECTIVE DATE AND VESTING.** The effective date of the Plan shall be the date of the order Confirming the Plan. Property of the estate shall vest in the Debtor upon confirmation of the Plan unless otherwise stated in the order confirming the Plan. Debtor may use the estate property in any manner or may sell the property without further order of this Court. Prior to and upon confirmation, the automatic stay pursuant to 11 U.S.C. §362 will remain in full force and effect on all real and personal property of the Debtor until the discharge or dismissal of this proceeding.

9. **POSTPETITION CLAIMS.** Claims allowed for postpetition debts incurred by Debtor may be paid in full and in such order and on such terms as the Trustee, in his sole discretion, may determine. Trustee may file to dismiss this case if Debtor incurs postpetition debts without the written consent of the Trustee and Debtor fails to keep such obligations current in payment.

10. **GENERAL PROVISIONS.**

a. If this case is filed as a joint Debtors' case, the Debtors' estate shall be fully consolidated for purposes of administration. Pursuant to §1322(b)(3) of the Bankruptcy Code, Trustee shall have the power to waive, in writing and on such conditions as the Trustee may impose, any default in Debtors' payment to the Trustee under this Amended Plan.

b. The automatic stay granted pursuant to 11 U.S.C. §362 and §1301 shall remain in full force and effect

FIGURE 11-1e. Chapter 13 plan (page 5).

until further order of this court.

DATED THIS _____ day of October, 1994.

LAW OFFICES OF JANETTE ANDERSON

_____   _____
Attorney for Debtor   Debtor

FIGURE 11-1f. Chapter 13 plan (page 6).

```
                        FORM 13-2
                      PLAN ANALYSIS

Debtor:
prior:Bankruptcy (  )      Chapter 13  (  )      Date _____
Estimated Length of Plan:  48 months

                              Trustee Use
                              §341 Meeting Date: _____
                              Continued:_____
                              Confirmed Date: _____
                              _____
                              _____
```

TOTAL DEBT PROVIDED FOR UNDER THE PLAN AND ADMINISTRATIVE EXPENSES

A. TOTAL PRIORITY CLAIMS
   1. Unpaid Attorney's Fees . . . . $ -0-
   2. Taxes . . . . $ -0-
   3. Other . . . . $_____
B. TOTAL PAYMENTS TO CURE DEFAULTS . . . . $ -0-
C. TOTAL PAYMENTS ON SECURED CLAIMS. . . . . $ 5,056.32
D. TOTAL OF PAYMENTS ON GEN. UNSECURED CLAIMS $26,224.87
E. SUBTOTAL $31,281.19
F. TOTAL TRUSTEE'S COMPENSATION (maximum of
   10% of Debtor's payments) . . . . $ 3,128.11
G. TOTAL DEBT AND ADMINISTRATIVE EXPENSES $34,409.30

RECONCILIATION WITH CHAPTER 7

H. INTEREST OF GENERAL UNSECURED CREDITORS IF CHAPTER 7 FILED
   1. Value of Debtor's interest in nonexempt
      property . . . . $ 149,393.70
   2. Plus: value property recoverable
      under avoiding powers. . . . . $
   3. Less: estimated Chapter 7 administrative
      expenses . . . . $ 14,939.37
   4. Less amounts payable to priority creditors
      other than costs of administration . . . . $
   5. Equals: estimated amount payable to
      general unsecured creditors if Chapter 7
      filed (if negative enter zero) . . . . $ 134,454.33
I. ESTIMATED DIVIDENDS FOR GENERAL UNSECURED
   CREDITORS UNDER CHAPTER 7 . . . . $ 134,454.33
J. ESTIMATED DIVIDEND UNDER PLAN . . . . $ 26,224.87

IF THERE ARE DISCREPANCIES BETWEEN THE PLAN AND THE PLAN ANALYSIS, THE PROVISIONS OF THE PLAN AS CONFIRMED CONTROL.

FIGURE 11-1g. Chapter 13 plan (page 7).

Name	Law Offices of Jeffrey S.Shinbrot
Address	3601 Wilshire Boulevard, Suite 900
	Beverly Hills, California 90211
Telephone	(310) 659-5444

☐ Attorney for Debtor(s)   (If applicable) Attorney's
☐ Debtor in Pro Per   State Bar I.D. No.

UNITED STATES BANKRUPTCY COURT
CENTRAL   **DISTRICT OF**   CALIFORNIA

List all names including trade names, used by Debtor(s) within last 6 years.

Chapter 13
Case No.

CONF:
TIME:
PLACE:

Social Security No. _____ Debtor
Social Security No. _____ Joint Debtor
Debtor(s) EIN No. _____

CHAPTER 13 PLAN AND
MOTION TO AVOID LIENS

NOTICE

THIS PLAN CONTAINS EVIDENTIARY MATTER WHICH, IF NOT CONTROVERTED, MAY BE ACCEPTED BY THE COURT AS TRUE. CREDITORS CANNOT VOTE ON THIS PLAN BUT THEY MAY OBJECT TO ITS CONFIRMATION PURSUANT TO BANKRUPTCY CODE §1324. ANY OBJECTION MUST BE IN WRITING AND MUST BE FILED WITH THE COURT AND SERVED UPON THE DEBTOR, DEBTOR'S COUNSEL (IF ANY), AND THE CHAPTER 13 TRUSTEE NOT LESS THAN FOUR (4) COURT DAYS PRIOR TO THE DATE FIXED FOR THE CONFIRMATION HEARING. ABSENT ANY SUCH OBJECTION, THE COURT MAY CONFIRM THIS CHAPTER 13 PLAN AND ACCEPT THE VALUATIONS AND ALLEGATIONS.

HOLDERS OF CLAIMS SECURED BY REAL PROPERTY WILL BE PAID ACCORDING TO THIS PLAN UNLESS AND UNTIL A CLAIM IS TIMELY FILED BY THE SECURED CLAIM HOLDER AND THAT CLAIM IS ALLOWED. HOLDERS OF ALL OTHER CLAIMS MUST TIMELY FILE PROOFS OF CLAIM IN ORDER TO BE PAID.

Debtor proposes the following Chapter 13 Plan and makes the following declarations:

I. PROPERTIES AND FUTURE EARNINGS OR INCOME SUBJECT TO THE SUPERVISION AND CONTROL OF THE TRUSTEE:
Debtor submits the following to the supervision and control of the Trustee:

1. Payments by Debtor of $_____ per month for _____ months. This monthly payment will begin within 30 days of the date the Petition was filed.

2. Other property: _____
(specify property or indicate none)

3. Amounts necessary for the payment of postpetition claims allowed under Bankruptcy Code § 1305.

II. MOTION TO AVOID LIENS ON EXEMPT PERSONAL PROPERTY
Notice is hereby given that the Debtor moves to avoid the following liens on exempt personal property pursuant to Bankruptcy Code §522(f)(2), and to treat such creditors as unsecured creditors only. (Motions to avoid judicial liens under Bankruptcy Code § 522(f)(1) must be brought by separate motion pursuant to appropriate Local Bankruptcy Rules.) Debtor's declaration in support of this motion is annexed hereto pursuant to Local Rule 111 (13). **If you object to the motion, you must file your objections within 20 days from the date this motion and plan is served on you.** Any objection to the motion will be heard on the date and at the time set for confirmation of the plan.

NAME OF CREDITOR   DESCRIPTION OF PROPERTY

_____   _____

_____   _____

FIGURE 11-1h. Chapter 13 plan (page 8).

III. CLASSIFICATION AND TREATMENT OF CLAIMS

1. CLASS ONE—Allowed Unsecured Claims entitled to priority under Bankruptcy Code § 507. Debtor will pay Class One claims in full in deferred payments, provided a proof of claim has been filed, as follows:

	PRIORITY CLAIM	MONTHLY PAYMENT	NUMBER OF PAYMENTS	TOTAL PAYMENTS
a. Administrative Expenses				
(1) Trustee's Compensation	(estimated at 10% of disbursement amounts)			
(2) Attorney's Fees..............	$ _____	$ _____	# _____	$ _____
b. Internal Revenue Service...........	$ _____	$ _____	# _____	$ _____
c. Franchise Tax Board	$ _____	$ _____	# _____	$ _____
c. Other..........................	$ _____	$ _____	# _____	$ _____

2. CLASS TWO—Claims secured by Real Property that is the debtor's PRINCIPAL RESIDENCE. The value as of the effective date of the Plan, of the series of payments to be distributed under the Plan on account of each secured claim provided for by the Plan, is equal to the allowed amount of such claim. Defaults shall be cured using a discount rate of _____ % per annum. Any obligation maturing by its terms before termination of this Plan shall be paid on or before its due date. Each creditor shall retain its lien.

	AMOUNT IN DEFAULT	MONTHLY PAYMENT	NUMBER OF MONTHS	TOTAL PAYMENT
Name of creditor				
Loan No..........................				
Cure of default...................	$ _____	$ _____	# _____	$ _____
Name of creditor				
Loan No..........................				
Cure of default...................	$ _____	$ _____	# _____	$ _____
Name of creditor				
Loan No..........................				
Cure of default...................	$ _____	$ _____	# _____	$ _____
Name of creditor				
Loan No..........................				
Cure of default...................	$ _____	$ _____	# _____	$ _____

3. CLASS THREE—Secured claims not secured solely by a security interest in Debtor's principal residence which are paid in full under the Plan. Class Three claims shall be paid in monthly payments as set forth below. Each creditor shall retain its lien until the plan is completed. Debtor is the owner of the property serving as collateral, is aware of its condition and where the Secured Claim is less than the Total Claim, believes its value is as set forth below under the heading "Secured Claim." The value as of the effective date of the Plan, of the series of payments to be distributed under the Plan on account of each secured claim provided for by the Plan, is equal to the allowed amount of such claim, based upon a present value computation using a discount rate of _____ % per annum.

NAME OF CREDITOR & LOAN NUMBER	TOTAL AMOUNT OF DEBT	SECURED CLAIM	UNSECURED AMOUNT	MONTHLY PAYMENT	NUMBER OF PAYMENTS	TOTAL PAYMENT
Name...........................						
Loan No...........................	$ _____	$ _____	$ _____	$ _____	# _____	$ _____
Name...........................						
Loan No...........................	$ _____	$ _____	$ _____	$ _____	# _____	$ _____
Name...........................						
Loan No...........................	$ _____	$ _____	$ _____	$ _____	# _____	$ _____
Name...........................						
Loan No...........................	$ _____	$ _____	$ _____	$ _____	# _____	$ _____
Name...........................						
Loan No...........................	$ _____	$ _____	$ _____	$ _____	# _____	$ _____

FIGURE 11-1i. Chapter 13 plan (page 9).

4. CLASS FOUR—Secured and Unsecured Claims for which the last payment is due after the final payment under the Plan is due. The value as of the effective date of the Plan, of the series of payments to be distributed under the Plan on account of each secured claim provided for by the Plan, is equal to the allowed amount of such claim. Defaults shall be cured using a discount rate of _____ % per annum. If more than two creditors, attach separate exhibit.

	AMOUNT IN DEFAULT	MONTHLY PAYMENT	NUMBER OF MONTHS	TOTAL PAYMENT
Name of creditor _____				
Loan No. _____				
1) Cure of default _____	$ _____	$ _____	# _____	$ _____
2) ☐ Other monthly payment (only if to be paid through Trustee) ____	_____	$ _____	# _____	$ _____
Name of creditor _____				
Loan No. _____				
1) Cure of default _____	$ _____	$ _____	# _____	$ _____
2) ☐ Other monthly payment (only if to be paid through Trustee) ____	_____	$ _____	# _____	$ _____

5. CLASS FIVE—Non-priority Unsecured Claims. Debtor estimates that non-priority general unsecured claims total the sum of $ _____. Class Five claims shall be paid as follows:

(Check one box only.)

☐ Class Five claims (including allowed unsecured amounts from Class Three) are of one class and shall be paid (pro rata) at _____ % of such claims. Unless the plan provides for payment of 100% to unsecured creditors, the debtor shall pay all disposable income to the trustee for the first 36 months and shall submit statements of income to the trustee on a semi-annual/annual basis. The amount of income shall be reviewed by the trustee who may petition the court to increase the monthly payments for cause.

OR

☐ Class Five claims shall be divided into subclasses as shown on the attached Exhibit and paid pro rata in each subclass as indicated therein. The Plan provides the same treatment for each claim within each subclass of Class Five. The claims of each subclass are substantially similar and the division into subclasses does not discriminate unfairly.

5. CLASS SIX—Post-Petition claims under Bankruptcy Code § 1305. Post-Petition claims allowed under Bankruptcy Code § 1305. Post-Petition claims allowed under Bankruptcy Code § 1305 shall be paid in full in equal monthly installments commencing no more than 30 days after entry of an order allowing such claims and concluding on the date of the last payment under the Plan, provided sufficient funds are available under the plan or amended plan.

IV. COMPARISON WITH CHAPTER 7—The value as of the effective date of the Plan of property to be distributed under the Plan on account of each allowed unsecured claim is not less than the amount that would be paid on such claim if the Estate of the Debtor were liquidated under Bankruptcy Code Chapter 7 on such date. The percentage distribution to general unsecured creditors in Chapter 7 is (estimate) _____ %.

V. PLAN ANALYSIS—TOTAL PAYMENT PROVIDED FOR UNDER THE PLAN

(a) CLASS ONE	
(1) Unpaid attorney's fees	$ _____
(2) Taxes	$ _____
(3) Other	$ _____
(b) CLASS TWO...	$ _____
(c) CLASS THREE	$ _____
(d) CLASS FOUR	$ _____
(e) CLASS FIVE	$ _____
(f) SUBTOTAL..	$ _____
(g)TRUSTEE'S FEES (Estimate 10% unless advised otherwise.)	$ _____
(h) TOTAL PAYMENTS...	$ _____

FIGURE 11-1j. Chapter 13 plan (page 10).

VI. ENLARGEMENT OF TIME FOR PAYMENTS

If the Plan provides for payments over a period of more than 36 months, cause exists as follows:

1. _____ The Plan proposes to pay at least 70% of unsecured claims.

2. _____ Other: _____.

VII. DEBTOR'S ABILITY TO MAKE PAYMENTS AND COMPLY WITH BANKRUPTCY CODE

Debtor will be able to make all payments and comply with all provisions of the Plan, based upon the availability to the Debtor of the income and property the Debtor proposes to use to complete the Plan.

This Plan complies with the provisions of Chapter 13 and all other applicable provisions of the Bankruptcy Code. Any fee, charge, or amount required to be paid under the United States Code or required by the Plan to be paid before confirmation has been paid or will be paid prior to confirmation. The Plan has been proposed in good faith and is not by any means forbidden by law.

VIII. OTHER PROVISIONS

1. The following executory contracts and unexpired leases are rejected: _____

_____

_____

2. Debtor assumes the following executory contracts and unexpired leases: _____

_____

_____

3. Debtor shall make regular payments directly to the following: _____

_____

_____

4. Debtor hereby abandons the following personal or real property: _____

_____

_____

5. Miscellaneous Provisions (specify): _____

_____

_____

6. **Debtor agrees that the Trustee is authorized to disburse ~funds after the date of confirmation in open court.**

IX. REVESTMENT OF PROPERTY

Any property of the estate shall not revest in the debtor until such time as a discharge is granted or the case is dismissed, subject to all liens and encumbrances not avoided herein. In the event the case is converted to a case under Chapter 7, 11 or 12 of the Bankruptcy Code, the property of the estate shall vest in accordance with applicable law. After confirmation of the Plan, the Chapter 13 Trustee shall have no further authority or fiduciary duty regarding use, sale or refinance of property of the estate, except to respond to any proposed use, sale or refinance as imposed by Chapter 13 General Order of this Court.

Dated: _____

_____
Attorney for Debtor(s)

I declare under penalty of perjury that the foregoing is true and correct.

Executed at _____, California.

Executed on: _____

_____
Debtor

_____
Joint Debtor

FIGURE 11-1k. Chapter 13 plan (page 11).

A plan must include:

1. The debtor must submit all or a portion of future earnings or other future income to the supervision and control of the trustee that is necessary for the plan. A plan must propose the amount of monthly payments the debtor gives to the Chapter 13 trustee. These monthly payments are paid from the debtor's earnings. Other future income also must be submitted, such as tax refunds. It is the trustee's responsibility to collect these monthly payments and then make distributions to the creditors.

2. The plan must provide for payment *in full* of all priority claims in deferred payments. These claims include all debts entitled to priority under Section 507, including certain taxes, back support/alimony, claims for wages or employee benefit plans, "lay-away" claims, administrative expenses, etc.[53] A Chapter 13 plan must propose to pay these priority claims in their entirety through the duration of the plan.

3. If the plan classifies claims, it must provide the same treatment for each claim within a particular class. For example, a debtor cannot provide for the same amount of payment to all unsecured creditors regardless of the respective size of their claims. However, a debtor may offer to pay all unsecured creditors 10 percent of their claims. This affords the same treatment to all claims within a particular class.

4. Pay all filing fees and court charges.[54] A pro se debtor may request to pay the bankruptcy filing fee in installments. These installments along with any other court charges, such as noticing charges, must be paid in full through a Chapter 13 plan.

5. Propose in good faith.[55] Numerous factors have been adopted as a guideline to determine good faith, including the amount of proposed payments and amounts of debtor's surplus; the debtor's employment history, ability to earn, and likelihood of future increases in income; the probable or expected duration of the plan; the accuracy of the plan's statement of debts, expenses, and percentage of repayment of unsecured debt and whether any inaccuracies are an attempt to mislead by the debtor; the extent of preferential treatment between classes of creditors; the extent to which secured claims are modified; the type of debtor to be discharged and whether any such debt is nondischargeable in Chapter 7; the existence of special circumstances, such as inordinate medical expenses; the frequency with which a debtor has sought relief under bankruptcy; the motivation and sincerity of the debtor in seeking Chapter 13 relief; and the burden the plan's administration would place upon the trustee. [See *In re Warren*, 89 B.R. 87 (9th Cir. BAP 1988).]

For example, it was found a Chapter 13 debtor's plan was not proposed in good faith where the debtor had filed Chapter 13 after a single debt was determined to be nondischargeable in his prior Chapter 7 case.[56]

6. The amount to be distributed to general unsecured claimants must be at least equal to the amount that such claimants would receive in a Chapter 7. This is often called the *best interest test.* In essence, unsecured creditors must receive (over time) what they would have been entitled to if the debtor had filed Chapter 7. Normally, this would consist of a pro rata share of any of the debtor's nonexempt assets. However, when the debtor has few or no unencumbered, nonexempt assets, the unsecured creditors would get little if anything in Chapter 7. Therefore, under these circumstances, it is possible to pay such creditors little if anything under a Chapter 13 plan. [See *Barnes v. Whelan*, 689 F.2d 193 (D.C. Cir. 1982) (where unsecured creditors were allowed only 1 percent repayment).]

7. Unless the plan is a 100 percent repayment plan, submission of all the debtor's disposable income for at least three years.[57] *Disposable income* is defined as income that is received by the debtor and that is not reasonably necessary to be expended for the maintenance or support of the debtor (or dependent), or, if the debtor is engaged in business, for the payment of expenditures necessary for the continuation, preservation, and operation of the business. In short, disposable income is all the extra money a debtor earns after subtracting all living expenses.

   Unfortunately, this requirement often calls upon the Court to determine if a debtor's expenses are "reasonably necessary." This requires a reluctant judge to determine the lifestyle of a debtor. This often proves to be a very uncomfortable examination. For example, it has been held that going out to dinner, entertaining people, buying toys for kids, or going to the movies is not "reasonably necessary" for maintenance or support of a debtor.[58] Also, the judge may have to determine such things as whether a debtor may support his 72-year-old mother[59] or make church tithes as well as the extent of any such church tithes.[60]

   A suggestion to all legal assistants is to obtain a proposed list of acceptable monthly expenditures from standing Chapter 13 cases. This will provide a guideline for such things as acceptable amounts spent on food, transportation, clothing, etc.

8. The holder of each allowed secured claim must either accept the plan, be given its collateral back, or the plan can "strip down" a secured creditor to the value of the property plus interest.

Commonly, the most disputed areas regarding the strip down of a secured claim are the value placed on the collateral and the interest rate to be applied. The valuation issue comes up most frequently in used car situations. As a practical note, it would be advisable for a legal assistant to obtain current *Kelly Blue Books*, which provide a value standardly accepted in many districts.

9. A feasible proposed plan. This simply means that the debtor will be able to make the payments as proposed in the plan.

There are also certain items a debtor *may* include in the plan. These are called permissive plan provisions and allow a debtor great flexibility to submit a plan which meets particular financial needs. Permissive plan provisions include dividing claims into classes, changing certain secured claims, curing defaults while continuing to make regular monthly payments, paying both secured and unsecured claims at the same time, paying postpetition claims, paying claims with property, revesting estate property back to the debtor, and assuming or rejecting leases. The scope of each of these permissive plan provisions must be understood to allow a paralegal to creatively formulate a plan to meet the needs of each client.

A plan may divide creditors or claims into classes as long as the debtor does not discriminate unfairly against any class.[61] The debtor may specifically classify and treat cosigned unsecured consumer debts differently (and better) from all the other general unsecured claims. This allows debtors to protect their cosigners, who are usually relatives or friends, from deficiency lawsuits.

Generally the priority claims are one class, the secured creditors are each in a separate class, and the unsecured creditors are one class. The ability of a debtor to separately classify different claims may be advantageous when one unsecured claim will be nondischargeable, such as a student loan. This would allow the debtor to provide a different treatment of the class (such as payment in full) from the other general unsecured claims (such as minimal payment).

However, there are limits on the debtor's ability to differently classify claims. The debtor cannot unfairly discriminate against any class. Whether separately classifying and treating claims is "unfair" discrimination is subject of much debate. For example, in our student loan scenario, many Courts conclude that such treatment is not allowed since it unfairly discriminates. [See *In re Lawson*, 93 B.R. 979 (Bankr. N.D. Ill. 1988).] However, other Courts conclude such treatment is appropriate. [See *In re Boggan*, 125 B.R. 533 (Bankr. N.D. Ill. 1991).]

Accordingly a four-part test has been developed by the Courts to determine whether a proposed separate classification and treatment are unfair.

First, does the discrimination have a reasonable basis? Next, can the debtor carry out the plan without discrimination? Also, is the discrimination proposed in good faith? Lastly, is the degree of discrimination directly related to the rationale for discrimination? [See *In re Leser,* 939 F.2d 669 (8th Cir. 1991).]

The debtor has the burden of proving the rationale for any discrimination proposed in the plan.[62]

A plan is also permitted to modify the rights of holders of secured claims (other than the debtor's mortgage on his own home) or unsecured claims. Under this provision a debtor is allowed to strip down certain secured claims.[63] This allows the debtor to bifurcate the claim of an undersecured creditor into two parts: a secured claim equal to the value of the property and an unsecured claim for any remainder. Thereafter, the debtor can pay in full the secured portion and merely lump the unsecured portion together with all the unsecured debts (which usually receive less than full payment).

For example, debtor purchased a new automobile for $30,000 and financed it through ABC Finance at a 27 percent interest rate. Two years later the car is worth $15,000. The debtor may modify ABC's rights by treating $15,000 as a secured claim and any remaining amounts as an unsecured claim (and paying as little as possible on the unsecured claim). Further, the debtor may also reduce the interest rate (usually to a market rate).

However, note that a debtor may not bifurcate any mortgage in real property that is secured solely by the debtor's principal residence.[64]

Nobelman v. American Sav. Bank
113 S.Ct. 2106 (1993)

Thomas, J.: This case focuses on the interplay between two provisions of the Bankruptcy Code. The question is whether Section 1322(b)(2) prohibits a Chapter 13 debtor from relying on Section 506(a) to reduce an undersecured homestead mortgage to the fair market value of the mortgaged residence. We conclude that it does and therefore affirm judgment of the Court of Appeals.

In 1984, respondent American Savings Bank loaned petitioners Leonard and Harriet Nobelman $68,250 for the purchase of their principal residence, a condominium in Dallas, Texas. In exchange, petitioners executed an adjustable rate note payable to the bank and secured by a deed of trust on the residence. In 1990, after falling behind in their mortgage payments, petitioners sought relief under Chapter 13 of the Bankruptcy Code. The bank filed a proof of claim with the Bankruptcy Court for $71,335 in principal, interest and fees owed on the note. Petitioners' modified Chapter 13 plan valued the residence at a mere $23,500—an uncontroverted valuation—and proposed to make payments pursuant to the mortgage contract only up to that amount (plus prepetition arrearages). Relying on Section 506(a) of the Bankruptcy Code, petitioners propose to treat the remainder of the bank's claim as unsecured. Under the plan, unsecured creditors would receive nothing.

The bank and the Chapter 13 trustee, also a respondent here, objected to petitioners' plan. They argued that the proposed bifurcation of the bank's claim into a secured claim for $23,500 and an effectively worthless unsecured claim modified the bank's rights as a homestead mortgagee, in violation of 11 U.S.C. Section 1322(b)(2). * * *

Under Chapter 13 of the Bankruptcy Code, individual debtors may obtain adjustment of their indebtedness through a flexible repayment plan approved by a Bankruptcy Court. Section 1322 sets forth the elements of a confirmable Chapter 13 plan. The plan must provide, *inter alia,* for the submission of a portion of the debtor's future earnings and income to the control of a trustee and for supervised payments to creditors over a period not exceeding five years. (citations omitted). Section 1322(b)(2), the provision at issue here, allows modification of the rights of both secured and unsecured creditors, subject to special protection for creditors whose claims are secured only by a lien on the debtor's home. It provides that the plan may

> modify the rights of holders of secured claims, other than a claim secured only by a security interest in real property that is the debtor's principal residence or of holders of unsecured claims, or leave unaffected the rights of holders of any class of claims. (citations omitted).

The parties agree that the "other than" exception in Section 1322(b)(2) proscribes modification of the rights of a homestead mortgagee. Petitioners maintain however, that their Chapter 13 plan proposes no such modification. They argue that the protection of Section 1322(b)(2) applies only to the extent the mortgagee holds a "secured claim" in the debtor's residence and that we must look first to Section 506(a) to determine the value of the mortgagee's "secured claim." Section 506(a) provides that an allowed claim secured by a lien on the debtor's property "is a secured claim to the extent of the value of the property"; to the extent the claim exceeds the value of the property, it "is an unsecured claim." Petitioners contend that the valuation provided for in Section 506(a) operates automatically to adjust downward the amount of a lender's undersecured home mortgage before any disposition proposed in the debtor's Chapter 13 plan. Under this view, the bank is the holder of a "secured claim" only in the amount of $23,500—the value of the collateral property. Because the plan proposes to make $23,500 worth of payments pursuant to the monthly payment terms of the mortgage contract, petitioners argue, the plan effects no alteration of the bank's rights as the holder of that claim. Section 1322(b)(2), they assert, allows unconditional modification of the bank's leftover "unsecured claim."

This interpretation fails to take adequate account of Section 1322(b)(2)'s focus on "rights." That provision does not state that a plan may modify "claims" or that the plan may not modify "a claim secured only by" a home mortgage. Rather it focuses on the modification of the "rights of holders" of such claims. By virtue of its mortgage contract with petitioners, the bank is indisputably the holder of a claim secured by a lien on petitioners' home. Petitioners were correct in looking to Section 506(a) for a judicial valuation of the collateral to determine the status of the bank's secured claim. It was permissible for petitioners to seek a valuation in proposing their Chapter 13 plan, since Section 506(a) states that "such value shall be determined … in conjunction with any hearing…on a plan affecting such creditor's interest." But even if we accept petitioners' valuation the bank is still the "holder" of a "secured claim" because petitioners' home retains $23,500 of value as collateral. The portion of the bank's claim that exceeds $23,500 is an "unsecured claim" component under Section 506(a). (citations omitted). [H]owever that determination does not necessarily mean that the "rights" the bank enjoys as a mortgagee, which are protected by Section 1322(b)(2), are limited by the valuation of its secured claim.

The term "rights" is nowhere defined in the Bankruptcy Code. In the absence of a controlling federal rule, we generally assume that Congress has "left the determination of property rights in the assets of a bankrupt's estate to state law," since such "property interests are created and defined by state law." *Butner v. U.S.,* 440 U.S. 48 (1979). * * * The bank's "rights" therefore, are reflected in the relevant mortgage instruments, which are enforceable under Texas law. They include the right to repayment of the principal in monthly installments over a fixed term at specified adjustable rates of interest, the right to retain the lien until the debt is paid off, the right to accelerate the loan upon default and to proceed against petitioners' residence by foreclosure and public sale, and the right to bring an action to recover any deficiency remaining after foreclosure. (citations omitted). * * *

In addition [to restrictions of the automatic stay upon the bank], Section 1322(b)(5) permits the debtor to cure prepetition defaults on a home mortgage by paying off arrearages over the life of the plan "notwithstanding" the exception in Section 1322(b)(2). These statutory limitations on the lender's rights however are independent of the debtor's plan or otherwise outside the Section 1322(b)(2)'s prohibition.

In other words, to give effect to Section 506(a)'s valuation and bifurcation of secured claims through a Chapter 13 plan in the manner petitioners propose would require a modification of the rights of holders of their security interest. Section 1322(b)(2) prohibits such a modification where, as here, the lender's claim is secured only by a lien on the debtor's principal residence.

The judgment of the Court of Appeals is therefore affirmed.

But if the mortgage claim is secured by both interest in realty and personal property, it may be modified.[65]

A Chapter 13 plan may also cure or waive any default.[66] This is usually an essential tool for most Chapter 13 debtor. For example, this provision allows debtors to "make up" back payments on their home, car, furniture, etc. Meanwhile, the loan is restored to its nondefault position (i.e., default interest rates that are triggered upon a debtor's failure to make payments are much higher), and debtors are allowed to continue to make their regular payments.

Note: The 1994 Amendments significantly changed the treatment of "cure" claims. Prior to the Amendments, the Supreme Court held that interest was required to be paid on mortgage arrearages paid by debtors. [See *Rake v. Wade*, 113 S.Ct. 2187 (1993).] However, the 1994 Amendments specifically included 11 U.S.C. Section 1322(e) to overrule *Rake v. Wade* and not mandate that interest be paid on such "cure" classes of arrears.

The Chapter 13 plan may also provide for payments on any unsecured claim to be made concurrently with payments on any secured claim or any other unsecured claim. This allows the various priorities of creditors to be paid at the same time. For example, a Chapter 13 plan may propose to pay priority tax debt and "cure" claims both through the first 18 months of the plan and pay unsecured claims for the remainder of the plan.

On any debt with the last payment due after the last payment under the plan, provide for the curing of defaults within a reasonable time if it also calls for keeping the payments current while the Chapter 13 is pending. This section gives the debtor the power to cure prepetition accelerations, as already discussed.

However, the "cure" must be accomplished within a "reasonable time." What constitutes reasonable is a flexible concept and must be determined in each Chapter 13 case depending on the circumstances.[67] For example, the following periods have been held to be "reasonable" in curing a home mortgage default: 30 months,[68] 14 months,[69] and 3 years.[70] In contrast, the following periods have been held *not* to be "reasonable" in curing a home mortgage default: 12 months,[71] over 6 months,[72] or 25 months.[73] Accordingly, the legal assistant should become familiar with the local rulings of the jurisdiction to ascertain the appropriate "reasonable" cure period.

A Chapter 13 plan may also provide for payment of all or part of an allowed postpetition claim.[74] Generally, the existence and amounts cf claims are determined as of the date of the petition.[75] However, in Chapter 13 certain postpetition claims may be asserted. These are all tax claims that become payable while the case is pending as well as all consumer debts that arise after the petition is filed, provided such debts are for property or services necessary for the debtor's performance under the plan. [11 U.S.C. Section 1305(a).]

A plan may also provide for payment of all or part of a claim with property of the debtor or the estate.[76] However, note that this section does not allow a Chapter 13 plan to be solely founded on liquidating equity in a debtor's assets. It is merely an optional provision for inclusion in a plan to provide for payment.[77] Commonly, the plan will include contribution of all tax refunds during the course of the plan period. This section allows the contributions of such funds.

A Chapter 13 plan may also provide for the vesting of all property of the estate, on confirmation of the plan or at a later time, in debtor or any other entity.[78] This provision, if used, would allow all estate property to be converted back to a debtor's property.

A plan may also provide for the assumption or rejection of unexpired leases or executory contracts. This last permissive provision allows the debtor to assume or reject unexpired leases or executory contracts through the plan. For example, a Chapter 13 plan may reject an ongoing vehicle lease. The debtor would surrender the vehicle to the leasing company. Any damages arising from the breach of the leasing contract are treated as an unsecured claim.

As a final note, the 1994 Amendments have placed a cloud over existing case law which remains unresolved. Prior to the 1994 Amendments, it was generally held that a Chapter 13 plan could not stretch out a debtor's home mortgage with a balloon payment coming due during the plan. [See *In re Davis*, 91 B.R. 477 (Bankr. N.D. Ill. 1988); *In re Rubottom*, 134 B.R. 641 (9th Cir. BAP 1991).] However, the Amendments added 11 U.S.C. Section 1322(c)(2), stating that, when the last payment on the original payment schedule of a debtor's home mortgage becomes due before the plan is over, the plan can provide for payment of the mortgage as modified. Accordingly, Bankruptcy Courts now are resolving disputes as to whether this new Code section allows a Chapter 13 debtor to "unwind" a balloon payment on a mortgage.

Formulation of a Plan

Formulation of a Chapter 13 plan requires some mathematical calculations. First all debts which must be paid through the plan must be determined. These include all priority debts, such as back taxes and alimony. Also, all "cure" amounts must be paid in full through the plan. This would include all late payments on a house or car. Finally, all secured claims which have been "stripped down" must be paid in full with interest through the plan.

Also, unsecured debts must receive as much as they would have gotten in a Chapter 7 case. To calculate this amount, the value of the debtor's nonexempt property is totalled. From this total, the amount of priority debts is subtracted. The remainder is what unsecured creditors would have received in Chapter 7 and is the amount they must be paid in Chapter 13. Finally, the Chapter 13 trustee's fees must be calculated. This amounts to 10% of the total amount paid over the course of the plan, including priority debts, cure debts, secured debts with interest, and the unsecured amount paid.

Once the total of all amounts to be paid through the plan is calculated, the debtor's disposable income must be ascertained. Disposable income is the amount of a debtor's earnings which remain after paying all living expenses. The monthly disposable income is the debtor's monthly plan payment.

Next, the paralegal must calculate the duration of the plan. The duration of the plan is also a mathematical function. In essence, the total amount to be paid through the plan is divided by the monthly plan payment. For example, $36,000 is the total amount to be paid under the plan. The debtor's disposable income, and therefore plan payment is $1,000. Accordingly, the duration of the plan is 36 months.

Unfortunately, most paralegals and attorneys go about formulating a plan backward. The total amount to be paid under the plan is calculated as stated above. However, then the debtor's budget figures (i.e., monthly expenses) are manipulated to come up with a desired disposable income to fit within either three or five years. This is an unadvisable method to formulate a plan. This method limits the debtor's monthly expenses to a point where the debtor surely will falter in making plan payments. In essence, this method dooms the debtor to fail in his or her Chapter 13 case.

Effect of Confirmation

The provisions of a confirmed Chapter 13 plan bind the debtor and each creditor, whether or not the claim of the creditor is provided for by the plan and whether or not the creditor has objected to the plan. Further, the confirmation serves to vest all the property of the estate in the debtor, free and clear of any claims of creditors provided for by the plan.

However, note as a practical matter that a debtor cannot reduce a secured claim by a plan through listing it as unsecured and thereby "treating it" (such as providing little if any distribution to such creditor).[79] Further, if a creditor does not receive specific notice that its secured claim is to be stripped down under Chapter 13, the creditor will not be bound.[80] Once a secured creditor has filed its proof of claim asserting secured status, the debtor must object to the validity and amount of such secured interest under F.R.Bankr.P. 3007.

MODIFICATION OF CHAPTER 13 PLANS

The debtor may modify a plan either before confirmation or after confirmation.[81] A debtor may modify the plan at any time prior to confirmation as long as it still satisfies the mandatory requirements of the Code. Additionally, the debtor may modify the plan after confirmation, but the plan as modified must be "reconfirmed." This means another hearing must be held and creditors given their chance to object.[82]

REVOCATION OF CONFIRMATION

A creditor may request revocation of an order confirming a plan. Any revocation request must be based upon the fraud of the debtor. A creditor's request for revocation of a plan is initiated as an adversary proceeding which means a summons and complaint must be filed and served. The adversary proceeding must be commenced within 180 days from the entry of the confirmation order.[83]

The elements required to be proven by the creditor to demonstrate a debtor's fraud are:

1. A materially false representation.
2. The representation was either known by the debtor to be false or was made without belief in its truth or was made with reckless disregard for the truth.
3. The representation was made to induce the Court to rely upon it.
4. The Court did rely upon it.
5. As a consequence, the Court entered a confirmation order. [See *In re Edwards*, 67 B.R. 1008 (Bankr. Conn. 1986).]

An example of confirmation revoked for fraud is where a debtor knowingly used different social security numbers in different bankruptcy cases, used aliases in some bankruptcy filings but not in others, revealed some addresses but not others, and failed to list creditors, all in an effort to avoid the filing of claims. [See *In re Scott*, 77 B.R. 636 (Bankr. N.D. Ohio 1987).]

Upon revocation, the Court must either dismiss or convert the case to Chapter 7 unless the debtor proposes (and the Court confirms) a modified plan within the time set by the Court.[84] Generally, confirmation will not be revoked for matters that a creditor could have objected to prior to confirmation,[85] or based on the fact that property received through the plan had actual value less than originally anticipated.[86] Revocation of an order confirming a Chapter 13 plan is a little used remedy since a debtor may seek to modify a plan, even if it was confirmed through fraud.

CHAPTER 13 DISCHARGE

The Chapter 13 discharge can be very broad in scope. Essentially, there are two separate types of discharge in Chapter 13 cases found, respectively, in 11 U.S.C. Sections 1328(a) and (b). The first type of discharge occurs upon completion of a debtor's payments under a plan, a "full performance" discharge. The other type of discharge is called a "hardship discharge" and occurs before all plan payments have been completed.

In a *full performance discharge,* the debtor is discharged from all prepetition and allowed postpetition unsecured debts. This includes most debts that would otherwise be nondischargeable under 11 U.S.C. Section 523, with limited exceptions.[87] The types of debts within Section 523 that are not discharged in Chapter 13 are support/alimony [Section 523(a)(5)], student loans [Section 523(a)(8)], and DUI claims [Section 523(a)(8)].[88] Additionally, a Chapter 13 discharge does not discharge claims for restitution or criminal fines.[89] Accordingly, once a Chapter 13 debtor has fulfilled all payments under the plan over the course of three to five years, all other debts within Section 523 will be discharged. The broad discharge of a full performance discharge includes claims based on fraud, willful and malicious injuries, property settlement, etc. Also note that long-term debts (which extend beyond the duration of the plan, such as a mortgage) will also not be discharged.

A *hardship discharge* is granted to a debtor who has not completed all payments under a plan under certain circumstances. To obtain a hardship discharge, the debtor must demonstrate that the failure to complete the payments was not within the debtor's control. Also, to receive a hardship discharge, the payments to the creditors under the plan must equal at least as much as the creditors would have received in Chapter 7 (best interest test). Finally, to obtain a hardship discharge the debtor must demonstrate that it would be impractical to modify the plan.[90]

A prime example of when a hardship discharge is granted is when a husband and wife file a joint petition and have been making plan payments for a few years. Then one of the spouses dies. The remaining spouse either is not working or is making barely enough to survive. In this situation a hardship discharge will be granted since the unforeseen death of the spouse was not within the control of the debtor. Further, it would be impractical to modify the plan since the remaining spouse has no disposable income. Finally, the debtors have made enough payments under the plan that unsecured creditors have received as much as they would if the case was initially filed as a Chapter 7 liquidation.

However, a hardship discharge is not as broad in scope as a full performance discharge. In fact, a hardship discharge is no broader than a discharge in Chapter 7. In essence, all the nondischargeable debts of 11 U.S.C. Section 523 are not discharged in a hardship discharge. Further, the long-term debts (those whose final payment is due after the final payment under the proposed plan) are not discharged as well.[91]

To obtain a hardship discharge, the debtor must file a formal motion with the Bankruptcy Court. [F.R.Bankr.P. 4007(d).] Thereafter, the Court must give at least 30 days' notice to all creditors in order that any 11 U.S.C. Section 523 nondischargeability complaints may be filed.

CONCLUSION

Chapter 13 is a reorganization alternative for individuals rather than liquidation through Chapter 7. Chapter 13 allows debtors to pay certain nondischargeable priority debts over time, allows debtors to catch up missed payments on secured claims, such as cars or houses, and allows debtors to strip down certain secured claims. Chapter 13 also allows debtors to pay back some of their unsecured debt over time, rather than sacrifice all of the debtor's nonexempt property. A legal assistant will often be requested either to formulate and draft a Chapter 13 plan or to formulate objections to such plans.

REVIEW QUESTIONS

1. What is a Chapter 13 plan? Who proposes this plan and when?

2. What are the mandatory elements of a Chapter 13 plan? What are the permissive elements of a Chapter 13 plan?

3. How do you formulate a Chapter 13 plan?

4. What is confirmation? What is the effect of a confirmed Chapter 13 plan?

5. Can a Chapter 13 plan ever be changed once it is confirmed? How?

6. What are the basis and deadline for revocation of a confirmed Chapter 13 plan?

7. What are the two types of Chapter 13 discharge? What are the differences?

ENDNOTES

[1]*In re Alexander,* 670 F.2d 885 (9th Cir. 1982).

[2]11 U.S.C. Section 101(24).

[3]*In re Hammonds,* 729 F.2d 1391 (11th Cir. 1984).

[4]*In re Le Maire,* 883 F.2d 1373 (8th Cir. 1989).

[5]*In re Hines,* 7 B.R. 415 (Bankr. S.D. 1980).

[6]*In re Howell,* 4 B.R. 102 (Bankr. M.D. Tenn. 1980).

[7]*In re Taylor,* 15 B.R. 596 (Bankr. D. Ariz. 1981).

[8]*In re Iacovoni,* 2 B.R. 256 (Bankr. D. Utah 1980).

[9]*In re Overstreet,* 23 B.R. 712 (Bankr. W.D. La. 1982).

[10]*In re Cole,* 3 B.R. 346 (Bankr. S.D. W.Va. 1980).

[11]Raised from $100,000 by the 1994 Amendments.

[12]Raised from $350,000 by the 1994 Amendments.

[13]See *In re Pearson,* 773 F.2d 751 (6th Cir. 1985); *In re Robertson,* 84 B.R. 109 (Bankr. S.D. Ohio 1988); *In re Jerome,* 112 B.R. 563 (Bankr. S.D. N.Y. 1990); *In re Young,* 91 B.R. 730 (Bankr. E.D. La. 1988).

[14]See *In re Koehler,* 62 B.R. 70 (Bankr. Neb. 1986); *In re Perry,* 56 B.R. 663 (Bankr. M.D. Ga. 1986).

[15]*In re McGovern,* 122 B.R. 712 (Bankr. N.D. Ind. 1989); *In re Lucoski,* 126 B.R. 332 (S.D. Ind. 1991). A thorough discussion of eligibility under Chapter 13 is found in Chapter 3, "Varieties of Bankruptcy Chapters."

[16]See Chapter 2, "Infrastructure of a Bankruptcy Case," for an analysis and procedures to claim exemptions.

[17]*In re Fisher,* 113 B.R. 718 (W.D. Okla. 1990).

[18]*In re Sininger,* 84 B.R. 115 (Bankr. S.D. Ohio 1988).

[19]*In re Sanders,* 78 B.R. 444 (Bankr. D. S.C. 1987).

[20]*In re Frascatore,* 98 B.R. 710 (Bankr. E.D. Pa. 1989).

[21]See *Lee v. Schweiker,* 739 F.2d 870 (3rd Cir. 1984); *In re Bennett,* 35 B.R. 357 (Bankr. N.D. Ill. 1984); *In re Berry,* 30 B.R. 36 (Bankr. E.D. Mich. 1983); *In re Marsh,* 28 B.R. 270 (Bankr. S.D. Ohio 1983).

[22]*In re Mast,* 79 B.R. 981 (Bankr. W.D. Mich. 1987); *In re Walls,* 17 B.R. 701 (Bankr. S.D. W.Va. 1982); *In re Colandrea,* 17 B.R. 568 (Bankr. D. Md. 1982).

[23]See Chapter 8, "Voidable Transfers" for discussion.

[24]11 U.S.C. Section 1321; F.R.Bankr.P. 3015.

[25]While the trustee, if advisable, is required to oppose discharge of the debtor, the trustee lacks standing to oppose dischargeability of a specific claim. [See *In re Dunn,* 83 B.R. 694 (Bankr. D. Neb. 1988).]

[26]Courts have interpreted this to mandate the attendance of the Chapter 13 trustee at confirmation hearings. [See 11 U.S.C. 1302(b)(2); *In re Colandrea,* 17 B.R. 568 (Bankr. D. Md. 1982).]

[27]11 U.S.C. Section 1302(b)(1)-(5); F.R.Bankr.P. 2015(b)(2).

[28]11 U.S.C. Section 1302(c).

[29]11 U.S.C. Section 1304(c).

[30]*In re Kutner,* 3 B.R. 422 (Bankr. N.D. Tex. 1980), appeal dismissed, 545 F.2d 1107 (5th Cir. 1981), cert. denied, 455 U.S. 945 (1982).

[31]11 U.S.C. Section 1329(a).

[32]11 U.S.C. Section 1328(d).

[33]11 U.S.C. Section 1303 and 1304(b); *In re Walls,* 17 B.R. 701 (Bankr. S.D. W.Va. 1982).

[34]11 U.S.C. Section 1302(d); 28 U.S.C. Section 586.

[35]28 U.S.C. Section 586(e).

[36]11 U.S.C. Section 1305(a) & (b).

[37]11 U.S.C. Section 1305(c).

[38]See Chapter 9, "Creditor Status, Priority, and Distribution Rights."

[39]Chapter 12 also provides a "codebtor" stay, but none of the other chapters have such a provision.

[40]11 U.S.C. Section 1301(1).

[41]*In re SFW, Inc.,* 83 B.R. 27 (Bankr. S.D. Cal. 1988).

[42]*Id.*

[43]11 U.S.C. Section 1301(d).

[44]11 U.S.C. Section 1301(c)(1).

[45]*In re Rhodes,* 85 B.R. 64 (Bankr. N.D. Ill. 1988).

[46]11 U.S.C. Section 1301(c)(2).

[47]11 U.S.C. Section 1301(c)(3).

[48]*In re Burton,* 4 B.R. 608 (Bankr. W.D. Va. 1980).

[49]11 U.S.C. Section 1321; F.R.Bankr.P. 3015.

[50]11 U.S.C. Section 1321.

[51]11 U.S.C. Section 1324; F.R.Bankr.P. 3020(b)(2).

[52]F.R.Bankr.P. 2002(b).

[53]11 U.S.C. Section 507.

[54]11 U.S.C. Section 1325(a)(2).

[55]11 U.S.C. Section 1325(a)(3).

[56]*In re Rasmussen,* 888 F.2d 703 (10th Cir. 1989).

[57]11 U.S.C. Section 1325(b)(1).

[58]*In re Kelly,* 841 F.2d 908 (9th Cir. 1988).

[59]*In re Tracey,* 66 B.R. 63 (Bankr. D. Md. 1986).

[60]*In re Bien,* 95 B.R. 281 (Bankr. D. Conn. 1989).

[61]11 U.S.C. Section 1322(b)(1).

[62]*In re Furlow,* 70 B.R. 973 (Bankr. E.D. Pa. 1987).

[63]11 U.S.C. Section 506.

[64]11 U.S.C. Section 1322(b)(2).

[65]*Wilson v. Commonwealth Mortgage Corp.,* 895 F.2d 123 (3rd Cir. 1990).

[66]11 U.S.C. Section 1322(b)(3).

[67]*In re Randolph,* 102 B.R. 902 (Bankr. S.D. Ga. 1989).

[68]*In re King,* 23 B.R. 779 (9th Cir. BAP 1982).

[69]*In re Smith,* 19 B.R. 592 (Bankr. N.D. Ga. 1982).

[70]*In re Van Gordon,* 69 B.R. 545 (Bankr. D. Mont. 1987).

[71]*In re Hailey,* 17 B.R. 167 (Bankr. S.D. Fla. 1982).

[72]*In re Mitchell,* 27 B.R. 288 (Bankr. S.D. Fla. 1983).

[73]*In re Brooks,* 51 B.R. 741 (Bankr. S.D. Fla. 1985).

[74]11 U.S.C. Section 1322(b)(6).

[75]11 U.S.C. Section 502(b).

[76]11 U.S.C. Section 1322(b)(8).

[77]*In re Anderson,* 21 B.R. 443 (Bankr. N.D. Ga. 1981).

[78]11 U.S.C. Section 1322(b)(9).

[79]*In re Simmons,* 765 F.2d 547 (5th Cir. 1985).

[80]*In re Linkous,* 990 F.2d 160 (4th Cir. 1993).

[81]11 U.S.C. Sections 1323 and 1329.

[82]11 U.S.C. Section 1329; F.R.Bankr.P. 2002(a)(6).

[83]11 U.S.C. Section 1330(a); F.R.Bankr.P. 7001(5).

[84]11 U.S.C. Section 1330(b); F.R.Bankr.P. 2002(a)(6).

[85]*In re Szostek,* 886 F.2d 1405 (3rd Cir. 1989).

[86]*In the Matter of Pence,* 905 F.2d 1107 (7th Cir. 1990).

[87]11 U.S.C. Section 1328(a).

[88]11 U.S.C. Section 1328(a)(2).

[89]11 U.S.C. Section 1328(a)(3).

[90]11 U.S.C. Section 1328(b).

[91]11 U.S.C. Section 1328(c).

12 *Chapter 11 Practice*

Several months after your firm has filed Chapter 11 for a client, your supervising attorney announces that the time has come to file a plan. She instructs you to make sure all the U.S. Trustee fees and monthly reports are current, make sure all cash collateral stipulations are on file, and verify that all fee applications have been prepared and submitted. Further, you are to gather all exhibits that would be useful in a disclosure statement.

Even the most simple Chapter 11 case requires a vast amount of pleadings and documents. This also means the number of deadlines and ongoing filing requirements increases exponentially. A paralegal's duties are critical to making a Chapter 11 case run smoothly. Chapter 11 also has certain terminology which is rarely found in other bankruptcy cases. A paralegal must know the specific deadlines in Chapter 11 as well as be familiar with the all documents required within each specific stage of Chapter 11.

INTRODUCTION

Chapter 11 is known as a "business reorganization." However, both business entities and individuals may avail themselves of Chapter 11 relief. Business entities may include sole proprietorships, corporations, partnerships, limited liability partnerships, etc. Further, Chapter 11 is not limited to reorganization.

Sometimes, the goal of Chapter 11 is to liquidate the business as an ongoing entity. This allows the current management to remain in place and allows a greater sales price for the business. The underlying policy of Chapter 11 reorganization is to preserve the jobs of a debtor's employees through the business's rehabilitation.

The difference between Chapter 11 and either Chapter 7 or Chapter 13 is that the debtor acts as the trustee for the case and is called a debtor-in-possession. Also, the debtor need not initiate monthly plan payments as in Chapter 13. In fact, the debtor is allowed at least four months to formulate and file a plan of reorganization, unlike Chapter 13. A Chapter 11 plan is likely to be much more complex than a Chapter 13 plan and is required to be accompanied by a document to describe the plan, called a disclosure statement. Another difference in Chapter 11 is that the creditors are allowed to vote on the debtor's plan.

PARTIES: DUTIES AND RIGHTS

As with Chapter 7 relief, almost all entities are eligible for Chapter 11.[1] Also as in Chapter 7, a Chapter 11 case may be voluntarily filed by a general partner or any duly authorized officer of a corporation. The filing fee of $800[2] must accompany the Chapter 11 petition.

The petition of a corporate Chapter 11 debtor must include a "corporate resolution" (i.e., corporate minutes) authorizing the filing of the petition. Further, the petition in a corporate Chapter 11 case must include a special Exhibit A. Exhibit A includes certain vital information regarding the corporate debtor, including:

- The debtor's employer identification number (TIN).
- Whether any of the debtor's securities are registered with the Securities and Exchange Commission (SEC).
- The SEC file number, as well as certain financial data (total assets, total liabilities, secured and unsecured debts with the number of holders of claims).
- The number of shares of preferred and common stock, along with the number of holders of such shares.
- A brief description of the debtor's business.
- The identity of any person holding more than 20% of the debtor's voting securities.
- The name of any corporations where debtor holds 20% or more of the voting securities.[3]

Along with the petition (and corporate resolution and Exhibit A), the master mailing list and a list of the 20 largest unsecured creditors must be filed in order to file an "emergency filing." Thereafter, the 15-day deadline is imposed upon the debtor to file the remaining documents that comprise the debtor's statements and schedules. These documents include the list of equity security holders (names and addresses of all equity security holders showing the number and kind of interests held),[4] the schedule of assets and liabilities,[5] the statement of financial affairs for debtor engaged/not engaged in business,[6] and a statement of executory contracts.[7]

In addition to the regular schedules that must be filed in every case under the Code, Chapter 11 cases require more documents at the outset of the case. The U.S. Trustee requires the Chapter 11 debtor-in-possession to provide detailed information regarding assets of the estate. Often this information is submitted in forms promulgated by the U.S. Trustee's Office or obtained through the U.S. Trustee's personal interview with the debtor. This information includes:

- The debtor's real property holdings.
- Proof that prepetition bank accounts have been closed and new debtor-in-possession banking accounts have been opened.
- Proof of insurance coverage on all estate property.
- Proof of the required certificates and licenses.
- A list of insiders.
- Recent financial statements.
- Projected cash flow statements.
- All recently filed federal and state tax returns.
- Information on trust agreements that involve a debtor.
- Proof that the Chapter 11 petition has been recorded.
- A physical inventory of all goods, machinery, and equipment.

A sample of the forms required by the U.S. Trustee's Office in the Central District of California is attached in Appendix A to this chapter. Failure to file this financial information within the deadlines provided by the U.S. Trustee's Office, usually within mere days of the filing of the petition, shall result in dismissal of the Chapter 11 case.

Additionally, the Chapter 11 debtor must file monthly financial reports with the Court. Copies of these reports must be sent to the U.S. Trustee's Office. A sample copy of the monthly reports required is attached in Appendix A to this chapter. Generally, these monthly reports itemize the monthly income and expenses of the debtor's business operations. The Chapter 11 debtor also is required to make quarterly payments to the U.S. Trustee's Office based upon a sliding scale. The current scale for U.S. Trustee's quarterly fees is attached in Appendix A to this chapter. The debtor's ongoing efforts and costs to maintain these continuing obligations throughout a Chapter 11 can be burdensome. A primary duty of a paralegal representing Chapter 11 debtors is to ensure these ongoing duties are maintained by the debtor.

The initiation of an involuntary Chapter 11 is virtually identical to filing an involuntary Chapter 7 case.[8] An involuntary Chapter 11 petition may be commenced against anyone except a farmer or a nonprofit corporation.[9] Note: An involuntary Chapter 11 petition cannot be commenced against a husband and wife as a joint case.[10] An involuntary petition is commenced by the filing of a petition by three secured or unsecured creditors owed in the aggregate of at least $10,000[11] of noncontingent unsecured (or undersecured) debt. Also, the debt must not be subject to a "bona fide dispute." Further, an involuntary Chapter 11 petition may also be commenced by any single creditor if the debtor has less than 12 creditors as long as such single creditor holds at least $10,000 in claims. Further, if the involuntary debtor is a partnership, any general partner may commence an involuntary case.

Once the involuntary petition is filed, the Bankruptcy Clerk issues a summons that must be served upon the debtor.[12] Service under the Bankruptcy Rules may be done by first class mail; personal service is not required.[13] The involuntary petition must allege only that the debtor is generally not paying its debts as they become due or that, within 120 days prior to the involuntary petition, a receiver was appointed to take charge of the property of the debtor to enforce a lien against the property.[14]

If an answer or response is filed by the debtor, an evidentiary hearing is held.[15] If a hearing is to be held, discovery is allowed. However, discovery is only allowed on the issue of nonpayment of debts when due and whether a bona fide dispute exists. Involuntary petitions are intended to be single-issue proceedings. Therefore, counterclaims against a petitioning creditor are not allowed unless it is to defeat the petition.[16]

After the hearing, the Court must either enter the order for relief, dismiss the petition, or enter other appropriate orders.[17] If a petition is dismissed, the Court may assess fees and costs against any and all petitioners, as well as both actual and punitive damages.[18] These sanctions are imposed against the creditor to discourage meritless involuntary proceedings.

The period after the involuntary petition is filed and before the entry of the order for relief is called the gap period. During this time the debtor may continue to operate any business it has, as well as use, acquire, or dispose of any property unless the Court restricts such actions.[19] However, a party may request the appointment of an interim trustee in an involuntary Chapter 11 even prior to the entry of the order for relief if necessary to preserve the property of the estate so as to prevent loss to the estate.[20]

The debtor in a Chapter 11 case is in charge of the administration of the Chapter 11 case and is the authorized representative of the estate.[21] Essentially, the debtor acts as the trustee and is called a debtor-in-possession (DIP). The DIP in a commercial bankruptcy is the management (i.e., officers, directors, partners, etc.) that existed as of the date of the petition.[22] The DIP is authorized to operate the business of the Chapter 11 debtor.[23] The DIP continues to operate the business unless and until the Court orders otherwise (such as through the appointment of a trustee).

The debtor-in-possession acts as a fiduciary, just as an appointed trustee would, and has substantially all the powers of a court-appointed trustee.[24] Such powers include the power to obtain turnover of estate property [11 U.S.C. Sections 542 and 543]; the power to void preferential, fraudulent transfers and unauthorized postpetition transfers [11 U.S.C. Sections 547, 548, and 549];[25] the power to void statutory and landlord's liens [Section 545]; and the power to abandon property [Section 554].[26]

The debtor-in-possession also has all the responsibilities of a trustee. These duties include being accountable for all property received,[27] examining proofs of claim if necessary,[28] furnishing information regarding the estate upon request,[29] filing periodic accountings and reports,[30] filing a plan of reorganization,[31] and filing any tax returns (both current and back tax returns).[32]

Additionally, the DIP has certain significant powers that allow it to continue to operate its business, such as the power to assume or reject executory contracts.[33] For example, debtors often file Chapter 11 to obtain relief from ongoing obligations, such as an unfavorable lease of commercial property or business equipment. Once rejected, such ongoing obligations cease. The damages arising from the breach caused by termination of such contracts are treated as prepetition claims. However, certain deadlines exist for a debtor to accept or reject certain executory contracts.

A lease of nonresidential real property (i.e., commercial office space, shopping center leased space, industrial leased property) must be accepted or rejected by a formal motion by the debtor. This "motion to accept lease" must be filed with the Bankruptcy Court within 60 days of the petition date. [11 U.S.C. Section 365(d)(4).] If the motion is never made, or untimely made, the lease is deemed rejected and the DIP must surrender the real property to the lessor.

Note: A motion to extend the time within which to assume or reject the lease on nonresidential property may be made by the debtor. However, such motion to extend must be made prior to the expiration of the 60-day period or the lease is forever lost. Further, a creditor (namely the landlord) can request the Court to set a time within which a debtor must assume or reject the lease prior to the expiration of the 60-day period.

The 1994 Amendments changed some key deadlines for the procedures regarding the assumption or rejection of leases on personal property (i.e., computers, machinery, equipment, telephone system, etc.). Under prior law, when a debtor filed Chapter 11 it had an unspecified period of time to determine whether to assume or reject a lease on personal property. Usually, the debtor made such determination at the very end of the case through its reorganizational plan. Of course, the creditor could always request the Court to compel the debtor to make a decision to assume or reject, but this placed an undue burden upon the creditor.

Under the 1994 Amendments, a debtor must perform all obligations under a personal property lease within 60 days of the petition.[34] In other words, the debtor must make lease payments within 60 days of the petition date or "reject" the lease. Rejection will treat the lease as a prepetition claim (with the postpetition lease payments generally being afforded administrative priority status). This shifts the burden to the debtor to bring a motion to excuse compliance in performing its obligations under the lease. [11 U.S.C. Section 365(d)(10).]

Accordingly, it is imperative that the legal assistant make note of the 60-day deadline with respect to nonresidential real property as well as non-household personal property leases. If the 60-day postpetition period lapses without affirmative action by the debtor, the debtor's rights are effectively waived with respect to such leases.

Debtors-in-possession also have the power to use, sell, or lease estate property.[35] This provides funds for distribution to creditors under a plan or allows the debtor to reinvest such funds in the business operations that generate profits to fund a plan. Note that when a debtor sells property free and clear of liens, such liens generally attach to the sales proceeds. Further, the debtor-in-possession has the ability to incur debt to facilitate the rehabilitation of its business.[36]

The debtor-in-possession also has the power to employ professionals. All professionals (including the debtor's attorney, all accountants, appraisers, auctioneers, realtors, property managers, etc.) must apply to the Court for authorization of their employment at the outset. [11 U.S.C. Section 327.] These employment authorization requests are commonly termed "employment applications."

The significance of failure to seek prior Court authorization for employment cannot be emphasized enough. In short, if no prior Court authorization is obtained, the professional most assuredly will be denied payment at a later date. [See *In re Marlin Oil Co.*, 83 B.R. 50 (Bankr. Colo. 1988) (where a professional was not allowed fees when authorization for employment was never sought from the Court).]

The consequences of untimely employment applications are also significant. If a professional fails to seek employment at the outset of the case (i.e., usually the same day the petition is filed), then all fees sought between the petition date and the actual date the employment application was submitted may be denied. For example, a Chapter 11 debtor's counsel inadvertently did not file his employment application until one month after the petition date. The Court may deny all fees and costs incurred by debtor's counsel for that one-month period. Accordingly, all employment applications should be timely submitted due to the ramifications of either failure to seek authorization or untimely requests.

The application for employment must include certain facts:

- The name and occupation of the person or firm to be employed (such as attorney, CPA, realtor, etc.).

- Facts demonstrating the necessity for the employment and the specific services to be rendered, including such things as the debtor's pending bankruptcy and the need for legal representation or the debtor's state court collection litigation, eviction litigation, etc.

- The reason for the selection of the particular professional to be employed, including facts regarding the proposed professional's experience level to render the proposed services. For example, a resume may be attached, if appropriate.

- Disclosure of the compensation agreement between the debtor-in-possession and the professional (i.e., $250 per hour for "partners" of a firm, $175 per hour for "associates," $65 per hour for "legal assistants," etc., plus reimbursement of expenses).

- The amount and source of any fees, retainers, or other compensation (including any contingency fee agreements) paid or agreed to be paid.

- Any fees, retainer, or other compensation paid or agreed to be paid within one year of the filing of the petition for services rendered in contemplation of the case.

Additionally, if the employment application is for a type of professional already employed by the estate (i.e., another attorney for the debtor), the application should specify the need for such dual professionals. For example, a Chapter 11 debtor sought and received authorization to employ a bankruptcy attorney to assist it in its Chapter 11 proceedings. Now the Chapter 11 debtor is seeking employment of another attorney to represent it in defense of a pending class action suit regarding products liability (e.g., IUDs).[37] In this instance, the employment application should state the need to hire counsel specializing in class action suits. Additionally, the employment application should include the services to be performed by each attorney so that the Court may ensure that duplication of services to the debtor (and therefore duplication of fees for the same service) will be avoided.

Additionally, the employment application must be signed by a person authorized to make the application. In other words, the debtor-in-possession signs the application to employ debtor's counsel, the creditors' committee chairperson signs the application to employ the committee's counsel, etc. It is generally not acceptable for professionals to sign their own employment applications.

Moreover, the application for employment must be accompanied by a "statement of disinterestedness" of the proposed professional. [F.R.Bankr.P. 2014.] The statement must be a verified statement (a declaration under the penalty of perjury or an affidavit of the proposed professional) stating the professional's connections with the debtor, creditors, or any other party in interest. In essence, the Court needs to ensure that the professional will not have any conflicts in representing the estate, such as prior or current representation of creditors.

An excellent example of an employment application seeking authorization to be employed as counsel for the debtor-in-possession is included in Appendix B to this chapter.

Once employed, professionals must thereafter formally apply to the Court for authorization of their fees. [11 U.S.C. Section 330, F.R.Bankr.P. 2016.] These applications are commonly called *fee applications.* Such fee applications are either interim fee applications or final fee applications. *Interim fee applications* may be submitted every 120 days. At the conclusion of representation, a *final fee application* is submitted, which encompasses all the interim fees (even if prior approval has been granted for the interim fee applications—such will be interim approval). Usually, final fee applications take place once the plan of reorganization has been confirmed.

The fee application should contain the date the order was entered approving the professional's employment. Also, the fee application should contain the date of the applicant's last fee application (i.e., no fee applications within 120 days for same professional). Additionally, a summary of the fees already approved and paid should be included. Any funds remaining in the retainer should be articulated.[38] Further, the fee application should contain a narrative summary of the significant events in the case during the time period for which fees are sought. Fee applications should include a statement of the source and amount of cash available to pay the requested fees. The legal assistant should also consult any local U.S. Trustee's guidelines for fee applications for specifics regarding the form and content of fee applications.[39] A sample of the U.S. Trustee's guidelines for fee applications for the Central District of California is included in Appendix C to this chapter.

Finally, as an exhibit to every fee application, a detailed itemized billing statement is included. Such billing statement should include the date, hourly rate, name of professional performing the task, a description of the task, the amount of time spent on the task, as well as the total amount charged for each task.

For example, each entry should be similar to the following:

Name	Hourly Rate	Date	Hours	Total Amt.	Description
JJA	$200.00/HR	1/1/95	0.5	$100.00	Telephone conference with attorney Jones re: settlement of stay lift matter "C."

Additionally, professionals are allowed reimbursement of certain expenses, if the reimbursement has been previously authorized by the Court through the employment application. Expenses may include such things as postage, long-distance telephone charges, messenger services, filing fees, travel expenses, facsimile charges, etc. Note: Most items such as staff overtime, luxury travel expenses, local meals, and normal overhead (rent, insurance, utilities, offices supplies, etc.) are generally not reimbursable. However, the actual and necessary reimbursable expenses for the respective period may be included in the professional's fee application. Such expenses should also be articulated in the itemized billing statement.

Creditors

The creditor structure in Chapter 11 cases is the same as in Chapter 7, 12, or 13. Both prepetition and certain postpetition creditors are affected by the case.[40]

In a Chapter 11 a creditor must file a proof of claim only if the debtor-in-possession fails to list that creditor's claim in its statements and schedules or if the claim is listed as disputed, contingent, or unliquidated.[41] However, a cautious creditor shall always file a proof of claim to preserve its priority status and to ensure that the amount of the claim is correct.

The Bankruptcy Court fixes a time within which proofs of claims must be filed. [F.R.Bankr.P. 3003(c)(3).] Usually, this is done after approval of the disclosure statement and prior to the confirmation of the plan. However, a debtor may request the Court to set a "bar date" for filing proofs of claim in order to assist in evaluating and analyzing proposed repayment schedules in any plan.

Once a bar date is set by the Court, all creditors must receive at least 20 days' notice of such deadline. [F.R.Bankr.P. 3003(c)(3), 2002(a). This 20-day notice period may not be reduced.[42] However, as in a Chapter 7 case, the time for filing a proof of claim may be extended as long as the request for extension is filed prior to the expiration of the set bar date.[43] Finally, proofs of claims may be amended once filed.

Creditors in Chapter 11 cases also may request stay relief in order to foreclose or repossess their property or liquidate their claim in state court.[44] Further, creditors may request dismissal of the Chapter 11 case or conversion to Chapter 7.[45] Additionally, within a Chapter 11 case, a creditor may request that a Chapter 11 trustee be appointed and thereby displace the debtor-in-possession from remaining as the managing entity of the estate's business. Creditors may also request the appointment of an examiner in a Chapter 11 case to investigate allegations of mismanagement by the debtor-in-possession. In essence, the appointment of a trustee or examiner requires some type of malfeasance on behalf of the debtor-in-possession. Standards for such appointment are discussed later in the chapter.

Further, creditors are allowed not only to cast their vote but also to file objections to any plans of reorganization filed by the debtor. Additionally, if the debtor's exclusivity period has lapsed, creditors may propose their own plans of reorganization.

Secured creditors often are entitled to their "cash collateral." Cash collateral is a term of art under the Bankruptcy Code. *Cash collateral* is defined as cash, negotiable instruments, documents of title, securities, deposit accounts, or other cash equivalents whenever acquired in which the estate and an entity other than the estate have an interest and includes the proceeds, products, offspring, rents, or profits of property subject to a security interest under the Code, whether existing before or after the commencement of a case under the Code.

In short, some secured creditors have an interest in not only the underlying property, but all the rents and profits generated by the property.[46] A prime example is a creditor secured by an apartment complex owned by a debtor. Assuming the mortgage has an assignment of rents clause (as do most security instruments), the creditor may also have a secured interest in the rents received by the debtor from the tenants of the building. These rents constitute cash collateral.

Cash collateral may not be used by a debtor-in-possession unless the secured creditor consents (which is rare), or if the Court authorizes the debtor's use of cash collateral. The usual course of action is for a creditor to request "sequestration" or conditional use of the cash collateral. Sequestration of cash collateral is placing the cash in a separate segregated account and not using it. Conditional use of cash collateral is the debtor's limited spending of the funds, usually to maintain the property and to make payments to the secured creditor. However, cash collateral is often the "lifeline" of the debtor in Chapter 11.[47] In other words, the cash generated is used to operate the business. In our preceding example, if the creditor were to sequester (or to take all rents and place them in a separate account and prevent the debtor's use of them), no funds would be available to operate the apartment complex (such as to pay for management fees, landscaping services, utilities, security, repairs, etc.).

More often than not, a creditor will be unsuccessful in obtaining a total sequestration of cash collateral. Accordingly, the best a creditor can usually hope for is to obtain an order from the Court conditioning the use of cash collateral on things such as periodic reporting to the creditor, as well as submission and approval of operating budgets.[48] However, before a Court can authorize the use of cash collateral, it must make factual findings of the value of the secured claims and collateral, and of the impairment or nonimpairment of those interests if cash collateral is to be used.[49]

Creditors' Committees

The unsecured creditors' committee is an official committee appointed by the U.S. Trustee's Office.[50] Generally, the unsecured creditors' committee shall consist of the persons, willing to serve, who hold the seven largest claims against the debtor. The U.S. Trustee's Office may also appoint an official committee of equity security holders (i.e., shareholders) if it deems it appropriate to do so. Note: The Court may review the U.S. Trustee's appointment of a committee and vacate the appointment if the Court finds it failed to comply with the requirements of the Code (i.e., 11 U.S.C. Section 1102). [F.R.Bankr.P. 2007(c).]

Generally, the official committee's duties are to investigate the debtor and monitor the operation of the debtor's business.[51] An official committee has numerous powers to aid it in its task of overseeing the DIP and obtaining the eventual confirmation of a plan of reorganization. An official committee also has the duty to consult with the debtor-in-possession regarding the case administration, participate in the formulation of a plan of reorganization, and request the appointment of a trustee or examiner if necessary. The committee is also allowed to lobby for rejections or acceptances of a proposed Chapter 11 plan. Further, if a debtor fails to file its plan within the exclusivity period, an official committee may propose a plan.

An official committee as a whole and the members thereof are fiduciaries and owe a fiduciary duty to the unsecured creditors of the estate and to each other.[52] In essence, the purpose of an official committee is to provide adequate representation of all parties with the same status as the committee (i.e., unsecured, equity holders, etc.). Often in Chapter 11 cases many, if not hundreds, of small unsecured creditors exist. For example, all prepetition trade creditors (such as the gardener, office supply vendor, window washers, architects, janitorial services) hold unsecured claims. An official unsecured creditors' committee provides these claimants with a "voice" in the bankruptcy proceeding when otherwise their respective claims would be too small to realistically invest in adequate representation.

An official committee is empowered to employ counsel to represent the committee.[53] Of course, the employment of a creditors' committee's attorney must also be approved by the Court. The employment application contents and procedure for a creditors' committee is virtually identical to that for employment of any of the debtor's professionals.

Furthermore, the fees and costs of the counsel for the committee will be payable as administrative and priority expenses *from the estate*.[54] In other words, the debtor-in-possession will pay the committee's attorney's fees. However, creditors' committee's attorneys must seek approval of their fees in the same manner as debtor's counsel (i.e., by means of fee applications).

Additionally, official committees are permitted to seek employment of accountants and other professionals. Again, the employment procedure and fee application procedure must be followed for such professionals to be paid. However, these authorized professionals also may be paid from the estate.

Lastly, the 1994 Amendments allow the individual committee members reimbursement of their court-approved expenses if such expenses are incurred in the performance of their duties.[55] These out-of-pocket expenses include such things as travel and lodging. This reimbursement is considered an administrative expense and is therefore also payable from the estate.

Trustee

There is a presumption in favor of allowing a debtor-in-possession to remain in possession of its business.[56] Generally, the Court will appoint a Chapter 11 trustee only upon the request of a party in interest if there is a showing of fraud, dishonesty, incompetence, or gross mismanagement by the debtor-in-possession.[57] Once appointed, the Chapter 11 trustee has the rights, powers, and duties of a debtor-in-possession. Finally, under the 1994 Amendments, creditors are able to elect their own trustee in Chapter 11 cases. [11 U.S.C. Section 1104(b).]

Examiner

If the Court does not appoint a trustee under Section 1104(a), the Court may appoint an "examiner." An *examiner* is essentially a trustee with limited powers and is appointed to conduct investigations into the financial affairs of the debtor.[58] The grounds for appointment of an examiner are that the appointment would be in the best interest of the estate or that the debtor's fixed, liquidated, unsecured debts exceed $5,000,000.[59]

Meanwhile, during all the cash collateral battles, valuation disputes, claim allowance litigation, stay relief warfare, avoidance suits, and trustee/examiner appointment quarrels, the debtor must maintain regular monthly reports and pay quarterly U.S. Trustee's fees. Further, despite all these bankruptcy activities and distractions, the debtor-in-possession is attempting to operate its business. Moreover, the debtor-in-possession is expected during this time to formulate a viable plan of reorganization to repay its creditors.

THE CONFIRMATION PROCESS

Debtor's Exclusivity Periods

11 U.S.C. § 1121 provides in pertinent part that only the debtor may file a plan for the first 120 days after the petition date. However, on request of a party in interest, the court may for cause reduce and or increase the 120-day period. Accordingly, the first 120 days from the petition date are commonly referred to as the debtor's *exclusivity period.*

To determine whether cause exists for extending or reducing the 120-day period several factors are considered, including the size and complexity of the case, how hotly contested the case has been, whether the debtor has shown progress through extraordinary diligence and skill in the face of major obstacles, the likelihood of success of the debtor's reorganizational activities, whether some progress has been made regarding acceptances, and whether the sheer mass, weight, volume, and complication of filings justify a shakedown period.[60] A universal theme for denial appears to be that the debtor is seeking the extension for an improper purpose, such as prolonging the process in order to pressure a creditor to accede to the debtor's demands.

The 1994 Amendments have added a new exclusivity period for certain types of debtors. Under 11 U.S.C. Section 1121(e) a debtor who has elected to be treated as a "small business" has an exclusivity period of 100 days after the petition within which to file a plan. To qualify as a "small business" debtor, all debts must be less than $2 million and the debtor's primary business may not consist of owning and operating real property. [11 U.S.C. Section 101(51C).] The benefit of electing to be a small business debtor is that no creditors' committees are elected and the small business debtor may combine the disclosure statement hearing with the plan confirmation hearing.

Finally, while not a true exclusivity deadline, the 1994 Amendments have implicitly imposed a 90-day deadline within which a single-asset real estate debtor may file a plan. A *single-asset real estate debtor* is one holding real property that generates substantially all of the gross income of a debtor and upon which no substantial business is being conducted by a debtor other than the operation of the real property. Further, single-asset real estate debtors must have no more than $4 million in aggregate noncontingent, liquidated secured debts. [11 U.S.C. Section 101(51B).]

The essence of the implicit 90-day deadline for single-asset real estate debtors is found in the new stay relief provisions of 11 U.S.C. Section 362(d)(3). Basically, if no plan of reorganization is on file within 90 days, the stay is lifted. The only defense the debtor has available is to commence monthly payments. Since secured creditors will undoubtedly hold all rents from such real estate as cash collateral, these rents probably will not constitute the necessary payments to defeat a stay relief request. Given the ramifications of stay relief granted upon the debtor's only property, if the plan is not on file in 90 days, then the debtor will lose its only asset and thus its only hope of reorganization.

Disclosure Statement

The first step in the confirmation process is drafting a disclosure statement that explains the plan to prospective voters. The disclosure statement must be approved by the Bankruptcy Court prior to any solicitations of acceptances of the plan.[61] Before a disclosure statement can be approved, after notice and a hearing, the Court must find that the proposed disclosure statement contains "adequate information" to solicit acceptances of a proposed plan of reorganization.[62] *Adequate information* means information of a kind, and in sufficient detail, as far is as reasonably practicable in light of the nature and history of the debtor and the condition of the debtor's books and records, that would enable a hypothetical reasonable investor, typical of the holders of claims against the estate, to make a decision on the proposed plan of reorganization.[63] Courts have developed a list of relevant factors required for adequate disclosure.

There is no set list of required elements to provide adequate information per se. A case may arise where previously enumerated factors are not sufficient to provide adequate information, and conversely a case may arise where previously enumerated factors are not required to provide adequate information.[64] The Court will determine which factors are relevant and required in light of the facts and circumstances surrounding each case.[65]

The elements to include when drafting a disclosure statement are articulated in *In re A.C. Williams*, 25 B.R. 173 (Bankr. N.D. Ohio 1982):

1. *Incidents that led to filing Chapter 11.* This section should include why the debtor was forced to file for relief. Some examples may be pending IRS seizure, pending foreclosure of property, pending execution of judgment through sheriff's sale, etc.

2. *A description of available assets and their value.* This section should include a list of all estate assets along with their values, such as a list of all inventory and the resale value, a list of all real property and the values therein, etc.

3. *The anticipated future of the debtor.* A capsulization of the general plan of reorganization, such as payment of certain classes through postpetition operations, the sale of certain properties to liquidate and distribute, the closing of certain divisions of operations, etc.

4. *The source of information of the disclosure statement.* Examples are the unaudited books and records of the debtor.

5. *A disclaimer.* Basic language that the Bankruptcy Court has not deemed the contents of the disclosure statement to be true and accurate, but merely that such information, if true, is sufficient information upon which a hypothetical investor may make an informed decision.

6. *The present condition of the debtor in Chapter 11.* This should include the postpetition financial status of the debtor, the status or outcome of any litigation during Chapter 11, any acquisitions or dispositions of property during Chapter 11, etc.

7. *A listing of the claims scheduled.* All claims of any priority along with the amounts and whether such claims are being disputed or litigated should be included.

8. *A liquidation analysis.* Usually included as an exhibit to the disclosure statement, this should include all assets and their "liquidation value" (or fire sale value), less all costs of sales. These assets are compared to all liabilities, namely, the amounts of creditors in order of priority. The goal is basically to show that, in the event of liquidation, unsecured creditors would not receive more than they would under the debtor's proposed plan.

9. *The identity of the accountant and the process used.* Include the name and address of the accountant as well as the method (i.e., cash or accrual).

10. *The future management of the debtor.* The identity, qualifications, and compensation of the proposed reorganized debtor's management should be included.

11. *Whether a plan is attached.* Attach a plan as an exhibit.

Other items that may be included in a disclosure statement (depending on the nature of the debtor's business) include projections of future income, historical financial information to support such future projections, appraisals, and market analyses.

Chapter 11 Plan Classification

A Chapter 11 plan of reorganization classifies claims and interests. Generally, each secured creditor is in a separate class. Classification of priority creditors is important only insofar as there are to be deferred payments. Finally, all unsecured claims should comprise one class. The Court can resolve classification procedures at a preconfirmation hearing. Upon motion, the Court is to determine classes of creditors and equity security holders for the purposes of the plan and its acceptance. [F.R.Bankr.P. 3013.]

Voting/Ballots

Once the disclosure statement is approved, the following are mailed by the plan proponent (i.e., the entity submitting the plan) to all creditors and equity security holders: the plan, the disclosure statement, the Court order regarding votes and confirmation, and the ballots. [F.R.Bankr.P. 3017(d).] The ballot sent to each creditor is Official Form No. 14. Thereafter, impaired creditors and shareholders file their ballots either accepting or rejecting the plan.

Essentially, a class of claims or interests is considered "impaired" under the Code unless the plan does one of the following three things: (1) leaves unaltered the legal, equitable, and contractual rights of such claim; (2) cures any default in a contract, reinstates the maturity of such contract, and compensates the holder for interest or damages; or (3) provides the holder of the claim cash *plus interest*[66] as of the effective date.[67]

All ballots must be filed by the deadline fixed by the Court. [F.R.Bankr.P. 3017(c).] Copies of all ballots submitted to the Court should be mailed to the plan proponent's attorney as well. Thereafter, the proponent of the plan tallies the ballots and files with the Court an official report of the accepting and rejecting votes. This report is termed "ballot results" and articulates the acceptances and rejections within each class. Also, the ballot results report indicates which classes are impaired. Finally, the ballot results should specify mathematically whether each class has "accepted" the plan (i.e., two-thirds in amount and one-half in number).

CHAPTER 11 PLAN AND CONFIRMATION

The Bankruptcy Court must hold an evidentiary hearing in ruling on Chapter 11 plan confirmation. However, this does not preclude the Bankruptcy Court from considering evidence presented by the parties at prior evidentiary hearings. The Court may take judicial notice of evidence presented during the administration of the estate.[68] To approve a reorganization plan, the Court must find that the proposed plan is "fair and equitable," meaning that the payment priorities of the Bankruptcy Code are met.[69]

The statutory elements necessary to confirm a plan under 11 U.S.C. Section 1129 are as follows:

(a) (1)   The plan complies with applicable provisions of Chapter 11 because it contains what is required for a plan and what is permitted for a plan. (See Sections 1122 and 1123).

(a) (2)   The plan proponent complies with the applicable provisions of this title. (The person is an entity that could file a plan and has made the appropriate disclosure.)

(a) (3)   The plan is proposed in good faith and is not by any means forbidden by law.

(a) (4)   Payment made or promised by the proponent, the debtor, or the person issuing securities or acquiring property under the plan for services or for costs and expenses in connection with the case or plan are disclosed to the court. Payment made preconfirmation and payment fixed postconfirmation must be reasonable and court-approved.

(a) (5)   The plan discloses the identity and affiliations of any individual proposed to serve, after confirmation, as a director, officer, or voting trustee of the reorganized debtor. The plan must disclose the identity of the insider to be employed/retained by the debtor and the nature of the compensation.

(a) (6)   Has regulatory commission having jurisdiction over the debtor postconfirmation approved any rate change provided for in plan?

(a) (7)   Acceptances/best interests. Must show that each member of an impaired class has either accepted the plan or will receive as much as if the debtor liquidated in Chapter 7.

(a) (8)   Acceptances/unimpaired. Must show that each class has either accepted the plan or is unimpaired. (If not, then proceed to "cramdown" [11 U.S.C. Section 1129(b)].

(a) (9)   Administrative expenses/involuntary gap expenses; other priority claims/prepetition taxes.

Administrative expenses and "gap" claimants will receive, on account of each claim, cash equal to the allowed amount of such claim (unless they agree to other treatment).

Wages, employee benefit claims, fishermen/grain storage claims, "lay-away" claims, and past due support claims will receive deferred cash payments on the effective date equal to the allowed amount of the claim. If the class has not accepted the plan, cash is paid on effective date equal to the claim.

Priority tax claims will receive deferred cash payments over a period not exceeding six years after the date of assessment of the claim, of an amount equal, on the effective date, to the allowed amount of the claim.

(a) (10)   The plan is accepted by one class that is impaired and not an insider.

(a) (11)   The plan is feasible and not likely to be followed by liquidation.

(a) (12)   Fees payable under Section 1930 are paid or will be paid on the effective date (i.e., court fees for noticing, etc.)

Many creditors may belong to a single class or a sole creditor may comprise an entire class. To be an "accepting" class a certain number of creditors within such class need to vote in favor of the plan. The dollar amount of such accepting creditors must be two-thirds of the total amount of claims within the class. Further, one-half the total number of actual creditors within a class must accept the plan. [11 U.S.C. Section 1126(c).]

If a plan is accepted by all classes, it is a *consensual plan*. A plan is *nonconsensual* if one or more classes reject the plan. However, despite the fact that not all classes vote in favor of a plan, it may still be confirmed. The process of confirming a plan despite the rejection of one or more classes is called cram-down.

If all the other requirements for confirmation are met, except acceptances, the court shall confirm (i.e., may "cram down") if the plan does not discriminate unfairly, and if it is fair and equitable with respect to each class of claims and interests that is impaired under but has not accepted the plan. [11 U.S. C. 1129(b)(1).] "Fair and equitable with respect to a class" includes the following:

- *Secured claims.* The claimant retains its lien and receives an amount in deferred cash payments totaling at least the allowed amount of such claim (i.e., the value the property). In the alternative, the plan may provide for the sale of the property with the proceeds to satisfy the claim. Also, secured claimants may receive the indubitable equivalent of their claims. An example of "indubitable equivalent" treatment is returning the property to the secured creditor.[70]

- *Unsecured claims.* The claimant receives or retains property of value equal to the allowed claim, or the holder of a junior claim neither receives nor retains property on account of such claim. This is called the absolute priority rule. In essence, all creditors are divided into a particular order or priority of payment (i.e., administrative priority claims are paid before priority tax claims which are paid before unsecured claims, etc.). The absolute priority rule requires that in order for a class to be paid, the class ahead of it (or prior in the distribution scheme) must be paid in full.

The provisions of a confirmed plan bind the debtor, any creditor, any equity security holder, and all others whether or not such parties accepted the plan. The confirmation of a plan also vests all of the property of the estate in the debtor. Finally, confirmation of the plan discharges the debtor from all debts (other than those provided in a repayment distribution through the plan). However, note that confirmation does not discharge a debtor if the plan provides for liquidation of all the debtor's assets or if the debtor does not engage in business after the confirmation of the plan. [11 U.S.C. Section 1141.]

CONCLUSION

A bankruptcy paralegal serves a key role in accomplishing the many procedural requirements within a Chapter 11 case. Often, paralegals are requested to draft all employment applications and fee applications, ensure all U.S. Trustee requirements are fulfilled, and calendar the multitude of deadlines arising in Chapter 11 cases. Further, the bankruptcy paralegal assists in assembly of the disclosure statement along with potentially hundreds of exhibits. Accordingly, Chapter 11 practice can be interesting and challenging for a bankruptcy paralegal.

REVIEW QUESTIONS

1. Who generally acts as the trustee in Chapter 11 cases and what is their title?

2. What are some of the differences between Chapter 11 cases and Chapter 13 or Chapter 7 cases?

3. What must a professional do to be employed by a Chapter 11 debtor? What must be included? What must a professional do to get paid by a Chapter 11 estate? List the requirements for this as well.

4. What is the deadline for nonresidential real property lease assumption? What is the deadline for acceptance of business personal property leases?

5. What is the purpose of an official unsecured creditors' committee? What are some of the official committee's duties?

6. What does a debtor's "exclusivity period" mean? What are these periods?

7. What is a disclosure statement? What is a plan of reorganization?

ENDNOTES

[1]Except for stockbrokers or commodity brokers.

[2]28 U.S.C. Section 1930(a)(3).

[3]Official Form No. 1, Exhibit A.

[4]F.R.Bankr.P. 1007(a)(3).

[5]F.R.Bankr.P. 1007(b).

[6]F.R.Bankr.P. 1007(a).

[7]F.R.Bankr.P. 1007(b).

[8]Except the filing fee is greater (i.e., $800). [28 U.S.C. Section 1930(a)(3).]

[9] 11 U.S.C. Section 303.

[10]*In re Benny,* 842 F.2d 1147 (9th Cir. 1988).

[11]Increased from $5,000 by the 1994 Amendments.

[12]F.R.Bankr.P. 1010.

[13]F.R.Bankr.P. 7004(b).

[14]11 U.S.C. Sections 3003(h)(1), (2).

[15]F.R.Bankr.P. 1013(a).

[16]F.R.Bankr.P. 1011(d).

[17]F.R.Bankr.P. 1013(a).

[18]11 U.S.C. Sections 303(i)(1), (2). See *In re Walden,* 781 F.2d 1121 (5th Cir. 1986).

[19]11 U.S.C. Section 303(f).

[20]11 U.S.C. Section 303(g).

[21]11 U.S.C. Section 323(a), (b).

[22]11 U.S.C. Section 1101, F.R.Bankr.P. 9001(5).

[23]11 U.S.C. Section 1108.

[24]11 U.S.C. Section 1107(a).

[25]See Chapter 8, "Voidable Transfers."

[26]See Chapter 2, "Infrastructure of a Bankruptcy Case."

[27]11 U.S.C. Sections 1106(a)(1) and 704(2).

[28]11 U.S.C. Sections 1106(a)(1) and 704(5).

[29]11 U.S.C. Sections 1106(a)(1) and 704(7).

[30]11 U.S.C. Sections 1106(a)(1) and 704(8) and (9).

[31]11 U.S.C. Section 1106(a)(5)

[32]11 U.S.C. Section 1106(a)(6).

[33]11 U.S.C. Section 365.

[34]This excludes personal property leased to an individual primarily for personal, family, or household purposes.

[35]11 U.S.C. Section 363(b), (c), and (f).

[36]11 U.S.C. Section 364(d).

[37]Assuming, of course, the class action plaintiffs have sought and obtained modification of the automatic stay in order to liquidate their claims.

[38]Retainer funds should be kept in the attorney-client trust account.

[39]The 1994 Amendments added in its entirety 28 U.S.C. Section 586(a)(3)(A), which requires the U.S. Trustee's Office to invoke procedural guidelines regarding fees in bankruptcy.

[40]The hierarchy of a particular creditor's claim and status in the repayment distribution is discussed in detail in Chapter 9, "Creditor Status, Priority, and Distribution Rights."

[41]11 U.S.C. Section 521(a), 1106(a)(2), 1111(a), and F.R.Bankr.P. 3003(c)(4).

[42]F.R.Bankr.P. 9006(c)(2)

[43]F.R.Bankr.P. 3003(c)(3).

[44]See Chapter 5, "Automatic Stay."

[45]See Chapter 7, "Dismissal/Conversion."

[46]The extent to which a secured creditor has a security interest in such rents or profits is determined by state law. [See *In re Village Properties, Ltd.*, 723 F.2d 441 (5th Cir. 1984), cert. denied 466 U.S. 974 (1985).]

[47]*In re Sel-O-Rak Corp.*, 24 B.R. 5 (Bankr. S.D. Fla. 1982).

[48]*In re Prime, Inc.*, 15 B.R. 216 (Bankr. W.D. Mo. 1981).

[49]*In re Center Wholesale, Inc.*, 759 F.2d 1440 (9th Cir. 1985).

[50]11 U.S.C. Section 1102.

[51]11 U.S.C. Section 1103(c).

[52]*In re Johns-Manville Corp.*, 52 B.R. 879 (Bankr. S.D. N.Y. 1985).

[53]11 U.S.C. Section 1103(a) and Section 328(a).

[54]11 U.S.C. Sections 1103(a), 330(a)(1), 503(b)(2), and 507(a).

[55]11 U.S.C. Section 503(b)(3)(F).

[56]*In re Paolino*, 53 B.R. 399 (Bankr. E.D. Pa. 1985).

[57]*In re Sharon Steel Corp.*, 871 F.2d 1217 (3rd Cir. 1989).

[58]11 U.S.C. Section 1106(b).

[59]11 U.S.C. Section 1104(c)(2).

[60]See, e.g., *In re Perkins*, 71 B.R. 294 (W.D. Tenn. 1987), where the district court affirmed the Bankruptcy Court's continued extensions of the exclusivity period (for a total of more than 800 days).

[61]11 U.S.C. Section 1125(b).

[62]11 U.S.C. Section 1125(b).

[63]11 U.S.C. Section 1125(a).

[64]*In re Metrocraft Pub. Services, Inc.*, 39 B.R. 567 (Bankr. N.D. Ga. 1984).

[65]*In re East Redley Corp.*, 16 B.R. 429 (Bankr. E.D. Pa. 1982).

[66]The 1994 Amendments altered 11 U.S.C. Section 1124 to require interest also be paid on this third option in order for the class to be considered unimpaired.

[67]11 U.S.C. Section 1124.

[68]*In re Acequia, Inc.*, 787 F.2d 1352 (9th Cir. 1986).

[69]See Chapter 9, "Creditor Status, Priority, and Distribution Rights."

[70]*In re Sandy Ridge Development Corp.*, 881 F.2d 1346 (5th Cir. 1989).

A U.S. Trustee's Office Requirements

NOTICE OF REQUIREMENTS FOR
CHAPTER 11 DEBTORS IN POSSESSION
("NOTICE OF REQUIREMENTS")

The United States Trustee has extensive monitoring and oversight responsibilities with respect to Chapter 11 estates pursuant to section 586(a)(3) of Title 28 of the United States Code. In order to fulfill these responsibilities, the United States Trustee has delineated certain duties, responsibilities and reporting requirements for Chapter 11 debtors in possession. Some must be performed immediately upon the filing of the petition (where the case is converted to Chapter 11, upon entry of the order of conversion or, in the case of an involuntary petition, upon entry of the order for relief), a significant number are required within seven days of the receipt of this Notice (the 7-Day Package), others are not required until several weeks after the petition is filed, and still others are required on an ongoing basis throughout the pendency of the bankruptcy. All requirements must be met in a complete and timely fashion unless waived in writing by the attorney or analyst assigned to the case.

The documents discussed in this Notice must be submitted to the United States Trustee, not the Bankruptcy Court.

Day-One Requirements

1. Close Out All Existing Books and Records

All books and records of the Chapter 11 debtor must be closed out as of the date the petition is filed.

2. Open a New Set of Books and Records

These are the debtor-in-possession books and records, which must be maintained throughout the bankruptcy.

3. Close All Existing Bank Accounts

All accounts that the debtor owns, has access to, or over which the debtor exercises possession, custody or control must be closed immediately upon filing.

4. Open New General, Payroll and Tax Bank Accounts

In business cases, a minimum of three new debtor-in-possession bank accounts (general, payroll and tax) must be opened in a bank that appears on the list of approved depositories, which can be obtained from the United States Trustee. In some limited cases, such as those involving individual non-business debtors, the debtor may obtain written permission from the attorney or analyst assigned to the case to maintain fewer debtor-in-possession accounts. All estate funds must be kept in these accounts. The new bank signature cards and printed checks must clearly indicate that this is a "debtor-in-possession" account, and the Chapter 11 case number must also appear on the face of the checks. If the debtor is required to segregate cash collateral, additional separate accounts must be established and maintained.

5. Obtain Insurance Coverage

The debtor must maintain appropriate insurance coverage for all estate property, including raw land. Listed below are the types of insurance coverage that are normally required for most bankruptcy estates. If the debtor does not have the required insurance coverage at the time of filing, it must be obtained immediately.

> *General Comprehensive Public Liability Insurance*
> *Fire and Theft Insurance*
> *Worker's Compensation Insurance*
> *Vehicle Insurance*
> *Product Liability Insurance*
> *Any other insurance coverage customary in debtor's business*

The debtor must also immediately notify its insurance carrier(s) and or agent(s) in writing, with a copy to the United States Trustee, that the United States Trustee must be notified of any cancellation of any insurance.

The 7-Day Package

Within seven days of the service of this Notice, the debtor must submit a package of required documents (the 7-Day Package) to the United States Trustee consisting of the following.

1. 7-Day Package Cover Sheet (Form UST-2)

The 7-Day Package Cover Sheet (Cover Sheet) (Form UST-2, attached) contains a list of the documents required to be included in the 7-Day Package. The debtor must check the box on the form corresponding to each document that is attached. If any document is not attached, an explanation must be provided. Inadequate explanations may result in the filing of a motion to dismiss or convert the case.

If any required document is not included in the 7-Day Package but is later submitted, the submission must include an additional Cover Sheet indicating which document is being submitted at that time.

2. Real Property Questionnaire (Form UST-5)

The debtor must submit a separate Real Property Questionnaire (Form UST-5, attached) for each parcel of real property the debtor leases, owns, has an interest in or is in the process of purchasing.

3. Proof of Closed/Opened Bank Accounts

The debtor must provide the United States Trustee with a copy of a bank statement for each prepetition bank account evidencing that the account has been closed. The debtor must also provide the United States Trustee with copies of all new bank signature cards together with evidence of the amounts transferred to the new accounts.

4. Proof of Insurance Coverage

The debtor must submit proof of current insurance coverage in the form of a statement, signed under penalty of perjury, that all insurance coverage required by the Notice of Requirements is in full force and effect. The declaration page of each policy showing the type and extent of coverage and expiration date must be attached to the sworn statement. The debtor must provide updated information automatically upon the expiration date set forth in each insurance policy.

5. Proof of Required Certificates and Licenses

The debtor must submit proof that the debtor holds all certificates and licenses required by federal, state and local law for the lawful operation of the debtor's business. The following is a list of licenses and certificates that are typically required:

> *Certificate that a corporation is active and in good standing in its state of incorporation.*
>
> *Certificate of Limited Partnership.*
>
> *Fictitious Name ("DBA") Statement filed with the county recorder.*
>
> *Liquor and Tobacco Licenses.*

6. List of Insiders

The debtor must submit a list of all insiders as defined in 11 U.S.C. § 101(31).

7. Prepetition Financial Statements

The debtor must submit copies of its most recent financial statements (audited and unaudited), including but not limited to a balance sheet, income (profit and loss) statement and a cash flow statement. The cash flow statement must contain a detailed statement of all receipts and disbursements.

8. Projected Cash Flow Statement

The debtor must submit a projected cash flow statement, covering the first sixty days of operation under Chapter 11. This statement must contain a detailed income and expense statement.

9. Federal Income Tax Returns, Federal and State Payroll Tax Returns and State Sales Tax Returns

The debtor must submit copies of all federal income tax returns filed for the three fiscal years immediately preceding the filing of the Chapter 11 petition. The debtor must also submit copies of the most recently filed federal and state payroll and state sales tax returns, including all schedules and attachments. All taxes must be timely paid and all tax returns must be timely filed during the pendency of the Chapter 11 proceeding. Copies of all future tax returns must be submitted to the United States Trustee within seven days of filing with the taxing authority. Copies of tax returns will be sealed and kept in a confidential file that will not be made available for public inspection.

10. Trust Agreements

The debtor must submit copies of any trust agreements to which the debtor is a party or under which the debtor holds, has possession of, or operates any personal or real property or business as a trustee or otherwise.

11. Proof of Recordation of Chapter 11 Petition

The debtor is required to record a copy of the Chapter 11 petition (exhibits may be omitted) with the recorder of each county or other applicable political subdivision for each parcel of real property owned or leased by the debtor or in which the debtor has an interest, and provide proof of recordation to the United States Trustee.

12. Physical Inventory of Goods, Machinery and Equipment

The debtor must conduct a physical inventory, including an itemized cost value, of all goods, machinery and equipment on hand as of the date of the petition, and a copy of the inventory must be submitted to the United States Trustee. Although this requirement is included in the 7-day package, often the inventory cannot be completed immediately. If this is the case, the expected date for completing the inventory — normally not more than 30 days after filing the petition — should be noted on the Cover Sheet.

WITHIN 15 DAYS OF FILING THE PETITION

Extension of Time to File Schedules and/or Statements of Affairs

The debtor's Schedules and Statements of Affairs are required by the Code to be filed *with the Bankruptcy Court* within 15 days of the filing of the petition. If unable to file in a timely fashion, the debtor must obtain a court order granting an extension of time to file. The motion and proposed order *is not filed directly with the Court,* but rather must be submitted to the United States Trustee for review and comment, after which the United States Trustee will file the motion and proposed order with the Court.

The motion and proposed order must comply with the usual format requirements for a motion filed with the Court (i.e., captioned and blue-backed) and must also include a separate page for the comments of the United States Trustee (the format for the comment page is attached). This comment page should be placed at the end of the motion if the proposed order is a separate document, or just before a proposed order included in the same document.

ADDITIONAL AND ONGOING REQUIREMENTS

1. Insider Compensation

Before any insiders (defined in 11 U.S.C. § 101(31)), including the owners, partners, officers, directors or shareholders of the debtor and relatives of insiders, may receive compensation from a Chapter 11 estate, the debtor must submit a Notice of Setting/Increasing Insider Compensation (Form UST-12, attached). The Notice of Setting/Increasing Insider Compensation must be served on the creditors' committee or the twenty largest unsecured creditors if no committee has been appointed, and proof of service must be submitted to the United States Trustee. *No compensation may be paid out to any insiders until 15 days after service of such notice, although such compensation may be accrued during this period.*

If, at any later time, the debtor proposes to increase the compensation of any insider, the debtor must submit and serve a new Notice of Setting/Increasing Insider Compensation as above. *No increase in insider compensation may be paid until 30 days after service of such notice.*

2. Financial Reports

The debtor must regularly submit financial reports to the United States Trustee. These reports are described in the "Notice of Financial Reporting Requirements," included in the "Chapter 11 Notices and Guides."

3. Quarterly Fees

Debtors in possession are required to pay a quarterly fee to the United States Trustee every calendar quarter (including any fraction thereof), based on disbursements made from the date the petition is filed until the date of entry of an order confirming a plan or dismissing or converting the case. Cases that have been administratively consolidated must still pay a separate fee for each case; however, cases that have been substantively consolidated need pay only one quarterly fee, beginning the first full quarter after consolidation. Operation during even one day of a quarter requires payment of the fee applicable for that quarter.

Fees are due no later than one month following the quarterly reporting period. In order to be confirmed, a Chapter 11 plan of reorganization must provide for payment of outstanding quarterly fees on or before the effective date of the plan. Payment of quarterly fees is due immediately upon entry of an order dismissing the case.

The amount of the quarterly fee varies, depending upon the dollar amount of disbursements made during the calendar quarter, with the minimum fee required regardless of the amount disbursed. The current Quarterly Fee Schedule, including the address to which checks should be mailed, is attached.

Quarterly fees may be paid by check payable to the United States Trustee. However, if any check is returned marked "insufficient funds," all future quarterly fee payments must be made by cashier's check, certified funds or money order. *Failure to pay the quarterly fee is cause for conversion or dismissal of the Chapter 11 case.*

4. Quarterly Status Reports

The debtor must submit to the United States Trustee and serve on the creditors' committee or the twenty largest unsecured creditors if no committee has been appointed, a quarterly status report of the progress of the case detailing any significant activity, including any litigation commenced either by or against the debtor. The report should include information relevant to progress toward filing a plan of reorganization and estimated date that a plan and disclosure statement will be filed.

5. Maintain Accounts in Approved Depository

It is the debtor's responsibility to maintain all cash of the estate in debtor-in-possession bank accounts in an approved depository throughout the pendency of the case. If a depository is acquired by an institution that is not an approved depository or if an institution loses its approved status, the debtor must immediately close accounts at such an institution and reopen the accounts in an approved depository.

6. Preparation and Filing of Income Tax Returns

Income tax returns, whether personal or business, state or federal, must be prepared and filed throughout the pendency of the bankruptcy.

7. On-site Audits and Inspections

The United States Trustee may conduct on-site audits and inspections, which may be unannounced, of the debtor's books, records and facilities to verify the information provided and to ensure that estate assets are appropriately safeguarded. Under 18 U.S.C. § 152, concealment of books, records or assets of a bankruptcy estate is a felony, punishable by a maximum sentence of 5 years imprisonment and a fine of $5,000.

8. Applications to Employ Professionals

Applications for employment of any professionals who will render services to the debtor-in-possession, whether or not the fees are to be paid by the estate or by a third party, must be noticed and may either be submitted to the United States Trustee (in which case no hearing is required unless requested by the United States Trustee) or made by noticed hearing and filed directly with the court. Counsel should consult the "Guide to Applications for Employment of Professionals and Treatment of Retainers," for specific procedural and substantive guidance on employment of professionals. The employment application should be submitted before the professional begins to render any services to the debtor-in-possession or the Chapter 11 estate. Where this is not possible, the application should be submitted within 15 days of the commencement of services.

9. Use, Sale or Lease of Estate Property

Where the court has authorized the use, sale or lease of property of the estate outside the ordinary course of business of the debtor, if an escrow is contemplated, a copy of the escrow instructions must be submitted to the United States Trustee. Within ten days after the close of escrow or completion of the sale, a certified copy of the escrow closing statement or, where no escrow was utilized, a sworn declaration showing the distribution of the proceeds of any sale of estate property must be submitted to the United States Trustee, and this requirement should be included in the order approving the sale.

10. Notice and Service on United States Trustee

Copies of all pleadings filed in a Chapter 11 case, including those filed in adversary proceedings and contested matters, must be served on the United States Trustee, whether or not the United States Trustee is a party to the proceeding.

11. Notice of Address Change

The debtor must notify the United States Trustee and the Bankruptcy Court of any change of address or telephone number within seven days after the change occurs.

12. Stipulations for Appointment of Trustee or Examiner

Stipulations for the appointment of a Chapter 11 trustee or examiner must be submitted to the United States Trustee for review and comment prior to filing with the court. The stipulation must include a separate page for the comments of the United States Trustee (the format to be used for the comment page is attached). This comment page should be placed at the end of the stipulation if the proposed order as a separate document, or just before a proposed order included in the same document.

NOTICE OF FINANCIAL REPORTING REQUIREMENTS FOR CHAPTER 11 DEBTORS IN POSSESSION ("FINANCIAL REPORTING REQUIREMENTS")

General Instructions

A Chapter 11 debtor-in-possession serves as a fiduciary for the benefit of the creditors and owners in the case. Providing complete and accurate financial information regarding the estate is part of the debtor's fiduciary duty. The Financial Report Forms ("Reports") that are to be used for this purpose are attached.

What Must Be Reported

Interim Statements are required for all bank accounts over which the debtor has possession, custody, control, access or signatory authority, even if the account is not in the debtor's name.

Operating Reports must include a narrative statement regarding the status of the reorganization effort, and any problems or issues that have arisen since the filing of the prior Operating Report.

Debtors are required to report on all their financial information. Any portion of the debtor's postpetition income that the debtor believes is not included in the estate should nevertheless be reported, with the source of the income specifically identified.

Reporting Periods

Interim Statements must be completed twice monthly (on the 15th and last day of each month, regardless of when the petition is filed) and must be submitted within 7 days after the last day of the applicable period.

Operating Reports must be completed on a monthly basis and must be submitted within 20 days after the last day of each month.

The Interim Statements and Operating Reports must be submitted whether or not any financial activity has occurred. If an unusual event occurs that will delay filing of any of the Reports, you must submit a written explanation of the delay in lieu of the Report. Insufficient explanations may result in the filing of a motion to convert or dismiss your case.

Applicable Accounting Rules

The Reports are designed to enable debtors in possession to complete them without professional assistance. However, if professionals are utilized, they should follow Generally Accepted Accounting Principles. Also, the reports should indicate whether inventories are maintained on LIFO, FIFO or another valuation method.

Interim Statements are to be prepared on a cash basis only. The Profit and Loss Statement contained in the Operating Reports is to be prepared on an accrual basis only. The term accrual denotes revenues that have been earned or expenses that have been incurred, whether or not cash has actually been received or paid. Assets listed on the schedules at fair market value should be converted to historical cost for purposes of the Reports unless otherwise specifically noted. All amounts should be rounded to the nearest dollar.

Completing the Reports and Use of Customized Reports

The Reports are meant to be generic so that they can be easily adapted to various types of businesses. Reports must be typed or completed in ink and *must be signed by the debtor-in-possession.* Any attachments must have the case name and case number noted. All blanks must be filled out completely. If any information requested on the report is inapplicable, this must be noted on the Report. If a Report is incomplete, it will be treated as if no Report had been submitted. If you believe that the Reports need significant modifications to be useful for your estate or if you already are preparing the Balance Sheet or Profit and Loss Statement, etc., in a format customized for your business, you should consult with the analyst assigned to your case, from whom you must obtain written permission before you may submit alternative reports.

Where to Submit Reports

Reports must be submitted to the United States Trustee. Do not file them with the Bankruptcy Court. Copies of the reports should also be submitted to the attorney for the debtor-in-possession and the chair of any creditors' committee appointed in the case.

Failure to Submit or Submission of Incomplete Reports

Failure to submit reports to the United States Trustee in a timely fashion may result in a motion to convert or dismiss the bankruptcy. The submission of reports that are incomplete or not prepared in accordance with this Guide will be treated as a failure to submit. All Reports signed by anyone other than the debtor-in-possession will be treated as not having been submitted.

Office of the United States Trustee

In re:	
	Debtor.
Chapter 11 Case No: _____	

DEBTOR IN POSSESSION INTERIM STATEMENT

Statement Number: _____

For the period FROM: _____

TO: _____

	General Account	Payroll Account	Tax Account
CASH ACTIVITY ANALYSIS *(Cash Basis Only)*			
A. Total Receipts per all Prior Interim Statements	$	$	$
B. Less: Total Disbursements per all Prior Statements			
C. Beginning Balance (A less B)			
D. Receipts during Current Period *(Attach Separate Listing if Necessary)* Description			
TOTAL RECEIPTS THIS PERIOD:			
E. Balance Available (C plus D)			
F. Less: Disbursements during Current Period *(Attach Separate Listing if Necessary)* Date Check No. Payee/Purpose			
TOTAL DISBURSEMENTS THIS PERIOD:			
G. Ending Balance (E less F)	$	$	$

H. (1) General Account:
    (a) Depository Name and Location: _____
    (b) Account Number: _____
  (2) Payroll Account: _____
    (a) Depository Name and Location: _____
    (b) Account Number: _____
  (3) Tax Account: _____
    (a) Depository Name and Location: _____
    (b) Account Number: _____

I. Other monies on hand *(Specify type and location)* (i.e., Certificates of Deposit, Petty Cash):
_____
_____

I, (Name/Title: _____), declare under penalty of perjury that the information contained in the above Debtor in Possession Interim Statement is true and complete to the best of my knowledge.

Dated: _____

_____
Debtor in Possession or Trustee

```
                Office of the United States Trustee
```

1. Profit and Loss Statement *(Accrual Basis Only)*
   A. Related to Business Operations:
   Gross Sales $ _____
   Less: Sales Returns and Discounts   _____
       Net Sales   _____
   Less: Cost of Goods Sold:
   Beginning Inventory at Cost   _____
   Add: Purchases   _____
   Less: Ending Inventory at Cost   _____
       Cost of Goods Sold   _____
           Gross Profit   _____
           Other Operating Revenues (Specify)   _____
   Less: Operating Expenses:
   Officer Compensation   _____
   Salaries and Wages — Other Employees   _____
       Total Salaries and Wages   _____
       Employee Benefits and Pensions   _____
   Payroll Taxes   _____
   Real Estate Taxes   _____
   Federal and State Income Taxes   _____
       Total Taxes   _____
   Rent and Lease Exp.
   (Real Property and Personal Property)   _____
   Interest Expense
   (Mortgage, Loan, etc.)   _____
   Insurance   _____
   Automobile Expense   _____
   Utilities (Gas, Electricity, Water,
   Telephone, etc.)   _____
   Depreciation and Amortization   _____
   Repairs and Maintenance   _____
   Advertising   _____
   Supplies, Office Expenses,
   Photocopies, etc.   _____
   Bad Debts   _____
   Miscellaneous Operating Expenses
   (Specify)   _____
       Total Operating Expenses   _____
           Net Gain/Loss from Business
           Operations   _____
   B. Not Related to Business Operations:
   Income:
       Interest Income   _____
       Other.Non-Operating Revenues
       (Specify)   _____
       Gross Proceeds on Sale of Assets   _____
       Less: Original Cost of Assets
       plus Expenses of Sale   _____
           Net Gain/Loss on Sale of Assets   _____
       Total Non-operating Income   _____
   Expenses Not Related to Business Operations:
       Legal and Professional Fees (Specify)   _____
       Other.Non-operating Expenses (Specify) _____
   Total Non-operating Expenses   _____
NET INCOME LOSS FOR PERIOD $ _____

2. Aging of Accounts Payable and Accounts Receivable (exclude pre-petition accounts payable):

		Accounts Payable	Accounts Receivable
Current	Under 30 Days	$	$
Overdue	31 - 60 Days		
Overdue	61 - 90 Days		
Overdue	91 - 120 Days		
Overdue	Over 121 Days		
TOTAL		$	$

3. Statement of Status of Payments to Secured Creditors and Lessors:

Creditor/ Lessor	Frequency of Payments per Contract / Lease (i.e., mo., qtr.)	Amount of Each Payment	Next Payment Due	Post-Petition Payments Not Made*	
				Number	Amount
		$			$

*Explanation for Non-Payment: _____

_____

4. Tax Liability:
   Gross Payroll Expense for Period: $ _____
   Gross Sales for Period Subject to Sales Tax $ _____

	Date Paid	Amount Paid*	Post-Petition Taxes Still Owing
Federal Payroll and Withholding Taxes		$	$
State Payroll and Withholding Taxes			
State Sales and Use Taxes			
Real Property Taxes			

*Attach photocopies of depository receipts from taxing authorities or financial institutions to verify that such deposits or payments have been made.

5. Insurance Coverage:

	Carrier/ Agent Name	Amount of Coverage	Policy Expiration Date	Premium Paid Through Date
Worker's Compensation		$		
Liability				
Fire and Extended Coverage				
Property				
Theft				
Life (Beneficiary: _____)				
Vehicle				
Other (Specify): _____)				
_____				

6. Questions:

   A. Has the Debtor in Possession provided compensation to any officers, directors, shareholders, or other principals without the approval of the Office of the United States Trustee?

     _____: Yes   Explain: _____

     _____: No

   B. Has the Debtor in Possession, subsequent to the filing of the petition, made any payments on its prepetition unsecured debt, except as have been authorized by the Court?

     _____: Yes   Explain: _____

     _____: No

7. Statement of Unpaid Professional Fees (Post-Petition Amounts *Only*)

Name of Professional	State Type of Professional (Attorney / Accountant / etc.)	Total Post-Petition Amount Unpaid
		$

8. Narrative Report of Significant Events and Events out of the Ordinary Course of Business: *(Attach separate sheet if necessary)*

_____
_____
_____
_____
_____
_____
_____
_____
_____

9. Quarterly Fees: (This Fee must be paid to the United States Trustee every calendar quarter)

Quarterly Period Ending	Total Disbursements for Quarter	Quarterly Fee	Date Paid	Amount Paid	Check No.	Quarterly Fee Still Owing
	$	$		$		$

I, (Name/Title: _____), declare under penalty of perjury that the information contained in the above Debtor in Possession Operating Report is true and complete to the best of my knowledge.

Dated: _____

_____

Debtor in Possession or Trustee

Attorney Name, Address and Telephone	File with U.S. Trustee within 7 days after the Chapter 11 petition is filed. Do not file in Bankruptcy Court.

Office of the United States Trustee

In re:	Chapter 11 Proceeding
Debtor.	Case Number: _____ - _____

7- DAY PACKAGE COVER SHEET

Mark One Box for Each Required Document

You must attach each of the following documents or a satisfactory explanation for your failure to attach a document. Failure to meet these requirements may result in the filing of a motion to dismiss or convert your case.

Document Attached	Previously Submitted	Explanation Attached	REQUIRED DOCUMENTS:
☐	☐	☐	1. Real Property Questionnaire (UST-5) for each parcel of real property
☐	☐	☐	2. Bank Statements evidencing that all pre-petition bank accounts have been closed
			3. Proof of Establishment Of debtor in possession bank accounts:
☐	☐	☐	A. General Account
☐	☐	☐	B. Payroll Account
☐	☐	☐	C. Tax Account
			4. Proof of insurance coverage: (Submit declaration pages)
☐	☐	☐	A. General comprehensive public liability insurance·
☐	☐	☐	B. Fire and theft insurance
☐	☐	☐	C. Worker's compensation insurance
☐	☐	☐	D. Vehicle insurance
☐	☐	☐	E. Product liability insurance
☐	☐	☐	F. Other customary insurance coverage
☐	☐	☐	5. Proof of required certificates and licenses
☐	☐	☐	6. List of insiders as defined in 11 U.S.C. § 101(31)
☐	☐	☐	7. Most recently prepared audited and unaudited financial statements
☐	☐	☐	8. Projected cash flow statement for first sixty days of operation
☐	☐	☐	9. Most recently filed State and Federal Payroll Tax Returns, Federal Income Tax Returns, and State Sales Tax Returns, with all schedules and attachments
☐	☐	☐	10. Copies of trust agreements to which Debtor is a party or under which Debtor holds property
☐	☐	☐	11. Proof of recordation of Chapter 11 petition
☐	☐	☐	12. Physical inventory of goods, machinery and equipment

Dated: _____, 19 _____.

_____
Attorney for Debtor in Possession or Trustee

Attorney Name, Address and Telephone Number	FILE WITH U.S. TRUSTEE ONLY - DO NOT FILE IN BANKRUPTCY COURT
Attorney for Debtor	

OFFICE OF THE UNITED STATES TRUSTEE CENTRAL DISTRICT OF CALIFORNIA	
In re: Debtor.	CHAPTER 11 CASE NUMBER
REAL PROPERTY QUESTIONNAIRE *(Form UST-5)* *Check One Box:* ☐ Owned ☐ Being Purchased ☐ Leased	

Within seven (7) days after the filing of the petition, every Chapter 11 Debtor in Possession which holds any interest in any parcel of real property shall provide the United States Trustee with a completed Real Property Questionnaire (Form UST-5). Included within the meaning of the phrase "any interest in any parcel of real property" are real property leases, land sales contracts, open escrows and other transactions under which the Debtor presently may not be a titleholder of record.

The United States Trustee deems the requested information necessary to carry out his statutory responsibilities to monitor and evaluate all pending Chapter 11 cases in this District. Therefore, failure to timely and fully submit this form for each parcel of real property may result in the filing of a motion to dismiss this case, convert this case to one under Chapter 7 or for appointment of a Trustee. Consequently, the Debtor is required to fully answer each question contained in each section of this Questionnaire that applies to the particular parcel of real property involved. A separate Questionnaire is to be filed for each parcel of real property. If additional space is required for any answer, a continuation sheet specifying the Section and Question involved should be attached.

SECTION ONE: PROPERTY OWNED OR BEING PURCHASED BY DEBTOR
A. Address of property including county and state in which it is located:
B. Legal Description of property (i.e., Lot and Tract Number, including Tax Assessor's I.D. Number):
C. Percentage interest in the property owned by the Debtor:
D. Date of Debtor's acquisition of the property: Purchase Price: $

E. Type of real property (i.e., single family residence, condominium, apartment bldg., office bldg., commercial, industrial, unimproved):

F. Description of property (i.e., square footage, number of units, number of offices, amenities, condition):

G. Development status of property:
   (1) Permits (type, date issued, expiration date):

   (2) In construction (date of commencement, estimated date and cost of completion, name of construction lender):

   (3) Rehabilitation (specify nature, cost and status of rehabilitation effort):

H. Present Fair Market Value: $

I. State source and basis of the above fair market value: (Attach a copy of the latest appraisal)

J. Does the property meet all federal, state and local requirements including, but not limited to health, building, safety, OSHA, earthquake and fire regulations? ☐ Yes ☐ No (If answer is "No," briefly explain and attach copies of any complaints, citations and/or recorded documents which specify the substance of the alleged violations.)

K. State the name of the titleholder of record as of the date of the filing of the Petition:

L. State the name of the Grantor of the property to the titleholder set forth in "K" above:

M. Is the titleholder, specified in "K" above, the Debtor in this Chapter 11 Proceeding? ☐ Yes ☐ No

N. State the date of the last transfer of any interest in the property and name of the transferor and transferee:

O. Was title to the property transferred to the Debtor within ninety (90) days prior to the filing of the Chapter 11 Petition? ☐ Yes ☐ No (If your answer is "Yes," state the reason for the transfer.)

P. If the Debtor is a partnership, did all of the general partners consent to the filing of the Chapter 11 Petition? ☐ Yes ☐ No (If your answer is "Yes," attach documentation to indicate such consent was given by all partners.) (If your answer is "No," explain why all did not consent and identify each non-consenting partner.)

Q. Is the property occupied? ☐ Yes ☐ No

R. Does the Debtor, its principals or any other person or entity related to the Debtor or its principals occupy or use any portion of the property? ☐ Yes ☐ No (If your answer is "Yes," state the name of the tenant, nature of the relationship to the Debtor and terms of the agreement, if any.)

S. Does any other person/entity other than the Debtor use, lease or occupy any portion of the property? ☐ Yes ☐ No (If your answer is "Yes," state name of such person/entity, whether it is related, affiliated or doing business with the Debtor or a principal of the Debtor, and state the terms of such use, lease or occupancy.)

T. Has the Bankruptcy Petition been recorded in the Office of the Recorder of the county in which this property is located? ☐ Yes ☐ No (If your answer is "Yes," state the Date of Recordation and Instrument Number or Book and Page Number.)

SECTION TWO: FINANCIAL STATUS OF OWNED PROPERTY

A. List voluntary encumbrances of record against the property (e.g., mortgages, stipulated judgments):

Lender Name	Current Principal Balance	Installment Amount	Frequency (Mo/Qtr/Yr)
1st:	$	$	
2nd:	$	$	
3rd:	$	$	
4th:	$	$	

Maturity Date	Date of Last Payment	Number of Delinquent Installments
1st:		
2nd:		
3rd:		
4th:		

B. List involuntary encumbrances of record against the property (tax, mechanics' and other liens, judgments, lis pendens):

(State type of lien, amount claimed and date of recordation)

C. Was a Notice of Default and/or a Notice of Sale recorded prior to the filing of the bankruptcy petition? ☐ Yes ☐ No
(If your answer is "Yes," state which document was recorded, the name of the lender, and the date of recordation.)

D. Property Taxes:

(1) Assessed value of property per latest real property Tax Bill: $

(2) Annual taxes and installment due dates:

(3) Indicate the due dates and amounts of any Tax Bills which have not been paid:

SECTION THREE: SALE OF PROPERTY

A. Has a real estate broker been employed? ☐ Yes ☐ No
(If your answer is "Yes," state the name of broker, name of the salesperson, date employed, company name, address and telephone number and the listing agreement expiration date.)

B. Has an Application to employ the broker been filed with the Court?
   ☐ Yes ☐ No

C. How long has the property been listed or advertised for sale with current broker?

D. Has any written offer been received? ☐ Yes ☐ No
   (If your answer is "Yes," state the terms of each such written offer.)

E. What is the date the property was first listed for sale with any broker?

F. What is the current listing price? $
   (Attach a copy of the Listing Agreement.)

G. Have other attempts been made to sell the property? (For each such attempt state the date, asking price and result.)

H. Explain other alternatives considered as to the disposition of the property (i.e., refinancing, capital infusion, stipulation with lender):

SECTION FOUR: PURCHASE OF PROPERTY

A. Is the Debtor currently purchasing this parcel of real property?
   ☐ Yes ☐ No (If your answer is "Yes," state the name, address and telephone number of the Seller.)

B. Is the Debtor a party to a Land Sales Contract or other arrangement by which actual title is to be taken at some pint in the future?
   ☐ Yes ☐ No (If your answer is "Yes," attach a copy of any written documents which state the terms of such transaction.)

C. If an escrow has been opened, state the escrow company name, name of escrow officer, address, and telephone number:
   (Attach a copy of the Purchase Agreement and Escrow Instructions.)

D. What is the purchase price? $

360

SECTION FIVE: PROPERTY LEASED BY DEBTOR AS A LESSEE
A. Address of property including county and state in which it is located:
B. Type of real property (i.e., single family residence, condominium, apartment bldg., office bldg., commercial, industrial, unimproved):
C. Description of property (i.e., square footage, number of units, number of offices, amenities, condition):
D. Is the Debtor or any principal of the Debtor affiliated with or related to the lessor? ☐ Yes ☐ No (If your answer is "Yes," explain the relationship.)
E. Does a written lease exist? ☐ Yes ☐ No (If your answer is "Yes," attach a copy of the Lease.)
F. Lease payment amount: $ per ☐ Month ☐ Quarter ☐ Year ☐ Other:
G. Number of pre-petition delinquent lease payments:
H. Total dollar amount of pre-petition delinquent lease and related payments: $
I. Specify the type, amount and date of any deposits paid to the lessor (i.e., security deposits, first and last months' rent):
J. Describe provisions in the lease for increases in lease payments:
K. Describe type of lease (i.e., triple net, minimum plus percentage of sales, gross lease) and state basic lease terms:
L. When did the lease commence? When is the lease termination date?

M. Does the lease provide any options to extend the term of the lease?
☐ Yes ☐ No
(If your answer is "Yes," describe each option.)

N. List the improvements made and fixtures installed by the Debtor (i.e., items so attached or integrated with the property so as to render them legally non-removable) and state the cost:

SECTION SIX: INSURANCE

A. State the following as to each policy of insurance: *(ATTACH A COPY OF EACH CURRENT POLICY OF INSURANCE)*

Type of Insurance	Name of Insurance Agent	Insurance Company Name	Policy No.	Amt. of Coverage	Exp. Date

B. If any policy payments are delinquent, so state and provide the amount and number of installments that are past due:

SECTION SEVEN: INCOME FROM RENTAL OF PROPERTY

A. What is the actual gross monthly income being received from rental of the property? $

B. What is the current occupancy rate and the square footage presently being lease?

C. If the property were fully leased, state the anticipated gross monthly income? $

The Debtor hereby gives Notice of Setting/Increasing Insider Compensation as indicated below (if additional space is required for any answer, attach a

362

D. Itemize the total monthly expenses *excluding* debt service:

E. Is there any person or entity managing the property? ☐ Yes ☐ No
(If your answer is "Yes," state the name, address and telephone number of the managing person/company and attach a copy of the management company's fidelity bond.)

F. What are the terms of the management agreement? (If written, attach a copy of the agreement.)

G. Is the manager of the property related to or affiliated with the Debtor in any way? ☐ Yes ☐ No
(If your answer is "Yes," explain the relationship or affiliation.)

H. Is any person and/or entity occupying any portion of the property at a reduced rental rate or at no rental charge? ☐ Yes ☐ No
(If your answer is "Yes," explain fully.)

I declare under penalty of perjury that the answers contained in the foregoing Real Property Questionnaire are true and correct to the best of my knowledge, information and belief. I have full authority to make the above answers on behalf of the Debtor in Possession.

Date:

Name and Title *(Please Type or Print)*:

Signature of Authorized Agent for Debtor in Possession:

continuation sheet specifying the question involved).

1. Name of insider:

2. Relationship to Debtor (i.e., owner, partner, officer, director, shareholder):

3. Date when relationship with Debtor commenced:

4. Position title:

5. Position description:

6. Assigned duties:

7. Date employed in current position:

8. If previously employed by Debtor within past two years in a different position, state date(s) and position(s):

9. Number of hours worked per week:

10. Total amount of compensation and payment interval:

(THIS FORM IS CONTINUED)

364

11. Breakdown of compensation (specify amount and payment interval):

Salary:

Perquisites (total, detail below):

Car Allowance:
Medical Insurance:
Life Insurance:
Business Expenses:
Other (specify):

12. Identify the source of the funds to be used to pay compensation specified in No. 10:

13. Date and amount of last increase in compensation:

14. Identify any creditor who asserts a security interest (whether or not Debtor disputes the validity thereof) in the receipts generated by the operation of the Debtor's business and the amount of its claim:

15. Specify all compensation, perquisites, loans, etc. received by insider from the Debtor during the twelve-month period immediately preceding the filing of the Chapter 11 Petition (Attach W-2,1099, Individual Payroll Cards and other related forms):

Compensation:
Loans:
Perquisites (specify):

I declare under penalty of perjury that the answers contained in the foregoing Notice are true and correct.

Name and title of authorized agent for Debtor:

Signature of authorized agent for Debtor: _____ Date: _____

ATTACH PROOF OF SERVICE ON THE CREDITORS' COMMITTEE OR THE TWENTY LARGEST CREDITORS IF NO COMMITTEE HAS BEEN FORMED.

IF THIS NOTICE PERTAINS TO SETTING COMPENSATION, IT MUST BE FILED AND SERVED FIFTEEN DAYS BEFORE ANY PAYOUT OF COMPENSATION, ALTHOUGH COMPENSATION MAY BE ACCRUED DURING THIS PERIOD.

IF THIS NOTICE PERTAINS TO AN INCREASE IN COMPENSATION, IT MUST BE FILED AND SERVED THIRTY DAYS BEFORE THE DATE WHEN THE PROPOSED INCREASE TAKES EFFECT.

QUARTERLY FEE SCHEDULE AND
PAYMENT INFORMATION

Debtors in possession are required to pay a quarterly fee to the United States Trustee every calendar quarter (including any fraction thereof), based on disbursements made from the date the petition is filed until the date of entry of an order confirming a plan or dismissing or converting the case. Cases that have been administratively consolidated must still pay a separate fee for each case; however, cases that have been substantively consolidated need pay only one quarterly fee, beginning the first full quarter after consolidation. Operation during even one day of a quarter requires payment of the fee applicable for that quarter.

Fees are due no later than one month following the quarterly reporting period. In order to be confirmed, a Chapter 11 plan of reorganization must provide for payment of outstanding quarterly fees on or before the effective date of the plan. Payment of quarterly fees is due immediately upon entry of an order dismissing a case.

Quarterly fees may be paid by check payable to the United States Trustee. However, if any check is returned marked "insufficient funds," all future quarterly fee payments must be made by cashier's check, certified funds or money order. *Failure to pay the quarterly fee is cause for conversion or dismissal of the Chapter 11 case.*

The amount of the quarterly fee owing depends on the amount of disbursements made during the calendar quarter and can be calculated using the chart below. However, a minimum fee of $250 is due each quarter even if no disbursements are made.

QUARTERLY DISBURSEMENTS			QUARTERLY FEE
$ 0	to	14,999.99	$250
15,000	to	149,999.99	500
150,000	to	299,999.99	1,250
300,000	to	2,999,999.99	3,750
3,000,000	to	and above	5,000

Quarterly Fees should be mailed to:

United States Trustee
P.O. Box 198246
Atlanta, GA 30384

B *Sample Employment Application*

JEFFREY S. SHINBROT, Esq.
State Bar No. 155486
8601 Wilshire Blvd.
Suite 900
Beverly Hills, CA 90211
Telephone: (310) 659-5444

Attorney for Debtor in Possession

UNITED STATES BANKRUPTCY COURT
CENTRAL DISTRICT OF CALIFORNIA

In re   )
)
)   Chapter 11
)
)   NOTICE OF APPLICATION TO
)   EMPLOY ATTORNEY FOR
)   DEBTORS-IN-POSSESSION.
)
)
            Debtors-in-possession.)
_____)
                                            [No hearing required]

        The application _____ (hereinafter
"Applicants"), respectfully represents as follows:
        1.   On May 25, 1995 the Applicants filed a petition under
Chapter 11 of the Bankruptcy Code.
        2.   Applicants propose to employ Jeffrey S. Shinbrot,
Esquire, to represent them in their capacity as Debtors-in-Possession
under Chapter 11 of the United States Bankruptcy Code.
        3.   Applicants propose to employ Mr. Shinbrot as he has
experience in matters of this nature and Applicants believe that Mr.
Shinbrot is well qualified to represent them as Debtors-in-possession
in these proceedings.
        4.   The legal services required will be legal advice and
guidance with respect to the powers, duties, rights and obligations
of the Applicants as Debtors-in-Possession, the formulation and
preparation of a Plan of Reorganization and a Disclosure Statement
for said plan, and to prepare on behalf of the Applicants all legal

documents as may be necessary, and to perform such legal services as are required in these Chapter 11 proceedings.

5.   To the best of the Applicants' knowledge, Mr. Shinbrot is a "disinterested person" as defined by 11 U.S.C. Section 101 (14) and has no connection with the creditors, or any other party in interest.

6.   Mr. Shinbrot is not a pre-petition creditor of the Applicants.

7.   Mr. Shinbrot has no interests adverse to the Applicants' Chapter 11 estate, and his employment would be to the best interest of this estate.

8.   Mr. Shinbrot has agreed to undertake this employment as attorney for Applicants if authorized by this Court and to be compensated in accordance with 11 U.S.C. Section 330, the Local Rules for the Central District of California and the Guidelines of the office of the United States Trustee. The Applicant has agreed to pay Mr. Shinbrot a $10,800.00 retainer, which has been placed in Mr. Shinbrot's segregated Attorney/Client Trust account.

9.   The source of the retainer is the Applicants and Mr. Shinbrot will adhere to the Guidelines of the office of the United States Trustee regarding applications for payment of Professional fees and expenses. No payments will be made without prior approval of the United States Bankruptcy Court.

WHEREFORE, the Applicants pray that this Court authorize the employment of Jeffrey S. Shinbrot, Esquire as attorney for the Debtors-in-Possession in these Chapter 11 proceedings.

DATED: June 5, 1995

<u>COMMENTS OF THE OFFICE OF THE UNITED STATES TRUSTEE</u>

( )   THE U.S. TRUSTEE TAKES NO POSITION.

( )   THE U.S. TRUSTEE HAS NO OBJECTION.

( )   THE U.S. TRUSTEE OBJECTS AND REQUESTS A HEARING.

( )   AN OBJECTION IS RAISED AND SET FORTH BELOW.

COMMENTS:

DATED: _____

OFFICE OF THE UNITED STATES
TRUSTEE

By: _____
Name: _____
Attorney for the
United States Trustee

Case Name: In re

Case Number:
Type of Document: Application to Employ Attorney, Declaration
                    of Counsel, Order Thereon.

JEFFREY S. SHINBROT, Esq.
State Bar No. 155486
8601 Wilshire Blvd.
Suite 900
Beverly Hills, CA 90211
Telephone: (310) 659-5444

Attorney for Debtor in Possession

UNITED STATES BANKRUPTCY COURT
CENTRAL DISTRICT OF CALIFORNIA

In re   )

)

)   Chapter 11

)

)   NOTICE OF APPLICATION TO
)   EMPLOY ATTORNEY FOR
)   DEBTORS-IN-POSSESSION.

)

)

     Debtors-in-possession.)

_____)   [No hearing required]

1.   TO ALL PARTIES IN INTEREST:

2.   NOTICE IS HEREBY GIVEN: that an Application to Employ Jeffrey S. Shinbrot as attorney for the above captioned Debtors-in-Possession has been submitted to the United States Trustee and that if you fail to file a written response within fifteen (15) days of the date of service of this Notice, the Court may treat such failure as a waiver of your right to oppose this Application and may grant the requested relief.

3.   A copy of the Application to Employ Jeffrey S. Shinbrot as attorney for the Debtors-in-Possession is available upon request by contacting The Law Offices of Jeffrey S. Shinbrot, 8601 Wilshire Blvd., #900, Beverly Hills, California, (310) 659-5444.

4.   Opposition to this Application, if any, must be filed in duplicate with the Bankruptcy Court and served on the office of the United States Trustee at 221 N. Figueroa Street, Suite 800, Los

Angeles, California 90012 and the Proposed-Attorney for the Debtor: Jeffrey S. Shinbrot, Esq. 8601 Wilshire Blvd. #900, Beverly Hills, CA 90211

DATED: June 6, 1995

                              _____

                              Jeffrey S. Shinbrot,
                              Proposed Attorney for Debtors-
                              in-Possession

JEFFREY S. SHINBROT, Esq.
State Bar No. 155486
8601 Wilshire Blvd.
Suite 900
Beverly Hills, CA 90211
Telephone: (310) 659-5444

Attorney for Debtor in Possession

UNITED STATES BANKRUPTCY COURT
CENTRAL DISTRICT OF CALIFORNIA

In re   )
)
)   Chapter 11
)
)   DECLARATION OF PROPOSED
)   ATTORNEY FOR DEBTOR IN
)   POSSESSION
)
        Debtors-in-possession.)
_____)   Bankruptcy Rule 2016(b)

                                          [No hearing required]

I, Jeffrey S. Shinbrot declare and state as follows:
        1.   I am an attorney at law, duly admitted to practice in
the State of California and to the United States District Court in
the Central District of California.
        2.   I am a "disinterested person" as defined by 11 U.S.C.
Section 101(14) and I have no connection with any creditor of the
above captioned debtors-in-possession, or any other party in
interest, or its respective attorney, I have no interests adverse
to the above captioned debtors' Chapter 11 estate, and I am
informed and believe that my employment would be to the best
interest of this estate.
        3.   I am not a pre-petition creditor of the debtors-in-
possession captioned above.
        4.   No agreement or understanding exists for a division of
fees between my offices and any other person whomsoever.

5.   The legal services required by the above referenced Chapter 11 debtors will be legal advice and guidance with respect to the powers, duties, rights and obligations of the Applicants as Debtor in Possession, the formulation and preparation of a Plan of Reorganization and a Disclosure Statement for said plan, and to prepare on behalf of the Applicants all legal documents as may be necessary, and to perform such legal services as are required in these Chapter 11 proceedings.

6.   I have received $10,800.00 retainer, which has been placed in my segregated Attorney/Client Trust account. I am informed and I believe that the source of this retainer is the debtors.

7.   I will adhere to the Guidelines of the Office of the United States Trustee regarding applications for payment of professional fees and expenses. No payments will be made without prior approval of the United States Bankruptcy Court.

8.   I am experienced in bankruptcy proceedings and have agreed to undertake this employment as attorney for the above referenced debtors-in-possession if authorized by this Court. The debtors will be billed at my normal hourly rate, as set forth in the retention letter attached hereto as Exhibit "A" and incorporated herein by this reference. A true and accurate copy of my firm resume is also attached hereto as Exhibit "B" and incorporated herein by this reference.

I declare under penalty of perjury that the foregoing is true and correct.

Dated this 5th day of June, 1995.

_____
Jeffrey S. Shinbrot,
Proposed Attorney for Debtors-
in-Possession

<u>COMMENTS OF THE OFFICE OF THE UNITED STATES TRUSTEE</u>

( )   THE U.S. TRUSTEE TAKES NO POSITION.

( )   THE U.S. TRUSTEE HAS NO OBJECTION.

( )   THE U.S. TRUSTEE OBJECTS AND REQUESTS A HEARING.

( )   AN OBJECTION IS RAISED AND SET FORTH BELOW.

COMMENTS:

DATED: _____

OFFICE OF THE UNITED STATES
TRUSTEE

By: _____
Name: _____
       Attorney for the
       United States Trustee

Case Name: In re

Case Number:
Type of Document: Application to Employ Attorney, Declaration
                    of Counsel, Order Thereon.

JEFFREY S. SHINBROT, Esq.
State Bar No. 155486
8601 Wilshire Blvd.
Suite 900
Beverly Hills, CA 90211
Telephone: (310) 659-5444

Attorney for Debtor in Possession

UNITED STATES BANKRUPTCY COURT
CENTRAL DISTRICT OF CALIFORNIA

In re   )
)
)   Chapter 11
)
)   ORDER ON APPLICATION TO
)   EMPLOY ATTORNEY FOR DEBTORS-
)   IN-POSSESSION
)
          Debtors-in-possession.)
_____)

                                        [No hearing required]

     Upon the Application of _____ in the above-
captioned Chapter 11 proceedings (hereinafter the "Debtors") for
Jeffrey S. Shinbrot, Esquire, to serve as bankruptcy counsel for the
Debtors, and upon the Declaration of Jeffrey S. Shinbrot as an
attorney duly admitted to practice in this Court, and the Court
being satisfied that Mr. Shinbrot represents no interest adverse to
the Debtors herein, or its estate in the matters upon which they are
to be engaged and that his employment would be in the best interest
of the bankruptcy estate, it is hereby
     ORDERED, that the employment of Jeffrey S. Shinbrot to serve as
bankruptcy counsel of the Debtor in these Chapter 11 proceedings is
approved and authorized with compensation to be fixed after notice
and a hearing pursuant to 11 U.S.C. §330, in accordance with the
foregoing application.

DATED: _____
                                THE HONORABLE ARTHUR M. GREENWALD
                                UNITED STATES BANKRUPTCY JUDGE

376

<u>COMMENTS OF THE OFFICE OF THE UNITED STATES TRUSTEE</u>

( )   THE U.S. TRUSTEE TAKES NO POSITION.

( )   THE U.S. TRUSTEE HAS NO OBJECTION.

( )   THE U.S. TRUSTEE OBJECTS AND REQUESTS A HEARING.

( )   AN OBJECTION IS RAISED AND SET FORTH BELOW.

COMMENTS:

DATED: _____

        OFFICE OF THE UNITED STATES
        TRUSTEE

        By: _____
        Name: _____
           Attorney for the
           United States Trustee

Case Name: In re

Case Number:
Type of Document: Application to Employ Attorney, Declaration
                    of Counsel, Order Thereon.

In re (SHORT TITLE)	CHAPTER 11 CASE NUMBER:
Debtor.	

NOTICE OF ENTRY OF JUDGMENT OR ORDER
AND CERTIFICATE OF MAILING

TO ALL PARTIES IN INTEREST ON THE ATTACHED SERVICE LIST:

1. You are hereby notified, pursuant to Local Bankruptcy Rule 118(1)(a)(iv) that a judgment or order entitled *(specify)*:

ORDER ON APPLICATION TO EMPLOY ATTORNEY FOR DEBTORS IN POSSESSION

was entered on *(specify date)*:

2. I hereby certify that I mailed a copy of this notice and a true copy of the order or judgment to the persons and entities on the attached service list on *(specify date)*:

Jon D. Ceretto

Dated:

Clerk of the Bankruptcy Court

By:_____
Deputy Clerk

Jeffrey S. Shinbrot, Esquire
8601 Wilshire Blvd., #900
Beverly Hills, California 90211

Office of the United States Trustee
221 N. Figueroa Street, #800
Los Angeles, California 90012

C ‎ *U.S. Trustee's Office Employment Guidelines*

*GUIDE TO APPLICATIONS FOR EMPLOYMENT OF
PROFESSIONALS AND TREATMENT OF RETAINERS
("EMPLOYMENT GUIDE")*

I. APPLICATIONS TO EMPLOY

A. General Information Required

The Bankruptcy Court must approve the employment of any attorney, accountant, appraiser, auctioneer, agent or other professional retained pursuant to §327, §1103 and §1114 of the Bankruptcy Code. Pursuant to Federal Rule of Bankruptcy Procedure 2014(a) and Local Rules 111(7)(d) and 141, an application to employ such a professional must include the following information.

1. The name and occupation of the person or firm to be employed.
2. Facts demonstrating the necessity for the employment and the specific services to be rendered.
3. The reason for the selection of the particular professional to be employed, including facts to substantiate that the proposed professional has attained a sufficient experience level to render the proposed services. The professional's personal and, if appropriate, firm resume

should be attached. If a trustee proposes to retain his or her own firm as counsel, the application must show a compelling reason why appointment of outside counsel is not feasible.

4. A declaration under penalty of perjury setting forth, to the best of the professional's knowledge, all of the professional's connections with the debtor, creditors, or any other party in interest, their respective attorneys and accountants, the United States Trustee and any person employed by the office of the United States Trustee, and whether the professional holds any interest adverse to the estate of the debtor. The declaration must contain facts, not merely legal conclusions.

5. The terms and conditions of the employment agreement, including the hourly rate charged by each professional (including partners, associates, and paraprofessional persons employed by the professional) expected to render services to or for the benefit of the estate.

6. If the professional is an attorney, the application must state the amount and source of any fees, retainers or other compensation (including any contingency fee agreements) paid or agreed to be paid, including any fees, retainers or other compensation paid or agreed to be paid within one year of the filing of the petition, for services rendered or to be rendered in contemplation of or in connection with the case, whether the fees, retainers or other compensation have already been paid, whether the retainer is an advance against fees for services to be rendered or earned upon receipt, whether all or any portion of the retainer is refundable, the services, if any, the client is entitled to receive in exchange for the retainer, the facts justifying the amount of the retainer, and a declaration under penalty of perjury demonstrating the need for a retainer, including any unusual circumstances that would justify a postpetition retainer.

7. If the application is made more than thirty days after the date postpetition services commenced, it must include a declaration under penalty of perjury explaining the delay and stating the amount of fees and expenses that have accrued during the period between the date postpetition services were commenced and the date of the application.

8. If the application is made more than sixty days after the date postpetition services commenced, the Notice of Application required by Bankruptcy Local Rule 141(2)(b) (see item I.B.4 below) must include a statement that retroactive employment is being requested and the date that services commenced. Normally only extraordinary facts will justify retroactive employment.

9. If more than one of a particular type of professional is being retained, each application must set forth the need for dual professionals, the ser-

vices to be performed by each, a statement that there will be no duplication of services and an explanation of how duplication will be avoided.

B. Form of Application and Procedures for Submission

1. The application must be signed by a person authorized to make the application, such as the debtor-in-possession, the Chapter 11 trustee, creditors' committee chairman, or an officer, general partner or other principal of the debtor-in-possession. It is not acceptable for counsel to sign on behalf of the applicant.

2. The application, together with a proposed order, must be submitted to the United States Trustee for review and comment prior to filing unless noticed and set for hearing pursuant to Local Bankruptcy Rule 111(7)(d), or otherwise ordered by the court. Applications will be processed by the United States Trustee in the regular course of business unless there is a demonstrated emergency. In an emergency case, counsel should telephone the attorney for the United States Trustee assigned to the case to arrange for expedited treatment.

3. The application must include a separate page for the comments of the United States Trustee (the format to be used for the comment page is attached to the "Notice of Requirements for Chapter 11 Debtors"). This comment page should be placed at the end of the application if the proposed order is a separate document, or just before a proposed order included in the same document.

4. Notice that the application has been submitted to the United States Trustee must be filed and served on the appropriate parties as specified in Local Rule 141(2)(b), prior to or on the same day that the application is submitted. Under local procedures established by the court in Santa Ana, the applicant must submit, with the application to employ, a separately blue-backed notice stating that notice of the application was served and no opposition was received by the applicant within fifteen days after service of the notice. Because this requirement inevitably delays the submission of the application to the United States Trustee, for purposes of the time periods discussed in paragraphs A.8 and A.9 above, the application will be considered as submitted on the date that the notice of application is served.

5. In addition to the information required to be included in the Notice of Application in Local Rule 141(2)(b), the Notice should include any terms, including "evergreen" provisions, that allow for payments or transfers of funds to the professional without any further notice or hearing.

II. RETAINERS

A. General Information

Any unearned portion of a prepetition or postpetition retainer that is an advance against fees must be deposited in a segregated trust account upon filing of the petition. If the prepetition retainer is earned upon receipt, the funds need not be segregated by the professional.

B. Accounting for Services Covered by a Retainer

1. Any professional who has received a prepetition or postpetition retainer must submit to the United States Trustee a monthly Professional Fee Statement (Form UST-6, attached) no later than the 20th day after the end of the month during which professional services were rendered, together with documentation supporting the charges for the professional services and expenses in the form required for professional fee applications in the "United States Trustee Guide to Applications for Professional Compensation." In addition, a copy of the Professional Fee Statement (without the supporting documentation) must be served on the official creditors' committee or, if no committee has been appointed, on the 20 largest unsecured creditors, and on those parties who have requested special notice. The Professional Fee Statement should include a statement that the supporting documentation can be obtained from the professional upon request.

2. The Professional Fee Statement must explicitly state that the fees and costs will be withdrawn from the trust account in the amount requested without further notice or hearing, unless an objection is filed with the clerk of the court and served upon the applicant(s) within 10 days after service of the Professional Fee Statement. If no objection is timely filed and served, the professional may withdraw the requested compensation without further notice, hearing or order. If an objection is timely filed and served, the professional should refrain from withdrawing any funds until the objection has been resolved by the court.

3. Notwithstanding the submission of the Professional Fee Statement, as long as the professional is performing services covered by a retainer, the professional must submit interim fee applications to the court every 120 days in the form and manner specified in the "Guide to Applications for Professional Compensation." Once the full amount of the retainer has been accounted for, no further Professional Fee Statements shall be filed.

4. Neither the United States Trustee nor any party in interest shall be estopped from raising objections to any charge or expense in any professional fee application filed with the court on the ground that no objection was lodged to the Professional Fee Statement.

5. *Special Note:* Some judges do not permit attorneys to draw down on retainers pursuant to the above procedures. Attorneys with retainers should thus make certain at the time of their employment what procedures are required by the judge to whom the case is assigned.

Attorney or Professional Name, Address and Telephone Number	FOR COURT USE ONLY
(If Applicable) Attorney for	
UNITED STATES BANKRUPTCY COURT CENTRAL DISTRICT OF CALIFORNIA	

In re:	CHAPTER 11 CASE NUMBER
	PROFESSIONAL FEE STATEMENT
	NUMBER: _____
Debtor.	MONTH OF _____, 19 _____

1. Name of Professional:
2. Date of entry of Order approving employment of the
   Professional:
3. Total amount of Pre-Petition payments received by the
   Professional: $
4. *Less:* Total amount of all Pre-Petition services rendered
   and expenses: <_____>
5. Balance of funds remaining on date of filing of Petition: $
6. *Less:* Total amount of all services rendered per prior Fee
   Statements: <   >
   (Line 6 is not used when filing Statement No. 1)
7. *Less:* Total amount of services and expenses this reporting
   period: <   >
8. Balance of funds remaining for next reporting period: $_____

YOU MUST ATTACH DETAILED DOCUMENTATION SUPPORTING THE PROFESSIONAL FEES
EARNED AND THE EXPENSES INCURRED DURING THIS REPORTING PERIOD. (THE AMOUNT
SPECIFIED ON LINE 7 ABOVE.) THE REQUIREMENTS SET FORTH IN PARAGRAPHS 3, 4,
AND 5 OF U.S. TRUSTEE GUIDELINE NO. 7 APPLY TO THE DETAIL REQUIRED IN THIS
STATEMENT. *(Attach only to U.S. Trustee's copy of this Statement.)*

---

9. Total number of pages of supporting documentation attached hereto: _____
10. The above is a true and correct statement of fees earned and expenses
    incurred during the indicated reporting period.

Dated:

_____   _____
Type Name of Professional   Signature of Professional

_____   _____
Type Name of Attorney for   Signature of Attorney for
Professional *(If applicable)*   Professional *(If applicable)*

385

In re (SHORT TITLE)	CHAPTER 11 CASE NUMBER:
Debtor.	

PROOF OF SERVICE BY MAIL

STATE OF CALIFORNIA
COUNTY OF LOS ANGELES

I am employed in the County of _____, State of
California, in the office of a member of the bar of this Court at
whose direction the service was made; I am over the age of 18 and
not a party to the within action; and my business address is as
follows:

On _____, I served the foregoing PROFESSIONAL FEE
STATEMENT on the interested parties at their last known addresses in
this action by placing a true and correct copy thereof in a sealed
envelope with postage thereon fully prepaid in the United States Mail
at _____, California, addressed as follows:

I declare under penalty of perjury that the foregoing is true and
correct.

Dated:

_____   _____
Print Name   *Signature*

GUIDE TO APPLICATIONS FOR PROFESSIONAL COMPENSATION ("FEE GUIDE")

I. BILLING GUIDELINES

A. General information

1. The United States Trustee will object to the payment of any professional fees at a time when the debtor-in-possession or Chapter 11 trustee has failed to file timely Operating Reports or Interim Statements or where other administrative expenses, such as quarterly fees and taxes, have not been paid in a timely manner.

2. The United States Trustee may request a hold back of an appropriate percentage on the award of interim compensation, but 100% of expenses are ordinarily allowable on an interim basis.

3. When a reorganization plan has been confirmed, final fee applications under § 330 of the Bankruptcy Code must be promptly submitted by all professionals who have been employed at the expense of the estate. Failure to act promptly may result in the United States Trustee bringing a motion to compel filing or to disgorge fees.

4. Final fee applications must cover all of the services performed in the case, not just the last period for which fees are sought, and must seek approval of all prior interim fee awards.

5. The Bankruptcy Court can limit notice of fee applications. The United States Trustee will oppose requests to limit notice to fewer than ten days, or to notice that does not include at least the United States Trustee, any committees, any secured creditors claiming a right to cash collateral, and any parties who have requested special notice.

6. No professional may be paid any amount for services rendered prior to the effective date of the plan, unless such payment has been approved by the court or as specified in the United States Trustee Employment Guide.

7. Whenever there is a substitution of counsel in a Chapter 11 case, withdrawing counsel shall file a final fee application within sixty days after the date provided in the order allowing withdrawal of representation. The United States Trustee will seek an accounting and return of any prepetition retainer or postpetition fee paid to withdrawing counsel if a timely fee application is not filed.

B. Professional Fees

1. Discuss strategy with client (i.e., the debtor, trustee, committee chair, etc.) both at the outset of the case and on an ongoing basis, at least quarterly. If a particular project is likely to require in excess of five thousand dollars of billable time, excluding travel and court time, the client should be consulted in advance and provided an estimate of the expected total cost for the project.

2. Consult with the client in advance on any expense disbursements in excess of one thousand dollars.

3. Delegate assignments, consistent with performance of high-quality work, to those who will provide the best value for the time spent. Counsel should consult the client with respect to the initial staffing and any staffing increases.

4. Do not charge for educating junior personnel in basic substantive or procedural rules, law or principles.

5. Do not charge learning time for replacing staff or professionals.

6. It is expected that most routine hearings and meetings will require only a single professional. Where two professionals routinely appear at meetings or hearings or whenever more than two are in attendance, specific justification must be provided in the fee application.

7. Internal conferences and meetings should be conducted only when necessary and appropriate.

8. Do not "double charge" for long distance travel time; i.e., when work is performed for this or another client while traveling, there should not be an additional charge for travel time. Also, where travel is on behalf of more than one client, it should be pro-rated among them.

9. Billing statements must be provided to the client on at least a monthly basis.

10. Neither hourly fees nor expense charges may exceed those applicable to non-bankruptcy clients.

11. Services should be billed at the hourly rate applicable when performed.

12. Any deviations from the requirements of this Guide are to be highlighted and explained.

C. *Reimbursable Expenses:* **The following expenses are reimbursable at actual cost only.**

1. Postage.
2. Long distance telephone charges.
3. Messenger and overnight delivery services.
4. Filing fees.
5. Computer research services.
6. Outside photocopy services.
7. Reasonable parking expenses.
8. Charges for meals during travel, but not to exceed $50.00 per day, per person.
9. Reasonable charges for meals provided in the course of an in-office business meeting with "outside" individuals.
10. Charges for transmitting facsimiles that do not exceed 1 dollar per page, if telephone expenses are not separately charged. Where the telephone expenses are separately charged, the charge for transmitting facsimiles is limited to 20 cents per page.*
11. In-house photocopy charges that do not exceed 20 cents per page.*
12. Charges for receipt of facsimile copies that do not exceed 20 cents per page.*

D. *Non-Reimbursable Expenses:* **Absent extraordinary circumstances, the United States Trustee will object to the following as not actual, necessary expenses.**

1. Staff overtime.
2. Travel expenses for "first class" or other luxury transportation.
3. Local meals for professional or support staff.
4. Normal overhead expenses such as rent, insurance, utilities, secretarial work, word processing, office supplies, docketing time, tending photocopy or facsimile machines, "opening file" administrative expenses, and other similar internal operating or overhead expenses.

*These charges are intended to approximate actual costs, given the difficulty of an accurate determination. To the extent that actual costs can be documented, they should be used. To the extent that non-bankruptcy clients are charged less, the lesser amount should be used.

II. APPLICATIONS FOR PROFESSIONAL FEES AND EXPENSES

A. General Information Required

The application for payment of professional fees and expenses shall contain the following information.

1. The entry date of the order approving employment and the date services commenced.

2. The date of the applicant's last fee application. Note, unless otherwise specifically approved by the court, applications for payment should not be filed more frequently than once every 120 days.

3. A summary of fees paid and costs reimbursed including:

   a. Advance fee payment received (identify whether the amount is the unused portion of a prepetition retainer, an earned on receipt retainer or a postpetition retainer).

   b. Advance fee payment remaining.

   c. Payments made pursuant to prior applications.

   d. Amount remaining to be paid pursuant to prior applications.

   e. Any amount reserved pending final fee application.

   f. Any portion of an earned on receipt retainer allocable to services documented in the current fee application.

4. A narrative summary of the significant events in the case during the relevant time period.

5. A brief statement for each major activity code category used, noting the total fees charged for that category and the particular benefits generated to the estate.

6. Fee applications by debtor's reorganization counsel should include a statement of the source and amount of cash available to pay the requested fees.

7. In Chapter 11 cases, fee applications by debtor's reorganization counsel should include a discussion of the prospects for reorganization and an estimate of when the disclosure statement and plan will be submitted.

8. In Chapter 7 cases, a statement by the trustee or trustee's counsel estimating when the final report will be filed and what further work must be performed before the estate will be in a position to be closed.

9. A notation and explanation of any items that deviate from any of the requirements of this Guide.

10. A declaration by the applicant's designated professional that the application complies with this Guide except as specifically noted and justified in the application and indicating the amount, if any, that the bill has been reduced as a result of discussion with the client (see Example 6, attached).

11. A written statement by the client that he/she has reviewed the billing and indicating what objections, if any, the client has not been able to resolve. If the client is unwilling to provide such a statement, the professional should indicate that the bill was provided to the client, the client was informed of this requirement and has declined to comply.

B. Billing Format—Professional Fees

1. The applicant's **Time and Billing Statement** shall be submitted in chronological order by activity code category (see below) in substantial compliance with the following format. The total hours and amount for each activity code category should also be provided (Example 1).

Activity Code Category

Name	*Type*	*Hourly Rate*	*Date*	*Hours*	*Total Amt.*	*Description*

"Type" refers to the type of professional performing the services: e.g., (P) for partner, (S) for shareholder, (O) for owner, (A) for associate, (PL) for paralegal. A key to the abbreviations used should be provided. An acceptable alternative would be to combine name and type by using initials, e.g., BHP to indicate Benjamin Harrison, partner, so long as a key to the full name and type coding is provided.

"Hourly Rate" is the rate applicable at the time the services were performed.

"Hours" should be calculated by tenths; no "lumping."

"Description" should include sufficient detail to identify the particular persons, motions, discrete tasks performed and other subject matters related to the service.

2. In addition to the Time and Billing Statement, the applicant shall submit:

Biographical Information—a brief biography for each billing professional (Example 5);

Monthly Summary of Fees—a summary showing the total amount billed on a monthly basis for each activity code category (Example 3);

Professional Activity Summary—a summary for each activity code category listing the name and type of professionals who billed under that category, each professional's billing rate, and the total hours and amount billed by that professional under that category (Example 2).

C. Billing Format—Expenses

Expenses (e.g., long distance telephone, copy costs, messengers, computer research, airline travel, etc.), should be listed by category and month incurred (Example 4). Unusual expense items or those in excess of $1000.00, should include the date incurred; description; amount and explanation of need. Backup documentation for all expenses should be retained whenever possible and made available on request.

D. Activity Code Categories

The following is a list of activity code categories that are applicable to most bankruptcy cases. Only one category should be used for any given activity and professionals should make their best effort to be consistent in their use of categories. This applies both within and across firms. Thus, it may be appropriate for all professionals to discuss the categories in advance and agree generally on how activities will be categorized. The application may contain additional categories as the case requires. For example, each litigation matter should have its own category. But every effort should be made to use the listed categories in the first instance and to coordinate the use of additional categories with other professionals in the case.

The following categories are generally more applicable to attorneys and trustees but may be used by all professionals as appropriate. Activities that are included in the category of § 330(a)(1) Chapter 7 trustee's services (Exhibit B to General Order 93-02) are prefaced with the notation "Ch-7:".

ASSET ANALYSIS AND RECOVERY: Identification and review of potential assets including causes of action and non-litigation recoveries. *Ch-7:* Review schedules; Investigate location and status of assets (internal); Initial contact with lessors, secured creditors, ABC, etc., if same can be accomplished from office; Turnover or inspection of documents, e.g., bank documents; UCC search review; Mail forwarding notices; Collection of accounts receivable; Letters re compliance with Local Rule 140.

ASSET DISPOSITION. Sales, leases (§ 365 matters), abandonment and related transaction work. *Ch-7:* Document notice of sale, abandonment, compromise, etc.; Appear at sale; Prepare certificate of sale, deed or other transfer documents; Abandon assets (draft papers for the trustee's signature); Attend sales; Place investments at the direction of trustee.

BUSINESS OPERATIONS: Issues related to debtor-in-possession operating in Chapter 11 such as employee, vendor, tenant issues and other similar problems.

CASE ADMINISTRATION: Coordination and compliance activities, including preparation of statement of financial affairs; schedules; list of contracts; United States Trustee interim statements and operating reports; contacts with the United States Trustee; general creditor inquiries. *Ch-7:* Objection to exemption; Reports re 707(b) motions; Notification of asset case; Approve proposed disbursements; Prepare exhibits to operating reports; Prepare text of operating reports, schedules re quarterly bond reports; Prepare schedules for 180-day status reports; Answer creditor correspondence and phone calls; Participate in audits; Answer United States Trustee questions.

CLAIMS ADMINISTRATION AND OBJECTIONS: Specific claim inquiries; bar date motions; analyses, objections and allowances of claims. *Ch-7:* Review claims and decide as to objectionable claims; Negotiate amendment or withdrawal of claims; Documentation and hearing on objections to claims.

EMPLOYEE BENEFITS/PENSIONS: Review issues such as severance, retention, 401K coverage and continuance of pension plan.

FEE/EMPLOYMENT APPLICATIONS: Preparation of employment and fee applications for self or others; motions to establish interim procedures. *Ch-7:* Acceptance and qualification; Documenting appointment of appraisers, brokers, professionals; Recruit brokers, appraisers, other professionals.

FEE/EMPLOYMENT OBJECTIONS: Review of and objections to the employment and fee applications of others. *Ch-7:* Review and comment on professional fee applications.

FINANCING: Matters under §§ 361, 363 and 364 including cash collateral and secured claims; loan document analysis.

LITIGATION: There should be a separate category established for each matter (e.g., XYZ Stay Litigation). *Ch-7:* Motions to dismiss; Monitor litigation; Attend hearings where adjustor may be a witness.

MEETINGS OF CREDITORS: Preparing for and attending the conference of creditors, the § 341(a) meeting and other creditors' committee meetings. *Ch-7:* Conduct 341(a) examination; Notice of continuance of 341(a).

PLAN AND DISCLOSURE STATEMENT: Formulation, presentation and confirmation; compliance with the plan confirmation order, related orders and rules; disbursement and case closing activities, except those related to the allowance and objections to allowance of claims.

CH-7 CASE CLOSING: Notice of intention to file final account; Prepare order to return books and records; Prepare financial exhibits to final account; Prepare narrative to final account; Appear at final hearing; Prepare order approving accounting and fixing fees; Approval of 3011 report.

The following categories are generally more applicable to accountants and financial advisors, but may be used by all professionals as appropriate.

ACCOUNTING/AUDITING: Activities related to maintaining and auditing books of account, preparation of financial statements and account analysis.

BUSINESS ANALYSIS: Preparation and review of company business plan; development and review of strategies; preparation and review of cash flow forecasts and feasibility studies.

CORPORATE FINANCE: Review Financial aspects of potential mergers, acquisitions and disposition of company or subsidiaries.

DATA ANALYSIS: Management information systems review, installation and analysis, construction, maintenance and reporting of significant case financial data, lease rejection, claims, etc.

LITIGATION CONSULTING: Providing consulting and expert witness services relating to various bankruptcy matters such as insolvency, feasibility, avoiding actions; forensic accounting, etc.

RECONSTRUCTION ACCOUNTING: Reconstructing books and records from past transactions and bringing accounting current.

TAX ISSUES: Analysis of tax issues and preparation of state and federal tax returns.

VALUATION: Appraise or review appraisals of assets.

EXAMPLE 1

PROFESSIONAL FEE STATEMENT FOR HARRISON & POLK

XYZ Stay Litigation

Name	Type	Hourly Rate	Date	Hours	Total Amt.	Description
Harrison B.	P	305.00	4/1/92	.1	30.50	Telephone conference with M. Fillmore from ABC re: stipulation to cancel hearing on XYZ's motion to lift automatic stay.
Arthur C.	A	155.00	4/1/92	1.6	248.00	Preparation of stipulation to cancel hearing on XYZ's motion to lift automatic stay.
Harrison B.	P	305.00	4/2/92	.4	122.00	Review of stipulation to cancel hearing on XYZ's motion to lift automatic stay.
			Totals	2.1	400.50	

Business Operations

Name	Type	Hourly Rate	Date	Hours	Total Amt.	Description
Harrison B.	P	305.00	4/1/92	1.5	457.50	Review Form 10-Q.
Polk J.	P	285.00	4/2/92	1.2	342.00	Meet with Debtor regarding next Board Meeting.
Pierce F.	PL	80.00	4/3/92	2.5	200.00	Review and summarize schedules and all contracts attached as exhibits to the real estate briefs.
Polk J.	P	285.00	4/4/92	1.0	285.00	Attend Board of Directors meeting.
			Totals:	6.2	1,284.50	

EXAMPLE 2

HARRISON & POLK
PROFESSIONAL ACTIVITY SUMMARY

XYZ Stay Litigation

Name	Rate	Hours	Amount
Partner			
Harrison B.	305.00	.5	152.50
Associate			
Arthur C.	155.00	1.6	248.00
Matter Totals:		2.1	400.50

Business Operations

Name	Rate	Hours	Amount
Partner			
Harrison B.	305.00	1.5	457.50
Polk J.	285.00	2.2	627.00
Paralegal			
Pierce F.	80.00	2.5	200.00
Matter Totals:		6.2	1,284.50

EXAMPLE 3

HARRISON & POLK
MONTHLY SUMMARY OF FEES

MATTER	APRIL	MAY	JUNE	TOTAL
XYZ Stay Litigation	400.50	587.00	939.00	1,926.50
Business Operations	1,284.50	2,642.00	727.00	4,653.50
Fee/Employment Applications	583.50	475.00	0	1,058.50
Case Administration	1,397.00	1,959.00	942.00	4,298.00
TOTAL FEES	3,665.50	5,663.00	2,608.00	11,936.50

EXAMPLE 4

HARRISON & POLK
EXPENSE AND DISBURSEMENT SUMMARY

EXPENSE CATEGORY	APRIL	MAY	JUNE	TOTAL
Litigation Support	30.00	20.00	35.00	85.00
Computer Legal Research	50.00	35.00	25.00	110.00
Outside Reproduction	20.00	0	40.00	60.00
TOTAL	100.00	55.00	100.00	255.00

EXAMPLE 5

BIOGRAPHICAL INFORMATION
HARRISON & POLK

PARTNERS

Benjamin Harrison

Mr. Harrison has extensive experience in the area of land acquisition as well as special expertise in antitrust law. In addition to his distinguished military service as a Colonel in the 70th Indiana Volunteers and as a Brevet Brigadier General he served as Commissioner for the Court of Claims; City Attorney; State Supreme Court Reporter and a Member of the U.S. Senate. Mr. Harrison was educated at Farmer's College and received his degree at Miami University.

James K. Polk

Mr. Polk received his degree from the University of North Carolina. He has overseen some major acquisitions and has a special emphasis on international property disputes. Mr. Polk has had a distinguished political career, having served as a Member of the Tennessee Legislature, a U. S. Representative, Speaker of the House of Representatives and Governor of Tennessee.

ASSOCIATE

Chester A. Arthur

Mr. Arthur is a corporate associate who graduated with honors from Union College of Schenectady. He has specialized experience relating to import-export duties having served as Collector of Customs for the Port of New York.

PARALEGAL

Frank Pierce

Specializes in civil litigation.
Graduate of Bowdoin College.

EXAMPLE 6

Declaration of Benjamin Harrison

1. I, Benjamin Harrison, am an attorney at law licensed in the State of California and admitted to practice in the Central District of California. I am the designated professional responsible for overseeing the billing in this matter and for assuring compliance with the Guidelines of the United States Trustee relating to billing. I have personal knowledge of the facts set forth herein, and if called upon to do so, could and would competently testify to those facts.

2. The fee application submitted by Harrison & Polk for the time period from April through June 1992 complies with United States Trustee Guidelines A and B except as specifically noted and justified in the application.

3. As a result of discussions with the client, the total bill for this time period was reduced by $150.00.

I declare under penalty of perjury that the foregoing is true and correct.

Executed on: _____

Benjamin Harrison

LAW OFFICES OF JANETTE ANDERSON
Janette Anderson, Esq.
420 West Roosevelt Road
Phoenix, Arizona 85003
(602) 253-7300
(602) 253-0033 Facsimile

Attorneys for Debtor

IN THE UNITED STATES BANKRUPTCY COURT
FOR THE DISTRICT OF ARIZONA

In re   )
)
)
)
)   NOTICE OF HEARING ON
)   DEBTOR'S OBJECTION TO
)   PROOF OF CLAIM OF
            Debtor.   )   BY
_____   )

    NOTICE is HEREBY GIVEN that a hearing will be held on Debtor's
objection to Proof of Claim of _____, _____., on the _____
day of _____, 1995, at _____ a.m./p.m., in the Bankruptcy
Court located at 2929 North Central Avenue, 10th Floor, Courtroom #4,
Phoenix, Arizona, which states as follows:
    The claims raised by _____ Proof of Claim have all been
previously adjudicated in Maricopa County Superior Court, Civil
Action Number _____, and us such, such claims are barred by
operation of law.
    Any person opposing the Debtor's Objection to Proof of Claim of
_____, shall file a written objection with the U.S.
Bankruptcy Court, P.O. Box 34151, Phoenix, Arizona 85067 and a copy
served upon Debtor's attorneys in care of _____, 420 West
Roosevelt, Phoenix, Arizona 85003., no later than _____ days prior to
the hearing.

Debtor shall immediately serve a Copy of this Notice of Hearing upon all parties-in-interest in this matter.

DATED this _____ day of _____, 1995.

U.S. BANKRUPTCY COURT

_____
By Deputy Clerk

ROBERT MOTHERSHEAD, P.C.
Attorneys at Law
420 West Roosevelt
Phoenix, Arizona 85003
(602) 253-7300
(602) 253-0033 - Facsimile
Mothershead, State Bar No. 005480
Attorneys for Debtor

IN THE UNITED STATES BANKRUPTCY COURT
FOR THE DISTRICT OF ARIZONA

In re   )   Chapter 11 Proceedings
)
)   No. 95-00459-PHX-RTB
)
)   **AFFIDAVIT OF MAILING**
                  Debtor.   )
_____)

    I am authorized to make this Affidavit on behalf of the Debtor, as an employee of Debtor's attorney, Robert Mothershead, am over the age of 18 years, and am otherwise competent to testify to the fact stated herein. I make this Affidavit as <u>prima facie</u> evidence that I personally mailed the **ORDER AND NOTICE OF TIME WITHIN WHICH TO FILE PROOFS OF CLAIM AND FOR HEARING ON DISCLOSURE STATEMENT,** a copy of which is attached, by first class mail, postage prepaid on this 18th day of September, 1995 to the following parties listed on Exhibit "A" attached herein:
    I have read the foregoing document and know of my own knowledge that the facts stated therein are true and correct.

_____
Affiant

    SUBSCRIBED AND SWORN to before me this _____ day of September, 1995.

_____
Notary Public

My Commission Expires:

_____

13 *Bankruptcy Procedure and Discovery*

What is the form to request employment of a professional by a debtor? What about a request to abandon property? What about a request that a debt be nondischargeable? Who is suppose to find out about these requests? How is that accomplished? What are the deadlines for opposition to these requests?

A bankruptcy paralegal is expected to know the form and procedure to file any of the dozens of documents filed in bankruptcy. Also, a paralegal's duties include providing appropriate notice to the correct parties. Finally, a paralegal must recognize the deadlines imposed in bankruptcy cases to ensure the rights of the client are preserved.

INTRODUCTION

This chapter will generally discuss the time limits imposed in bankruptcy and the notice provisions of the Federal Rules of Bankruptcy Procedure and the Bankruptcy Code. Further, the types of documents and pleadings that must be filed to accomplish commonly requested relief under the Bankruptcy Code will be covered, along with the applicable notice requirements of such requests. Finally, the basic discovery rules and procedure within a bankruptcy proceeding will be addressed.

The Federal Rules of Bankruptcy Procedure (F.R.Bankr.P.) were promulgated by the Supreme Court of the United States and govern bankruptcy procedure nationwide. However, Rule 9029 of F.R.Bankr.P. allows Bankruptcy Courts to adopt local rules to the extent that they are not inconsistent with the Federal Bankruptcy Rules. Accordingly, most Courts have adopted rules that will further govern the procedure specific to such Court's cases. Therefore, it is imperative that the legal assistant obtain a copy of such local rules and ensure that all procedures are in full compliance.

BANKRUPTCY PROCEDURE

Various types of documents are filed in bankruptcy and are given different names. The following addresses the different types of documents and when they are needed.

Petition

The document initiating proceedings under the Bankruptcy Code is called the "petition." No other document or pleading in bankruptcy is termed a petition in order to avoid confusion. For example, when in state or District Court a "petition for allowance of fees" would be filed, in bankruptcy such a request is called an "application."

Motions

As a general rule, a request for an order, except when an application is authorized by the F.R.Bankr.P., shall be by written "motion," unless made during a hearing. [F.R.Bankr.P. 9013.] A copy of the motion must be served upon the trustee, United States Trustee, debtor (or debtor-in-possession), as well as those persons articulated in the specific rules. However, if the F.R.Bankr.P. or local rules do not indicate who receives service, then service shall be made on the persons specified by the Bankruptcy Court. [*Id.*] In essence, Rule 9013 governs the procedure when there is no entity against whom relief is sought.

Applications

Further, the F.R.Bankr.P. and/or Code provide for a few limited instances where a request for a court order must be made by application. For example, applications to employ professionals [Rule 2014], applications for compensation and reimbursement of expenses [Rule 2016], application for permission to pay filing fee in installments [Rule 1006(b)(1)], application for appointment of creditors' committee organized before order for relief [Rule 2007(a)], application for entry of final decree on consummation of a Chapter 11 plan [Rule 2015(a)(6)], application for removal [Rule 9027(a)], and application to shorten the period of notice [Rule 9006(d)] are all made via application instead of motions. The difference between a motion and an application is that an application does not usually involve an adverse party but does require some judicial consideration, the application of statute or rule, and a resulting action. Therefore, these types of requests require none of the formalities and safeguards of notices and hearings that are characteristic of civil litigation.

Additionally, applications do not need to be served upon someone unless the Court directs. As a practical matter, most local rules require that applications be served upon at least the U.S. Trustee's Office.

Contested Matters

Request for an order in a contested matter is made by a motion served on the parties against whom relief is sought. An opportunity for hearing is offered. Unless the Court orders otherwise, no response to a motion needs to be filed under Rule 9014. However, failure to respond could result in the request being granted. Certain types of litigation, for example, stay litigation [Rule 4001(a)], are not treated as adversary proceedings but are considered contested matter proceedings from the beginning. Examples of such contested matters are dismissal or conversion [Rule 1017(d)], objection to confirmation [Rule 3020(b)(1)], relief from stay [Rule 4001(a)], avoiding a lien on exempt property [Rule 4003(d)], and the assumption, rejection, or assignment of executory contracts [Rule 6006(a)].

The key issue in a contested matter proceeding is that the motion must be served in the manner provided for the service of a summons and complaint by Rule 7004. Additionally, other specific rules that are generally applicable only to adversary proceedings apply to contested matters [i.e., F.R.Bankr.P. 7021, 7025, 7026, 7028-37 (discovery rules), 7041, 7042, 7052, 7054-56, 7062, 7064, 7069, and 7071].

Further, contested matters may require a "double caption." That is, the caption appears as the general administrative case and directly below the caption is another caption indicating the "movant" and the "respondent" and reading *Contested Matter "XYZ"*[1] below the bankruptcy case number.

Adversary Matters

A request to obtain certain types of orders must be made by initiating an adversary proceeding. Adversary proceedings are analogous to a civil lawsuit in

District Court. Adversary proceedings are commenced by filing a complaint, a filing fee, and a summons. The summons must thereafter be served on the defendants. The following matters must be filed as adversary proceedings under F.R.Bankr.P. 7001:

1. To recover money or property (except a proceeding to compel the debtor to deliver property to the trustee or a proceeding to abandon property or the trustee's disposition of property under 11 U.S.C. Section 725, i.e., estate property returned to secured creditor).
2. To determine the validity, priority, or extent of a lien or other interest in property [other than a proceeding by debtor to avoid a lien on exempt property under 11 U.S.C. Section 522(f)].
3. To obtain approval for the sale of the interest of the estate and a co-owner in property.
4. To object to or revoke a discharge.
5. To revoke an order of confirmation of a Chapter 11, Chapter 12, or Chapter 13 plan.
6. To determine the dischargeability of a debt.
7. To obtain an injunction or other equitable relief.
8. To subordinate any allowed claim or interest, except subordination through a plan.
9. To obtain a declaratory judgment regarding any of the preceding entries.
10. To determine a claim or cause of action removed to Bankruptcy Court.

Adversaries are, in essence, mini-lawsuits within a bankruptcy case. An adversary contains a double caption. The party bringing the adversary is the *plaintiff* and the adverse party is the *defendant*. Adversaries are assigned "adversary numbers" by the bankruptcy clerk. These adversary numbers should be indicated below the actual bankruptcy case number in the caption.

Further, all the F.R.Bankr.P. under Part VII (i.e., Rules 7001–7087) apply to adversaries. These rules govern the procedural aspects of litigation, including most of the discovery provisions of bankruptcy that are applicable to adversary proceedings. For the most part the rules of adversary proceedings either incorporate or are adaptations of most of the Federal Rules of Civil Procedure.

Proof of Claim/Proof of Interest

In a category of its own is a "proof of claim." This document is filed by a creditor to assert the amount of money owed by the debtor as well as the status of the claim, such as secured, priority, or unsecured. Likewise, a "proof of interest" is filed by equity security holders (i.e., stockholders) to assert the number of shares held as well as the type of shares (i.e., common or preferred).

Objections

The F.R.Bankr.P. provide that a party protesting a particular request or course of action do so by filing an "objection." *Objections* are within the main administrative case (i.e., not contested or adversary matters). Examples are "Objection to Confirmation of Chapter 13 Plan" or "Objection to Debtor's Motion to Compel Trustee to Abandon Property."

Notice

One of the primary and crucial tasks assigned to a legal assistant is to ensure that proper notice is provided to all parties who must be noticed, with sufficient time to respond. Who is required to receive notice and how much time they are given to respond are governed by the F.R.Bankr.P., local rules, or by the Bankruptcy Court. Additionally, proof of the notice must be filed with the Bankruptcy Court. These notice requirements are commonly called "noticing."

In particular matters only one or a few persons must be noticed of a proposed request or course of action. However, in other situations every party in the bankruptcy case must be noticed, including the debtor, creditors, trustees, U.S. Trustee, all parties in interest, all parties who make a notice of appearance, and all parties' attorneys. As one can imagine, noticing may be onerous at times.

Notices may take many forms, but two types of notices are particularly common. One of these routine notices is the "notice of hearing" of a particular request, which articulates the date, time, and location of the hearing, declares the nature of the request sought, and states the deadlines to file objections. A sample of a notice of hearing is shown in Figure 13-1.

The other type of notice is sometimes called *negative notice*, or *bar notice*. In these cases no actual hearing is set unless a party objects to the request sought. These notices must include the details of the request sought and the objection deadline. A sample of a negative notice of hearing is shown in Figure 13-2. If no objection is filed by the deadline, the party requesting the proposed conduct may file a *certificate of no objection*. The certificate of no objection states the date of the notice and declares that no objections had been filed by the deadline. Usually, the requesting party will file the certificate of no objection along with a proposed form of order for the judge to enter. If an objection is filed in a negative notice matter, the court will set a hearing in due course. Local rules will govern who is then responsible for the noticing.

OFFICES OF JANETTE ANDERSON
Janette Anderson, Esq.
420 West Roosevelt Road
Phoenix, Arizona 85003
(602) 253-7300
(602) 253-0033 Facsimile

Attorneys for Debtor

IN THE UNITED STATES BANKRUPTCY COURT
FOR THE DISTRICT OF ARIZONA

In re:	)	Chapter 11 Proceedings
	)	
	)	Bk No. PHX-GBN
	)	
	)	NOTICE OF HEARING ON
	)	DEBTOR'S OBJECTION TO
	)	PROOF OF CLAIM OF
Debtor.	)	BY
	)	

NOTICE IS HEREBY GIVEN that a hearing will be held on Debtor's objection to Proof of Claim of _____, _____., on the _____ day of _____, 1995, at _____ a.m./p.m., in the Bankruptcy Court located at 2929 North Central Avenue, 10th Floor, Courtroom #4, Phoenix, Arizona, which states as follows:

The claims raised by _____ Proof of Claim have all been previously adjudicated in Maricopa County Superior Court, Civil Action Number _____ and as such, such claims are barred by operation of law.

Any person opposing the Debtor's objection to Proof of Claim of _____, shall file a written objection with the <u>U.S. Bankruptcy Court, P.O. Box 34151, Phoenix, Arizona 85067</u> and a copy served upon Debtor's attorneys in care of _____, <u>420 West Roosevelt, Phoenix, Arizona 85003</u>, no later than _____ days prior to the hearing,

Debtor shall immediately serve a copy of this Notice of Hearing upon all parties-in-interest in this matter.

DATED this _____ day of _____, 1995.

U.S. BANKRUPTCY COURT

_____
By Deputy Clerk

FIGURE 13-1. Notice of Hearing.

ROBERT MOTHERSHEAD, P.C.
420 West Roosevelt Phoenix, Arizona 85003
(602) 253-7300
(602) 253-0033 Facsimile
Mothershead, State Bar No. 005480

Attorney for Debtors/Plaintiffs

IN THE UNITED STATES BANKRUPTCY COURT
FOR THE DISTRICT OF ARIZONA

In re:	Chapter 7 Proceeding
EUGENE A. MAYFIELD and DORIS J. MAYFIELD,	Bk. No. 91-09155-PHX-RTB
	Adv. No. 94-0099-PHX-RTB
Debtors.	NOTICE OF FILING OF MOTION FOR APPLICATION FOR ENLARGEMENT OF TIME PURSUANT TO RULE 9006 WITHIN WHICH TO FILE A NOTICE
EUGENE A. MAYFIELD and DORIS J. MAYFIELD,	AND APPLICATION OF REMOVAL PURSUANT TO RULE 9027
Plaintiffs, v.	
RUSSELL. D. ROBINSON,	
Defendant.	

Notice is hereby given that a Motion for Application for Enlargement of Time Pursuant to Rule 9006 Within Which to File a Notice and Application of Removal Pursuant to Rule 9027, has been filed by Eugene A. and Doris J. Mayfield in the above-referenced case, for reasons outlined as follows:

Debtors filed Chapter 7 on August 5, 1991. Defendant, Russell Robinson, filed a State court action on or about March 16, 1992 against Debtors based upon a personal guarantee of Debtors in regard to a contract breach action, in the Superior Court for the District of Arizona, Case No. CV 92-05039, (hereinafter "State Court Action"). Debtors answered such State court complaint asserting as a defense their discharge, entered December 10, 1991, in this case. Thereafter, Debtors filed this adversary complaint to determine the dischargeability of their obligation to Defendant herein. Meanwhile, the State court action has proceeded and is still pending against Debtors. Removal of the State court action is appropriate pursuant to 28 U.S.C. 1334 and 1452(a) since the action is a civil action (breach of contract/guarantee).

Enlargement may be granted upon a showing of excusable neglect. Here, Debtors excusable neglect was their lack of legal knowledge and lack of legal counsel in both the State court action as well as this pending adversary.

Any objection/response shall be in writing, filed with the Clerk of court and a copy served upon the movant's attorney, ROBERT MOTHERSHEAD, P.C., 420 West Roosevelt, Phoenix, Arizona 85003, on or before February 14, 1995.

If a party in interest timely objects to the motion and requests a hearing, the matter will be placed on the calendar to be heard by Judge Redfield T. Baum. Only those objecting and parties in interest will receive notice of the hearing on any objections.

DATED this _27_ day of January, 1995.

ROBERT MOTHERSHEAD, P.C.

By Robert Mothershead

FIGURE 13-2. Negative Notice.

As noted earlier, the Court is given significant authority to regulate notices. This authority, in conjunction with the F.R.Bankr.P. 9029 that allows the adoption of local rules for any bankruptcy district, makes the noticing requirements differ significantly from district to district. Accordingly, the importance of conforming to the local rules cannot be overly stressed to the legal assistant. Bankruptcy procedure discussed in this chapter in no way attempts to incorporate the many varieties of local rules throughout the nation.

The specific type of pleading or document along with the appropriate notice requirements under the Federal Rules or Code, if any, is now discussed for some of the more common pleadings and requests.

Motions

The following requests are made through motion practice. Unless otherwise specified, such motions need not include any double caption or contested matter designation, and they are included in the general administrative file of the bankruptcy case.

Abandonment

When a request to abandon property from the estate under Section 544 is made by someone *other than the trustee*, it is done by a *motion to compel trustee to abandon estate property.*[2] An opportunity for hearing (i.e., possibly negative notice) must be afforded. The notice of motion to compel trustee to abandon estate property must be given to all creditors, committees, the trustee, the U.S. Trustee, and all parties in interest. If a party objects within 15 days of the mailing of the notice, a hearing will be set in due course. [F.R.Bankr.P. 6007.]

Avoid Lien Under 11 U.S.C. Section 522(f) [on exempt property]

A request to avoid a lien on property that the debtor claims as exempt is made by a motion. A notice of motion to avoid lien on property pursuant to 11 U.S.C. Section 522(f) must be given to the party holding the lien and the debtor (if the debtor does not file the request). An opportunity for a hearing must be afforded. The amount of applicable time for the notice is as the Court directs (usually contained in local rules).

Relief from the Automatic Stay

Any request to modify, terminate, or annul the automatic stay (filed by a creditor) is made by a *motion for relief from the automatic stay.* This motion usually contains a double caption as well as a "Contested Matter [ABC]" designation (the contested matter letter is assigned by the Clerk of the Court). A notice of the motion must be given to at least the debtor and trustee (check local rules to ascertain if junior lienholders and/or the top 20 unsecured creditors and/or any official committee must also be noticed). An opportunity for hearing must be afforded. Less than 30 days is required for notice on any hearing since otherwise the stay is automatically terminated under Section 362(e). [F.R.Bankr.P. 4001(a), 9014.] Check local rules for noticing deadlines.

Set Bar Date for Proofs of Claim

A *motion to set bar dates within which to file proofs of claim* is usually made by the debtor in Chapter 11 cases. [F.R.Bankr.P. 2002(f)(3).] No opportunity for a hearing on this motion is necessary. Once granted, the "order setting bar dates for proofs of claim" (usually a proposed form of order is submitted with the motion) must be sent to all parties on the master mailing list. Twenty days' notice of the bar date is necessary. [F.R.Bankr.P. 2002(a)(8).]

Approve Settlement

A *motion to approve compromise or settlement* is generally filed by any party to the settlement. An opportunity for hearing must be afforded to the debtor, trustee, all creditors and all parties in interest. [F.R.Bankr.P. 2002(a)] Twenty days' notice of the notice of motion to approve compromise (or settlement) must be given.

Request to Assume or Reject Executory Contract or Unexpired Lease

A *motion to assume (or reject) executory contract (or lease)* is usually filed by the debtor-in-possession or the trustee. An opportunity for hearing must be afforded to all parties to the contract or lease through a "notice of motion to assume (or reject) executory contract (or lease)." The amount of time necessary for the notice is as the Court directs or may be outlined in local rules. [F.R.Bankr.P. 6006.] Note: Some executory contracts and/or leases may be assumed or rejected through confirmation of a plan.[3]

Convert from Chapter 7

A *motion to convert to Chapter [11, 13, 12]* is usually filed by the debtor. [F.R.Bankr.P. 1017(d).] An opportunity for hearing must be afforded the debtor, trustee, creditors, and equity holders (if any) by a "notice of motion to convert to Chapter [11, 13, 12]." Twenty days' notice is required. [F.R.Bankr.P. 2002(a).] Check local rules for procedure when the debtor has absolute right to convert. The debtor has absolute right to convert from Chapter 7 to either Chapter 11 or 13 as long as the debtor is eligible and the case has not previously been converted. [11 U.S.C. Sections 706(a) and (d).] Therefore, some courts allow ex parte requests or the mere filing of a praecipe with the clerk.

Convert from Chapter 11

A *motion to convert to Chapter [7, 13, 12]* generally is filed by any creditor or the debtor. [F.R.Bankr.P. 1017(d).] An opportunity for hearing must be afforded the debtor, trustee, creditors, and equity holders (if any) by a "notice of motion to convert to Chapter [7, 13, 12]." Twenty days' notice is required. [F.R.Bankr.P. 2002(a).] Check local rules for procedure when the debtor has absolute right to convert. The debtor has absolute right to convert from Chapter 11 to Chapter 7 unless the debtor is not the debtor-in-possession, the case was originally commenced as an involuntary case under Chapter 11, or the case was previously converted to Chapter 11 other than at the debtor's request. [11 U.S.C. Section 1112(a).] Therefore, some courts allow ex parte requests or the mere filing of a praecipe with the clerk.

Convert from Chapter 13

A *motion to convert to Chapter [7, 11, 12]* generally is filed by any creditor or the debtor. [F.R.Bankr.P. 1017(d).] An opportunity for hearing must be afforded the debtor, trustee, and creditors by a "notice of motion to convert to Chapter [7, 11, 12]." Twenty days' notice is required. [F.R.Bankr.P. 2002(a).] Check local rules for procedure when the debtor has absolute right to convert. The debtor has absolute right to convert from Chapter 13 to Chapter 7 if the case has not previously been converted and the debtor is eligible for relief under the intended chapter. [11 U.S.C. Section 1307(a).] Therefore, some courts allow a debtor's ex parte request or the mere filing of a praecipe with the clerk.

Dismissal (Chapter 7, 11, or 13)

A *motion to dismiss* may be filed by any party in any of the chapters. Twenty days' notice is required. [F.R.Bankr.P. 2002(a)(5).] Check local rules for procedure for Chapter 13 when the debtor has absolute right to dismiss. [11 U.S.C. Section 1307.] In Chapter 13, some courts allow ex parte requests or the mere filing of a praecipe with the clerk.

Obtain Credit

A *motion to incur debt* or *motion to obtain credit* is usually filed by the debtor in reorganization cases. An opportunity for hearing must be afforded parties as the Court directs by a "notice of motion to incur debt [obtain credit]." Noticing deadlines are as the Court prescribes or may be found in local rules. [See 11 U.S.C. Section 364.]

Reopen Case

A *motion to reopen case* is usually filed by the debtor. An opportunity for hearing must be afforded to all parties as the Court directs (or according to local rules) via a "notice of motion to reopen case." [11 U.S.C. Section 350; F.R.Bankr.P. 5010.]

Appoint Examiner

In Chapter 11 cases, creditors usually file any *motion to appoint examiner.* An opportunity for hearing must be afforded to all parties as the Court directs (or according to local rules) via a "notice of motion to appoint examiner." [11 U.S.C. Section 1104(b).]

Reduction or Enlargement of Exclusivity Period to File Chapter 11 Plan.

A *motion to enlarge exclusive period within which debtor may file a plan* is filed by the debtor. Likewise, a *motion to reduce exclusive period within which debtor may file a plan* is usually filed by creditors. [11 U.S.C. Section 1121(d).] An opportunity for hearing must be afforded by a "notice of motion to enlarge [reduce] exclusive period within which debtor may file a plan" to all parties as the Court directs (or according to local rules), with noticing deadlines as the Court directs.

Redemption of Property.

A *motion for redemption of property* is filed by the Chapter 7 debtor. An opportunity for hearing must be afforded the parties and noticing deadlines are as the Court dictates (or according to local rules). [11 U.S.C. Section 722; F.R.Bankr.P. 6008.]

Stay Relief from Codebtor Stay (Chapter 13)

A *motion for relief from the codebtor stay* is filed by a creditor. This generally requires a double caption along with the contested matter designation. An opportunity for hearing must be given through "notice of motion for relief from the codebtor stay" to the parties against whom relief is sought, namely the debtor, the trustee, and the codebtor. Unless the debtor or the codebtor files a response within 20 days of the motion, the codebtor stay automatically lapses. [See 11 U.S.C. Section 1301(d); F.R.Bankr.P. 4001.]

Appoint Trustee in Chapter 11 Case

A *motion to appoint a trustee* is usually filed by creditors. An opportunity for hearing, via a "notice of motion to appoint a trustee," must be given to the parties as the Court directs with noticing deadlines as the Court directs (or as governed by local rules). [See 11 U.S.C. Section 1104; F.R.Bankr.P. 9013.]

Applications

Instead of motions, some of the Rules and/or Code sections require certain requests to be made by application. Certain applications must be noticed to particular parties while others need not be noticed whatsoever.

Compensation of Professionals

An *application for interim [or final] compensation for services and reimbursement of expenses* is filed by the party the professional represents (i.e., creditors' committee will file application for the creditors' committee accountant; debtor will file application for debtor's attorney). The debtor, trustee, and all creditors must be noticed via "notice of application for compensation for services and reimbursement of expenses" with at least 20 days' notice. [11 U.S.C. Section 331; F.R.Bankr.P. 2016, 2002(a)(7).]

Employment of Professionals

An *application for authorization to employ [professional (such as attorney, accountant, special counsel, etc.)] for [party whom professional represents (such as debtor, official creditors' committee, etc.)]* is filed ex parte and no opportunity for hearing must be afforded. [11 U.S.C. Section 327; 1103; F.R.Bankr.P. 2014.]

Complaints

The following requests for relief are "adversary matters" and are initiated by the filing of a complaint, adversary filing fee ($120), and adversary cover sheet. A summons also must be issued for each defendant to the adversary. Service of the summons and complaint may be made by a personal service or by first class mail. [F.R.Bankr.P. 7004(a) and (b).] The summons must be served within 10 days of the issuance. [F.R.Bankr.P. 7004(f).]

The form of complaints (and all other pleadings within the adversary) always has double captions and always has an adversary number (assigned by the Clerk of the Court upon filing of the complaint), which must be included in conjunction with the actual bankruptcy case number.

If the complaint is duly served, the defendant has 30 days after the issuance of the summons within which to file an "answer" (or 35 days if the United States is a defendant).

The following are some of the more common complaints filed as adversary proceedings:

Avoidance of lien [under Section 506].

Avoidance of transfer [under Section 544, the trustee's "strong-arm clause"].

Avoidance of statutory lien [under Section 545].

Avoidance of preference [under Section 547(b)].

Avoidance of fraudulent transfer [under Section 548].

Avoidance of postpetition transfer [under Section 549].

Avoidance under Section 550 [transferee's liability].

Complaint objecting to discharge in Chapter 7 or Chapter 11 [Section 727 or 1141; F.R.Bankr. P. 4004, 4005].

Complaint seeking an exception to discharge [Section 523; F.R.Bankr.P. 4007; 2002(f)(6)].

DISCOVERY IN BANKRUPTCY

Discovery in bankruptcy is necessary in virtually all adversary matters and is appropriate in most contested matters. The formal discovery techniques in bankruptcy are basically identical to those in federal District Court. Further, bankruptcy provides certain other avenues for more informal discovery, such as the 341 First Creditors' Meeting.

For example, if a trustee has brought a complaint to void a fraudulent transfer, it would be very difficult to prove each element without the deposition of the debtor or transferee, or interrogatories regarding the event, etc. Also, if a creditor brings a nondischargeability complaint [Section 523] based on fraud, it will undoubtedly be beneficial to find out all the debtor's witnesses from the Rule 26 disclosure statement. Finally, in stay relief matters, each party's asserted value of the property is generally the focus. Accordingly, the identity and qualifications of the appraisers is necessary information in order to prevail at the final hearing.

Therefore, what follows is a discussion of the commonly used (and sometimes necessary) discovery devices in bankruptcy along with appropriate response dates. The penalty for failure to abide by the discovery rules of bankruptcy is covered also.

341 First Creditors' Meeting

This is generally the first opportunity to question the debtor regarding certain transactions (the whereabouts of missing property, questions regarding the statements and schedules such as values for certain exemptions, etc.) or the debtor's intentions (whether he intends to reaffirm, when a plan will be filed, etc.). Along with the statements and schedules filed, this may lead to further discoverable matters. The 341 First Creditors' Meeting is recorded (usually electronically) and the record is kept by the U.S. Trustee's Office for 2 years.

2004 Debtor's Examination (Rule 2004)

A "2004 debtor's exam" may actually be an examination of *any entity*. However, the scope of the examination must relate only to the acts, conduct, or property or to the liabilities and financial condition of the debtor, or to any matter that may affect the administration of the debtor's estate or the debtor's right to a discharge. Nonparties may be subpoenaed for attendance at a 2004 examination (witness fees and mileage costs must be provided for nonparties).

Depositions (Rule 7030)

Depositions are oral testimony given by parties to an action as well as by nonparties (witnesses may be compelled to attend a deposition through a subpoena). F.R.Bankr.P. 7030 incorporates F.R.Civ.P. 30 in its entirety. Leave from the Court must be granted for taking more than ten depositions by any of the parties or if the party to be deposed has already had a deposition taken.

A notice in writing of the deposition must be provided to the party deposed and include the time, date, and location of the deposition as well as the name and address of each person to be examined. A party to the action may also be required to produce documents in conjunction with the deposition as long as it is in compliance with F.R.Bankr.P. 34. If a subpoena duces tecum is to be served on the person to be examined, a list of the materials to be produced must be included.

Depositions may be in front of a court reporter, may be taken electronically, or even may be made telephonically (if the parties agree).

Interrogatories (Rule 7033)

Interrogatories are basically written questions seeking specific detailed information. F.R.Bankr.P. 7033 incorporates F.R.Civ.P. 33 in its entirety. Interrogatories may be served upon parties to an adversary, and they must be answered (or objected to) within 30 days from the date of service. Also, the answers must be signed under oath by the person making the answers. Any more than 25 interrogatories (including all subparts) will require leave of the Court.

Request for Production (Rule 7034)

A request for any party to produce documents (writings, bank account statements, contracts, etc.) must be in writing, and it must set forth the specific item to be produced or general categories (i.e., "any and all bank account statements from 1993 to present"). The response is due 30 days from the date the request for production is served. Even a person who is not a party may be compelled to produce documents via a subpoena.

Discovery Disclosure Statement (Rule 7026)

F.R.Bankr.P. 7026 incorporates F.R.Civ.P. 26 in its entirety. A new provision under Rule 26 requires initial disclosure be exchanged between all parties to an action of virtually all witnesses, documents, damages, and expert witnesses. This information must be disclosed in what is commonly referred to as the *Rule 26 disclosure statement* (not to be confused with the Chapter 11 disclosure statement regarding a plan of reorganization). The Rule 26 disclosure statement must be in writing and is due relatively quickly after the answer is filed (40 days). Further, the disclosure statement must be updated on a regular basis (usually every 30 days) to include new information obtained through discovery or otherwise. Rule 26 states that the disclosure statement must be filed with the Court; however, most local rules waive this requirement. [See F.R.Civ.P. 26(a)(4).]

Further, the Rule 26 disclosure statement must be given to the other party notwithstanding any excuses, such as that an investigation is incomplete or the other party's disclosure statement is feeble or has not been made at all. [Rule 26(a)(1).]

Discovery Disputes

Any party who fails to make discovery is subject to sanctions. F.R.Bankr.P. 7037 incorporates F.R.Civ.P. 37 in its entirety. When a party does not comply with discovery requests, then the discovering party may make a *motion for order to compel*. The motion is appropriate whether the discovery request is the Rule 26 disclosure statement, depositions, interrogatories, etc. Note: Evasive or incomplete responses are treated as failures to respond. If the Court grants the motion to compel or if the discovery is made after the motion to compel has been filed, the Court can grant the requesting parties their attorney's fees in bringing the motion to compel.

If the order compelling discovery is entered and the party *still* fails to make the requested discovery, the Court may grant sanctions against that party. Sanctions may range from taking the facts as true (if questions are not answered), refusing to allow the party to introduce certain matters into evidence, striking out that party's pleadings, or even entering a default judgment against that party. [Rule 37(b)(1).]

Accordingly, the penalty for failure to comply with a discovery request can be not only costly (having to pay the other side's attorney's fees) but can result in losing the case entirely.

REVIEW QUESTIONS

1. What is the difference between a contested matter and an adversary proceeding?
2. What requests can be accomplished through an application?
3. When is it necessary to file an adversary?
4. When is it necessary to file a contested matter?
5. What are some informal discovery techniques unique to bankruptcy?
6. What types of discovery techniques parallel the F.R.Civ. P.?

ENDNOTES

[1]The Bankruptcy Clerk will assign a letter for contested matters (usually beginning with A and progressing serially, sometimes as far as MMMM, for example.)

[2]A trustee's request to abandon property is accomplished through a notice.

[3]See Chapters 11 and 12, "Chapter 13 Practice" and "Chapter 11 Practice," for deadlines for particular commercial property leases and commercial personal property leases.

Glossary

abandonment. A formal process whereby property of the estate is removed from the estate after the bankruptcy is filed and is thereby no longer available for liquidation or distribution to creditors. [See 11 U.S.C. Section 541.]

adversary. A lawsuit within a bankruptcy case that must be initiated by filing and serving a summons and complaint upon the opponent and procedurally must parallel the bankruptcy rules of discovery. Adversary matters are assigned an adversary case number to be used in conjunction with the bankruptcy case number. Usually adversary matters include dischargeability complaints, preference, and fraudulent transfer complaints, etc.

application. A formal request filed within the administrative case such as to employ professionals, etc. No summons is required.

automatic stay. An injunction that prohibits certain creditor collection activity against both debtor and estate property, including repossession, garnishment, seizures, collection letters, etc. The automatic stay is imposed immediately upon the filing of the bankruptcy petition. [See 11 U.S.C. Section 362.]

ballots. Creditors of Chapter 11 cases must vote to accept or reject a proposed plan by filing a form with the Bankruptcy Court in a proscribed format.

Bankruptcy Act. Bankruptcy statutes that existed before the enactment of the Bankruptcy Code (prior to 1978) and that apply to all cases filed before the enactment of such Code.

Bankruptcy Appellate Panel (BAP). A court that hears appeals from Bankruptcy Court decisions. Each BAP court consists of three judges sitting simultaneously on the bench. Such BAP judges most often also serve primarily as lower court bankruptcy judges.

Bankruptcy Code. Title 11 of the United States Code including all current relevant bankruptcy statutes for all bankruptcy cases.

Bankruptcy Court. A federal court whose exclusive jurisdiction is bankruptcy cases. Bankruptcy Courts are the trial level courts of bankruptcy cases which means they hear evidence and make determinations based upon the evidence. Bankruptcy cases are automatically referred to the Bankruptcy Courts from the District Courts.

Bankruptcy Forms. Official forms for use in bankruptcy cases.

Bankruptcy Rules. F.R.Bankr.P. 1001 through 9035. Bankruptcy Rules govern procedure in bankruptcy cases such as certain deadlines and discovery procedures.

cash collateral. The funds generated by secured property such as rents, issue, or profits, which are also considered secured by the lending creditor through the underlying loan and security documents. Cash collateral may consist of rental amounts collected from nonparty tenants of apartment complexes, funds charged for hotel rooms, golf course greens fees, etc.

Chapter 7. Liquidation bankruptcy, also sometimes referred to as "straight" bankruptcy. All nonexempt assets of the debtor are collected and liquidated (sold) by the trustee and the funds are used to pay distributions to creditors.

Chapter 9. Municipality bankruptcy (such as Orange County, etc.).

Chapter 11. Business reorganization bankruptcy. However, debtors may be not only corporations and partnerships but also individuals. Chapter 11 debtors generally operate as debtors-in-possession, which equates to holding the same responsibilities to creditors as a trustee. Chapter 11 is one of the most complex, involved, and lengthy of the bankruptcy chapters, requiring disclosure statements and plans, ballots, monthly operating reports, etc.

Chapter 12. Family farmer reorganization bankruptcy. Specific criteria for eligibility purposes exist to be considered a "family farmer." Chapter 12 debtors are also required to file plans to repay their creditors over time and must file regular financial reports to disclose their income and expenses.

Chapter 13. Consumer reorganization bankruptcy. Only individuals (or husbands and wives) may file under Chapter 13. Business entities are excluded, except for sole proprietorships. Eligibility for Chapter 13 requires that debtors have regular disposable income to be contributed to the plan. Chapter 13 debtors must file plans to pay creditors over a period of three to five years from such extra income. A Chapter 13 trustee is appointed to collect the extra income from the debtors and make distributions to the creditors.

complaint. A formal initial document starting an adversary proceeding such as a preference action, nondischargeability action, etc. In essence, a complaint starts a lawsuit within a bankruptcy case. The adversary is assigned a separate adversary number in conjunction with the bankruptcy case number. Adversary complaints usually must be accompanied by a filing fee and appropriate cover sheet. Complaints must be accompanied by a summons and served in the appropriate manner under the F.R.Bankr.P.

confirmation. In reorganizational cases (Chapters 11, 13, and 12), the Bankruptcy Court's official approval of a plan via confirmation order.

contested matter. A proceeding within a bankruptcy case that is initiated by filing and serving a motion and notice upon appropriate parties. Contested matters follow a substantial number of the discovery rules associated with adversary matters. Usually contested matters include stay relief motions. [See F.R.Bankr.P. 9001.]

core matter. Bankruptcy judges may hear and make final determinations regarding all bankruptcy cases and all "core proceedings." However, "noncore" matters must be submitted to the District Court for final determination after the proposed findings and conclusions have been made by the Bankruptcy Court. [See 28 U.S.C. Section 157.]

creditor. The individual or entity to whom funds are owed. Creditors are generally prohibited from various collection activities against the debtor during the bankruptcy and are afforded certain rights, such as to file proofs of claim to assert the priority and amounts they are owed, seek relief from the automatic stay, object to dischargeability, object to plans in reorganizational cases, and cast votes in Chapter 11 cases.

cross-collateralized property. Supplementary real or personal property used to secure a loan in addition to the initially secured property purchased by the funds borrowed. Cross-collateralization allows the secured creditor to repossess or foreclose upon not only the initial property purchased but the additional property as well.

debtor. The individual or entity who has filed for bankruptcy (voluntarily) or against whom bankruptcy has been filed (involuntarily). Debtors owe the funds or obligations to creditors. "Debtor" is used in all the bankruptcy chapters (7, 9, 11, 13, 12) to describe the entity/individual to whom the automatic stay applies.

debtors' exam. A formal investigative procedure whereby a creditor or trustee serves a written request to appear in order to obtain information regarding the debtor's financial circumstances and transactions. Debtor's exams are also referred to as 2004 exams with a format much akin to a deposition, including a court reporter to record all questions and answers during the exam.

debts. Financial obligations owed to others such as taxes, balances owed on credit cards, mortgages, car loans, medical bills, etc.

deposition. A discovery technique that requires the physical appearance of the opponent and/or witnesses to answer questions under oath. Court reporters are often present to transcribe the questions and answers made during depositions or a deposition may be electronically recorded in special circumstances.

discharge. The elimination of the debtor's personal liability on obligations.

disclosure statement. In Chapter 11 cases the document that describes in detail the financial circumstances of the debtor as well as the proposed plan of reorganization. Disclosure statements are sent to all creditors and parties in interest once the Bankruptcy Court has determined the disclosure statement contains sufficient information. They are invariably lengthy, substantial documents.

disclosure statement (discovery). A written statement exchanged between parties to an adversary proceeding that discloses all information including inter alia theories of their cause of action or defense, proposed witnesses, expert witnesses, and exhibits.

discovery. In contested and adversary matters, the method through which factual information is obtained from the opponent or other nonparty sources.

dismissal. The expulsion of a case or adversary matter from the Bankruptcy Court, either voluntarily through stipulation of the parties or upon request of the debtor, or involuntarily such as when a case is filed in bad faith.

disposable income. The monthly amount of a debtor's income remaining after all reasonable monthly living expenses are deducted.

distribution. The amounts ultimately paid to the creditors through the bankruptcy.

District Court. Automatic reference of all bankruptcy cases to the Bankruptcy Court from the District Court. Parties may thereafter request the District Court to "withdraw the reference," which would allow the District Court to hear the bankruptcy case at the trial level. Otherwise, District Courts have jurisdiction to hear all appeals from the Bankruptcy Court. *See also* Bankruptcy Appellate Panel for appeals from the Bankruptcy Court.

estate. Generally, all property the debtor owns at the time of the filing of bankruptcy except property specifically excluded or claimed and approved as exempt. [See 11 U.S.C. Section 541.]

exclusion. Property in which the debtor holds a beneficial interest and which restricts the debtor's transfer of interest is not property of the estate and is excluded, such as a debtor's interest in a spendthrift trust or in an ERISA qualified plan.

executory contract. When a debtor has an ongoing contract with some portion of the contract remaining to be performed by both parties, the contract must be listed on the appropriate schedules and assumed or rejected within specific time periods. Executory contracts include shopping center leases, vehicle leases, equipment leases, etc. [See 11 U.S.C. Section 365(d)(4).]

exemption. Individual debtors may claim certain of their property free from bankruptcy proceeding liquidation and distribution. The Bankruptcy Code provides a specific listing of the nature and amount of such items that may be claimed exempt. For example, 11 U.S.C. Section 522(d)(2) allows up to $1,200 of equity in a vehicle. Additionally, certain states have "opted out" of federal exemptions and provide detailed itemization of exemptions that may be claimed. In the cases of such "opt out" states, the state law exemptions must be used rather than federal exemptions.

ex parte. A motion that requests the court to act upon a matter without notice to other parties in the case.

feasibility. Whether a plan will likely succeed based upon the financial information presented.

fiduciary. A party who acts on behalf of others. Trustees are fiduciaries of the estate and unsecured creditors. Unsecured creditors' committee members are fiduciaries among themselves as well as to all other unsecured creditors. The debtor-in-possession acts as a fiduciary of the estate.

First Creditors' Meeting. A meeting that must be attended by debtors in all chapters. Also referred to as the 341 Meeting, it is held with the trustee as the presiding officer in Chapter 7, 12, or 13 cases or the U.S. Trustee as the presiding officer in Chapter 11 cases. Debtors are questioned under oath as to the information within the statements and schedules filed with the Court, the appropriateness of the jurisdiction of that district, and, in reorganization cases, the status of the debtor's plan. All creditors of the bankruptcy case are notified of the date and time of the First Creditors' Meeting and may attend to question debtors regarding their financial circumstances, the circumstances regarding that creditor's specific obligation, or the debtor's intent to reaffirm, redeem, or surrender collateral.

fraudulent transfer. Money or property transferred from the debtor to another before the filing of the bankruptcy in order to stop creditors from receiving the property in bankruptcy. [See 11 U.S.C. Section 548.]

homestead. The exemption amount provided for a debtor's equity interest in his or her residence, for example, under 11 U.S.C. Section 522(d)(1), $7,500.

income and expense statement. A form filed with the Bankruptcy Court by the debtor stating in a prescribed format the monthly financial budget of the debtor.

interrogatories. A written discovery request that asks a set of questions of the opponent and requires answers in the form of "yes" or "no" as well as factual information such as dates, the identity of potential witnesses along with addresses, financial information such as bank account numbers, etc.

involuntary. Creditor-initiated Chapter 7 or Chapter 11 cases. It is necessary to have three creditors with aggregate debt of over $10,000 (or one creditor with aggregate debt of $10,000 if there are fewer than 12 creditors altogether).

master mailing list. Form filed with the Bankruptcy Court by the debtor that identifies in a prescribed format the identities and addresses of the debtor, creditors, trustee, U.S. Trustee's Office, and parties in interest.

monthly operating reports. Reports filed by the reorganizational debtor (i.e., Chapter 11 or Chapter 13 sole proprietor cases) with the Bankruptcy Court in a prescribed format that disclose the income and itemized expenses on a monthly basis.

motion. A formal request filed within the administrative case (same case number as the main bankruptcy). Motions include such matters as abandoning property, sanctions, assume/reject executory contracts, etc. No summons is required.

noncore matter. Bankruptcy judges may hear and make final determinations regarding all bankruptcy cases and all "core proceedings." However, "noncore" matters must be submitted to the District Court for final determination after proposed findings and conclusions have been made by the Bankruptcy Court. [See 28 U.S.C. Section 157.]

nondischargeable. Obligations or debts that remain owed by the debtor despite the filing of the bankruptcy.

notice. Written notification of a hearing or proposed event within the bankruptcy proceedings. Notices usually include a response/objection deadline and details of the particular event that is "noticed out" to parties.

oversecured creditor. The value of property upon which the creditor holds a lien is more than the amount of the secured debt.

petition. The initial form filed with the Bankruptcy Court by the debtor (in voluntary cases) or by unsecured creditors (in involuntary cases), which initiates the bankruptcy case. The petition identifies in a prescribed format relevant information regarding the identity and location of the debtor, the chapter under which the case is filed, the choice of venue, etc.

plan. In Chapter 13, 12, and 11 cases, the document that outlines the method of payment/distribution to creditors. Plans must be approved by the Court. In Chapter 11 cases, creditors must vote to accept or reject such plan.

preferential transfer. A payment made by the debtor to a creditor before filing bankruptcy for past-due debt. A trustee or debtor-in-possession may file an adversary complaint to force the paid creditor to return the payment to the estate. [See 11 U.S.C. Section 547.]

priority debt. These types of obligations get paid from the estate before unsecured debts and include such things as recent tax obligations, approved bankruptcy estate professional fees that occur after the petition, spousal support, etc.

professional. In reorganizational cases all professionals who are to be paid from estate funds, such as attorneys, accountants, property managers, auctioneers, etc., must seek approval for employment from the Bankruptcy Court and must disclose all potential conflicts of interest with the debtor.

proof of claim. The document filed by creditors with the Court that states the amount and priority of the debt owed the creditor by the debtor.

quarterly fees. Amounts owed to the U.S. Trustee's Office from the Chapter 11 estate for every period of three months or each portion thereof from the petition date through the confirmation date. The quarterly fee amount owed for each quarter is based upon the amount of funds the Chapter 11 estate expends each quarter and is considered an administrative expense.

reaffirmation agreement. An agreement between a debtor and a creditor where the debtor reobligates to pay amounts owed to the creditor notwithstanding the filing of the bankruptcy or any discharge. [See 11 U.S.C. Section 524.]

rescission. When a party later decides to not perform on a contract or agreement that was entered into. Right of rescission is allowed to Chapter 7 debtors in regard to reaffirmation agreements up to 60 days after the agreement is entered into or until discharge, whichever occurs later.

redemption. In Chapter 7 cases only, the debtor is allowed to pay secured creditors a "lump sum" that totals the value of the property upon which the secured creditor holds a lien.

request for admissions. A written discovery request that requires the opponent to admit or deny certain statements of fact and/or law.

request for production. A written discovery request that requires the production of documents or things, such as tax records, bank account records, payment records, trust documents, etc.

Schedule A. A form filed with the Bankruptcy Court by the debtor that lists in a prescribed format all the debtor's real property interests, such as residence, apartment complex holdings, time-share property, etc.

Schedule B. A form filed with the Bankruptcy Court by the debtor that lists in a prescribed format all the debtor's personal property interests, such as vehicles, appliances, bank accounts, jewelry, etc.

Schedule C. A form filed with the Bankruptcy Court by the debtor that states in a prescribed format the property debtor claims as exempt.

Schedule D. A form filed with the Bankruptcy Court by the debtor that states in a prescribed format the secured creditors of the estate.

Schedule E. A form filed with the Bankruptcy Court by the debtor that states in a prescribed format the priority of creditors of the estate.

Schedule F. A form filed with the Bankruptcy Court by the debtor that states in a prescribed format the unsecured creditors of the estate.

Schedule G. A form filed with the Bankruptcy Court by the debtor that states in a prescribed format the executory contracts of the debtor.

Schedule H. A form filed with the Bankruptcy Court by the debtor that states in a prescribed format the codebtors' claims of the estate.

secured collateral. Specific property that a debtor has agreed to allow a creditor to repossess or foreclose upon under state law should the debtor default on payments on a loan from the creditor, such as a vehicle under a motor vehicle sales contract or a residence under a deed of trust.

secured debt. An obligation owed by the debtor whereby the creditor may foreclose or repossess the underlying property under state law upon the default of debtor in the repayment of the debt.

statements and schedules. Required documents filed by the debtor with the Court that become public information. Such documents contain information regarding the debtor's assets (property), liabilities (debts), income and expenses, exemptions claimed, ongoing contract obligations, and financial transactions of the debtor including business transactions or holdings.

statement of financial affairs. A form filed with the Bankruptcy Court by the debtor that articulates in a prescribed format detailed financial transactions of the debtor.

stipulation. An agreement (usually ultimately reduced to writing) wherein the parties agree to certain facts or an entire agreement that resolves a disputed matter. Stipulations must be noticed in the appropriate manner (depending on the nature of the underlying dispute).

subpoena. A formal written command to make a physical appearance (usually at a deposition, court hearing, or trial, etc.).

subpoena duces tecum. A discovery request that requires either the opponent or a third-party witness to appear and produce documents or things.

surrender. The debtor voluntarily returns secured collateral to the lender.

trustee. A fiduciary appointed by the U.S. Trustee's Office to oversee all cases in Chapters 7, 12, 13, and sometimes Chapter 11 cases. The trustee's responsibilities in liquidation cases is to collect all nonexempt assets, liquidate those assets, determine whether preferential or fraudulent transfers have occurred, and file complaints in Bankruptcy Court to regain those funds transferred, investigate whether the debtor has committed any wrongdoing that would prohibit discharge or justify dismissal, analyze and object to improper proofs of claim filed by creditors, and ultimately make distributions to the allowed proofs of claim.

undersecured creditor. When the value of property upon which a creditor holds a lien is less than the amount of the secured debt owed to the creditor.

unsecured creditors' committee. The official committee appointed by the U.S. Trustee's Office consisting of the largest seven unsecured creditors, if willing to serve, to act as fiduciaries on behalf of all unsecured creditors of the estate. Official committees may employ counsel who is paid from estate assets. Duties are to investigate the debtor's financial affairs and oversee administration of the case.

unsecured debt. An obligation owed by the debtor wherein the only relief a creditor is entitled to outside bankruptcy is to file a state court law suit and obtain judgment. Under the Bankruptcy Code, unsecured debts are entitled to one of the lowest priorities, which means they get paid last if funds exist to that extent. Unsecured debts include personal loans, most credit card balances, medical bills, etc.

U.S. Trustee's Office. An administrative office of the executive branch of the government (not a division of the judiciary branch such as the Bankruptcy Court). The role of the U.S. Trustee's Office is to appoint and oversee all trustees in each bankruptcy case, and oversee administration of Chapter 11 cases in which the debtor is acting as debtor-in-possession. The U.S. Trustee often plays an active role in Chapter 11 cases, including requiring debtors to file with the Trustee's Office additional initial informational documentation or forms regarding the business operations and assets of the estate. The U.S. Trustee's Office may also make recommendations regarding dismissal, conversion, and confirmation of Chapter 11 cases.

voluntary. The debtor initiates the bankruptcy proceedings. Voluntary proceedings can be filed under any Chapter (i.e., 7, 11, 13, 12, or 9).

votes. Creditors of Chapter 11 cases may enter a vote by use of a ballot to accept or reject a proposed plan in order to effectuate or prevent confirmation of the plan. [See 11 U.S.C. Section 1126 for voting requirements.]

withdrawal of the reference. Upon the filing of a bankruptcy petition, the District Court automatically refers the case to the Bankruptcy Court to hear the case as the trial court. A party in interest may request that the District Court withdraw the automatic reference for sufficient cause and hear the bankruptcy case in part or in its entirety as the trial court. [See 28 U.S.C. Section 157(d).]

witness fee. The federal witness fee, under 28 U.S.C. Section 1821, is $40 per day plus mileage.

Index

Abandonment, 37-40, 265
  motion for, 410
  secured creditors, 37-38
  trustees, 38
Accounting/auditing, as activity
    code category, 394
Administrative dismissal, 179-83
  Chapter 13 Trustee's dismissals,
    182-83
  court dismissals, 180-82
  United States Trustee's Office dis-
    missals, 181-82
Adversary matters, 405-6
"After acquired property," 32
Alimony, as nondischargeable debt,
    157-59
Allowance of claim, 251-53
America West Airlines, Inc., 47
Applications, 404-5, 414
Appointment of trustee/interim
    trustee, chronological order,
    40
Asset analysis and recovery, as activ-
    ity code category, 392
Asset disposition, as activity code
    category, 393

Automatic stay, 118-53, 260
  actions prohibited by, 123-24
  codebtor stay, 146-48
  definition of, 119-20
  duration of, 125
  function of, 120-21
  Motion for Relief from Automatic
    Stay, 126-28, 410-11
  policy, 120-23
  purpose of, 120-21
  scope of, 121-23
  statutory exclusions from, 125-
    36
  stay relief, 137-45
    burden of proof, 145
    cause and lack of adequate pro-
      tection, 137-42
    expedited, 146
    lack of equity and inability to
      reorganize, 142-44
    single-asset real estate, 144-45
  stay relief motions, hearing on,
    145-46
  violations of, 148-49

Badges of fraud, 222

BAFJA, *See* Bankruptcy Amend-
    ments and Federal Judgeship
    Act of 1984 (BAFJA)
Bankruptcy, 1
  collective nature of, 2
  first legislation regarding, 9
  types of, 44
Bankruptcy Act (1898), 9-10
Bankruptcy Amendments and Fed-
    eral Judgeship Act of 1984
    (BAFJA), 10
Bankruptcy Appellate Panel (BAP),
    25
Bankruptcy case, infrastructure of,
    21-43
  Bankruptcy Code, 27-29
  Bankruptcy Court system, 24-25
  bankruptcy estate, 29-34
  parties, 21-24
Bankruptcy case law, precedent of,
    26-27
Bankruptcy chapters, 44-66
  Chapter 7, 38, 45-46, 256-82
  Chapter 9, 29, 44, 46
  Chapter 11, 29, 44, 47-48, 60-64,
    321-40

Bankruptcy chapters (*Cont.*)
  Chapter 12, 29, 44, 48
  Chapter 13, 29, 44, 49, 283-319
  comparison of, 60-64
  differences between, 60-64
  eligibility requirements, 49-59
  goal of, 60
Bankruptcy Code, 4-7, 10, 27-29
  bankruptcy rules, 8
  local rules, 8-9
  Official Bankruptcy Forms, 7
  substantial chapters of, 28-29
Bankruptcy Court, 1-2
  appeals from, 25
  bankruptcy judges, 25
  system, 24-25
Bankruptcy documentation, *See* Documentation
Bankruptcy estate, 29-34
  abandonment, 37-40
  estate property, categories of, 30-
    32
  exemptions, 35-37
Bankruptcy judges, 25
Bankruptcy law, 1
  goals in, 2-3
  history of, 7-10
  policy of, 2-3
  structure of, 1
Bankruptcy petition, 69-73, 404
  filing of, 1
Bankruptcy procedure, 403-15
  adversary matters, 405-6
  applications, 404-5, 414
  complaints, 414-15
  contested matters, 405
  motions, 404, 410-13
  notice, 407-10
  objections, 407
  petition, 404
  proof of claim/proof of interest,
    406-7
  See also Discovery
Bankruptcy proceedings (Chaps. 7
  and 13 cases), chronological
  events in, 40-41
Bankruptcy Reform Act (1978), 10
Bankruptcy Reform Act (1994), 10,
  13-20
  commercial bankruptcy issues
    (Title II), 16-18
  consumer bankruptcy issues (Title
    III), 18-19

governmental bankruptcy issues
  (Title IV), 19-20
  improved bankruptcy administra-
    tion (Title I), 14-16
Bar notice, 407
Barnes v. Whelan, 306
Beezley v. California Land Title Co.,
  169
Bereziak v. Bereziak, 158
Best interest test, 306
BFP v. Resolution Trust Corp., 223-25
Billing guidelines, 387-89
  general information, 387
  non-reimbursable expenses, 389
  professional fees, 388
  reimbursable expenses, 389
Bonnett v. National Bank of Petersburg,
  166
Business analysis, as activity code
  category, 394
Business operations, as activity code
  category, 393
Business reorganization, *See* Chapter
  11 bankruptcy
Butner v. U.S., 310

Case administration, as activity code
  category, 393
Cash collateral, 329
Certificate of no objection, 407
Chapter 1, Bankruptcy Code, 28
Chapter 3, Bankruptcy Code, 28
Chapter 5, Bankruptcy Code, 28
Chapter 7 bankruptcy, 38, 45-46, 256-
  82
  comparison of, 60-61
  deadline for complaints, chrono-
    logical order, 41
  debtor's rights, 260-73
    abandonment, 265
    automatic stay, 260
    avoidance of liens on exempt
      property, 260-61
    avoidance of transfers to protect
      exemptions, 261
    claim exemptions, 260
    discharge, 265-67
    freedom from discrimination,
      261-65
    reaffirmation, 267-68
    redemption, 268-71
    reopening case, 272-73
    Statement of Intent, 271-72

    surrender, 271
    timing/procedure (redemption),
      271
  debtor's role, 257-60
    duties of, 259
    eligibility of, 257
    schedules, 259-60
    voluntary vs. involuntary cases,
      257-59
  eligibility requirements, 49-50
  exempt property, 45
  general timeline for, 278-79
  practice, 256-82
  trustee, 273-77
    appointment of, 273
    avoiding powers of, 275-76
    compensation, 277
    disbursement, 276
    duties of, 274-75
    eligibility/qualifications of,
      273
    liability/indemnity, 277
    liquidation, 276
    powers of, 275
    role/capacity of, 273-74
Chapter 7 case closing, as activity
  code category, 394
Chapter 9 bankruptcy, 29, 44, 46
Chapter 11 bankruptcy, 29, 44, 47-
  48
  comparison of, 60-64
  confirmation process, 332-35
    Chapter 11 plan classification,
      335
    debtor's exclusivity periods, 47,
      332-33
    disclosure statement, 333-34
    voting/ballots, 335
  eligibility requirements, 50
  fee applications, 327-28
  Financial Reporting Requirements,
    349-65
  Notice of Requirements, 341-48
  parties, 321-32
    creditors, 328-30
    creditors' committees, 330-31
    debtor, 321-24
    debtor-in-possession (DIP), 324-
      27
    examiner, 331-32
    trustee, 331
  plan confirmation, 335-38
  practice, 320-40

Chapter 11 plan:
  classification, 335
  plan confirmation, 335-38
  reduction/enlargement of exclusivity period to file, motion for, 413
Chapter 12 bankruptcy, 29, 44, 48
  eligibility requirements, 55-59
Chapter 13 bankruptcy, 29, 44, 49, 283-319
  automatic stay, 286
  Chapter 13 plans, 293-312
  codebtor stay, 290-91
  comparison of, 60-61
  confirmation process, 293-312
  contingent claims, 285
  creditors, 289-90
  debtor status, 287
  discharge, 315-16
  disputed debt, 285
  eligibility requirements, 50-55
  fraudulent conveyances, 287
  nonliquidated obligations, 285
  parties, 283-93
  powers, 286-87
  practice, 283-319
  preferences, 287
  regular income requirement, 51, 284-85
  trustee, 287-89
Chapter 13 plans, 293-312
  defaults, 311
  elements of, 305-7
  formulation of, 312-13
  illustration of, 294-304
  modification of, 314
  payment of allowed postpetition claim, 311
  payment on claim with property of debtor/estate, 312
  payment on unsecured claims, 311
  permissive plan provisions, 307
  revocation of confirmation, 314
  types of, 293
Chapters, 44-66
  differences between, 60-64
  goal of, 60
Circuit Courts, 26-27
Claim exemptions, 260
Claim(s), 22, 241-42
  allowance of, 251-53
  definition of, 241-42

fraud, 162-67
  fully secured, 252
  oversecured, 252
  proofs of, filing, 250-51
  undersecured, 252
Claims administration and objections, as activity code category, 393
Closure of case, chronological order, 41
Codebtor stay, 146-48
  motion for relief from, 413
Compensation, trustee, 277
Composition plan, 293
Concealment offenses, 5
Confirmation process, 23
  Chapter 11 bankruptcy, 332-35
    Chapter 11 plan classification, 335
    debtor's exclusivity periods, 332-33
    disclosure statement, 333-34
    voting/ballots, 335
  Chapter 13 bankruptcy, 293-312
Consensual liens, 242
Consensual plan, 337
Consumer debts, 190, 269
  codebtor stay, 146-48
  definition of, 146
Consumer-related property, 269
Contested matters, 405
Conversion, 178-79, 195-96
  definition of, 178
  See also Dismissal
Corporate finance, as activity code category, 394
Court dismissals, 180-82
Creditor requested dismissal, 186-90
  Chapter 7, 186
  Chapter 11, 188-90
  Chapter 13, 187-88
Creditors, 1, 22, 241, 277-78
  offenses by, 5-6
  priority creditors, 244-47
  secured creditors, 242-44
  super superpriority creditors, 250
  superpriority creditors, 249-50
  unsecured creditors, 247-48
Creditors' committee, 23, 330-31

Data analysis, as activity code category, 394
Debtor, 1, 21-22

automatic stay, benefit to, 119-20
  surplus to, 249
  willful failure of, 185
Debtor-in-possession (DIP), 40, 181-82, 324-27
Debtor's rights, 260-73
  abandonment, 265
  automatic stay, 260
  avoidance of liens on exempt property, 260-61
  avoidance of transfers to protect exemptions, 261
  claim exemptions, 260
  discharge, 265-67
  freedom from discrimination, 261-65
  reaffirmation, 267-68
  redemption, 268-71
  reopening case, 272-73
  Statement of Intent, 271-72
  surrender, 271
  timing/procedure (redemption), 271
Debtor's role, 257-60
  duties of, 259
  eligibility of, 257
  schedules, 259-60
  voluntary vs. involuntary cases, 257-59
Debtor's Statement of Intention, 94, 96
Dewsnup v. Timm, 62-64
Discharge, 154-77, 265-67
  Chapter 7 bankruptcy, 265-67
  Chapter 13 bankruptcy, 315-16
  definition of, 154-55
  denial of, 155-56
  effect of, 173-74, 194-95
  nondischargeable debts, 156-70
  plaintiffs in nondischargeability actions, 170-72
  sanctions available to debtor, 173
  See also Nondischargeable debts
Discharge order, chronological order, 41
Disclosure of Compensation of Attorney for Debtor, 110-13
Disclosure statement, 321
Discovery, 415-19
  depositions (Rule 7030), 416
  discovery disclosure statement (Rule 7026), 417

Discovery (*Cont.*)
  discovery disputes, 417-18
  interrogatories (Rule 7033), 416
  request for production (Rule
    7034), 417
  341 First Creditor's meeting, 415-
    16
  2004 Debtor's Examination (Rule
    2004), 416
Dismissal, 178-95
  administrative dismissal, 179-83
  creditor requested dismissal, 186-
    90
  definition of, 178
  due to lack of eligibility, 184-86
  motion to dismiss, 412
  substantial abuse filing, 190-92
  voluntary, 192-94
    involuntary vs., 179
  See also Conversion
Disposable income, 51
Disputed debt, 285
District Courts, 24-27
Documentation:
  document preparation services,
    115-16
  initial, 67-117
DUI injuries, as nondischargeable
  debts, 162
Durrett v. Washington Nat. Ins. Co.,
  224

Eligibility requirements:
  Chapter 7 bankruptcy, 49-50
  Chapter 11 bankruptcy, 50
  Chapter 12 bankruptcy, 55-59
  Chapter 13 bankruptcy, 50-55
Emergency filing, 180, 322
Employees benefits/pensions, as ac-
  tivity code category, 393
Employment applications, 325-27
  facts to include in, 326
  sample, 367-79
  statement of disinterestedness, 327
  untimely, consequences of, 325-
    26
Employment guidelines (U.S.
  Trustee's Office), 380-402
  billing guidelines, 387-89
    general information, 387
    non-reimbursable expenses, 389
    professional fees, 388
    reimbursable expenses, 389

form of application/procedures
  for submission, 382
general information required, 380-
  81
professional fees/expenses, 390-
  402
  activity code categories, 392-94
  billing format—expenses, 392
  billing format—professional
    fees, 391-92
  example statements, 395-99
  general information required,
    390-91
retainers, 383-86
  accounting for services covered
    by, 383-84
  general information, 383
  Professional Fee Statement, 383,
    385-86
Enabling loans, 216
Equity, 142
Equity security holders, 23
Estate property, categories of, 30-32
Examiner, 23, 331-32
  motion to appoint, 413
Exemptions, bankruptcy estate, 35-
  37
Expedited stay relief, 146
Extension plan, 293

False oaths, 5
Farming operation test, 55
Farmout agreement, 33
Federal Rules of Bankruptcy Proce-
  dure, 6-7, 32, 40-41, 137, 148,
  209, 404-5, 410
Fee/employment applications, as ac-
  tivity code category, 393
Fee/employment objections, as ac-
  tivity code category, 393
Fiduciary defalcation, as nondis-
  chargeable debt, 167
Final fee application, 327
Financial Reporting Requirements,
  349-65
Financing, as activity code category,
  393
Floating liens, 217
Fraud:
  badges of, 222
  constructive, 223
Fraud claims, as nondischargeable
  debts, 162-67

Fraudulent conveyances, 218-29
  defenses to, 228-29
  definition of, 218
  examples of, 223
  policy of, 219-20
  under federal law, 220-28
    "actual fraud," 222-23
    "constructive fraud," 223-28
    transfer date, 222
    transfer of debtor's property,
      221-22
  under state law, 220-21
F.R.Bankr.P., *See* Federal Rules of
  Bankruptcy Procedure
Full performance discharge, 315
Fully secured claims, 252

Gap period, 230, 258-59
Goal, chapters, 60
Governmental fines/penalties, as
  nondischargeable debts, 160
Grogan v. Garner, 172

Hardship discharge, 315-16
Hill v. Fidelity Fin. Svcs., 233
Homeowners' association dues, as
  nondischargeable debts, 162

Initial documentation, 67-117
  petition, 69-73
  preparation of, 69
  Schedule A (real property), 73, 74
  Schedule B (personal property),
    73, 75-79
  Schedule C (property claimed as
    exempt), 80, 81
  Schedule D (creditors holding se-
    cured claims), 80, 82
  Schedule E (creditors holding un-
    secured priority claims), 83-84
  Schedule F (creditors holding un-
    secured nonpriority claims),
    85, 86
  Schedule G (executory contracts
    and unexpired leases), 85, 87
  Schedule H (codebtors), 85, 88
  Schedule I (current income), 85-92
  Schedule J (current expenditures),
    89-114
In re A. C. Williams, 333
In re Andrews, 161
In re Austin, 163

In re Bedingfield, 158
In re Boggan, 307
In re Brown Iron & Metal, Inc., 228
In re Caldwell, 188
In re Campbell, 157, 187
In re Carmen, 278
In re Carr, 233
In re Carroll, 270-71
In re Carter, 287
In re Chastant, 155
In re Ciavarella, 233
In re Cloverleaf Farmer's Co-Op, 56-58
In re Copman, 186
In re Couch, 155
In re Cycle Accounting Services, 155
In re Davis, 312
In re Dolin, 155
In re Doughtery, 166
In re Dunston, 163
In re Edwards, 314
In re Energy Cooperative, Inc., 245
In re Fostvedt, 53
In re Harris, 160
In re Hollar, 210
In re Hyers, 168
In re Jackson, 155
In re James R. Corbitt Co., 246
In re Joshua Slocum, Ltd., 226
In re King, 160
In re Kleitz, 30
In re Kress, 191
In re Landmark Hotel & Casino, Inc., 47
In re Latimer, 187
In re Lawson, 307
In re Leser, 308
In re Loya, 53-54
In re Lundell Farms, 139
In re Maytag Sales & Service, Inc., 235
In re Moreno, 167
In re National Service Corp., 122
In re Oklahoma P.A.C. First Ltd. Partnership, 142
In re Owens, 289
In re Perry, 287
In re Planned Systems, Inc., 138
In re Pretner, 166
In re Raff, 157
In re Reece, 287
In re Revco Drug Stores, Inc., 47
In re Ritz Theatres, Inc., 139
In re Rubottom, 312
In re Scott, 314

In re Stonegate Secur. Svcs., Ltd., 122
In re Suburban Motor Freight, Inc., 227
In re Tillery, 287
In re Tyson, 149
In re Vernon Sand & Gravel, Inc., 245
In re V.N. Deprizio Construction Co., 16, 206-7
In re Walton, 191-92
In re Warren, 188
In re Wheeler, 233
In re Williamson, 171
In re Willis, 233
Insider, 209
Insolvency, 226
Interim fee applications, 327
Ipso facto clauses, 34
Irreparable harm, 291

Johns-Manville Corp., 15
Judicial liens, 243

Kelly Blue Books, 307

Litigation, as activity code category, 393
Litigation consulting, as activity code category, 394

Matter of Allison, 163-65
Matter of Sommersdorf, 291-93
Matter of Tolona Pizza Products Corp., 214-16
Meetings of creditors, as activity code category, 394
Midlantic Nat'l Bank v. N.J. Dept. of Environmental Protection, 38-40
Miracle Church of God in Christ, The, 50
Motion, to avoid lien, 262-64, 410
Motion for order to compel, 417-18
Motions, 404, 410-13
  for abandonment, 410
  for redemption of property, 413
  for relief from automatic stay, 410-11
  for relief from the codebtor stay, 413
  reduction/enlargement of exclusivity period to file Chapter 11 plan, 413
  to appoint examiner, 413
  to appoint trustee, 413
  to approve settlement, 411
  to assume (reject) executory contract (lease), 411
  to avoid lien, 410
  to convert from Chapter 7, 411
  to convert from Chapter 11, 412
  to convert from Chapter 13, 412
  to dismiss, 412
  to incur debt, 412
  to obtain credit, 412
  to reopen case, 413
  to set bar dates for proofs of claims, 411

Necessary property, 144
Neeley v. Murchinson, 171-72
Negative notice, 407, 409
New Debtor Syndrome, 190
New value, 212
  subsequent, 216-17
Nobelman v. American Sav. Bank, 154, 308-10
Nonconsensual plan, 337
Nondischargeable actions:
  burden of proof, 172
  deadlines, 170-71
  procedural aspects of, 170-72
  procedure, 171-72
Nondischargeable debts, 156-70
  alimony, 157-59
  debts incurred to pay otherwise nondischargeable taxes, 161-62
  debts omitted from schedules, 168-69
  DUI injuries, 162
  fiduciary defalcation, 167
  fraud claims, 162-67
  governmental fines/penalties, 160
  homeowners association dues, 162
  prior bankruptcies, 170
  property settlement, 157-59
  student loans, 161
  support, 157-59
  taxes, 159-60
  willful and malicious injuries, 167-68
Nonliquidated obligations, 285
Northern Pipeline Construction Co. v. Marathon Pipe Line Co., 10
Notice of Available Chapters, 111, 114

Notice of hearing, 407, 408
Notices, 407-10
  negative notice, 407, 409
  notice of hearing, 407, 408

Objections, 407
Objections to exemptions, chrono-
  logical order, 41
Offenses by creditors, 5-6
Official Bankruptcy Forms, 7
Ohio v. Kovacs, 39
Omnibus administrative chapters, 27
Oversecured claims, 252

Parties, bankruptcy, 21-24
  Chapter 11 bankruptcy, 321-32
  Chapter 13 bankruptcy, 283-93
  creditors, 22
  creditors' committee, 23
  debtor, 21-22
  equity security holders, 23
  examiner, 23
  professional persons, 24
  trustee, 22-23
  United States Trustee, 23
*Penn Terra Ltd. v. Dept. of Environ. Re-
  sources,* 130-34
Petition, 69-73, 404
  filing of, 1
Petition date, chronological order,
  40
Plan and disclosure statement, as activity code category, 394
Postpetition interest, 248-49
Postpetition transfers, 229-31
  defenses to, 230-31
  unauthorized transfers, elements
    of, 230
Practice:
  Chapter 7, 256-82
  Chapter 11, 320-40
  Chapter 13, 283-319
Preferential transfers actions, 201-18
  account of antecedent debt, 207-8
  creditor receives more than in
    Chap. 7 case, 210-11
  defenses to, 211-18
    consumer debts under $600, 218
    contemporaneous transactions,
      211-13
    enabling loans, 216
    floating liens, 217

ordinary course of business,
  213-16
spousal/child support transfers,
  217-18
statutory liens, 217
subsequent new value, 216-17
elements of, 204-11
insolvency presumed during 90
  days prepetition, 208
policy of avoidable transfers, 202-4
property of the debtor, 205-6
to the benefit of a creditor, 206-7
transfer of property, 204-5
transfer within 90 days of bankruptcy filing, 209
transfer within 91 days and one
  year of filing if creditor an insider, 209-10
Prior bankruptcies, as nondischargeable debts, 170
Priority creditors, 22, 46, 244-47
  classification/order of claims by,
    244-47
Professional fees/expenses, 390-402
  activity code categories, 392-94
  billing format—expenses, 392
  billing format—professional fees,
    391-92
  general information required, 390-
    91
Professional Fee Statement, 383, 385-
  86
Professional persons, 24
Proof of interest, 406-7
Proofs of claim, 406-7
  chronological order, 41
  filing, 250-51
  motion to set bar dates for, 411
Property of the debtor, 205-6
Property settlement, as nondischargeable debt, 157-59
"Pro rata" distribution, 243-44
Punitive-type debts, 248

Quarterly fee schedule and payment
  information, 366

Rake v. Wade, 26, 311
Reaffirmation, 267-68
Reconstruction accounting, as activi-
  ty code category, 394
Redemption of property, 268-71

motion for, 413
Regular income, definition of, 284
Regular income requirement, Chap-
  ter 13 bankruptcy, 51
Remainder of statements and sched-
  ules, chronological order, 40
Reopening a case, 272-73
  motion for, 413
Reorganization, definition of, 45
Repurchase agreement (repo), 134
Restriction on a transfer, 34
Retainers, 383-86
  accounting for services covered by,
    383-84
  general information, 383
  Professional Fee Statement, 383,
    385-86
Rule of substantial compliance, and
  Official Forms, 7

Schedule A (real property), 73, 74
Schedule B (personal property), 73,
  75-79
Schedule C (property claimed as ex-
  empt), 80, 81
Schedule D (creditors holding se-
  cured claims), 80, 82
Schedule E (creditors holding unse-
  cured priority claims), 83-84
Schedule F (creditors holding unse-
  cured nonpriority claims), 85,
  86
Schedule G (executory contracts and
  unexpired leases), 85, 87
Schedule H (codebtors), 85, 88
Schedule I (current income), 85-92
Schedule J (current expenditures),
  85, 89-114
  Debtor's Statement of Intention,
    94, 96
  Disclosure of Compensation of At-
    torney for Debtor, 110-13
  master mailing list, 111
  Notice of Available Chapters, 111,
    114
  Statement of Financial Affairs, 94,
    97-110
  Summary of Schedules, 94, 95
Schedules, 259-60
  quarterly fee schedule and pay-
    ment information, U.S.
    Trustee's Office, 366
  Summary of, 94, 95

Secured claims, 337
Secured creditors, 22, 46, 242-44, 329
    abandonment, 37-38
    consensual liens, 242
    judicial liens, 243
    "pro rata" distribution, 243-44
    statutory liens, 242-43
Serial filers, 184
Settlement:
    motion to approve, 411
    property, as nondischargeable
        debt, 157-59
Single-asset real estate, 144-45
Single-asset real estate debtor, 332-33
Spousal/child support transfers, as
        exception to preference excep-
        tions, 217-18
Stare decisis, 26
Statement of disinterestedness, and
        employment applications, 327
Statement of Financial Affairs, 94,
        97-110
    assignments/receiverships, 104-5
    books/records/financial state-
        ments, 108-9
    closed financial accounts, 106
    current partners/officers/direc-
        tors/shareholders, 110
    former partners/officers/direc-
        tors/shareholders, 110
    gifts, 105
    income from employment/opera-
        tion of business, 103
    income other than from employ-
        ment/operation of a business,
        103
    inventories, 109-10
    losses, 105
    nature/location/name of busi-
        ness, 108
    other transfers, 106
    payments related to debt counsel-
        ing/bankruptcy, 105-6
    payments to creditors, 103-4
    prior address of debtor, 107
    property held for another person,
        107
    repossessions/foreclosures/re-
        turns, 104
    safe deposit boxes, 106-7
    setoffs, 107
    suits/executions/garnishments/
        attachments, 104

withdrawals from a
        partnership/distributions by
        a corporation, 110
Statement of Intent, 271-72
Statutory liens, 217, 242-43
Stay relief, 137-45
    burden of proof, 145
    cause and lack of adequate protec-
        tion, 137-42
    expedited, 146
    lack of equity and inability to re-
        organize, 142-44
    single-asset real estate, 144-45
Stay relief motions, hearing on, 145-
        46
Stewart v. Gurley, 143-44
Straight bankruptcy, *See* Chapter 7
        bankruptcy
Student loans, as nondischargeable
        debts, 161
Substantial abuse filing, 190-92
Substantially contemporaneous ex-
        change, definition of, 212-13
Summary of Schedules, 94, 95
Super discharge, 60, 173
Super superpriority creditors, 250
Superpriority creditors, 249-50
Support, as nondischargeable debt,
        157-59
Surplus to debtor, 249

Taxes, as nondischargeable debt,
        159-60
Tax issues, as activity code category,
        394
Taylor v. Freeland & Kronz, 35, 260
341 First Creditors' Meetings, 61,
        181, 250, 277, 278, 279, 415-16
    chronological order, 41
Transfer, 222, 227
    gap period, 230, 258-59
    restriction on, 34
Trustee, 22-23, 273-77
    abandonment, 38
    appointment of, 273
    avoiding powers of, 275-76
    Chapter 7 bankruptcy, 273-77
    Chapter 11 bankruptcy, 331
    Chapter 13 bankruptcy, 287-89
    compensation, 277
    disbursement, 276
    duties of, 22, 274-75
    eligibility/qualifications of, 273

liability/indemnity, 277
liquidation, 276
motion to appoint, 413
powers of, 275
role/capacity of, 273-74

Undersecured claims, 252
Uniform Commercial Code (UCC), 1
Uniform Fraudulent Conveyance
        Act (UFCA), 221
Uniform Fraudulent Transfer Act
        (UFTA), 221
*United Sav. Ass'n v. Timbers of Inwood
        Forest*, 139-41
United States Trustee's Office, 23
    address, 366
    dismissals, 181-82
    employment guidelines, 380-402
    Financial Reporting Requirements,
        349-65
    Notice of Requirements, 341-48
    quarterly fee schedule and pay-
        ment information, 366
    requirements, 341-66
    unsecured creditors' committee,
        330-31
Unsecured claims, 337-38
Unsecured creditors, 22, 247-48
    tardily filed claims, 247-48
    timely filed proofs of claim, 247
U.S. Trustee v. Harris, 191-92
U.S. v. Whiting Pools, Inc., 30

Valuation, as activity code category,
        394
Voidable transfers, 199-240
    authority to bring, 231-33
    collection of, 231
    definition of, 199-200
    duties of legal assistants in, 200-
        201
    fraudulent conveyances, 218-29
        defenses to, 228-29
        definition of, 218
        policy of, 219-20
        under state/federal law, 220-28
    postpetition transfers, 229-31
        defenses to, 230-31
        elements of unauthorized trans-
            fers, 230
    preferences, 201-18
        defenses to, 211-18

Voidable transfers (*Cont.*)
  elements of, 204-11
  policy of avoidable transfers, 202-4
  transfer of property, 204-5
  statutes of limitations of, 233-35

Voluntary dismissal, 192-94
  after stay relief request, 185-86
  Chapter 7 cases, 192-94
  Chapter 11 cases, 194
  Chapter 13 cases, 194
  involuntary vs., 179

"Wage earner" reorganizations, *See* Chapter 13 bankruptcy
Weissman v. Hasset, 277
Willful and malicious injuries, as nondischargeable debts, 167-68
Willful failure/lack of prosecution, 185